Modern Western Civilization

A STUDENT'S SYNOPSIS AND GUIDE TO THE HISTORY OF MODERN EUROPEAN WORLD

2

Since 1848

Nelson Klose
Professor of History
San Jose State College, California

INCORPORATING THESE USEFUL FEATURES:

***Great Significance
**Important Topics
*Secondary Importance

Cross Referenced to Leading Texts
and Supplementary Readings

Dictionary of Terms

Selected Documents of Importance

Barron's Educational Series, Inc.
Woodbury, New York

All inquiries should be addressed to
Barron's Educational Series, Inc.
113 Crossways Park Drive
Woodbury, New York 11797

Library of Congress Catalog Card No. 65-16323

PRINTED IN THE UNITED STATES OF AMERICA

CONTENTS

RESTORATION AND RENEWED REVOLUTION, 1815-1848

THE ASSERTIONS OF NATIONALISM, 1849-1871

DEMOCRACY, THE NEW INDUSTRIALISM, AND THE NEW IMPERIALISM, 1871-1914

*Weapons Development and Space Research
**Sigmund Freud (1856-1939) and the New Psychology
*Keynesian Economics
Philosophy
History: Spengler and Toynbee

You will find this concise history and guide useful because of its concentration upon the essential subject matter of college courses in Modern Civilization and courses in Western, European, and World History. The great emphasis, of course, is upon Europe, the main source of world change since the middle ages. Instead of lengthy commentary and description, significant factual subject matter is presented in topical form and with adequate detail for most purposes. The structure, substance, and interpretation of our heritage of modern world civilization are made readily apparent so that the student may more easily grasp mental outlines of subject matter. This presentation represents a somewhat selective choice of subject matter based upon a consensus of the emphasis given by historians to the multitude of topics that comprise modern history. Since the student will probably use this guide along with a more detailed textbook, the sequence of subject matter has been arranged to parallel as nearly as possible the organization of most textbooks now in use. Each Part of the book is an independent unit so that the student may start with any Part according to where his particular course begins and need study earlier Parts only as he finds a need to do so. Subject matter has been organized with proper respect for chronology. All headings for Parts, Chapters, and topics are forthright and descriptive rather than fanciful or journalistic. The author has had many years experience teaching history survey courses, including such courses in European civilization, and has prepared this guide in the light of such experience.

Special Features. Important additions to this concise history serve the student as a means of quick reference for locating information. 1] Chapters are prefaced by chronologies which provide a kind of outline of the subject matter covered by the

chapter and give important dates the student may need to remember. The Table of Contents itself is an outline of the
main chronological periods of modern history. 2] Chapters are
followed by typical questions to study in reviewing for examinations. 3] Chapter bibliographies will help in finding books
providing more detail on special subjects. 4] Maps should be
studied until one has a mental image of the location of important points in geography. 5] At the back of the book are to be
found copies or excerpts from many of the great documents
of western civilization. In context considerable attention has
been given to providing full discussion of many of the documents of Modern History. 6] A dictionary of important, difficult terms and vocabulary, 7] lists of heads of state of the various nations, 8] and the index are also provided for reference
purposes. 9] Asterisks (*) are used to indicate the relative
importance of topics.

Use of Asterisk. Attention to the asterisks prefacing each
topic will assist the student and teacher in concentrating attention according to the relative importance of subjects. This
feature is particularly appropriate for a study guide in Modern
Civilization where it is literally impossible to "cover" everything of importance. The evaluation of the relative importance
of topics represents a consensus based upon a study of textbooks, books of selected readings and documents, and subjects
covered by examination questions available for the use of students and teachers.

Three asterisks (***) indicate topics of the greatest significance, two asterisks (**) indicate important topics, one
asterisk (*) indicates topics of secondary importance, and
topics not marked are of least relative significance but too
important to omit. This provision of asterisks should help the
student gain perspective, but, since opinions vary, the students
should be alert to his instructor's judgment of the significance
of topics covered in lectures. To be well prepared for examina-

tions, the student should "overlearn" the more important topics and study the others as time permits. He should underline subject matter that needs to be reviewed more than once and consciously consider its importance while doing so.

How to Use the Review Questions. Review questions follow each chapter. These questions, of several types, have been carefully prepared to give the student types of questions at the level of difficulty he is likely to encounter in college objective examinations. They may be used as study exercises and should give the student substantial preparation for examination questions over important subjects. For excellent reasons, instructors prefer to use multiple-choice items; therefore, more space has been given to this type. The name "best-answer" is a more accurate description of this type of question. If these questions are ideally framed, the student will often find that there are several possible responses that appear to be correct; therefore, the student needs to consider each response carefully and select one that seems to provide the "best answer" for that item. He should analyze the separate responses and not impulsively throw down the first answer that appears to be satisfactory. In reviewing, remember that it is just as important to understand why a statement is not true as to know that it is true.

Dictionary of Important and Difficult Terms. A full dictionary and glossary has been added to provide convenient definitions for difficult, confusing, and more important terms. The student should check this list at the beginning of the course and mark those terms and definitions he does not understand well and concentrate his study upon them.

To the Instructor. The teacher who wishes to replace the traditional textbook with selected readings of sources, documents, and interpretative articles should find this concise history sufficient to supply the basic factual subject matter of his course. Classroom time can then be used for lectures on special subjects, discussion, and the use of other teaching methods and devices instead of dictating essential subject matter of his course. Several inexpensive paperback histories, of which so many are now available, could be substituted for the traditional textbook. Lists of currently available paperbacks are provided here after each chapter. Many new titles are constantly being issued. For these see Bowker's guide to *Paperbound Books in Print*. Tables have been provided here to aid the teacher in correlating (keying) this book with currently available supplementary readings and standard textbooks.

Why Study and How. Some students enroll in required general education courses with more or less conscious reservations regarding their value. The attractions of the immediate goals and of the more tangible rewards of vocationally oriented studies distract attention from the very real values of an understanding of the larger environment offered by history courses. The sophisticated student will accept these values as pointed out here. A few reminders on how to study will help one to get a better start.

Why Study Western Civilization. As trite as it seems, a correct understanding of the nature of history is needed to help some students to see why it is useful knowledge. History is an interpreted record of all of man's experience in a framework of time and place. The study of History selects those parts of man's past that give a useful understanding of the present. The content of written history is determined by what is relevant to the present; thus it is really useful knowledge of the present and future that the past brings us. History is a great accumulation of information and understandings of man's past experience. For man to ignore this is to commit himself to a cultural amnesia that discards all the values of experience. It is the work of the historian to select and explain the most pertinent and valuable parts of this heritage to laymen and students. Then in the light of his needs man can decide what part of his heritage represents something he should preserve and what parts he should discard. The knowledge of origins of things brings man as much understanding as any kind of information. Western Civilization, a cultural rather than a "practical" subject, gives students a larger view and perspective of our whole culture than does any other study. History is no longer an account of facts about wars and rulers and laws.

The word "civilization" takes in economic changes, science, thought, art, and literature. Thus, history is a vehicle for educating the student relative to a variety of information and understanding that he needs to become well prepared to do his part as a citizen and leader. For the individual, history brings meaning to the news and discussions brought to him by our media of communication—the printed word, radio, television, and other means. Certainly, in a world as small as ours today, one needs to know all he can about his neighbors. History provides a foundation for studying other subjects: government and other social sciences, law, journalism, education, literature, and others. A student who has not learned his history can hardly be well educated.

How to Study History. The student has taken a long step toward mastering history courses if he consciously and fully accepts their usefulness to him personally. Then he needs to seek to understand it for his further development rather than memorizing a minimum of facts to pass a forthcoming examination. There is not enough space here to give the student who is having difficulty with history all the directions he needs. He should use one of the various "how to study" books in order to remedy his weaknesses in writing papers and reports, in preparing for and taking examinations, in reading efficiently, in taking lecture notes, and organizing his notes. Self-examination will help him to discover his weaknesses in study habits. He may have to discover what methods of study are best suited to himself. He needs to realize that history requires self-discipline as much as other subjects do and that previous exposure in a similar course should not provide an excuse to neglect his present course. Space does not permit historians to make explicit why each topic is included in a textbook or lecture, but the student must trust the experience and judgment of his authors and teachers in the selection of such information.

A few concrete and more important suggestions on how

to study may suffice for many students. One needs to react to his reading instead of trying to absorb it passively; he should avoid being too relaxed but should be active in looking up terms, using reference books, and in thinking about relationships. Reading should be done with a conscious objective; decide what you are reading for. Do your first reading of subject matter before your instructor lectures on the subject. You will gain much more from the lecture this way. The lecture most likely deals with the most important subject matter of the course, or it may supplement other material. Avoid busywork that is time consuming but does not require thought. Making outlines and brief summaries force one to think as he looks for key information and ideas. Make marginal notations in lecture and other notes and in expendable books that you own; do this to indicate difficult material that you need to study again and in order to avoid wasting time reviewing material you already know. In studying history it is especially helpful to make use of maps in order to obtain a mental picture of the location of events. This book will be helpful in establishing a chronological framework in which to place events. A student of Western Civilization will also need to give much attention to concepts; for example, "absolute monarchy," "scientific socialism." He needs to identify a multitude of names of persons, places, laws, and events. The multiplicity of facts and ideas will necessitate the development of a sense of proportion as to what is relatively more important.

Look upon your study of each course as one of the tasks of your job of attending college. Your grades earned are a measure of your success in your job. Earn better grades by closely following directions of your instructor, by doing assignments as if they were instructions from an employer who is paying you well. Try to earn high grades; they are the measure of how well you are doing your job as well as of how much you are learning. Do your studies with the conviction that you are gaining experience for doing still more important work later. From this approach learning should follow naturally.

The student of Modern Western Civilization may need first to orient himself with reference to the larger scene by briefly reviewing the main periods of history—ancient, medieval, and modern. Modern Western Civilization begins in Europe, for through Europe was transmitted the heritage of the ancient world of the Near East, of Greece, of Rome, and of the middle ages.

Ancient History.   The Greeks and the Romans of ancient times conserved, enlarged, and transmitted the heritage of the several civilizations that preceded them in the regions bordering the eastern Mediterranean. To mark the boundary between the termination of the history of the ancient world and the beginning of the middle ages, many historians have found that the year 476 A.D. serves as a convenient and realistic date. In that year one of the kings at the head of the German conquerers deposed the last of the Roman emperors and left the throne vacant. This event symbolized the downfall of the great Roman empire, a reality that had long since occurred in the repeated barbarian invasions of Italy. But it must be emphasized that the dates chosen to bracket the periods of history do not represent any real break between such periods. Transition from one age to another comes gradually, and dates of important events merely serve as convenient and somewhat arbitrary boundaries by which historians organize subject matter.

Medieval History.   The middle ages (medieval period) covers a time of approximately a thousand years from about 500 A.D. to 1500. The early middle ages up to 1000 A.D. have often been referred to as the "Dark Ages" because of the continued decay of the civilization of the ancient world and the political anarchy of these centuries. The second 500 years of the medieval period witnessed a strong emergence from the earlier conditions of decay and semi-barbarism. These changes were especially rapid from about 1050 to 1270, a period known as the high middle ages. During the high middle ages the worst anarchy of feudalism ceased, the authority of the Church increased, the cities and commerce revived, and the universalists stimulated intellectual growth. The most typical of medieval institutions—the Church, feudal society, and the gilds in the cities—developed their characteristic form and spirit during this time.

Modern History. Modern history begins with the Renaissance. The Renaissance is a period of transition from medieval into modern times and overlaps those two periods. During the Renaissance the typical medieval institutions underwent important changes. The Renaissance represents the revival of the worldly, individualistic outlook of ancient times, as contrasted with the spiritual and social mindedness fostered by the pervasive influence of the medieval Church. The revival of the secular spirit began with the Revival of Learning in Italy in the 1300's and lasted until about 1500. The Renaissance in northern Europe, however, began later and extended through the first century of the modern age to approximately 1600. More fully, the term *Renaissance* refers to several significant developments: the intensified growth of trade and cities, the revival of learning, the rise of national literature in the vernacular, the flowering of the fine arts in northern Italy, progress in invention and science, the emergence of individualistic ethics, the supplanting of the gilds by capitalistic enterprise, voyages of exploration and discovery, and the rise of strong monarchies. Now, with this outline of the periods of history before 1500, we are better prepared to study the details of Modern Western Civilization at our beginning of about 1500.

THE GEOGRAPHY AND PEOPLES OF EUROPE

Europe is not a continent in its physical geography but is a great irregular peninsula extending westward from Asia. Europe is treated as a continent because of its historic cultural unity which, more than any physical barrier, has separated it from Asia. The diversity of races or ethnic groups in Europe also needs to be known as a foundation for the study of Europe since so many references to these differences will be made.

Land Outlines of Europe. In the east, Europe is hardly separated from Asia by the Ural Mountains; along the South it is bounded by the Caucasus Mountains and the Black Sea. The Mediterranean separates Europe geographically from North Africa. Yet North Africa, as well as the Near East, has always been closely related to the European world. On the west is the Atlantic Ocean and on the north is the Arctic Ocean. Attached to the mainland mass of Europe are several peninsulas: the Balkan Peninsula, Italy, the Iberian Peninsula, Denmark, and the Scandinavian Peninsula. Large outlying islands belonging to Europe in the Mediterranean are Crete, Sicily, Sardinia, Corsica, and the Balearic Islands. On the northwest are the islands of Britain and Ireland. Important bodies of water lying next to these land extensions of Europe include the Aegean Sea, the Adriatic Sea, the English Channel, the North Sea, and the Baltic Sea. The very irregular coastline of Europe affords harbors and access to the sea for nearly all the nations of Europe.

Mountains, Rivers, and Plains. Continental Europe has been divided fairly effectively by barriers of mountains and rivers that have given rise to many distinct nation-states. The Pyrenees Mountains separate Spain from France; the Alps enclose the northern limits of Italy; the Carpathians form a half-circle around Hungary. The Apennines give most of Italy a rugged or mountainous terrain, and the Balkan Mountains do the same for that region. The Sudeten Mountains enclose the western part of Bohemia. Much of the southern part of both France and Germany is covered by other, lower mountains. Scotland and most of Scandinavia are also rugged with mountain landscape.

The rivers of Europe have served both as barriers and as routes of transportation. Adequate rainfall throughout the year, except in Spain, maintains Europe's rivers in a full, even flow suitable for inland water-borne traffic. The largest river, the Volga in Russia, flows into the Caspian Sea. The lengthy Danube originates in central Germany, flows through the Hungarian Plain, between Rumania and Bulgaria and, finally, into the Black Sea. The Rhine, the most important river of Europe, is one of several navigable rivers that flow across the northern plain into the North and Baltic seas. The three most important rivers in France are the Seine, the Loire, and the Rhone. The Vistula and the Niemen flow out of the Polish plain into the Baltic Sea. England's most important river is the Thames.

A wide and continuous coastal plain across northern Europe begins in southeastern France and extends across Germany and Poland and merges into the great inland plains of Russia that extend to the Urals. The agricultural plains of Europe have provided bread and meat to feed the heavy populations of Europe since historic times. Other rich agricultural plains of considerable significance are the Hungarian and Bohemian plains, the plain of the Po River in northern Italy, and the lowlands of southern Britain. Other countries possess smaller agricultural plains. The Pripet marshes along eastern Poland formerly interrupted transportation across the plains.

Climate and Minerals. The northerly latitudes of Europe might rightfully lead one to expect a cold climate like that of Canada and Labrador. But the warm waters of the Gulf

Stream in the Atlantic bring beneficial warmth and rainfall. Winters are relatively mild; cool and moist summers are conducive to the growth of food-producing vegetation. Europe, except in the east, is not subject to the sharp and sudden changes produced by the weather cycles of the continental climates of Russia, of North America, and of Asia.

The mountainous parts of Europe are rich in mineral deposits. Britain's early Industrial Revolution was nourished by her deposits of coal and iron. These same minerals in the Saar, in Belgium, in Germany, in Upper Silesia, and in Styria founded industry there. Western and central Europe has been favored with rich, loamy soils. The edges of the plain along the southern shores of the North and Baltic seas are poor, sandy, and marshy. The Ukraine of Russia is a highly fertile plain.

The Peoples of Europe.   The racial composition of Europe is pretty thoroughly mixed, but certain ethnic groups, based primarily on language characteristics, are clearly identifiable. 1] Latin nationalities—Italian, French, Spanish, Portuguese, and Rumanian—occupy much of southern Europe. 2] The Germanic peoples occupy the main areas of northern Europe, particularly Britain, Germany, and Scandinavia. 3] A third large group are the Slavic peoples of eastern Europe—Poles, Russians, Czechs, Slovaks, and Balkan groups. Three smaller but numerous peoples are 1] the Greeks, 2] the Celtic people of Ireland, Scotland, Wales, and Brittany, and 3] the Magyars of Hungary. Somewhat related to the Magyars are the Finns, Estonians, and Turks. Still other distinct peoples are the Basques of northwestern Spain and southern France, the Albanians, the Moors of Spain, and Jews, who are scattered over almost all of Europe. Language and racial differences and geography tended to form these peoples into separate nations. However, invasions, migrations, colonization, and intermarriage have thoroughly blended these different peoples in many parts of the continent. For most peoples the language

groups show little if any correspondence with racial characteristics as determined by physical features. The peoples of
Europe were not isolated from each other but nearly always
maintained contacts that resulted in such diffusion of cultural
traits throughout Europe as to create a sub-continent of cultural unity with local variations.

Correlation of *Modern Western Civilization*, Vol. II with **Recent Textbooks**
(1815 to the Present)

Brinton, et al., II 2nd ed.	Burns II, 6th ed.	Craig	Easton
		10–28, 69–80	531–534
187–214	673–709	2–9, 91–96	523–527, 630–643
223–234	711–716	28–37, 48–54, 59–68, 80–150	534–537, 598–605, 608–612
240–242	720–724	161–196	605–608
249–253, 265–273	728–733, 735–739	197–236, 251–257	543–559
74–80, 180–184, 278–297	739–746	38–47, 54–59	559–565
215–219, 313–340	673–709, 796–829	150–160, 260–266, 290–309	567–596, 643–660
234–239, 242–248, 273–278	716–720, 724–728, 733–735, 748–750	237–247, 310–328, 335–394	612–616, 624–628
253–262	768–795		619–625
297–309		247–251, 395–408, 417–438	559–565
	746–747	328–335, 408–410	
343–371	751–760	267–290, 439–463	616–619, 668–695
371–385	760–765, 838–850	464–488	698–707
385–403	850–866	498–525	707–712
403–414	866–876	526–543	712–721
417–455	892–904	554–580	723–740
478–480, 503–535	904–915	543–553, 600–622, 653–681	757–778
459–478, 480–501	877–891	581–599, 623–652	740–755
539–552	918–937	682–712	778–790
552–574	938–967	713–755	790–799
577–610	1009–1014	761–796	799–805, 825–837
577–616	970–1009	797–814	807–825, 837–839, 845–851
619–660		814–825	839–845
663–687	1016–1040	490–497	853–887

Correlation of *Modern Western Civilization*, Vol. II with **Recent Textbooks**
(1815 to the Present)

CHAPTERS	Ergang, "Since Waterloo" 2nd ed.	Ferguson & Bruun Part II 3rd ed.	Palmer
1. Concert of Europe	27–47	647–648, 662–664	443–454
2. Social Movements	68–127	651–656, 665–669	421–443, 495–502
3. Revolutions, 1830, 1848	48–67	656–662, 669–688	454–495
4. Napoleon III	128–148	689–694	502–513
5. Italy and Germany	149–170	695–714	513–526
6. Austria and Russia		715–721	
7. Social Developments	225–229	739–750	555–577, 592–612
8. Political Developments	171–252, 91–110, 328–351	731–734, 756–767	527–530, 577–592
9. The United States		780–786	539–545
10. Russia and the Dual Monarchy	278–316	721–726, 726–731	530–539
11. Smaller States	316–323	734–736	627–637
12. New Imperialism	253–277	750–753, 767–779, 786–792	545–554, 613–627, 637–639
13. Background of WW I	352–368	793–804	660–670
14. World War I	369–397	806–820	670–694
15. Peace Settlements	398–412	821–831	694–703
16. Russian Revolution	433–457	844–853	704–751
17. Western Nations	413–432, 458–510	832–843, 854–872	752–764, 785–800
18. Fascism	511–547	873–889	800–816
19. Background of WW II	564–587	901–916	774–784, 816–826
20. World War II	588–656, 752–809	918–935	827–848
21. After the War	672–706, 727–751	936–942, 956–966, 970–978	848–851, 858–868
22. Cold War	657–671, 810–842	942–956, 978–983	868–876
23. Revolt Against Imperialism	548–563, 706–726	890–900, 966–969, 984–997	765–777, 851–858
24. Science and Thought		998–1012	

Correlation of *Modern Western Civilization*, Vol. II with **Recent Textbooks**
(1815 to the Present)

Starr, et al., II	Strayer, et al., II	Stromberg	Swain, II
	151–154, 166–171	458–474	229–237
366–375, 378–385	154–166, 194–200	450–452, 457–474	256–271, 345–366
385–406	171–191	455–457, 479–493	238–245, 271–291
	236–249	502–507	295–305
	249–272	507–516	305–315
	275–281		320–323, 393–408
	200–233, 336–366	499–502, 516–523, 552–555, 575–591	367–390, 503–522
461–477	272–275, 307–313, 332–336, 367–371	550–565	315–320, 324–341, 523–530
407–411, 484–490	284–307		437–459
477–481	371–373	565–571	408–434, 531–533
481–484			
411–459	313–329, 385–402	528–545	465–499
490–496	377–413	596–609	533–542, 545–554
505–512	413–445	613–627	554–577
	444–455	627–634	578–591
513–519	508–522	651–656	595–616
525–532	455–463, 466–486	640–649, 656–662	639–667
519–525	508–511, 523–540	649–651	617–636, 667–678
532–535	540–549	669–690	725–730
535–545	552–577	695–713	730–750
619–634	595–611	734–743	750–756
644–653	584–591, 624–639	719–734	756–765
548–577, 634–644	487–495, 611–624	745–748	681–721
581–615	495–505	662–664, 743–748	766–770

Correlation of *Modern Western Civilization*, Vol. II with **Recent Textbooks**
(1815 to the Present)

CHAPTERS	Thompson 2nd ed.	Wallbank & Taylor, II 4th ed.
1. Concert of Europe	107–138	173–180
2. Social Movements	92–106	147–172, 180–187
3. Revolutions, 1830, 1848	139–155, 156–210	187–211
4. Napoleon III	217–230, 241–247	220–223
5. Italy and Germany	263–271, 274–301	213–220
6. Austria and Russia	271–274, 302–312	223–225
7. Social Developments	250–262, 372–421	241–267, 351–376, 406–417
8. Political Developments	237–241, 247–250, 321–382	225–229, 376–392
9. The United States		275–288
10. Russia and the Dual Monarchy	333–335, 444–453	225–234, 392–399
11. Smaller States	312–318, 428–448	234–240, 399–404
12. New Imperialism	231–237, 453–487	288–342
13. Background of WW I	488–507	417–429
14. World War I	513–562	429–454
15. Peace Settlements	575–608	454–461
16. Russian Revolution		471–480
17. Western Nations	563–574, 611–661	461–470, 485–496
18. Fascism	662–689	480–485
19. Background of WW II	690–717	523–544
20. World War II	721–770	544–560
21. After the War	773–791	583–597
22. Cold War	791–803, 828–850	567–582, 597–602
23. Revolt Against Imperialism	804–827	497–522, 590–597
24. Science and Thought	853–893	603–617

Correlation of *Modern Western Civilization*, Vol. II
with **Recent Books of Selected Reading**

Correlation of *Modern Western Civilization*, Vol. II
with **Recent Books of Selected Reading**

COLLEGE TEXTBOOKS

Albrecht-Carrié, René, *Europe since 1815* (New York, Harper, 1962).

Beik, Paul H., and Laurence Lafore, *Modern Europe, A History since 1500* (New York, Holt, Rinehart and Winston, 1961).

Brace, Richard M., *The Making of the Modern World from the Renaissance to the Present* (2nd ed., New York, Holt, Rinehart and Winston, 1961).

Boak, A. E. R., Albert Hyma, and Preston Slosson, *The Growth of Western Civilization*, Vol. II (4th ed., New York, Appleton, Century, Crofts, 1951).

Brinton, Crane, John B. Christopher, and Robert L. Wolff, *A History of Civilization*, Vol. II (2nd ed., Englewood Cliffs, N.J., Prentice-Hall, 1960).

Burns, Edward McNall, *Western Civilizations, Their History and Their Culture*, Vol. II (6th ed., New York, W. W. Norton, 1963).

Craig, Gordon A., *Europe since 1815* (New York, Holt, Rinehart and Winston, 1961).

Easton, Stewart C., *The Western Heritage* (New York, Holt, Rinehart and Winston, 1961).

Ergang, Robert, *Europe since Waterloo* (2nd ed., Boston, D. C. Heath, 1961).

Ferguson, Wallace K., and Geoffrey Bruun, *A Survey of European Civilization*, Part II (3rd ed., Boston, Houghton, Mifflin, 1962).

May, Arthur J., *A History of Civilization, The Story of Our Heritage. The Mid-seventeenth Century to Modern Times* (New York, Scribners, 1956).

Palmer, R. R., *A History of the Modern World* (2nd ed., New York, Knopf, 1963).

Schapiro, J. S., *Modern and Contemporary European History, 1815-1952* (Boston, Houghton, Mifflin, 1953).

Schevill, Ferdinand, *A History of Europe from the Reformation to the Present Day* (Rev. ed., New York, Harcourt, Brace, 1951).

Slosson, Preston, *Europe since 1815* (New York, Scribners, 1954).

Starr, Chester G., *et al., A History of the World*, Vol. II (Chicago, Rand, McNally, 1960).

Strayer, Joseph R., Hans W. Gatzke, and E. Harris Harbison, *The Course of Civilization*, Vol. II (New York, Harcourt, Brace, 1961).

Stromberg, Roland N., *A History of Western Civilization* (Homewood, Ill., Dorsey Press, 1963).

Swain, Joseph W., *The Harper History of Civilization*, Vol. II (New York, Harper and Bros., 1958).

Thompson, David, *Europe since Napoleon* (2nd ed., Knopf, 1963).

Wallbank, T. Walter, and Alastair M. Taylor, *Civilization Past and Present* (4th ed., Scott, Foresman, 1961).

BOOKS OF SELECTED READINGS

Anderson, Eugen N., *et al., Europe in the Nineteenth Century. A Documentary Analysis of Change and Conflict*. Vol. I, 1815-1870; Vol. II, 1870-1914 (Indianapolis, Bobbs-Merrill, 1961).

Beatty, John Louis, and Oliver A. Johnson, *Heritage of Western Civilization* (Englewood Cliffs, N.J., Prentice-Hall, 1958)

Bernard, Leon, and Theodore B. Hodges, *Readings in Modern Civilization* (New York, Macmillan, 1962).

Carroll, Harry J., Jr., *et al., The Development of Civilization. A Documentary History of Politics, Society, and Thought* (Chicago, Scott, Foresman, 1962).

Mosse, George L., *et al., Europe in Review. Readings and Sources since 1500* (Chicago, Rand McNally, 1957).

Schrier, Arnold, *et al., Modern European Civilization. A Documentary History from the Renaissance to the Present* (Chicago, Scott, Foresman, 1963).

Stearns, Raymond Phineas, *Pageant of Europe. Sources and Selections from the Renaissance to the Present Day* (Rev. ed., Harcourt, Brace, 1961).

Weber, Eugen, *The Western Tradition from the Renaissance to the Atomic Age* (Boston, D. C. Heath, 1959).

RESTORATION AND RENEWED REVOLUTION

1815-1848

The Congress of Vienna restored the system of monarchy and aristocracy, but democratic and national aspirations had been implanted in Europe by the French Revolution and were now nourished by the bourgeoisie everywhere. In 1820-1821 demonstrations and revolt protested the Restoration of the old system. These revolts were crushed. In 1830 the bourgeoisie revolutions were more successful. The failures of 1848 in Italy and Germany were redeemed in the successful unification achievements of the next two decades. This period on the whole was one of great scientific, industrial, and cultural progress.

1799	*Montenegro won independence*
1804-1813	*Serbia won brief independence*
1814	*Ferdinand VII suspended liberal constitution of 1812 in Spain*
*1815	*Congress of Vienna*
	Holy Alliance formed; Quadruple Alliance formed.
1817	*Serbia won autonomy*
1818	*Congress of Aix-la-Chapelle*
1819	*Carlsbad Decrees in Germany*
1820	*Congress of Troppau met*
	Liberal revolts in Spain, Portugal, Naples, and Greece
1821	*Congress of Laibach*
1821-1829	*Greek Rebellion*
1822	*Congress of Verona*
	Great Britain abandoned the Quadruple Alliance
*1823	*Monroe Doctrine announced*
1827	*Turkish navy destroyed at Navarino*
	Greece won independence
1830	*Serbia won full independence*

* More important dates.

1. The Reaction and the Concert of Europe, 1815-1830

The great powers which rearranged Europe at Vienna continued to cooperate to some extent. The challenges to the settlements came from liberals and nationalists who opposed the restored aristocratic and monarchical system of Metternich. These early nationalist and liberal movements seethed beneath the surface but were suppressed with the consent and aid of the reactionary powers of the Quadruple Alliance. Prince Metternich himself served as the leader of the reaction. To him democracy meant anarchy and revolution. His policies brought restrictions against public meetings, censorship of the press, and spying upon teachers. Limitations were placed on travel into his own country, Austria. In Germany and Italy secret societies organized to carry on the fight for liberalism and nationalism.

The International Congresses. To deal with problems that arose, a series of congresses were held by the victorious allies at Aix-la-Chapelle (1818), Troppau (1820), Laibach (1821), and Verona (1822). The last three conferences asserted the right of armed intervention in other states and arranged armed intervention to suppress the revolts in Spain and Italy. When Canning became minister in 1822 the conferences ceased as he refused to intervene in the domestic affairs of the European nations.

***The Concert of Europe.* In 1815 the victors agreed to two separate leagues: the Holy Alliance and the Quadruple Alliance. The Holy Alliance originated with Alexander I of

Russia and was accepted by Austria and Prussia in deference to Alexander and his idealism. The Russian tsar, a religious mystic, sincerely wished that Christian principles of justice, charity, and peace might be applied by the sovereigns of Europe. Other diplomats cynically distrusted the whole idea and it actually had little practical significance. It was viewed as a move to preserve benevolent despotism against democracy. The term "Holy Alliance" is often used in reference to the Quadruple Alliance. Both alliances included the same three members, but Britain formed the Quadruple Alliance by joining as its fourth member. The conference at Aix-la-Chapelle in 1818 brought the withdrawal of allied troops on French soil and the restoration of France as a partner in European affairs. When France joined the Quadruple Alliance in 1818, the league became a Quintuple Alliance, also called the Concert of Europe. The whole movement to cooperate in international affairs is popularly known as the "Holy Alliance." The term usually excludes Britain, since she refused to cooperate at all after 1822. The challenges of nationalism and democracy to the Vienna settlement came soon after 1815. Revolutionary movements broke out in Spain, Portugal, and Sicily in 1820. The middle class and intellectuals opposed the restoration of the old order.

Revolutionary activity in Spain, Italy, and Portugal. In Spain in 1814 the new Bourbon king, Ferdinand VII, suspended the liberal constitution of 1812 and restored the Jesuits and the Inquisition and decided to reconquer the New World colonies then in revolt. In 1820 when Ferdinand had finally gathered a large force at Cadiz to sail for the reconquest of the colonies, the men mutinied and called upon the rest of Spain to join them in demanding a liberal constitution. The revolt spread to other cities. The king then granted a constitution which remained in effect only a few years. Similar revolutions followed in Piedmont, Naples, and Portugal. The secret society of *Carbonari* (charcoal burners) led the unsuccessful revolt in Naples. Secret police put down the revolt in the Papal States. The revolutions alarmed the great powers and soon lost the support of their own people. In Portugal the Braganza family returned in 1821, but continued strife enabled her colony of Brazil to make good her independence in 1822. At Troppau in Silesia the Quadruple Alliance met and adopted the Troppau Protocol under which Austria was authorized to send an army which crushed the uprising in Naples in 1821 and in 1823. Ninety-five thousand French troops entered Spain and set off a reign of terror that crushed the liberals and restored Ferdinand VII. But Britain's Castlereagh protested the principle of intervention as decided upon at Troppau. When Canning succeeded Castlereagh in 1822 he took a still stronger stand against intervention and proposed armed opposition to intervention in Latin America.

***The Monroe Doctrine.** The Spanish colonies in revolt posed a further problem for the Quadruple Alliance. The colonies had taken advantage of the substitution of Napoleon's brother Joseph for the Spanish Bourbon king in 1808 and had declared their independence. Britain had rushed to trade with the new republics in America and, therefore, did not wish to see Spanish power restored. Ferdinand of Spain requested that the Quadruple Alliance assist him to recover his lost colonies. It was feared that French aid might be secured for their reconquest. Castlereagh had already refused to sign the Troppau Protocol which asserted the principle of intervention. His successor Canning gave diplomatic recognition to the twenty new republics in Central and South America and proposed an alliance with the United States to prevent reconquest of the former Spanish colonies. The terms of the proposal included a self-denying clause that would have limited United States expansion to its south and would have committed the United States too strongly to joint action with

Great Britain. Besides, Britain represented a monarchical system opposed to the American principle of representative government. President Monroe issued instead an independent warning to the European powers that the Americas were no longer open to colonization or political interference by Europe. This was the statement of the famous Monroe Doctrine which was to become more significant later. This warning and the existence of the British fleet prevented interference in America by the reactionary forces of Spain and France.

*The Carlsbad Decrees. A liberal movement in Germany just before and during the years immediately after the defeat of Napoleon secured written constitutions and limited reforms there. But Metternich was waiting for the suitable occasion to repress liberal movements in Germany. The occasion came in 1817. In the German universities students had organized societies known as the *Burschenschaften*; their purpose was to work for liberty and for the unification of Germany. The *Burschenschaften* demonstrated rather innocently at a national meeting called at Wartburg in 1817, but Metternich gave the affair a sinister interpretation. In 1819 an assassination of a suspected Russian agent, Kotzebue, led the German Diet to pass the Carlsbad Decrees. The decrees provided for the dissolution of patriotic societies and removal of liberal professors. The Decrees provided for censorship, spying, and other methods for suppression of liberal activities. Nevertheless, the German secret societies continued to foment liberal thinking.

Balkan independence movements. In the Balkans the nationalist sentiments of the French Revolution found expression in uprisings of the Christian peoples against the yoke of the Mohammedan Turks. In 1806 Russia invaded the Balkans. At the Vienna Conference she squelched discussion of the Turkish problem in order that she might be free to aid rebel Christians. Montenegro first won independence in 1799. In

Serbia in 1804 George Petrovich (1766-1817), also known as Karageorge, won independence for his country, but the government was crushed in 1813. Milosh Obrenovich (1781-1860) led another revolt. He won autonomy for Serbia in 1817 and full independence in 1830. Serbia became the nucleus of present Yugoslavia.

The Greeks revolted against Turkey in conjunction with the uprisings of 1820-1821. The Holy Alliance did not dare suppress this movement of a Christian people for independence. Instead, Europe favored aid to the rebels. The Greek Rebellion raged from 1821 to 1829. Each side resorted to the massacre of whole enemy towns. Britain, France, and Russia sent in warships which destroyed the Turkish navy at Navarino (1827). Russian aid finally forced Turkey to grant independence to Greece in 1829. Later, a Bavarian prince took the throne in Greece as King Otto I. During these years Moldavia and Wallachia, parts of Rumania, were granted autonomy as well as Serbia. In the general enthusiasm in Europe for Greek independence, the poet Byron and others volunteered to aid the rebels.

REVIEW QUESTIONS

Multiple-choice:
1. The chief means for bringing agreement among nations to preserve the Vienna settlements was   1) an international organization of all nations   2) the Congress system   3) the Holy Alliance   4) resort to a code of international law.

2. The first nation to abandon the others in providing for enforcement of the principles laid down at Vienna was   1) France   2) Russia   3) Austria   4) Prussia   5) Great Britain.

3. The leading nation in the founding of the Holy Alliance was   1) Russia   2) France   3) Spain   4) Italy   5) Austria.

4. The addition of which nation to the Quadruple Alliance created the Quintuple Alliance?   1) Spain   2) Britain   3) France   4) Germany.

5. The Monroe Doctrine was declared, because 1) Great Britain was threatening to take the Spanish colonies in America 2) there was fear that France might aid Spain in the reconquest of the new republics in America. 3) some colonies planned to rejoin the mother country 4) Portugal was planning the reconquest of Brazil.

6. Which statement is not true about the Monroe Doctrine? 1) Only American military power prevented the reconquest of Latin America 2) the pronouncement originated at the suggestion of the British 3) the Doctrine had little significance until after 1850 4) the British fleet stood ready to enforce the principles of the warning.

7. Which was *not* an aim of Metternich's system? 1) The preservation of Austria 2) the preservation of peace 3) preservation of the monarchical system 4) the full restoration of the institutions of the Old Regime.

8. The influence of Metternich in Germany resulted in 1) victory for the *Burschenschaften* 2) the Peterloo massacre 3) the Carlsbad Decrees 4) the restoration of the Holy Roman Empire.

9. National independence movements in the Balkans were supported by all the powers *except* 1) Russia 2) Turkey 3) France 4) Britain.

FOR FURTHER READING

HARDBOUND:

Halevy, E., *The Liberal Awakening, 1815-1830* (2nd ed., 1949).

Henderson, E. F., *A Short History of Germany* (1931).

Kissinger, Henry A., *A World Restored* (1958). Diplomacy after the Vienna Conference.

May, Arthur, *The Age of Metternich, 1814-1848* (1933). Brief introduction.

Mowat, R. B., *States of Europe, 1815-1871* (1922). Emphasizes diplomatic history.

Perkins, Dexter, *The Monroe Doctrine* (1933). The best study.

Phillips, Walter A., *War of Greek Independence* (1897).

Temperley, H. W. V., *Foreign Policy of Canning* (1925).

PAPERBOUND:

Artz, Frederick B., *Reaction and Revolution, 1814-1832* (Torchbooks). Europe after the defeat of Napoleon.

Fulford, Roger, *George the Fourth* (Capricorn).

May, Arthur, *The Age of Metternich, 1814-1848* (Berkshire). Useful brief account.

ESSAY TYPE REVIEW QUESTIONS FOR MID-TERM AND FINAL EXAMINATIONS

1. What action did the Holy Alliance take to repress democracy and nationalism?

2. Explain the origin, meaning, and application of the Monroe Doctrine.

3. State the conservative viewpoint and philosophy.

4. Discuss the origin, meaning, and expression of romanticism.

5. Explain the relationship of nationalism and liberalism. Where and how did these movements express themselves after 1815?

6. What factors delayed and later advanced the industrialization of the United States?

7. Explain the philosophy of utilitarianism. Who were its leading exponents?

8. Distinguish between Utopian and Scientific Socialism. Explain three of four of the main doctrines of Marx.

9. What is the difference in the forces behind the revolutions of 1830 and 1848? In which did notable failures occur and what is the significance of each of these movements taken separately.

10. How did Belgium win independence? Discuss fully.

11. What were the various political factions in France and why were various groups discontented with the government of Louis Philippe?

12. How did Louis Napoleon come to power in France?

1729-1797	*Edmund Burke*
1748-1832	*Jeremy Bentham*
1760-1825	*Saint-Simon*
1771-1858	*Robert Owen*
1772-1837	*Fourier*
1798-1857	*Comte*
1806-1873	*John Stuart Mill*
1807-1815	*Napoleonic wars cause factories to be built in the United States*
1809-1865	*Proudhon*
1811-1882	*Louis Blanc*
1814-1876	*Bakunin*
1818-1883	*Karl Marx*
1827	*Steam locomotives built in England*
1830	*Social legislation passed in Britain after this time*
*1848	Communist Manifesto
1867	Das Kapital *published*

2. Political, Economic, and Social Movements of the Early Nineteenth Century

Much of the impetus of the nineteenth century reform movements is attributed to the forces released by the French Revolution and the reaction to such forces. But rapid improvements in the technology of production also brought changes in social organization. In attempting to solve the problems of contrasting poverty and wealth created by the Industrial Revolution, thinkers advanced new ideas for economic and political organization. Political philosophies found expression in the practical world through political movements and political parties.

CONSERVATISM, ROMANTICISM, NATIONALISM

These broad movements are associated first with the Napoleonic era and the decades immediately following.

**Conservatism. The social philosophy of conservatism, which continues to the present time, arose as an intellectual response to the French Revolution and to the Age of Reason. Conservatism represented a defense of the old order against violent and sudden changes in its institutions. The outstanding voice of conservatism was Edmund Burke (1729-1797). In 1790 he wrote his *Reflections on the Revolution in France.* This new conservatism cautioned against any complete break with the past as a way of introducing an ideal government or

11

society. After the Restoration, thinkers in various nations, men like Friedrich von Gentz of Austria, elaborated the defense of conservatism. To the individualism of the bourgeoisie and the equalitarianism of the proletariat, the conservatives reacted by advising caution in breaking with the tried and proven. Conservatives pointed to the lessons of history, experience, and tradition. Conservatives defended the system of privileged classes, social stability, and class stratification; they defended the old institutions of monarchy, of aristocracy, and of the Church. Conservatism was both a reaction against rationalism and a successor to social theory that defended divine-right absolutism of the Old Regime. The conservatives distrusted intellectuals and defended religion. Opposing conservatism was the philosophy of liberalism, discussed later in this chapter.

Romanticism. An attitude toward art and society known as romanticism flourished in the generation after the French Revolution. This movement in art represented a reaction against the formality, elegance, harmony, and restraint of classicism. In philosophy, romanticism revolted against rationalism and in its place exalted instinct, feeling, and emotion. Romanticism defended individualism, idealism, and freedom. But it was not entirely a forward-looking attitude, since it was fascinated with the medieval past and often upheld traditionalism. One aspect of romanticism was its revival of religion, both Protestant and Catholic.

Rousseau, the early romanticist, was widely read, since he disagreed with the rationalists. He advocated a return to nature, but as a romanticist he rebelled against the restraints and the conventions of organized society. A part of the movement was democratic in its exaltation of the common man, but other romanticists were monarchist in their political philosophy. The term *romanticism* is associated particularly with the world of art.

In Germany romantic writers with liberal ideas included Schiller, Heine, and Goethe. In England there flourished such romantic poets as Wordsworth, Coleridge, Byron, Shelley, and Keats. In their novels Sir Walter Scott in England and Victor Hugo in France revived the medieval past of their respective countries. In American literature the romantics included Irving, Cooper, Poe, Hawthorne, Byrant, Emerson, Thoreau, and Whitman. Romanticism flourished in music. The characteristic formality of the minuet and the precision of the sonata gave way to great symphonies and operas. Romantic composers in Germany included Brahms, Schubert, Mendelssohn, Weber, and Wagner. Rossini and Verdi in Italy, Franck and Berlioz in France, Listz in Hungary, Chopin in Poland, and in Russia Rimsky-Korsakov, Glinka, Moussorgsky, and Tschaikovsky composed great new music. Opera, often related to patriotism, revived the romantic medieval past.

Nationalism and liberalism. Nationalism, another powerful force in the post-Napoleonic world, is most simply defined as the strong devotion of people toward their own country. Nationalism is a special attachment to the features that make a given country unique—its language, culture, distinct racial characteristics (if any), its customs and traditions, and the unification under a single government of the geographic area occupied by a people. Nationalism often retrogresses to a narrow feeling of superiority over other countries. It also represents a resentment against foreign or imperial controls and the accompanying desire of a people for independence of foreign rule or even foreign influence. We have seen that nationalism surged during and after the French Revolution as disunited peoples such as the Germans and Italians wished for unity and subject peoples such as the Poles, Finns, Greeks, and Belgians wanted self-government. Romanticism reinforced the emotional basis of nationalism. Each movement strove for some kind of freedom. Middle class business people supported nationalism for what it could do to consolidate markets at home and extend and protect the domestic and foreign business interests of a nation. Thus, nationalism is more closely associated with the bourgeoisie than with the aristocracy, for the privileges of the aristocracy gave them a vested interest in preserving vestigial feudalistic units of government which they ruled as princes. Historians, philosophers, and artists advanced or exploited nationalist themes. In most of the nineteenth century, liberalism went in hand with nationalism, because nationalism then was supported by democratic elements who wished to throw off the rule of foreign autocrats. Today, nationalism among colonial peoples is still often allied with liberalism. But in advanced industrialized nations nationalism represents a conservative attitude opposed to the innovation of internationalism, which is supported by liberals today.

THE INDUSTRIAL REVOLUTION

The beginnings of the Industrial Revolution have been traced as a part of an earlier historical period. After 1815 the tempo of the change from agriculture to industry increased. Before 1830 the factory system had made its greatest progress in England, but after 1815 France also, to a limited extent, was undergoing its own industrial revolution.

Transportation progress. The growth of railroad transportation over Europe paralleled the growth of industry. However, earlier improved transportation was provided by the construction of roads and canals well before the French Revolution. After 1800 the Scottish engineer Macadam began the construction of hard-surfaced roads of broken stone. Improved transportation was needed to gather raw materials for the factories and to distribute finished products. The boom in railway building began when steam locomotives were developed in Britain about 1827. Several thousand miles of track were in use by 1850. Railroads stimulated coal-mining and iron production. Robert Fulton's invention of the practical steamboat in 1807 began the widespread use of the steamboat, which proved so important in widening markets over the world.

Industrial progress. Among the important aids to industrial progress was the development of better communications. The penny post was introduced in England in 1840. The telegraph, invented by Samuel Morse, came into use after 1850 and in the next decade the trans-Atlantic cable began successful operation. Everywhere newspapers and magazines became numerous and gained wide circulation.

After England, France increased her industrialization. Germany and Italy suffered from a lack of the political unity that was needed to provide a large area of protected markets for national industry. Railroad construction there grew rapidly after 1840. The rest of Europe, except for parts of Austria, remained pre-industrial for a few more decades.

Industrialization in the United States. In America the introduction of the factory system was delayed by a lack of labor and the attractiveness of other opportunities. The exploitation of the immense resources of timber, soil, fur-bearing animals, and minerals engaged pioneers in the extractive industries, and the nation for long remained a great exporter of raw materials. The production of cotton, wheat, and meat were oustanding agricultural industries producing exports that were exchanged for the industrial goods of Europe. Capital was employed more profitably in shipping and commerce, in agriculture and extractive industries, and in land speculation. The development of transportation facilities and private and public improvements in a frontier land required much capital, including borrowed money drawn from Europe. Great stimulus to American industry came first when British goods were excluded during the Napoleonic Wars, particularly the War of 1812 with Great Britain. Industrial progress continued after 1815 under tariff protection, a means of excluding foreign competition by nations retarded in their industrial development. During the 1840's and 1850's heavy immigration for the first time brought an adequate labor supply. Turnpikes, steamboats, canals, and railroads provided transportation facilities for gathering raw materials and marketing finished goods. The Civil War won political predominance of manufacturing and other business interests of the North over the South. Favorable political climate after 1860 nourished a still more rapid growth of American business society.

***Effects of industrialization.** The great problem arising from industrialization was the sharp separation of owners and workers into two classes, capitalists and the proletariat. No institutions existed for the protection of workers from gross exploitation; therefore, workers did not share the product of industry but worked long hours often under harmful conditions. In time the machines introduced the problem of industrial unemployment. Industrial capitalism superseded commercial capitalism as the factory system grew.

Accompanying the industrial and agricultural revolutions was a great increase in population, an increase due to the greater availability of foodstuffs and to the rising standard of living. Medical science, sanitation, and freedom from war extended the average life span and thus helped increase the population.

Urbanization, the growth of large cities, resulted from the construction of factories that attracted workers by providing their livelihood. Crowded, ugly, and unsanitary factory towns became a concomitant of the growth of industry. Urban problems of pure water, sewage disposal, fire and police protection, and sanitary housing had not yet become a public responsibility. Important shifts in population occurred as agricultural areas lost migrants to urban, industrial areas. The earlier rural conflicts of peasants and landlords receded, and in the nineteenth century workers, fighting from barricades or protesting in great demonstrations, struggled against bourgeois capitalists.

ECONOMIC THOUGHT AND ACTION

In the early nineteenth century, social thought to a considerable extent dealt with the conflict between the rising middle class and the aristocracy. Later social thought concerned itself more with the improvement of the lot of the submerged working class. The term *liberalism* has added new meanings so that its use often causes confusion, but one needs to realize that it may have different meanings to different people and in different contexts. It originally meant liberation of businessmen and others from restraints of government, religion, and so on. In our own time the word expresses a philosophy that advocates government intervention on behalf of persons in the lower economic brackets. The early liberals fought for political freedom and humanitarianism; modern liberals work for the economic freedom of individuals and for humanitarianism.

**Bentham and Utilitarianism. Jeremy Bentham (1748-1832), an English philosopher and reformer, judged man's institutions by their utility. The utility of anything in question was measured in terms of the happiness and freedom from pain it would produce. Democracy and freedom, Bentham said, would produce the greatest happiness for the greatest number. Government might intervene if needed to promote the greatest total satisfaction. Bentham wrote his major work in 1789, but his philosophy became an active force through his disciples in England after 1820. His son James Bentham and the thinker John Stuart Mill (1806-1873) developed his ideas further. Mill advocated education as an aid in the solution of man's problems. He advocated freedom from government interference in man's activities, except when necessary to protect people from each other. He advocated a maximum of personal freedom except in such things as compulsory payment of taxes and service in the military forces. These views appealed to the middle class. Mill, as a rationalist and humanitarian, believed in government regulation to prevent injustice and exploitation.

Social reform.   Legislation to prevent exploitation and abuse of workers by middle class employers originated with humanitarian Tories. The British Parliament passed successive "Factory Acts" beginning in 1802. These acts limited working hours of apprentices and children and fixed age limits below which children could not work. Women and children were excluded from employment in mining after 1842. Local boards of health and poor relief laws were passed after 1830. France and Germany passed acts providing very limited regulation of working hours for children. Germany and France promoted public education even before the Industrial Revolution, but England lagged behind the Continent in promoting education.

When labor began to organize in England, Parliament passed Combination Acts against such activities. In 1824 the Combination Acts were repealed because of the agitation of working class friends. Strikes continued to be regarded by common law as conspiracy against the public interest. Not until 1871 did trade unions (labor unions) gain full legal recognition. The labor movement lagged on the Continent.

Comte and Positivism.   On the Continent the philosophy nearest related to English Utilitarianism was the Positivism of Auguste Comte (1798-1857). This German philosopher is best known as the founder of sociology, the science of human society. Comte was an empiricist in his approach to the study of man's social behavior: truth was to be ascertained only by observation or experience and not through religion or metaphysics. He believed men were motivated by altruism and not by self-interest alone, as Bentham taught. Comte proposed a Religion of Humanity as a means of improving men's relations with each other and of promoting social progress.

SOCIALISM AND OTHER REFORM PROPOSALS

After 1830 many varieties of socialism were advocated as solutions for maladjustments created by the spread of industrialism over Europe. Socialists share the belief that the social ownership of various economic resources and productive facilities is needed and the extreme differences in individual incomes are not justifiable. Socialists favor economic as well as political equality as social ideals. Capitalism, they argue, has failed to solve the problems created by the Industrial Revolution. Socialism arises especially from the demands of the industrial proletariat for a greater share of the good things produced by modern industry.

**The Utopian Socialists. Early socialist thought is usually referred to as Utopian Socialism because of its unrealistic approach to economic problems. The Utopians were humanitarians and philanthropists and did not advocate revolutionary violence as a means of introducing reforms. They favored the example of successful communitarian colonies.

Count Henri de Saint-Simon (1760-1825), the first of the French Utopian Socialists, originated the famous socialist principle: "From each according to his capacity and to each according to his needs." His numerous followers were mainly responsible for the spread of his ideas. He advocated social supervision of the production and distribution of goods and the abolition of private property.

Charles Fourier (1772-1837) advocated improvement of

individuals by providing a proper environment. He proposed organizing "phalanxes" of about 1700 individuals living in self-sufficient socialist communities. Many Fourierist colonies were set up in the United States where land was cheap, but they quickly broke up because they often attracted a large number of misfits. The appeal of individual opportunity on the outside was too strong for the more industrious.

Louis Blanc (1811-1882) exposed the evils of laissez-faire society and proposed political action as an approach to economic and social reform. He favored state-sponsored national workshops cooperatively owned and run by workers, with individuals being reworded according to need rather than productivity. Blanc's idea was subverted by the revolutionary government in France in 1848: instead of creating genuinely productive workshops, unproductive work relief was provided and it discredited the movement. Blanc differed from the Utopians because he did not advocate socialist colonies but government subsidies of workshops to provide jobs.

Robert Owen (1771-1858) was England's most prominent Utopian Socialist. Owen, a philanthropist who had made a fortune in cotton milling, was appalled at conditions in the textile industry. He created a model industrial community at his New Lanark Mills, where he reduced hours, increased wages and improved living conditions. At the same time, he actually increased the productivity of workers and company profits. New Lanark became a model for all of Europe. Owen experimented with an ideal community he organized at New Harmony, Indiana, but the community failed because of the shortcomings of its members and the attractions of free enterprise on the outside.

***Marxian (scientific) Socialism.** Karl Marx (1818-1883) and Frederick Engels (1820-1895) of Germany originated the type of socialism (better called communism) which became the basis of the Bolshevik Revolution in Russia. Marx, an exile from Germany, met Engels in Paris in 1844; an intellectual partnership sprang up between the two. In 1848 they published the *Communist Manifesto*. After 1848 Marx went to England. In 1867 he published the first volume of his most famous work, *Das Kapital* (*Capital*).

Marx's thought is best known for his economic, or materialistic, interpretation of history and his theory of the class struggle. 1] He stressed the influence of man's economic environment—the way people make a living—as fundamental in determining the political, social, and cultural institutions of society. Previously historians had explained history in terms of intellectual or other determining factors. The present full recognition of economic factors is due to the influence of Marx. 2] Marx explained that man's history had always been one of struggle between classes. In his time the struggle between the industrial capitalists and the working proletariat had been joined. Eventually, he said, capitalism would collapse and the proletariat would emerge victorious and create a classless society under which the means of production would be owned by the new proletarian state. Marx sought to make workers class-conscious—to think that the interests of workers were opposed to those of capitalists. Marx advocated international cooperation among workers and class loyalty instead of national loyalty. 3] Marx's theory of surplus value stated that the difference between the wage paid the worker and the market value of the goods he produces is surplus value and that this value, under capitalism, is confiscated. It is paid to property owners when it should go to workers, he said. Labor is the only factor of production. Capitalist economic theory states that land, labor, capital, and management are all factors of production and each deserves its income return. Many of Marx's predictions have failed to be realized. The poor have not grown poorer but have come to share in the wealth created by the capitalist-owned factories. Man shows an attachment to religion that Marx never expected.

Marx's influence is due more to his *Communist Manifesto* than to his other works; its enormous influence is evident in the present Communist governments and in the writings and deeds of numberless followers of Marxian thought. Marx was influential because he found a great following among working people themselves, whereas earlier socialists had not.

Anarchism. The goal of anarchism was the destruction of capitalism and of organized government. Pierre-Joseph Proudhon (1809-1865) is the outstanding early anarchist. Proudhon wished, like the socialists, to improve the lot of the worker. Since anarchists opposed organized government as a form of oppression, many at first opposed communism. According to Proudhon, society should consist of free and equal individuals who collaborate for efficiency in production.

Michael Bakunin (1814-1876), a Russian nobleman, became anarchism's greatest advocate. He proposed a collective society, one of federal communities in each of which property would be held in common. Bakunin advocated violence—terrorism, insurrection, assassination—as means of destroying the state. Anarchists were responsible for innumerable bombings and assassinations over Europe in the late nineteenth century. Anarchists trust in the essential goodness of human nature and advocate voluntary economic cooperation. Anarchism has arisen mainly in countries where great oppression existed.

REVIEW QUESTIONS

Multiple-choice:

1. The French Revolution had the immediate effect of strengthening which attitude in Britain? 1) Conservatism 2) liberalism 3) Romanticism 4) Chartism.

2. The movement of Romanticism 1) was uniformly opposed to religion 2) was both conservative and liberal in its attitude toward political questions 3) sought to preserve the rationalism of the Old Regime 4) drew much of its inspiration from Voltaire.

3. Nationalism was most closely identified with which? 1) the bourgeoisie 2) the aristocracy 3) peasantry 4) the proletariat.

4. The Industrial Revolution was delayed in the United States for all reasons *except* 1) alternative opportunities for the investment of capital 2) superior quality of imported manufactures 3) lack of sufficient labor supply 4) insufficient technical skills.

5. Legislation to limit the exploitation of workers originated at first with 1) middle-class liberals 2) the classical economists 3) humanitarian Tories 4) Christian Democrats.

Matching:

6. Edmund Burke	a. Wrote novels that revived the medieval past
7. Rousseau	
8. Sir Walter Scott	b. Best known advocate of utilitarianism.
9. Macadam	c. Noted as the British voice of conversatism
10. Fulton	
11. Jeremy Bentham	d. Advocated socialist communities, called "phalanxes."
12. John Stuart Mill	
13. Auguste Comte	e. Founder of sociology
14. Saint-Simon	f. The greatest of the romanticists
15. Charles Fourier	g. A classical economist
	h. Engineer of improved roads
	i. Earliest French Utopian Socialist
	j. Founder of Utilitarianism
	k. Identified with water transportation

Completion:

16. The French socialist who favored the organization of national workshops was named .....

17. The best known of the English Utopian Socialists was a) ...... who established an experimental colony at b) ...... Indiana.

18. The socialism advocated by Marx and Engels is known as a) ..... Socialism. These two leaders were joint authors of the b) ..... in 1848. Marx's best known work, written in German, was called c) ...... Marx thought of the class struggle as one between the capitalists and workers whom he designated by the special term, the d) . . . . . . Marx predicted the eventual collapse of e) . . . . .

19. An early French anarchist was named a) . . . . . and the best known Russian anarchist was named b) . . . . . .

FOR FURTHER READING

HARDBOUND:

Cheyney, Edward P., *An Introduction to the Industrial and Social History of England* (1923).

Clapham, John H., *The Economic Development of France and Germany* (1923).

Day, Clive, *History of Commerce* (1938).

Dietz, Frederick C., *The Industrial Revolution* (1927). Brief.

Hammond, J. L., and Hammond, B., *The Rise of British Industry* (1934). Short survey.

Heston, Herbert, *Economic History of Europe* (1936).

Paine, Thomas, *The Rights of Man.*

Russell, Bertrand, *Freedom versus Organization, 1814–1914* (1934). Narrative of the liberal movement.

Schumpeter, Joseph, *Capitalism, Socialism, and Democracy* (1942).

Toynbee, Arnold, *Lectures on the Industrial Revolution of the Eighteenth Century in England* (1884). By the historian who popularized the term "Industrial Revolution."

Woodward, Ernest, *The Age of Reform, 1815-1870* (1938). Applies to Britain.

PAPERBOUND:

Ashton, T. S., *Industrial Revolution: 1760-1830* (Galaxy).

Barzun, Jacques, *Classic, Romantic, and Modern* (Anchor).

Burke, Edmund, *Reflections on the Revolution in France* (Galaxy; Liberal Arts). The conservative reaction to the French Revolution.

Halevy, Elie, *The Growth of Philosophical Radicalism* (Beacon). Covers English reforms of the early nineteenth century.

Mill, John Stuart, *Utilitarianism* (Liberal Arts). The best classic statement of the theories of the Utilitarians.

Wishy, Bernard, ed., *Prefaces to Liberty: John Stuart Mill's Political Writings* (Beacon).

1814-1824	*Louis XVII, king of France*
1818	*German Zollverein established*
1819	*"Peterloo" massacre*
1820	*Revolution failed*
1824-1830	*Charles X, king of France*
1829	*Religious disabilities removed in Britain*
*1830	*July, Revolution in France*
	Belgium won independence
	Revolutions spread over Europe
*1830-1848	*Louis Philippe, king of France*
*1832	*British Reform Bill of 1832*
1833	*Negro slavery abolished in the British Empire*
*1839	*Belgium independence recognized and neutrality guaranteed*
*1846	*Corn Laws repealed*
*1848	*February, Revolution in France*
	Second French Republic established
	December, Louis Napoleon elected president
	Revolution spread all over Europe
	Chartist movement in Britain failed
1848-1916	*Franz Joseph, emperor of Austria-Hungary*
*1849	*Frankfort Constitution drafted; rejected by King Frederick William*
1850	*"Humiliation of Olmutz."*

3. The Revolutions of 1830 and 1848

The failure of the revolutions of 1820 merely postponed the gains that the liberals and the bourgeoisie were to make at the expense of the conservative and reactionary classes. France in 1830 and Britain in 1832 took the lead in transferring power from the aristocracy to the middle classes, actually upper middle classes. The struggle of the middle class and workingmen for a voice in government, as well as the national aspirations of various European peoples, accounts for the uprisings of 1830 and 1848. The example of the successful and rising democracy of the United States was no small factor in encouraging the strivings for popular government in Europe.

THE REVOLUTIONS OF 1830

The reactionary period following the Napoleonic Wars gave way to liberalism in the 1830's. In most countries of Europe the liberals revolted or otherwise fought for a greater voice in the government of their countries.

**France after the Restoration. Louis XVIII (1814-1824), who became king of France after the restoration of the Bourbons, was no "ultraist" like those who wished to restore the Old Regime. His return did not bring a return of the government of the pre-Revolutionary France, since most of the reforms had become permanent. Louis endorsed the constitution of 1814, which granted Frenchmen equality before the law, offered freedom of the press and religion, and created a bicameral legislative body. But many "ultra-royalists" among the clericals and the restored nobility had learned nothing and had forgotten nothing and longed for the days before

26

1789. However, the next thing, the Ultraist Charles X (1824-1830), did take steps to restore the Old Regime. In 1825 Charles attempted to compensate the emigres for their estates confiscated in the Revolution. The compensation money was to be raised by reducing the interest on the national bonds held by the bourgeoisie. Another set of laws permitted the Jesuits to return to France, and Catholics were given additional control over education. The climax came in July, 1830, when Charles issued decrees dissolving a newly elected liberal chamber and disfranchising the liberal, wealthy bourgeoisie. In the ensuing revolt in Paris, the bourgeoisie were joined in the barricades by workers and students, and the army refused to attack them. Charles X abdicated and took refuge in England. The aged Lafayette persuaded the revolutionists to accept the liberal Louis Philippe, nephew of Charles X. The constitution was amended to make the king definitely subordinate to the Chambers. Thus the bourgeois monarchy had to suppress both reactionaries and radicals in order to retain power.

**Reaction in England after 1815. The ruling Tories in Britain continued to fear the disruption and horrors of the Revolution. When war orders were cancelled after the defeat of Napoleon, unemployment and depression caused severe distress which led to mass meetings of protest. The ruling Tories in Parliament reacted by striking at radical propaganda. They passed the Six Acts of 1819 which deprived the people of such fundamental rights as holding public meetings, bearing arms, and the free press. Working class leaders and middle-class exponents of the liberal ideas of Utilitarianism (such as those of Jeremy Bentham and James Mill) were now actively calling for reforms in government. Middle-class liberals favored such measures as the abolition of special privileges and a popular school system. In the wave of fear and repression, a crowd that had gathered to hear political speakers was fired upon at Manchester in what came to be known as the "Peterloo" massacre (1819). The king, George IV, a man of despicable character, did nothing to make the government more popular. After 1822 moderate and more popular Tories came to power and began introducing reforms to lessen the harshness of the penal codes, to reduce the special privileges of Anglicans, and to withdraw trade restrictions of the old mercantile system. England withdrew from the Quadruple Alliance, aid was given the liberals in Portugal and Greece, and the new republics were recognized in Latin America.

The British Reform Bill of 1832. English liberalism gained further victories in 1828 when civil restrictions against religious noncomformists were repealed and in 1829 when the Wellington ministry achieved Catholic emancipation (by abolishing the political disabilities of the Catholics). The philosophic reformers, followers of Bentham, now concentrated on the larger issue of parliamentary reform. The basis of representation had not been changed since medieval times, yet great population changes had occurred as between different sections of England. Large industrial cities were without representation in Parliament. The reformers wished to abolish the "Rotten Borough System," which included the "rotten" boroughs (parliamentary electoral districts which because of depleted population were easily controlled by local landlords), "pocket" boroughs (where the lord had the right to appoint a representative to Parliament), and "borough-mongering" (whereby rich men bought nominations to seats in Parliament). A clear cut issue now developed between Whigs and Tories. Tories opposed the Parliamentary reforms.

In 1831 a Whig ministry under Earl Grey came into power and replaced the Tory ministry of the Duke of Wellington. The Whigs introduced the Parliamentary Reform Bill, but it suffered defeat. New parliamentary elections gave the Whigs a great victory in a hard-fought contest. The Reform Bill passed the Commons but was thrown out by the Lords. Prime Minister Grey won the assent of King William IV to a plan to create new peers (members of the House of Lords) who would vote for the Reform Bill. The threat sufficed and the Lords passed the Bill. This reform was the equivalent of the July Revolution (1830) in France; it was a victory for the liberal businessmen over the nobility and actually effected a revolution. It redistributed representation in Parliament so as to give fairer representation to the middle industrial region of England that had been increasing its population at the expense of the old agricultural regions to the south and east. It extended the voting privilege to the middle classes. But the great masses of farm and industrial workers remained disfranchised; their enfranchisement would come in two later, orderly revolutions—the reform bills of 1867 and of 1884.

Belgian independence (1830, 1839). Belgium (formerly Austrian Netherlands), transferred to Holland at Vienna in 1815, had much reason to be discontented with her forced marriage to the Dutch. The Dutch government in general dominated the larger population of Belgium. To the religious differences between Catholic Belgium and Protestant Netherlands was added economic discriminations against the Belgians. The example of revolution in France set off rioting in Brussels. Dutch concessions came too late, and troops sent to suppress the uprising were defeated. Belgium drew up her own constitution in November, 1830. France and England approved Belgian independence and the reactionary powers were too occupied with revolts in their own lands to intervene. The great powers agreed to Belgian independence in 1830, but the Dutch did not give recognition until 1839. At the same time, Belgian independence and neutrality guaranteed by the European powers and respected until 1914 when Germany invaded her in defiance of the "scrap of paper." In the 1830's Belgium in her domestic affairs won a fairly liberal constitution and accepted the German prince Leopold as her king. Belgium prospered with the growth of industry. In 1848 the suffrage was extended and the number of voters doubled.

Spread of the revolution. Almost all parts of Europe in one way or another followed the revolutionary lead of France in 1830. Many German states overthrew their harsh sovereigns and others won moderately liberal constitutions. Demands for political unity and freedom were met with extremely repressive measures passed at Metternich's behest by the Frankfurt Diet. These measures limited the action of legislative assemblies and protected the authority of the thirty-six German kings against further concessions to liberals. German scholars in the universities found means of fostering a spirit of nationalism in spite of the repression. They turned particularly to the study of the history of Germany. Leopold von Ranke (1795-1886) published the sources of German history to make them available to other scholars. He established a reputation as one of the world's great historians. G. W. F. Hegel, a philosopher and historian, published his *Philosophy of History*. He wrote that each age produced a great nation that fulfilled a mission to dominate civilization. Germany would play such a role in the future but must prepare herself by building a powerful military state. But the nationalist Hegel was not a liberal. He envisaged the Hohenzollerns as the future leaders of a German monarchical state.

Liberal outbursts occurred in Spain and Portugal. Spain too became after a time a constitutional monarchy in name but was ruled by a succession of dictators. Metternich sent Austrian troops into Italy to suppress uprisings and restore legitimate rulers. In 1852 Portugal's military dictatorship gave way to a parliamentary government and more stability. Secret nationalist societies in Poland fomented revolt in 1830. The Poles set up a provisional government; it took Russia nearly a year to crush the revolt. But in effect Poland became more thoroughly repressed than ever when it was made a province of Russia.

THE REVOLUTION OF 1848 IN FRANCE

In the great wave of revolutionary activity in 1848 about fifty uprisings occurred. These movements struck for both more liberal governments and for national independence, where such aspirations had not been satisfied. The working class made demands for socialist measures.

***Causes and character of the Revolutions of 1848.** The purpose of the European revolutions in 1848 was to extend the popular gains made during the French Revolution. In general, they represented the urban lower middle class and the workers rather than the upper middle class that had been prominent in earlier revolutionary movements. Everywhere, people were seeking more liberal governments and the end of feudal vestiges. Among subject peoples arose the demand for self-government and in Italy and Germany for unification of the nation. The unemployment accompanying the economic crisis of 1846-1847 helped to trigger the uprisings. The competition of machinery with hand weavers and spinners and low wages in the factories added to the unrest. Crop failures, including the "potato famines" in Ireland and Germany, caused much suffering and actual starvation.

**France under Louis Philippe. The most significant political developments continued to occur in France, since she was the most modern and the greatest power on the continent until the unification of Germany in 1870. The dissatisfaction with the regime of Louis Philippe lies in the background of the Revolution of 1848 in France.

Louis Philippe represented the middle-class virtues of simplicity, thrift, and industry. The wealthy industrialists

prevented reform measures to improve the lot of the workers
or to share the increasing wealth with them. There was much
labor unrest and agitation. Bondholders resisted reductions
in interest rates, and industrialists kept protective tariffs in
effect. In the thirties the king resisted the somewhat aggressive foreign policies of Thiers and forced him to resign in
order to prevent war. In 1840 the unprogressive Guizot became prime minister to the king and served until 1848. The
government promoted economic prosperity, and trade increased rapidly. An aggressive foreign policy and military adventures were avoided. Working class discontent was suppressed. Many Frenchmen were unhappy with the dullness
and lack of idealism of the government and desired a more
vigorous foreign policy rather than one that made compromises to avoid war.

***Political elements in France.** In the 1840's various par-
ties and other elements in France were divided into factions
that were somewhat characteristic of her subsequent political
life and somewhat typical of other participants in revolutionary movements in some other parts of Europe. 1] The bourgeoisie, in control, wished to preserve the gains of the French
Revolution but did not wish to share their power with the
workers. 2] The socialists were made up of the working classes
who followed the teachings of Saint-Simon and Louis Blanc.
The workers usually took the lead in revolutionary causes.
3] The republicans, a fast-growing faction, included not only
workers but intellectuals—writers, teachers, and scientists.
Conservative and reactionary groups included   1] the Legitimists who represented the Bourbon family and were supported
by the aristocracy. This group was the most reactionary of all.
2] The peasants became a conservative force after coming
into full possession of their landholdings. 3] The clericals,
those who favored a more powerful Catholic Church, bitterly
opposed the revolutionary changes for all the losses inflicted

upon them. 4] The Bonapartists, militaristic followers of the Napoleonic tradition, wished France to assert its military power once again. Their leader was Louis Napoleon who had been imprisoned after an attempt to start an uprising to gain control of France.

***The February Revolution in France.** In the late 1840's the increasing opposition to the policies of the minister Guizot were fomented at "reform banquets," where middle-class spokesmen indulged in oratory and resolutions against the government. Opponents of the government prepared a huge banquet in Paris to be held in a working-class section of the city on February 22, 1848. When the government forbade this banquet that had been planned by radicals, students, workers, and others joined in throwing up barricades, and street fighting began. The National Guard joined the agitators and demanded extension of the suffrage. Louis Philippe, to avoid further bloodshed, decided to abdicate and fled to England. A republic was proclaimed and a provisional government set up. The powerful socialists won the adoption of Louis Blanc's idea of national workshops to provide productive employment for the jobless. The jobs provided proved to be only a form of uneconomic work relief and discredited the whole program. Bourgeois republicans and other moderates took alarm at the wasteful unemployment relief and the radical demands of the socialists and workers. In elections held in April for a national assembly, other factions combined to defeat the socialists and the new government began to eliminate the national workshops. In June a socialist uprising was bloodily crushed by the regular army led by General Cavaignac, a moderate republican.

The republicans and conservatives drew up a constitution providing a strong president elected by universal suffrage. France's Second Republic had been created. In December, 1848, a new election was held to choose the president. Louis

Napoleon, a nephew of Napoleon I, won election by an overwhelming majority, and conservatives won control of the
assembly. Louis Napoleon won not only the support of the
Bonapartists but of others, because he bore the aura of the
great Napoleon. Peasants, the middle class, and others had
now become convinced that France needed a strong government to keep the radical workers under control. The assembly
increased the powers of the president in the summer of 1849.
In 1850 the assembly restricted the suffrage and enacted legislation that increased the control of the Catholic Church over
education. Louis Napoleon used his influence to discredit the
assembly. He toured the provinces to popularize himself further and took other steps in preparation for the coup d'état by
which he was to overthrow the Second Republic and establish
the Second Empire.

SPREAD OF THE REVOLUTIONS OF 1848

In 1848 revolution in France once again gave the signal
for the outbreak of similar movements elsewhere in Europe.

**Revolutionary movements in Germany.   In 1818 a practical
beginning toward German unification was begun in the
Zollverein (tariff union) under Prussian leadership. By the
1830's over half the German states had joined the union. It
was fortunate that Austria was excluded because of her stubborn opposition to any kind of German unity that would
destroy her hegemony there. In the revolutionary movements
of 1830 political reform had made only a little progress and
repression continued as before. Nevertheless, liberal agitation
by nationalists and business classes gave rise to a new spirit
that favored reform and unification.

Following the rash of revolutionary outbursts in March,
1848, several leaders called the famous assembly at Frankfurt
to write a liberal constitution for a federated government for

Germany. The Frankfurt Assembly split over the issue of including non-Germanic people and over the issue of a constitutional monarchy. The Greater Germany faction disagreed with the Little Germany faction over the inclusion of Austria and parts of other lands with alien peoples. Nevertheless, after a year a constitution was prepared which called for a limited monarchy and the inclusion of only German states. King Frederick William IV of Prussia, after the liberals had grown weaker, now discourteously refused to accept the crown under a limited monarchy and from the hands of a bourgeois assembly. But Frederick William himself then tried to create a federal union under Prussia. Austria took advantage of the weak and vacillating king and forced him to drop the plan. The king agreed, in the Treaty of Olmutz (1850) with Austria, to restore the former weak Confederation (Bund). Thus, Germany relapsed into its old Bund with its capital at Frankfurt. The larger liberal movement for unification in Germany was soon crushed, and many of the more radical leaders went into exile; many emigrated to the United States.

Revolution in Austria. Austria too was shaken by the revolutionary movements of 1848. The people of Vienna rose and drove the repressive Prince Metternich out of office, and the Emperor of Austria bowed to the revolutionary demands for a parliament and similar democratic reforms. The Hungarians set up their own government at Budapest; the Austrians were thrown out of Lombardy and Venetia; the Czechs took steps toward home rule. The uprising of Louis Kossuth in Hungary forced Metternich to resign. The Poles revolted, too. As elsewhere, the force of the liberal uprisings failed quickly after March, 1848. Bohemian revolutionists called a Pan-Slavic Congress at Prague, seeking to unify the Slavic peoples under Austria. But this movement was crushed in June by an Austrian army under Prince Windischgratz. The same general took control of Vienna, and the Emperor Ferdinand, who had given in to the rebels, was now forced to abdicate in favor of his nephew Francis Joseph (1848-1916). The Italians were defeated. In 1849 the Hungarian uprising was savagely crushed with Russian aid and the other uprisings were suppressed. Subsequently, limited reforms were undertaken by the Austrian government.

Revolution in Italy. The main objective of the revolution in Italy was to drive out the Austrians. In this the states of Lombardy and Venetia took the lead in 1848. Other states supported the movement against the Austrians. Among these were Sardinia under Charles Albert, Pope Pius IX, and the king of Naples. The revolt in Italy turned into a complete failure, however. The pope soon repudiated the unification movement, and the king of Naples withdrew after he had overthrown the liberal regime that had just been set up there. The Sardinians were defeated. The reforms of the revolution were quickly rescinded. The revolution of the republicans and their war against the pope antagonized the moderates. Italy was split between constitutional monarchists and radical republicans. When the pope repudiated the unification movement, the people of Rome revolted and set up a republic early in 1849. But Louis Napoleon sent troops to Rome to restore Pius IX. The revolution failed in Italy, because of Austrian military power and disunity among the Italians. From the experience of 1848 Italian patriots concluded that the republic of Mazzini was impractical and that the pope could not serve as the leader of a united Italy.

Repeal of the Corn Laws in Britain. The landed aristocracy in Britain had long taken advantage of its control of Parliament to maintain high tariffs on food grains, a means of increasing profits to a small class of landowners but one which increased the cost of food to workers. In 1838 an Anti-Corn

Law League was organized; the league was sponsored by two able and wealthy factory owners, John Bright and Richard Cobden who were hostile to the landed interests. Many other tariffs had already been reduced or repealed. The Anti-Corn Law League and the liberals fought for repeal in the press and in Parliament. The famine in Ireland helped build up sentiment for repeal. Sir Robert Peel, who also was a factory owner, took the lead in winning the final victory with repeal in 1846. Repeal enabled Britain to import cheaper foodstuffs for workers. By 1860 this free trade principle had been extended to nearly all goods that had been formerly protected. Britain's advantage in manufacturing enabled her to compete successfully with other nations, and there was no longer any advantage in preserving the protective principle but national profit to be gained by its repeal. In fact, England's industrial prosperity and output now rapidly increased. Not idealism but Britain's ability to meet foreign competitors in manufactures explains the adoption of free trade at this time.

English reforms and the Chartist movement. After the Reform Bill of 1832 the English Whigs reorganized themselves into the Liberal Party, and the Tories renamed themselves the "Conservatives." Even the Conservatives accepted some gradual reform. In 1833 Negro slavery was abolished throughout the empire; as the reform was carried out in subsequent years, plantation operators in the British West Indies and other colonies suffered great distress. After many years of agitation the working hours of women and children in factories were reduced to ten hours in 1847.

Since the Reform Act of 1832 still left most Englishmen disfranchised, radical agitators and working class sympathizers undertook to extend the franchise and other reforms. The agitation produced a movement, quite radical for the time, known as the People's Charter or Chartism. The Chartist demands were: 1] universal manhood suffrage, 2] the secret ballot, 3] annual parliamentary elections, 4] equal electoral districts, 5] payment of salaries to members of parliament, and 6] abolition of property qualifications for members of the House of Commons. The Chartists presented their first petition to Parliament in 1839 but it was overwhelmingly voted down. The Chartists tried to intimidate Parliament with a monster petition in 1848 and a mass demonstration, but Parliament stood firm and the movement faded out. All of the provisions were later realized except annual elections which were impractical anyway. But the Chartist movement itself failed in 1848. The earlier repeal of the Corn Laws had made food cheaper, and the steady improvement of living conditions deprived the movement of much of its force for the time being.

Effects of the revolutionary movements elsewhere. In the Netherlands in 1848 King William II granted a new constitution which made ministers partly responsible to the legislature and extended the suffrage. The Scandinavian countries, Denmark and Sweden, gradually adopted economic and political changes in keeping with the industrial and liberal growths of the times. In 1849 Denmark won a more liberal constitution. In 1848 Switzerland adopted a new constitution, which provided a federal system similar to that of the United States. This helped solve the long struggle between conservative rural Catholic cantons and the liberal rural Protestant cantons.

REVIEW QUESTIONS

Multiple-choice:

1. The main cause of the Revolution of 1830 in France was 1) the desire of the Paris working class for the vote   2) the attempt of Charles X to restore absolute monarchy   3) the failure

of the middle class to win control of the monarchy   4) disappointment of the French imperialists.

2. The revolution of 1830 reflected mainly the aspirations of 1) the working class   2) the lesser nobility   3) the clergy   4) the middle class.

3. The British Reform Bill of 1832 was passed because   1) new industrialized population centers were inadequately represented in Parliament   2) the agricultural sections needed better representation   3) there was need to represent the colonies in Parliament   4) agricultural laborers agitated for the vote.

4. Which French Monarch did not belong to the Bourbon line? 1) Louis Philippe   2) Louis XVIII   3) Charles X   4) Louis Napoleon.

5. The English Reform Bill of 1832 was passed   1) as a result of a monster petition   2) after a threat to create many new peers in the House of Lords   3) by a coalition of Whigs and Laborites 4) only after considerable mob violence.

6. The dissatisfaction with the rule of Louis Philippe was to a large extent due to   1) failure of the bourgeoisie to earn profits 2) the idea that the king was not the legitimate heir   3) a desire for national glory and prestige.

7. Belgian independence was substantially won in   1) 1815 2) 1848   3) 1820   4) 1830.

8. Belgium won her independence from   1) Germany   2) Spain   3) Holland   4) Austria   5) France.

9. The free trade principle was adopted by Britain in 1846 because   1) of English idealism   2) England enjoyed industrial leadership and could meet foreign competition in manufactures 3) the laboring class had come to power   4) English agriculture could meet foreign competition.

10. The Chartist movement demanded all *except*   1) universal manhood suffrage   2) equal electoral districts   3) woman suffrage   4) payment of salaries to members of Parliament.

11. The Chartist movement   1) ended in both immediate and permanent failure   2) was bloodily suppressed   3) failed but most of its demands subsequently realized   4) represented the demand for a written constitution.

12. The revolutions of 1848   1) encountered success in many countries but failed in many others   2) won few victories anywhere   3) were almost universally successful   4) succeeded only in southern Europe.

13. Revolutionary movements in the nineteenth century usually originated first in   1) Germany   2) England   3) France   4) Russia.

14. In Poland the revolution of 1830 resulted in   1) concessions to Polish demand for self-government   2) complete defeat of the revolt   3) a grant of self-government by Russia.

15. At the Frankfurt Assembly the German liberals drew up a constitution for a unified Germany that   1) excluded non-German peoples   2) provided for a republic   3) rejected representative government   4) sought unification under Austrian leadership.

Matching:

16. Charles X	a. French prime minister in the 1840's
17. Hegel	b. Hungarian radical nationalist
18. Ranke	c. Became emperor of Austria
19. Guizot	d. Abdicated his throne in 1830
20. Kossuth	e. Philosopher identified with German nationalism
21. Francis Joseph	
22. John Bright	f. Won repeal of the Corn Laws
23. Robert Peel	g. German leader at Frankfurt Assembly
24. Louis Napoleon	h. Author of patriotic history
	i. Sent troops to restore the pope in Rome
	j. Advocated repeal of the Corn Laws

Completion:

25. The revolutionary movements of 1830 were directed mainly against a) ..... but those of 1848 included socialists against the b) ......

26. A new political party that arose in Britain in the 1830's took the name ..... Party.

27. A political faction favoring increased power of the Church in France was known as the ......

28. The Austrian demand that Prussia abandon plans for the unification of Germany is known as the humiliation of ......

FOR FURTHER READING

HARDBOUND:

Barr, Stringfellow, *Mazzini: Portrait of an Exile* (1935).

Hamerow, Theodore, *Restoration, Revolution and Reaction: Economics and Politics in Germany 1815-1871* (1958).

Hammond, John and Barbara, *The Age of the Chartists, 1832-1854: A Study of Discontent* (1930).

Hawarth, T. E. B., *The Citizen King* (1961). France under Louis Philippe.

Hovell, Mack, *The Chartist Movement* (1918).

King, Bolton, *Mazzini* (1903). Biography.

Leys, M. D. R., *France between Two Empires, 1818-1848* (1955). A survey of the period.

Valentin, Veit, *1848: Chapters of German History* (1940).

Whitridge, Arnold, *Men in Crisis: The Revolution of 1848* (1949).

PAPERBOUND:

Berlin, Isaiah, *Karl Marx: His Life and Environment* (Galaxy). By a specialist on Marxism; somewhat unfriendly.

Bruun, Geoffrey, *Revolution and Reaction, 1848-1852: A Mid-Century Watershed* (Anvil). Brief survey with reading selections.

Marx, Karl, and Engels, Friedrich, *The Communist Manifesto* (Gateway). Reprint.

Robertson, Priscilla, *Revolutions of 1848* (Torchbooks). Shows relations of the different revolutions and their social backgrounds.

Tocqueville, Alexis de, *Recollections* (Meridian).

Wolf, John B., *France, 1814-1919: The Rise of a Liberal Democratic Society* (Torchbooks).

THE ASSERTIONS OF
NATIONALISM

1849-1871

The outstanding feature of the period from 1848 to 1871 was the assertion of aspirations to national independence, national unification, or defense against threats to national interests. The outstanding successes were in Italy and in Germany where independence and unification were both achieved in a series of wars. In one form or another, other assertions of nationalism occurred. In the United States the Union was preserved in the Civil War and in Mexico the French puppet regime was overthrown. In Hungary occurred a movement that was only partially successful, and Poland suffered a net setback. Ireland began her demands for "Home Rule" during this period, but for centuries she had been resisting the rule of England.

*1848   *Louis Napoleon elected president of the Second French Republic*
*1851   *Louis Napoleon overthrew the Second French Republic*
*1852-1870 *Napoleon III ruled as Emperor of France during the Second Empire*
*1854-1856 *Crimean War*
*1856   *Treaty of Paris ended the Crimean War*
 1862   *Napoleon made Maximilian emperor in Mexico*
*1870-1871 *Franco-Prussian War*
*1870   *Napoleon III abdicated*

4. Napoleon III and the Crimean War

Louis Napoleon (1808-1873) cleverly and cautiously schemed to overthrow the Second Republic of France under which he had been elected president. The seemingly irreconcilable differences between middle class and working class presented an opportunity for a strong man who promised to preserve order. After three years the president substituted an empire for the republic and made himself Emperor Napoleon III. He was really much of a modern dictator but also a clever politician who made his rule acceptable to most factions. His foreign wars appealed to the imperial spirit of the French people. Louis Napoleon was a nephew of Napoleon I.

NAPOLEON III'S DOMESTIC POLICIES

Napoleon III's attempts to please all factions in France caused some to observe that he was all things to all men.

The coup d'état of Louis Napoleon (1851). Evidence indicates that France did not really want a republic. Not only the election of a man to the presidency who had twice tried to seize control of France, but the election of a great majority of monarchists to the French parliament in 1849 indicates the desire for strong government. The republic might have been overthrown quickly except that Bourbons, Orleanists, and Bonapartists all were contenders for candidates of their respective royal lines. Napoleon made public appearances by which he augmented his popularity. He cultivated the support of Catholics, other conservative elements, and the moderates. He filled the army with the followers and executed a carefully planned coup d'etat on December 2, 1851. The country ratified his seizure of power by an overwhelming majority. A year later he made himself Emperor Napoleon III and inaugurated the Second Empire. Again France, in a plebiscite, approved his action.

Domestic policies of Napoleon III.   Emperor Napoleon III (1852-1870) maintained his dictatorship under the guise of a constitutional monarchy. He offered the shadow but not the substance of self-government. Legislation was initiated by an appointive senate. He distracted the people with imperial ventures, and, to maintain sufficient political base for his government, he catered to the desires of the different factions. The opposition of the republicans was weakened and "official" candidates were favored in elections. The Emperor built a political machine to control everything from local government to the national parliament. In his usual indirect way, he muzzled the powerful French press. Intellectuals were suppressed in the universities. Many leading French liberals went into exile. The support of Catholics was initially won by the Falloux law which gave the Catholic Church control of education and financial support to its schools. Church support was cultivated by deference, recognition, and encouragement of the Catholic Church. Banquets and balls open to the public provided gay social life with the appearance of a democratic society. The bourgeois and the conservative peasants gave the Emperor the most support, but the Empire never really received enthusiastic support of the nation.

Economic policies.   France shared the world prosperity of the 1850's, and Napoleon received credit for the fact that workers were employed and better off than ever before. The general prosperity was due to the increase in the world's money supply that resulted from the gold discoveries in California and Australia. Also a world trade revival occurred after the depressed conditions of the 1840's. Napoleon III took a genuine interest in the welfare of the poor, and the conditions of the working class materially improved. Charities were established and social security subsidized in a kind of welfare state. Paris was rebuilt and beautified as part of a vast public works program. Widened streets made barricades difficult to improvise.

Napoleon encouraged various forms of business activity and industrial development. Steel works and railways were built and shipping modernized with large iron steamships. The notable Credit Mobilier was founded to provide financing for large-scale enterprises. The Emperor, won over to free trade principles, reduced tariffs but antagonized protectionists among French businessmen by doing so. In all, France enjoyed her share of the world's prosperity of the 1850's.

NAPOLEON III'S FOREIGN VENTURES

By several military ventures Napoleon III sought to revive France's prestige, to increase the size of its empire, and to divert the public. Napoleon supported the principle of nationalism at several times. He helped the Italian nationalists, supported the Poles, and favored the independence of the Confederate States of America. Some of his foreign adventures, as may be seen below, show that Napoleon was cognizant of the value of winning Catholic support for his regime.

***The Crimean War (1854-1856).** Napoleon III followed an aggressive foreign policy even though he had made an early promise that the Empire meant peace. He engaged in a half dozen wars to extend his prestige and bring glory and territory to France. His outstanding involvement was the Crimean War against Russia. The war originated in the ancient enmity of Russia and Turkey. Napoleon managed to intervene on the pretext of defending Roman Catholics against Greek Catholics. Great Britain did not wish to see Russia gain control of the Black Sea and of its outlet to the Mediterranean. In 1854 Britain and France agreed to an alliance with Turkey and declared war on Russia. The allies decided to attack Russia at Sebastopol in the Crimea, and most of the war was simply a siege of that Black Sea port. Under the leadership of Cavour, Sardinia joined France in the war in order to win her friendship for Cavour's plan to end Austrian domination of Italy. The war ended with the capture of Sebastopol.

The Treaty of Paris (1856). At Paris the participants in the Crimean War drew up the terms of the peace. 1] The tsar gave up his claim as defender of the Greek Christians and 2] renounced special privileges in Serbia and Rumania. 3] The treaty guaranteed the independence and integrity of the Ottoman Empire. 4] The Black Sea was neutralized, and 5] the Danube opened to ships of all nations. 6] Certain rules of international law were changed so that Great Britain relinquished rules by which she had earlier interfered with the ships of neutrals on the seas.

The war increased the prestige of Napoleon and won favor for Sardinia in her plans against Austria. The failure of Austria to enter the war left her isolated and almost without friends while Britain and France listened to Sardinia's plans against Austria. France and Britain had fought as allies for the first time since the Crusades, a fact which calls attention to the weakness of France and the growing strength of Russia.

Napoleon's other foreign wars. Napoleon's first military intervention was his use of force in 1849 to restore the rule of Pius IX in the Papal States. His other foreign ventures were the intervention in Algeria, the establishment of the French protectorate in Indo-China, the seizure of islands in the Pacific, the cooperation to help Sardinia drive out the Austrians in 1859, and the establishment of a puppet regime in Mexico.

In the latter, Napoleon joined the reactionary elements in Mexico to subvert the Mexican Republic. At this time (1862) Napoleon needed some foreign victory that would help bolster his waning popularity in France. This violation of the Monroe Doctrine aroused the United States government to prepare to aid democratic forces in Mexico. Napoleon abandoned the puppet regime of the Emperor Maximilian who was executed by the victorious Mexicans under their native liberal leader Juarez. During the Civil War in the United States, Napoleon tried unsuccessfully to win British cooperation in a plan to break the Union blockade of the Confederacy so that cotton might be obtained for the textile mills of Europe. Napoleon definitely favored the cause of the Confederacy and felt assured it would succeed.

Downfall of Napoleon III (1870). The latent dissatisfaction under Napoleon III began to show itself more openly during his intervention in Italy in 1859 when various French factions objected for one reason or another. The withdrawal of French troops from Mexico greatly discredited Napoleon, and repeated concessions had to be made to his critics in parliament. Steps had to be taken to relax his absolutist rule until, in 1869-1870, he had to change the constitution to one that created genuine constitutional government. The defeat and humiliation of France in the Franco-Prussian War (See Chapter 5) and the capture of Napoleon himself by the invading Germans, finally ended the Empire, and Napoleon went into exile in England.

REVIEW QUESTIONS

Multiple-choice:
1. Napoleon III ruled 1) under the guise of constitutional government 2) without benefit of a constitution 3) conceded a constitution toward the end of his regime 4) by observing both the spirit and the letter of the French constitution.

2. In which matter did Napoleon III fail? 1) Providing the French with diversion and glory of imperial adventures 2) bringing economic prosperity 3) quieting discontent with his regime 4) satisfying the clerical faction.

3. Louis Napoleon's acts to secure the support of the workers included all *except* 1) a kind of social security system 2) creating jobs by public works projects 3) maintaining the national workshops as advocated by Louis Blanc 4) promoting the general prosperity of France.

4. Napoleon III's role in foreign affairs was mainly one of 1) acquiring colonies and supporting nationalism 2) upholding reactionary regimes wherever necessary 3) aggression against France's neighbors 4) supporting anti-clerical factions.

5. In summing up the rule of Napoleon III it is probably most accurate to conclude that he 1) attained and kept power by sheer force and ruthlessness 2) kept power by cunning, deceit, and demagoguery 3) ruled by playing the different factions against each other 4) was a complex figure who brought order to France by combining qualities of a dictator, politician, and statesman.

6. The concessions made by Napoleon before his rule was terminated seem to indicate that dissatisfaction with his government was strongest among 1) the clericals 2) the republicans 3) the socialists 4) the peasants 5) the monarchists.

7. In the American Civil War Napoleon 1) maintained strict neutrality 2) favored the cause of the Confederacy 3) favored the North 4) vacillated from one position to another.

8. In his foreign policy Napoleon III's most remarkable departure from France's past was 1) the war against Russia 2) fighting on the same side with Britain 3) fighting on the side of Turkey 4) the pursuit of an imperialist policy.

9. The Crimean War was fought 1) in the vicinity of Sebastopol in the Crimea 2) in the Baltic region 3) in the Balkans 4) in Palestine.

10. The most important outcome of the Crimean War was 1) achievement of independence by the Balkans 2) the defeat of the allies 3) the expansion of Turkey 4) various changes in international law.

FOR FURTHER READING

HARDBOUND:

Binkley, Robert C., *Realism and Nationalism, 1852-1871* (1935). Stimulating survey of the general history of this period.

Corley, T. A. B., *Democratic Despot* (1961). The regime of Napoleon III.

Guedella, Philip, *The Second Empire* (1937).

Guérard, Albert, *Napoleon III: An Interpretation* (1914). A careful study that is somewhat sympathetic with the complex personality of Louis Napoleon.

Simpson, Frederick A., *Louis Napoleon and the Recovery of France, 1848-1856* (1953).

———, *The Rise of Louis Napoleon* (1909; reprinted 1925).

Thompson, J. M., *Louis Napoleon and the Second Empire* (1955). Scholarly.

PAPERBOUND:

Brogan, D. W., *French Nation: From Napoleon to Petain, 1815-1940* (Colophon).

Cobban, Alfred, *A History of Modern France* (Penguin).

Williams, Roger L., *World of Napoleon III, 1851-1870* (Collier).

Woodham-Smith, C. M., *The Reason Why* (Everyman).

*1848   *Failure of the republican revolutions in Italy and Germany*

1849   *Victor Emmanuel II became king of Sardinia*

1850's   *Years of prosperity; industrial growth in Germany*

1850   *Cavour appointed minister by the king*

           "Humiliation of Olmutz" forced Prussia to abandon plans of unification of Germany

1851   *Bismarck became converted to German unification*

1852   *Cavour made premier*

*1854-1856 *Crimean War. Sardinian troops sent to aid the allies against Russia*

1858   *Plombieres agreement allied France and Sardinia against Austria*

*1859   **Austro-Sardinian War. Defection of Napoleon III*

           Peace of Villafranca between Austria and Sardinia

           Bismarck serves as Prussian minister in Russia

1860   *Garibaldi's conquest of Sicily and Naples*

1861   *Kingdom of Italy proclaimed. Cavour died.*

1862   *Bismarck became prime minister in Prussia*

*1864   *The Danish War fought by Prussia and Austria*

*1866   *Alliance of Prussia and Italy formed*

           **Austro-Prussian War won Venetia for Italy. Prussia defeated Austria. Bismarck dissolved the German Confederation and set up the North German Confederation and annexed the small German states of the north*

* 1870-1871   *Franco-Prussian War*
* 1870   *Italian annexation of the Papal States; Rome made the capital of Italy*
* 1871   *Treaty of Frankfurt confirmed Prussian victory over France. German Empire proclaimed; William I became kaiser and Bismarck chancellor.*

5. The Unification of Italy and Germany

The decade of nationalism of the 1860's witnessed the unification of Germany and Italy and their victory over foreign domination. Fortunately for the two nations other powers did not intervene. The unification of the two nations was achieved almost simultaneously as they cooperated against common enemies, Austria and France. The unification of Germany completely altered the balance of power on the continent.

THE UNIFICATION OF ITALY (1859-1870)

The Congress of Vienna preserved the disunity of Italy by undoing the work of Napoleon Bonaparte and by restoring the legitimate ruling families of 1789. Austria's possession of Lombardy and Venetia, and control of Austrian despots elsewhere, kept Italy under the domination of one foreign power or another, a condition that extended as far back as Spain's control of southern Italy in 1500. In 1850 southern Italy, known as the Kingdom of the Two Sicilies, was ruled by a king of Spanish Bourbon origin. The Papal States, located in central Italy, remained under the temporal government of the popes. Austria dominated the various states in the north. Napoleon had aroused a spirit of nationalism that survived in spite of Austrian intervention in 1820-1821 and in 1831. This rebirth of the Italian spirit is called the *Risorgimento;* its most active agency was the underground *Carbonari* society. Between 1859 and 1870 Italy realized her dream of unity in five major steps, which will be discussed later after plans for unification are surveyed first.

***Italian unification plans.*   Three alternative plans of unification, each advocated by a particular faction, were considered by Italian patriots. 1] Joseph Mazzini, an idealist and the outstanding leader of the *Risorgimento,* favored a democratic republic. He published educational propaganda and organized his followers in an association called Young Italy; this movement seemed too radical to the upper classes. 2] A second proposal, supported by conservatives, called for a confederation headed by the pope. The merit of this plan was that it solved the question of how to unify Italy without confiscating the pope's territorial holdings. 3] The third, a moderate plan and one which actually took effect, called for unification under the leadership of the liberal monarchy of the Kingdom of Sardinia, a large state which also included Savoy and Piedmont. As already seen, the liberal uprisings in Italy failed as they did elsewhere, and Austria maintained her oppression. But Sardinia adopted a liberal constitution (and the wise and patriotic new king, Victor Emmanuel II,) and successfully resisted Austria. The failure of the republicans in 1848 and the diminishing appeal of papal leadership at the head of a conservative national government—all these increased the attractiveness of the Sardinian plan. The failure of 1848 also taught Italians that they would need foreign aid to achieve unification, for they would have to overcome the power of Austria.

****Cavour's leadership in Sardinia.*   After 1849 the new king of Sardinia, Victor Emmanuel II (1849-1878), upheld the new constitution against threats from Austria, and thus Sardinia became the hope for the unification of all Italy. In 1850 the king made Count Camillo di Cavour (1810-1861) minister of agriculture and commerce and in 1852 made him premier. Cavour became the outstanding leader in the unification movement.

Cavour, a liberal and nationalist of noble birth, early gave himself to the study of the economic and political problems of Italy and prepared himself thoroughly by education and by travel in France and England. As premier, Cavour devoted himself to making Sardinia an example of a liberal, prosperous, and progressive state that would serve as a magnet to the rest of Italy. He particularly improved her agriculture, but promoted her commerce and her highway and railroad system. In the province of Piedmont the Catholic clergy were unusually strong and numerous and constituted the largest opposition to a liberal government. But Cavour secured the enactment of a series of laws that reduced the hold of the clergy upon the states. He confiscated half the Church lands in Sardinia as part of this anti-clerical policy. Cavour, a political realist, cultivated the favor of France and Britain by joining them in the Crimean War.

The first step: the Austro-Sardinian War (1859).   Each of these five steps in the unification of Italy represents the addition of a parcel of new territory. In the Crimean War, Cavour sent troops into the siege of Sebastopol as a way of placing Britain and France under obligation and of obtaining a hearing for Italy at the peace conference after the war. In 1858 in the Plombières agreement, Cavour won Napoleon III's alliance in a war against Austria; Napoleon's price was the cession of Savoy and Nice to France. Cavour used every kind of propaganda to incite anti-Austrian feeling all over Italy and made well-known plans for war. The war began when Austria demanded demobilization of Cavour's troops. Sardinia won two important victories at Magenta and at Solferino in 1859. But before the Austrians were driven out of all their important positions in Italy, Napoleon negotiated a separate peace with Emperor Francis Joseph of Austria in the Peace of Villafranca (1859). Under the terms of this agreement Austria gave up Lombardy but retained Venetia. Napoleon's sudden abandonment of Sardinia is explained by   1] his fear of heavy losses of

men in an extended war (he was not as callous as Napoleon
I), 2] the realization that a united Italy might be a threat to
France, 3] the preparations made by Prussia to mobilize
against France, and 4] the opposition of the clericals in
France. But Sardinia had won her first territorial accession
from Austria, the province of Lombardy.

The second step: acquisition of the North-Central States
(1859). When Sardinian victories seemed to promise the
ejection of Austria, all Italy reacted in a wave of enthusiasm
that alarmed Napoleon and threatened to lead to confiscation
of the Papal States; such an event would discredit Napoleon
in the eyes of his Catholic supporters in France. In this initial
wave of nationalism, Tuscany, Romagna, Parma, and Modena
arose and were annexed to Sardinia. Savoy and Nice were
ceded to France as the price of Napoleon's consent to the consolidation of these several provinces under Sardinia.

*The third step: Garibaldi's conquest of Sicily and Naples
(1860). Another of the famous leaders in Italy's unification
was the soldier of fortune Giuseppe Garibaldi. At the head of
his Thousand Red Shirts and with the secret encouragement of
Cavour, Garibaldi sailed from the harbor of Genoa and easily
won Sicily. He next entered and took Naples. When Garibaldi
proceeded with organizing his conquests as a separate state,
Cavour forced him to accede to Italian wishes and release his
conquests to Sardinia. The cession was confirmed by plebiscite.

In 1861, representatives from the conquered states proclaimed Sardinia to be the Kingdom of Italy. Cavour, exhausted by his strenuous labors, died the same year.

The fourth step: alliance with Prussia for the conquest of
Venetia (1866). Cavour's policy of biding his time to await
circumstances that would favor Italy was adhered to by his
successors. In 1866 Prussia made an alliance with Italy and

declared war on Austria. Austria defeated the Italian forces, but when Prussia defeated Austria, Venetia was transferred to Italy. Thus, Italian unification went hand in hand with German unification.

The fifth step: annexation of Rome and the Papal States (1870). In 1870, German and Italian unification again proceeded together and were, in fact, completed together. When the Franco-Prussian War broke out, Napoleon withdrew his garrison from the Papal States and his defeat at Sedan left the Italians completely free to occupy Rome without fear of French intervention. The Italians occupied Rome, and the pope was left with only an enclave which became the Vatican state. At the same time Rome became the capital of all Italy.

THE UNIFICATION OF GERMANY

In Germany, as in Italy, the Napoleonic invasions awakened the spirit of nationalism. The efforts of German liberals and nationalists failed in their efforts immediately after the Congress of Vienna. Nevertheless, the dissolution of the Holy Roman Empire, the German Confederation established at Vienna, the Frankfurt Assembly, and the Zollverein—all in different ways furthered eventual unification. The almost-successful movement of 1848 emphasized the obstacles and introduced a spirit of hard-headed realism hitherto lacking among the German leaders. Over the longer period, France and Austria frustrated unification in Germany, just as they had done in Italy. France knew that her influence would be overshadowed by a united Germany. Germany did not want union with Austria's non-German peoples, and Austria had always blocked German unification under any leadership other than her own. As late as 1850, Austria had forced the Prussian king, at the "humiliation of Olmutz," to abandon plans to unify Germany under Prussia.

**Germany in the 1850's. After 1849, Germany remained under conservative governments, but she grew economically stronger during the worldwide prosperity of the 1850's. Germany underwent a rapid phase of industrialization. Research and business enterprise combined with a disciplined and intelligent working class brought phenomenal industrial expansion after 1850. Capitalists in various businesses wanted all the advantages of uniformity of laws, of currency, and so on, as well as the advancement of foreign trade that strong government would offer. The historian Treitschke, before 1870, converted enthusiastic audiences to his conviction that unity should come under the leadership of Prussia, the strongest and most progressive of the German states. The Hohenzollerns in Prussia had created an efficient bureaucracy there. Prussia, therefore, offered a model government, a nucleus like Sardinia in Italy, around which the rest of the nation might gather itself.

***Otto von Bismarck (1815-1898). After William I came to the throne of Prussia in 1861 he prepared to strengthen the army in order to fulfill Prussia's mission in Germany. The Chamber of Deputies refused the necessary appropriations and thereby precipitated a serious crisis. At this point Otto von Bismarck won appointment as the king's chief minister; he defied the opposition in Parliament and soon unified Germany.

Bismarck, the outstanding figure in European politics after 1861, descended from a long line of Brandenburg landowning nobility—one of the Junker class so devoted to Prussia. He held a strong contempt for parliamentary democracy and for liberals. Until around 1851, Bismarck opposed German nationalism and unity, but, as a Prussian delegate to the German Diet under the Confederation, he gained an insight into Austria's dislike of Prussia and her moves to block German unity. Bismarck became a German and ceased to be a Prussian. In 1859 he went to Russia as minister from Prussia and won Russian friendship. Soon afterward in France he learned to be contemptuous of the ability of Napoleon III. In 1862 Bismarck's friends secured his appointment as prime minister in Prussia. Bismarck believed that Germany would be united by "blood and iron" and not by oratory or by parliamentary maneuvers. A leader without scruple, he resorted to cunning, deceit, or force, as he chose, to advance his ends. When parliament refused to vote the budget to strengthen and reform the Prussian army, Bismarck found the money by collecting taxes in defiance of the liberals in the Prussian parliament and of constitutional government. The struggle went on for four years, but Bismarck proceeded with his work of creating a strong German army.

*The first step: the Danish War (1864). Three wars constituted the three steps in German unification. The first step, the Danish War, developed out of the complicated dispute with Denmark over the German province of Holstein and the half-German province of Schleswig. When Denmark annexed Schleswig, Prussia and Austria together declared war against Denmark and forced the cession of the provinces. Bismarck intended that a quarrel over the disposition of the spoils would bring war with Austria. Bismarck made an alliance with Italy and made indefinite promises to Napoleon III in order to assure the neutrality of France; he already had an agreement with Russia that assured her neutrality.

**The second step: the Seven Weeks' War (1866). In the brief war with Austria that followed, Prussia had the advantage of a superior new rifle, the "needle gun" with three times the fire power of the Austrian muzzle loading guns. The Prussian army commander, General von Moltke had thoroughly organized the Prussian army so as to take advantage of the railway and telegraph, which had not been important factors in previous European wars. Austria's defeat in seven weeks and the Peace of Prague gave the disputed Danish provinces to Prussia. Austria agreed to withdraw from German affairs. The peace terms were lenient so as not to engender a spirit of revenge among the Austrians.

Other German states had entered the war against Prussia. Bismarck dealt with them as best suited his purposes. He dissolved the Confederation and created the North German Confederation. He gave lenient peace terms to the large south German states of Bavaria, Wurtemberg, Baden, and Hesse. The north central German states were annexed to Prussia under the North German Confederation.

***The third step: the Franco-Prussian War (1870-1871).** Napoleon III could not ignore the aggrandizement of Prussia even though he approved the principle of nationalism. But the Austro-Prussian War ended too soon for France to intervene. In vain, Napoleon repeatedly reminded Bismarck of his vague promises of compensation for France's neutrality in the Prussian wars. Napoleon's weakening position in France and the retreat from Mexico made him desperate for a foreign war by which he could restore his prestige. Bismarck also needed war with France to provide the opportunity for Prussian absorption of the other German states.

The affair of the Ems Dispatch (1870) offered the occasion for Bismarck and Napoleon to bring about a war that both governments wanted. In 1869 the Spanish crown became vacant and was offered to Leopold of Hohenzollern-Sigmaringen. Bismarck encouraged Leopold, knowing that Napoleon would oppose what would appear to be a threat of German encirclement of France. Leopold abandoned the throne when France objected. Napoleon's foreign minister pressed the point further by demanding that the Hohenzollerns promise *never* to accept the Spanish throne. The Prussian king, William I, sent a dispatch from Ems communicating the French demands to Bismarck. Bismarck omitted certain words from the message before releasing it to the press. He made it appear that each nation had been insulted by the other. It produced the effect Bismarck desired. Napoleon's advisers now pressed him to declare war, which was done in July, 1870.

Bismarck had previously isolated France by winning the good will of Italy and Russia. The Liberal government of Gladstone in England had no love for the autocrat Napoleon, and Austria had little desire to join her ancient Gallic enemy. In the Franco-Prussian War that followed Bismarck won quick victories against the poorly organized French forces at Sedan and Metz. Napoleon himself was captured but later released to go into exile in England. In France, the Third Republic was formed and continued the resistance until the Germans took Paris early in 1871. France surrendered in January, 1871.

The Treaty of Frankfurt (1871).   The treaty of peace provided for   1] the French surrender of Alsace-Lorraine to Germany and   2] for the payment of a large indemnity to Germany. A German army of occupation was to remain until the indemnity was paid. The German army made a triumphal entry into Paris.

At the time of the French surrender William I of Prussia was crowned as the Emperor of Germany at Versailles. Before the war Bismarck had won over the south German states by showing written proofs of Napoleon's demands for German territory, and they, therefore, agreed to an alliance with Prussia, while their subjects enthusiastically hailed the Prussian cause as their own. The south German states entered the North German Confederation which was then transformed into the German Empire, and Kaiser William I of Prussia was proclaimed emperor in the Hall of Mirrors in Versailles in January, 1871. Bismarck became chancellor, the "Iron Chancellor."

REVIEW QUESTIONS

Multiple-choice:

1. Which was the most prominent obstacle to the unification of both Germany and Italy?   1) Austria   2) the Papacy   3) privileged classes of each country   4) France.

2. One factor that helped to bring about Italian unification was   1) Napoleon III's support of the principle of nationalism   2) the presence of French troops in Rome   3) the support of Austria-Hungary   4) the Russian threat to Austria-Hungary.

3. The Italian leader who played a role in unification nearest to that of Bismarck in Germany was   1) Garibaldi   2) Victor Emmanuel II   3) Cavour   4) Mazzini.

4. Which state took the lead in Italian unification?   1) Naples   2) the Papal States   3) Sardinia   4) Venetia.

5. Which war was accompanied by the completion of unification by both Italy and Germany?   1) the Austro-Sardinian War   2) the Franco-Prussian War   3) the Crimean War   4) the First Balkan War.

6. The objections of the pope to Italian unification were overcome by   1) a change of policy by the papacy   2) an agreement between Cavour and the pope   3) pressure from Napoleon III upon the pope   4) the withdrawal of French troops, which permitted Italian troops to take over Rome.

7. Which was *not* an aid to the unification of Germany?   1) the Zollverein   2) the German princes   3) growth of industry in Germany   4) the Seven Weeks' War.

8. Bismarck came to realize that the main obstacle to German unification was   1) Austria   2) Italy   3) France   4) Britain   5) the German princes.

9. Particularly helpful in completing the unification in both Italy and Germany were   1) appeals to nationalistic sentiments   2) youth movements   3) democratic movements   4) skillful diplomacy to isolate the main opposing country.

10. Which does *not* describe correctly the government of one of the three main parts of Italy in 1859?   1) A Spanish puppet

king ruled the Kingdom of the Two Sicilies   2) Austria dominated the northern states   3) central Italy was ruled under the Papal States   4) a native monarchy ruled southern Italy and Sicily.

11. Who was the leader of the faction that favored Italian unification under a liberal republic? 1) Cavour 2) Mazzini 3) the pope 4) Garibaldi.

12. Italy added Venetia in which war? 1) Franco-Prussian 2) Austro-Prussian 3) Austro-Sardinian 4) Danish War.

13. Bismarck avoided French intervention in the first two wars for unification 1) by winning limited objectives before France could mobilize 2) by isolating France by diplomacy 3) by promising Napoleon III compensation for his neutrality 4) because Napoleon rigidly adhered to his doctrine of nationalism even though it meant a strong German state.

14. Bismarck won the war against Austria quickly because 1) only a quick war would bring sure victory 2) Italy won substantial victories against Austrian forces at the same time 3) Austria had to divert troops to crush the Bohemians 4) the German army employed the latest technology of warfare but Austria did not.

15. By the Treaty of Frankfurt, France 1) lost Alsace-Lorraine to Germany 2) only had to pay a large indemnity 3) was required to abandon the Second Empire.

16. The Franco-Prussian War occurred because 1) Napoleon III needed a military victory to stay in power 2) Bismarck provoked France to attack 3) Both Bismarck and Napoleon III wanted war 4) neither wanted war but were driven to it by their supporters.

FOR FURTHER READING

HARDBOUND:

Bismarck, Otto von, *Reflections and Reminiscences* (1898). By the Iron Chancellor himself.

Darmstaedter, Fredrick, *Bismarck and the Creation of the Second Reich* (1948). Excellent recent political study.

Friedjung, Heinrich, *The Struggle for Supremacy in Germany, 1859-1866* (1935). The Prussian victory over Austria.

Henderson, William Otto, *The Zollverein* (2nd ed., 1959). The economic origins of German unification.

King, Bolton, *A History of Italian Unity, Being a Political History of Italy from 1814 to 1871* (2 vols., 1912).

Lord, R. H., *Origins of the War of 1870* (1924). Study of the diplomacy.

Ludwig, Emil, *Bismarck* (1919). Good biography.

Polnay, Peter De, *Garibaldi: The Man and the Legend* (1961).

Smith, D. Mack, *Cavour and Garibaldi, 1860* (1954).

Thayer, W. R., *The Life and Times of Cavour* (1911). A classic.

Trevelyan, George, *Garibaldi* (1958). A one-volume edition. Excellent writing and informative.

Trevelyan, Janet, *A Short History of the Italian People* (1920). Standard survey.

Veit, Valentine, *The German People: Their History and Civilization from the Holy Roman Empire to the Third Reich* (1946).

PAPERBOUND:

Albrecht-Carié, René, *Italy from Napoleon to Mussolini* (Collier).

Barraclough, Geoffrey, *Origins of Modern Germany* (Capricorn).

Binkley, Robert C., *Reaction and Nationalism, 1852-1871* (Torchbooks). An account of the Second Empire.

1801-1825	*Alexander I, tsar of Russia*
1825-1855	*Nicholas I, tsar of Russia*
1825	*Decembrist Revolt*
1830	*Revolt in Poland crushed*
1848	*Liberal nationalist movements crushed in the Austrian Empire*
1848-1916	*Francis Joseph, emperor of Austria*
1855-1881	*Alexander II, tsar of Russia*
1856	*Reforms begin to be introduced by Alexander II*
1860-1861	*Provincial diets restored in Austria*
*1861	*Serfdom abolished in Russia*
1863	*Polish uprising crushed*
1864	*Zemstvos created by edict of Alexander II*
1866	*Attempted assassination of Alexander II caused him to abandon reforms*
*1867	*The* Ausgleich *permitted Hungary equal status with Austria under the Dual Monarchy*
1870	*Approximate beginning of more violent revolutionists in Russia: anarchists and nihilists*

66

6. Austria and Russia, 1848-1871

These two great powers of eastern Europe were both far behind the nations of western Europe in the development of democratic institutions. Both governed restless subject nationalities.

THE DUAL MONARCHY

In 1859 the Austrian Empire began to break into many parts before the impact of successive nationalistic blows, beginning with the loss of Lombardy to Italy.

Austria after 1850. Austria succeeded in crushing the nationalistic liberal uprisings of 1848 with Russian aid and remained a stronghold of conservatism. Metternich's successor, Schwarzenberg, resumed the absolutism and centralization of the preceding decades. After the death of Schwarzenberg, Alexander Bach used secret police and the army to extend and uphold the Austrian bureaucratic system throughout the empire. Hungary displayed great resentment over the rigid centralization of the Bach system. The Austrian defeat suffered in Italy in 1859 made the government reconsider the introduction of reforms in Austria.

During 1860 and 1861 provincial diets were restored and the imperial government announced it would move toward a constitutional system but such reforms as were made carefully preserved the control of the German element. Nationalism in Bohemia, Rumania, and Croatia asserted itself in minor ways in keeping with the spirit of this decade. Francis Deák, a moderate Hungarian nationalist who opposed Louis Kossuth's radicalism that demanded complete independence, urged a policy of non-collaboration until Hungary's liberties won in 1848 were restored.

The Ausgleich (1867). Defeat in the war with Prussia in 1867 forced Austria to compromise with Hungary, the strongest of the dissident nationalities. These discussions produced the *Ausgleich* (compromise) of 1867. Henceforth, Austria and Hungary constituted a unique Dual Monarchy known as Austria-Hungary, both under the same sovereign, the Emperor Francis Joseph. Hungary became an independent state with the emperor of Austria serving as the king of Hungary and providing a joint government with Austria in foreign policy and in military affairs. Otherwise, each part of the Dual Monarchy governed itself under a separate parliament. The two national parliaments coordinated their joint responsibilities through committees. This arrangement was really the result of a bargain made between the Germans and Magyars whereby the other minorities—Czechs, Slovaks, Serbs, Croats, and Rumanians—were kept in subjection. The Magyars dominated their minorities as did the Austrians. The new arrangement sharpened the determination of the minorities to work for eventual independence.

RUSSIA

Russia, far removed from the democratic influences released by the Enlightenment and the French Revolution, remained the most backward European nation during the nineteenth century. The nobility, the Church, and usually the tsars continued to resist the reforms that some wished to introduce from the West. By 1820 Alexander I had renounced his earlier liberalism as a mistake and had begun to repress liberal ideas in Russia. Polish nationalism was repressed and Finnish nationalism was checked during the first wave of liberal up-risings after 1815.

**Alexander I and Nicholas I.   Tsar Alexander I (1801-1825) a complex personality, had toyed with the idea of introducing liberal reforms, until the revolutions of 1820 caused him to concede that Metternich was right in opposing liberalism. Alexander adopted repressive policies in the last years of his reign. Before 1815 a considerable number of liberals among the nobility had begun to attack serfdom, the system of priv-ilege, and the principle of autocracy in government. No nu-merous middle class had yet developed in Russia.

When Alexander I died in 1825 his successor Nicholas I (1825-1855) faced the unexpected, liberal Decembrist revolt (December, 1825) against his succession. Having experienced this inaugural uprising, Nicholas was confirmed in his anti-liberal and repressive ideas. He did study the problem of serf-dom and other problems but avoided stirring up any discus-sion. He instituted still more severe censorship and repression of political and religious dissenters. After the revolt in Poland in 1830 he introduced more repressive measures there than ever. Nicholas helped Austria subdue the Hungarians in 1849 and encouraged Prussia also to stiffen resistance to liberalism. Since 1818 secret societies had organized to work for a con-stitution, to limit the power of the tsar, and remedy the back-wardness of Russia.

By intervention in foreign nations, Nicholas won territory in the 1820's from the Ottoman Empire and Persia. As a way of weakening the Turks, he gave aid to the Greeks in their war for independence. The continuation of his policies of protect-ing the Orthodox Greek Catholics in Turkey and of aggression against Turkey led to the Crimean War. But now France and Britain began a policy of active support of Turkey in order to prevent Russian expansion at the expense of the Turks. This war revealed the ineffectiveness of the tsar's government: corrupt and inefficient officials failed to deliver provisions for the army. At the same time, the serfs rose in a series of revolts.

***Alexander II's emancipation of the serfs.* Alexander II (1855-1881), intelligent and tolerant, recognized the need to modernize his country and introduced numerous reforms for several years after 1856. Restrictions upon freedom of speech, press, travel, and education were relaxed. But these limited reforms served only to save the autocratic system by timely concessions.

Reformers had long agreed that serfdom should be abolished. After several years of study of how best to free the serfs, Alexander issued a manifesto in 1861 abolishing serfdom, but it required several years to complete the emancipation. The peasants were allowed to keep a large part of the land they had cultivated. The nobles were compensated fully and immediately by the government for the loss of their land. The peasants were obliged to repay the government in annual installments over a period of forty-nine years. Freedom for the forty million serfs did not bring a complete or satisfactory solution to the peasants' problems. The peasants did not receive enough land, and much of the best soil remained in possession of the nobles. The annual redemption payments proved quite burdensome. Peasants lost the use of the pastures and woodlands of their former masters. The progress of agriculture was slowed because ignorant serfs were inexperienced in the management of the land. The serfs had been under a status closely resembling that of the Negro slaves in the United States who were freed at the same time. Both reforms created problems of difficult readjustment. Some peasants went to work in factories, which had been absorbing an increasing number of workers for some time.

The Zemstvos (1864). By edict, Alexander introduced district assemblies, or zemstvos, of elected representatives from the nobility, the towns, and the peasants. These assemblies gained control over schools and roads. The district zemstvos chose representatives to the provincial zemstvos. The zemstvos had power to tax themselves for local government financing. No national assembly was provided, but the local assemblies did provide experience in self-government.

Alexander's other reforms included reform of the judicial system. The principles of equality before the law, public trials, and the jury system were introduced. Political offenders, however, came to be tried in separate courts under procedures less fair to the accused.

Polish revolt of 1863. The spread of liberal ideas and the ever-present nationalism brought on an uprising in Poland in 1863. The rebellion was suppressed and followed by drastic measures; leaders of the revolt were exiled or executed. The Catholic Church of Poland suffered the loss of extensive lands and the suppression of the monasteries.

**Russian political reactionaries and reformers.* A large group of Russians positively opposed the liberal reforms being adopted in Europe after 1830. These nationalists or Slavophils upheld autocracy and orthodoxy as peculiarly fitting for Russians. The Slavophils opposed the copying of European culture and favored preservation of the old, unique ways of Russia. The church and conservative masses supported this Russian nationalism. The split between the Slavophils and the "Westernizers" dates back to the time of Peter the Great and continues to the present time; it often produced sudden changes in policy as one group or the other won control. The Westernizers wished Alexander to continue his liberalism. Westernizers and reformers increased in number with the rising middle class of industrialists and professional men. However, an assassination attempt, in 1866, against Alexander caused him to abandon reform. He now turned reactionary and reduced the privileges he had granted to the courts, journals, and schools. Since the schools had been responsible for much reform agitation, they were now restricted and were supervised by government inspectors. Students and teachers were spied upon. Spies once more sought out the critics of the government and those who advocated reform.

The outstanding early leader of reform and advocate of constitutional government and socialism was the moderate Alexander Herzen (1812-1870). After being exiled to France and Germany, Herzen wrote pamphlets to express his ideas; his writings were smuggled into Russia and encouraged Alexander to make his early reforms. After 1870 more violent types of reformers became active in Russia.

REVIEW QUESTIONS

Multiple-choice:

1. The liberal revolts of 1848 in Austria   1) were quite successful   2) were crushed by Prince Metternich   3) were crushed with Russian aid   4) were crushed with Prussian aid.

2. Austria's defeats in foreign wars had the effect of   1) making Austria more determined to suppress subject nationalities   2) winning complete independence for Hungary   3) winning near independence for Hungary in accordance with the ideas of Francis Deák   4) making Croatia independent.

3. Russia's strongest subject nationality was the   1) Finns   2) Poles   3) Rumanians   4) Lithuanians.

4. The Crimean War resulted in all the following in Russia *except*   1) the abdication of the reigning tsar   2) a series of revolts by the serfs   3) revealing inefficiency and corruption.

5. The serfs were freed in Russia   1) at the time of the American Civil War   2) after the Napoleonic Wars   3) in 1905   4) in the revolution of 1848.

6. The most liberal of the Russian tsars from 1825 to 1900 was   1) Alexander II   2) Alexander III   3) Nicholas II   4) Alexander I.

7. The Russian tsars generally resisted the terrorism and revolt by 1) resorting to more repressive measures 2) ignoring them 3) making concessions to demands for democracy 4) calculated repression and concession.

8. The freed peasants remained dissatisfied for all reasons *except* 1) they were required to pay burdensome installments to repay their former masters 2) they were not permitted to move to industrial jobs 3) they were not given sufficient land 4) they were kept in an underprivileged and unequal status.

9. The repressive policies followed in Russia reflect the thinking of the 1) Slavophils 2) Westernizers 3) anarchists 4) followers of Herzen.

Matching:

10. Schwarzenberg
11. Alexander Bach
12. Francis Deak
13. Louis Kossuth
14. Nicholas I
15. Alexander II
16. Alexander Herzen
17. Alexander I

a. Wanted complete independence for Hungary
b. Tsar during Napoleonic Wars
c. Metternich's immediate successor
d. The Decembrists revolted against him
e. Propagandist who advocated moderate reforms in Russia
f. Emperor of Austria
g. Used secret police in Australian Empire
h. He freed the serfs
i. Moderate Hungarian nationalist

FOR FURTHER READING

HARDBOUND:

Carr, Edward, *Michael Bakunin* (1937).

Clark, Chester, *Franz Joseph and Bismarck: The Diplomacy of Austria before the War of 1866* (1934).

Graham, Stephen, *Tsar of Freedom: the Life and Reign of Alexander II* (1925).

Hecht, David, *Russian Radicals Look to America, 1801-1917* (1932).

Jaszi, Oszkar, *The Dissolution of the Habsburg Monarchy* (1929).

Redlich, Josep, *Emperor Francis Joseph of Austria: A Biography* (1929).

Taylor, Alan, *The Hapsburg Monarchy, 1809-1918: A History of the Austrian Empire and Austria-Hungary* (1948).

PAPERBOUND:

Karpovich, Michael, *Imperial Russia, 1801-1917* (Berkshire). Brief and useful.

ESSAY TYPE REVIEW QUESTIONS FOR MID-TERM AND FINAL EXAMINATIONS

1. What policies did Napoleon III follow in order to please the various political factions in France?

2. State the various foreign ventures of Napoleon III.

3. What were some important consequences of the Crimean War?

4. Name several nationalist movements of the 1860's. Which ones were successful?

5. What were the three plans that were considered for the unification of Italy?

6. What various preparations did Cavour make for the unification of Italy?

7. What were the five steps in the unification of Italy?

8. What factors finally brought about the success of German unification? How did Bismarck overcome the various opponents of German unification?

9. What was accomplished in the three steps by which German unification occurred?

10. What do you see in common between the unification of Italy and of Germany.

11. Explain the structure of the German Empire created in 1871.

12. Describe the government of the Dual Monarchy of 1867.

13. Explain the failure of Russia to make liberal reforms up to 1890. Why did the emancipation of the serfs leave them dissatisfied?

DEMOCRACY, THE NEW
INDUSTRIALISM, AND
THE NEW IMPERIALISM

1871-1914

The movements toward industrialism and democracy in Europe since 1815 showed the most progress in western and central Europe. Great Britain, France, Switzerland, and some of the smaller countries on the Atlantic made the greatest progress. The United States became recognized as a great industrial and world power during this period. Germany had the most efficient governmental administration and caught up with Britain industrially but lagged in the growth of democracy. Northern Italy and a part of Austria shared much of the new industrial progress of the rest of Europe. In those countries where industrialism had developed, political and social problems and their solution followed parallel lines but varied as to the factors peculiar to each country. Political backwardness and autocratic government persisted in eastern Europe where industrial growth lagged. Russia suffered most of all from repressive autocracy and economic backwardness. Nationalism developed in eastern Europe in spite of political backwardness. Economic nationalism gave rise to imperialism on the part of the advanced industrial nations of western Europe and created some of the basic causes of World War I. There is a remarkable similarity in the political and social developments in the industrialized nations of the western world during this period.

1869-1882	*Charles Darwin*
1820-1903	*Herbert Spencer, English conservative philosopher*
1822-1895	*Louis Pasteur*
1844-1900	*Nietzsche, German philosopher*
1847-1922	*Georges Sorel, French syndicalist*
*1848	*Communist Manifesto issued by Marx and Engels*
1850	*Beginning of rapid expansion of railroads over the world*
*1859	*Darwin published* Origin of Species
1864	*First International of the Marxists*
*1865	*End of Civil War confirmed the rise of the business interests to power in the United States*
1869	*Ecumenical Church council called, first since 1563*
1870	*Infallibility of the pope declared in matters of faith and morals*
1870's	*Beginning of the New Industrialism, or Second Industrial Revolution. Rapid expansion of industry in the United States and Germany*
1880's	*Electric generating plants set up*
1883	*Fabian Society organized in England*
1900	*Automobiles powered by combustion engines coming to be manufactured in large numbers.*

7. Economic and Social Developments

After 1870 the United States and many nations of western Europe began to feel the full force of what is called the "New Industrialism," another stage in the Industrial Revolution. New theories of social and political thought, such as Marxism, took the place of Utopian socialism. The improvement of living and working conditions of industrial workers had hardly begun. The expansion of industry made the problem proportionately more important than ever. The history of the various movements to improve the living standards and status of workers emphasizes the enormous impact of Karl Marx's influence. However, significant differences developed among those who drew their inspiration from Marx's ideas.

THE NEW INDUSTRIALISM

A new wave of industrial expansion and technological progress beginning about 1870 is known as the Second Industrial Revolution. Outstanding economic changes of this period were the expansion of industry in many countries, the growth of steamship and railroad transportation, and the mass production of low-cost steel. This new industrialism was partly based on the products of chemistry—such as coal tar derivatives and cellulose products. Another cause was the use of mass production methods made possible by assembly line production based on the use of interchangeable parts. In the more advanced industrial nations science teamed up with industry to bring new products to the marketplace. The telegraph and the telephone permitted more rapid communications. Electricity and the combustion engine began to replace steam as a source of power.

The spread of industry.   Factory production in industry developed on the continent first in France, Belgium, and Holland, then in northern Italy, Switzerland, and in Germany. Overseas, the United States had become strongly industrialized in the northeast by 1860. At about this same time Japan began to import the technology of the West. The greatest challenges to British industry after 1870 came from the rapid expansion of manufacturing in Germany and in the United States. The American Civil War not only was a victory for the business and industrial interests of the Northeast but in itself released and accelerated great industrial energies. Japan deliberately planned to make herself a workshop for Asia just as her model, England, functioned in Europe. London, which long since had become the financial center of the world, still served in this role. Annually, England reaped hundreds of millions of pounds in interest and service charges from her investments and from such business services as shipping and such financial services as insurance. Germany's rivalry as an industrial nation, as much as her military power, made her a threat to British supremacy.

Improved transportation facilities.   Steamships in internal waterways and on the oceans worked a great revolution in transportation after Fulton built his successful steam-propelled ship in 1807. Steamboats gathered raw materials for European factories and later redistributed the finished goods and exchanged them for foodstuffs for the industrial populations of Europe. After 1850 thousands of miles of railroads opened the hinterlands to the trade of the whole world. Electric-powered railroads and trolley cars served thickly-populated areas by 1900. The invention of the internal combustion engine before 1900 provided the advantages of automobile transportation. The invention of the airplane foreshadowed the coming of much faster passenger transportation in a later period. Of these developments, the railroad had the greatest effects in the period discussed here. For one thing, railroads provided a huge market for the iron and steel industries, but, more important, steel rails spread over undeveloped areas all over the world and opened them to settlement and provided transportation for bulky raw materials produced by farms, mines, and forests everywhere.

New industries and inventions. Most fundamental of the new industries was the mass production of steel which was made possible by the development of the Bessemer process in England and in America during the 1850's. The knowledge of how to harness and use electricity worked a great transformation in civilization. Electricity provided a kind of power more easily controlled and transmitted than steam or water power of earlier decades. Electricity not only literally dispelled the darkness that man had endured earlier but found immediate application in derivative industries, such as telephony. Industries based on new chemicals and new chemical processes arose. Such industries included the production of celluloid, rayon, and other cellulose products.

Agriculture. The urban demand for foodstuffs and raw materials furnished a greater market and created incentive for increased production and efficiency on the farms of Europe and America. In America, the South prospered from the export of slave-produced cotton after 1800 and the North and West from the export of wheat and meat. The invention of the reaper by McCormick in America in the 1830's was followed by numerous other agricultural inventions. Refrigeration and rapid transportation of bulky farm commodities opened distant markets for the produce of millions of acres of land brought under cultivation by pioneer settlers in the United States and Canada. European agriculture, particularly in Great Britain, suffered from the import of foreign foodstuffs, but protective tariffs gave some shelter as was true notably in Germany where the influential Junker class kept much of the German market for foodstuffs for the products of their own large estates. The agriculture of France was dominated by the peasant proprietors.

New knowledge of chemical fertilizers increased production in the older countries. Scientific agriculture in the Western World postponed the fulfillment of the predictions of Malthus. Plant and animal breeding and selection, better cultivation practices, large-scale farming with the use of machines, and control of diseases all helped to increase the output of farms.

The consolidation of business firms. The victory of the economic liberals brought the abolition of such government monopolies in business as had existed under mercantilist doctrines. But laissez-faire policies left the way open for businessmen's monopolies, and the advantages of business consolidation became increasingly apparent by 1870. 1] Mass production introduced efficiency in the use of machinery, in the gathering of raw materials, and in the use of materials and labor. 2] Ruinous competition could be avoided and prices fixed to maximize profits. 3] Large-scale marketing of the finished product could add to profits. 4] Workers were controlled better under powerful corporations, and great economic power could be used to influence governments to adopt friendly policies. In Europe and America, after 1870, aggressive businessmen organized business combinations under such devices as pools, trusts, mergers, holding companies, and alliances. In Europe monopolies extending across national boundaries were called *cartels.* The large capital requirements of giant combinations brought in an age of financial capitalism in the place of industrial capitalism, and financiers came into control of business rather than the industrialists themselves. Business combinations were encouraged in Europe where government control had long been accepted. But in the United States corporate wealth brought the threat of complete domination of government by financial and industrial plutocrats.

The Sherman Act (1890) and the Clayton Act (1914) and other measures subjected business to an increased degree of control.

SOCIAL THOUGHT AND ACTION

The ideas of Karl Marx influenced many leaders who dealt with the social problems created by the further spread of the Industrial Revolution, but many reformers disagreed with parts of Marxian theory. Many conservatives employed the ideas of Darwin to rationalize their social theories.

**Marxism after 1870. After 1870 it became evident that Marx's predictions were not being borne out. Instead of becoming worse the condition of workers improved. Real wages and living standards increased. Democracy grew rapidly through the extension of the suffrage, the secret ballot, the spread of education, and the generally increasing adoption of democratic devices and the expansion of opportunity for the masses. All these disproved Marxian teachings and weakened its appeal. The First International Workingmen's Association, founded with Marx's participation in 1864 in London, had failed by 1876. In 1889 the Second International was organized and suffered from the same internal dissensions as the first. Revisionist Marxists disagreed with the orthodox Marxists, and it became apparent, especially after the outbreak of World War I, that workers felt more national loyalty (patriotism) than class loyalty.

Revisionist socialism in different forms challenged orthodox Marxianism. The revisionists recognized that great gains were being won and would be extended not by violence but by political processes. In England the Fabian socialists took the lead and won many improvements in the condition of the working class. In Germany, the revisionist Edward Bernstein in the 1890's denied the concept of the class struggle and ad-

vocated evolutionary socialism. The orthodox Marxists denounced revisionism (moderate socialism) as a betrayal of the
working class. These orthodox Marxists, led by Nikolai Lenin
(1870-1924) in Russia, opposed all collaboration with capitalism and worked to engender the class struggle as preparation
for the day of revolution. Lenin advocated stronger measures
against capitalism where Marx would have left it to die of its
own weaknesses. Lenin called for a rigidly disciplined revolutionary organization. Unlike Marx and Engels, Lenin advocated despotic, police-state dictatorship of the proletariat. As
the profound differences between them appeared, Leninists
(communists) regarded the revisionists (socialists) as outright
enemies.

Labor movements.   The growth of industry and the wage-
earning class was accompanied by the formation of the trade
unions. Craft unions organized the skilled workers first. Industrial unions were organized to unite all workers within a
single industry regardless of skills of the members. In England
and America national confederations of unions united the
separate craft unions into great national organizations.

Trades unions were formed first in England and then on
the continent. For the most part these unions were responsible,
moderate, and gradualistic in their pursuit of working class
goals. The syndicalists, however, pursued their goals with more
violence. In England the Reform Bill of 1867 opened the way
for political influence of workers, and Parliament passed
several acts in 1874 and 1875 to permit unions to picket, strike,
and raise funds. Consumer cooperative societies were organized all over Europe as another means of self-help among
workers and other classes. Near the turn of the century the
achievements by socialists of large programs of social insurance
legislation greatly alleviated in most European countries the
insecurity caused by such threats as unemployment, accidents,
sickness, and old age.

Christian socialism. Christian socialism arose to contradict the Marxian thesis that religion was an opiate to keep the masses satisfied with earthly miseries for promises of future rewards. Christian socialism became a potent influence in Europe. Pope Gregory VI took the lead in calling upon employers and workers to be guided by Christian principles in their relationships. Leo XIII (1878-1903) condemned the atheism of the Marxists and advocated restraint in the assertion of property rights. Workers parties and trades unions were endorsed by the pope.

Fabian socialism. English aversion to revolutionary socialism and preference for gradualistic tactics brought forth the Fabian Society in 1883. The name indicates the movement's preference for the tactics of the Roman general Fabius who defeated the enemy by attrition rather than by forcing a major frontal assault. The Fabians worked for the socialist state by educating the workers and hoped to achieve their goals through normal political processes and labor unions. The Fabians who included many intellectuals, worked for economic and social reforms and organized the Independent Labor Party, a forerunner of the present Labor Party. Leaders of the Fabians were Sidney and Beatrice Webb, George Bernard Shaw, and H. G. Wells.

Syndicalism. An outgrowth of anarchism and Marxism was the labor movement of syndicalism, which organized workers over entire industries. This radical movement became active after 1890; its leading theorist was the Frenchman Georges Sorel (1847-1922). Syndicalists opposed the socialized state as one likely to be arbitrary in dealing with workers and favored organization of *syndicats* or trade unions which would control each industry. Weapons prominently used by the syndicalists were sabotage and the general strike by which a nation might be paralyzed.

Conservatism. A late prominent advocate of laissez-faire economics was the English philosopher Herbert Spencer (1820-1903). Spencer, an old-fashioned liberal, is now classified as a conservative, since he upheld private property rights, favored individualism, and opposed the interference of the state in economic and social matters. Spencer's views applied Darwin's competitive struggle in nature to human society and thereby upheld business competition and opposed state poor relief but favored private charity. Businessmen sometimes actually justified their ruthless elimination of competitors as the survival of the fittest. Spencer found a large following in England and America during his lifetime but now receives little attention.

RELIGION

Organized religion had to reckon with the teachings of Marxism, Darwinism, and scientific thought and methodology.

Catholic Doctrine. The experiences of the papacy with republican governments in the French Revolution, in the revolutions of 1848, and with Italian nationalists in 1870 bred a deep distrust of liberal causes. But after 1815 reactionary or conservative governments, that of Napoleon III for example, enlarged the powers of the clergy. Conservatives needed the Church as a defense against liberalism and socialism. Reactionary and conservative regimes, therefore, enlarged the Church's educational and censorship functions.

In 1864 Pope Pius IX (1846-1878) issued the *Syllabus of Errors*, which condemned those liberal teachings which advocated separation of church and state, secular education, and religious toleration. The *Syllabus* condemned other liberal modern ideas, such as divorce and civil marriage. In 1869 the pope called an ecumenical (general) Church council, the first since the Council of Trent ended in 1563. This Council at the

Vatican in 1870 declared the pope to be infallible when he officially defined doctrines of faith or morals. This redefinition of the papal authority aroused considerable opposition among the governments of Britain, France, Germany, and Austria, but another pope, Leo XIII (1878-1903), a skillful diplomatist, did much to allay apprehension over papal claims. He sought to reconcile and minimize the differences of modernism with the Church but still tried to counteract the forces of materialism. In the encyclical *Rerum novarum* (1891) Leo XIII condemned both Marxist materialism and capitalist exploitation of the workers.

Science and theology. Protestant leaders found themselves busiest combating the findings of science, since their followers asserted the right to judge for themselves the quarrel of theology and science. The Catholic popes upheld Church doctrine against the teachings of science, but some Church modernists sought a reconciliation with the theory of evolution. Protestant theologians arose to dispute the conclusions of Darwinism and other findings of science that contradicted what the churches had been teaching. They fought science by ridicule or sought out and exploited weaknesses in its evidence or reasoning. Fundamentalists found refuge by faith in the Bible as being divinely inspired and by simply ignoring science. Many Protestants became atheists or agnostics.

Some scholars, engaging in "higher" criticism, studied the origins of the Bible by the critical methods used by historians in testing the accuracy of documents. They showed that some parts of the Bible had been lost, that others had changed from the originals, or that evidence was lacking for certain events. The study of comparative religion showed how Christianity was not unique but resembled many other religions. A popular *Life of Jesus* by the French writer Ernest Renan supplied natural explanations of the miracles associated with the life of Jesus.

SCIENCE AND PHILOSOPHY

Many branches of science made enormous progress in the last half of the nineteenth century. The theory of evolution found application in various sciences. The applications of science helped man to understand himself and his environment much better; the life sciences enabled man to combat disease, and to produce more foodstuffs; chemistry and other physical sciences gave rise to new industries and enabled men to live better in many ways.

***Darwin and the theory of evolution.** Charles Darwin (1809-1882) presented his theory of evolution in the book *Origin of Species* in 1859. The book explained how plant and animal species had evolved from earlier forms. Earlier scientists had suggested evolutionary development of present forms of life.

The earlier study of geology by the great Sir Charles Lyell and the study of fossilized plant and animal life by paleontologists supplied data on the age of the earth and on the evolution of life forms. In 1863 Lyell's book on *The Geological Evidences of the Antiquity of Man* supplied new information regarding man's development.

Darwin believed that plants and animals underwent chance modifications which enabled some to survive and reproduce themselves better than other individuals. "Natural selection" over long periods of time brought about new species. The "struggle for existence" by which certain forms of life survived troubled the religious minded; the theory of evolution explained man's origin in terms of nature and, therefore, seemed to contradict the Bible. Like the theory of Copernicus, it seemed to make man less important; besides, it made man a product of evolution from lower forms of life. Other scientists soon came to accept biological evolution and added to its proofs or modified the theory. Gregor Mendel in the 1860's accounted for change in the species by mutations. Much of the debate over Darwinism was among intellectuals who applied it to social theory. It was used to justify laissez-faire economic competition. The able English scientist, Thomas H. Huxley, became the leader in the defense of Darwin's findings.

Louis Pasteur (1822-1895). Pasteur's great work was the study of minute or microscopic forms of plant and animal life. Through the use of the improved microscope, Pasteur showed that microscopic life, or "germs," caused diseases. He showed that these organisms could be killed by heating or pasteurization. He demonstrated the importance of sanitation in combating disease and the possibilities of immunization by inoculation with serum that gave a harmlessly mild form of the disease. The German physician Robert Koch (1843-1910) developed the science of bacteriology and identified the bacilli of several diseases. Vaccines and serums were then found for preventing these diseases by giving immunity to individuals.

Friedrich Nietzsche (1844-1900). Possibly the most prominent philosopher in Europe after Schopenhauer was Friedrich Nietzsche. On account of ill-health, Nietzsche retired from his professorship in 1879 and produced a combination of philosophy and poetry in his writings. He attacked most contemporary thought except Darwinism. He revolted against the teachings of the German pessimistic philosopher Arthur Schopenhauer, who had renounced life. From Darwinism, Nietzsche concluded that man should look forward to the evolution of a better man, the "superman." He condemned the Christian values of charity and compassion and upheld such animal qualities as courage, aggressiveness, and ruthlessness as qualities that would produce higher forms of life. He was scornful of all measures to minimize the suffering of the poor and unfortunate. In 1889 the philosopher broke completely and spent his last years in insanity.

REVIEW QUESTIONS

Multiple-choice:

1. The most important improvement in transportation in use in 1870 was   1) the steamship   2) the automobile   3) steam railroads   4) electric railroads.

2. A large nation that became an industrial giant between 1870 and 1900 was   1) Germany   2) Russia   3) France   4) Japan.

3. Which new industry or invention was of *least* importance in 1880?   1) Electricity   2) railroads   3) steel   4) industries based on chemistry.

4. The agriculture of which country did not receive tariff protection from New World agricultural exports?   1) France   2) Germany   3) Britain.

5. A great new threat to the laissez-faire competitive economic system was introduced after 1870 by   1) government monopolies granted as revenue measures   2) the organization of labor unions   3) the rise of nationalized industries   4) monopolistic business combinations.

6. After 1860 the most widely adopted tactic of the working classes to improve their lot relative to employers was the   1) adoption of syndicalism   2) organization of Marxist societies and political parties   3) political alliances with the landowning class against the bourgeoisie   4) organization of Christian socialist parties.

7. Which did *not* bring about a diminution of the influence of orthodox Marxism?   1) Revisionist socialism   2) growth of nationalism   3) organization of the internationals   4) a real improvement in the conditions of workers.

8. Marx's theory was modified by Lenin when Lenin advocated   1) national socialist parties   2) active, rigidly organized revolutionary societies instead of waiting for capitalism to die on schedule   3) infiltration of middle class political parties   4) alliance with middle class moderate reformers.

9. All of these offered *moderate* solutions for betterment of the working class *except* 1) syndicalism 2) consumer cooperatives 3) Christian socialism 4) trade unions.

10. Noted for their advocacy of working for a socialist society by the gradual means of education and political processes were the 1) Christian socialists 2) syndicalists 3) Social Democrats 4) Fabians.

11. Protestant modernists 1) sought reconciliation with the Roman Church 2) accepted the findings of science 3) agreed with the fundamentalists 4) advocated radical labor movements.

Completion:

12. The fulfillment of the predictions of ..... were postponed in Europe by the vast increase in the production of foodstuffs in overseas areas.

13. A monopoly extending across national boundary lines is often called a ......

14. Revisionist socialists in England were called the ..... socialists.

15. The man who came to be the greatest leader of the orthodox Marxists was ......

16. In England the revisionist socialists organized a political party which came to be called the ..... Party.

Matching:

17. Sidney Webb
18. Sorel
19. Herbert Spencer
20. Pope Pius IX
21. Leo XIII
22. Ernest Renan
23. Louis Pasteur
24. Thomas H. Huxley
25. Friedrich Nietzsche
26. Schopenhauer

a. Militantly condemned various forms of modernism
b. Defended the Darwinian theory
c. A Fabian leader
d. German pessimist
e. Tactful pope who sought to quiet fears of papal claims
f. Germ theory of disease
g. Syndicalist theorist
h. Developed smallpox vaccine
i. Former popular defender of conservatism and property rights
j. *Life of Jesus*
k. Philosopher of the superman

FOR FURTHER READING

HARDBOUND:

Barnes, Harry Elmer, *An Intellectual and Cultural History of the Western World* (1937). A useful survey for all periods.

Cheyney, Sheldon, *A New World History of Art* (1956).

Clough, Shepard B., and Cole, Charles W., *Economic History of Europe* (1948).

Cole, George, *Fabian Socialism* (1943). Favorable to Fabianism.

Friedell, Egon, *A Cultural History of the Modern Age.*

Gardner, Helen, *Art through the Ages* (1936).

Hayes, Carlton J. H., *A Generation of Materialism, 1871-1900* (1941). Survey of cultural and political developments.

Heaton, Herbert, *Economic History of Europe* (1948).

Houghton, W. E., *The Victorian Frame of Mind* (1957).

Randall, John H., *The Making of the Modern Mind* (1940).

Shryock, Richard H., *Development of Modern Medicine* (1936).

Tyler, David, *Steam Conquers the Atlantic* (1939).

Webb, Sidney and Beatrice, *History of Trade Unionism* (1957). By the founders of Fabian Socialism.

PAPERBOUND:

Berlin, Isaiah, *Karl Marx* (Oxford). Somewhat hostile.

Bernstein, Edward, *Evolutionary Socialism* (Schocken).

Darwin, Charles, *Origin of Species* (Dolphin).

Eiseley, Loren, *Darwin's Century* (Anchor).

Fremantle, Anna, *Little Band of Prophets* (NAL). A study of the Fabian socialists.

Hughes, H. Stuart, *Consciousness and Society: European Social Thought, 1890-1930* (Vintage).

Huxley, Julian, *Evolution in Action* (NAL). By a foremost interpreter of science.

————, *et al., A Book That Shook the World* (Pittsburgh). A collection of essays on Darwinism.

Irvine, W., *Apes, Angels, and Victorians* (Meridian).

Kaufmann, Walter, *Nietzsche* (Meridian).

Marx, Karl, and Engels, Friedrich, *Basic Writings on Politics and Philosophy* (Anchor). Selections from the originals.

Mayo, H. B., *Introduction to Marxist Theory* (Oxford).

Pledge, H. T., *Science Since 1500: A Short History* (Torchbooks).

Ruggiero, G. de., *The History of European Liberalism* (Beacon). The classic account of liberalism in differernt countries.

Shaw, George Bernard, *Fabian Essays in Socialism* (Dolphin). First published in 1887.

Usher, A. P., *A History of Mechanical Inventions* (Beacon). Inventions that made the Industrial Revolution possible in England and elsewhere.

Wilson, Edmund, *To the Finland Station* (Anchor). Survey of radical movements since the French Revolution.

1837-1901	*Queen Victoria reigned in Great Britain*
*1861-1865	*Civil War in the United States*
*1867	*Second Reform Bill passed in Britain*
1868	*Disraeli's first ministry began*
1869	*Disestablishment Act ended Irish Catholic taxation to support the Anglican Church*
*1870's	*Kulturkampf waged in Germany; Centrist Party organized*
1871	*Paris Commune led uprising against French National Assembly*
1872	*Secret ballot introduced in Britain*
1875	*Beginning of the Third Republic in France*
	Social Democrat Party organized in Germany
1878-1900	*Humbert I, king of Italy. Italy makes little progress towards democracy*
*1884	*Gladstone won passage of the Third Reform Bill*
1886	*Gladstone failed to win passage of Irish Home Rule*
1888-1918	*William II, kaiser in Germany*
1890	*Bismarck's resignation accepted by Kaiser William II*
1893	*Independent Labor Party organized in Britain*
1894-1906	*Dreyfus Affair in France*
1898	*Spain lost her overseas colonies in the Spanish-American War*
1900-1914	*Period during which extensive social and progressive measures were enacted in most countries of the Western World*
1901	*Taff Vale decision threatened British trade unions*

1905	*French anti-clericals repealed the Concordat of 1801*
*1911	*Parliamentary Act of 1911 broke power of the House of Lords*
1918	*Women granted suffrage in Britain*

8. Political Developments in the Western Nations

The period of 1871-1914 was one of great industrial progress and one which ended with the development of political and social democracy in the countries of western Europe and in the United States. In the early part of this period universal manhood suffrage was realized in most of western Europe. Most of the battles of this era were fought in parliaments and in political campaigns rather than from behind street barricades. The clashes occurred between representatives of capital and of organized workers rather than between aristocrats and bourgeoisie. Those favored by wealth, education, or birth continued to serve as leaders for the masses and the upper classes. Not the rights of individuals against tyrannical governments or of the nation against privileged classes, but the working class struggle for economic gain and security constituted the political issues of this time. The functions of governments increased with the expansion of national education programs and social legislation. Compulsory military training was adopted in nearly all of Europe.

GREAT BRITAIN

In her domestic politics Great Britain continued to become more democratic during the last half of Queen Victoria's long reign (1837-1901) and under her successors, Edward VI (1901-1910) and George V (1910-1936). The struggle against royal tyrants had long since ceased with the failure of George III's schemes to control Parliament. The monarchs became figureheads who served ceremonially and symbolically as the heads of state. Altogether, Britain's stable parliamentary government, commercial and industrial strength, and naval power maintained her position of leadership in Europe and in world affairs.

**The Reform Bill of 1867. The Reform Bill of 1832 brought a political victory to the well-to-do business classes over the landed aristocracy. It redistributed representation in Parliament but extended the suffrage only enough to include about an eighth of all adult males.

The Reform Bill of 1867 was needed to give urban workers a direct voice in government. John Bright and William Gladstone, leaders of the Liberal Party, favored the extension of the suffrage; the working class had long been petitioning for the right to vote. By 1865 seats in Parliament needed to be redistributed again as the cities had greatly increased their population. The success of the democratic government of the Union in the American Civil War supported the arguments of those who favored more democracy in the English government. When the Reform Bill was introduced in 1866 it was defeated by Conservatives and dissident Liberals. In 1867 the Conservative leader Benjamin Disraeli introduced the bill that was enacted. Popular demonstrations had convinced Disraeli that the bill would soon pass in spite of any opposition, and he wanted the Conservative Party to gain credit for its passage. As enacted, this law doubled the electorate.

**Gladstone and the Liberal Party. William Ewart Gladstone (1809-1898) became prime minister for the first time in 1868. The voters returned the Liberals to power, because they realized that Gladstone and his party were really responsible for the passage of the Reform Bill of 1867. Many measures were now passed by the Liberal Parliament. Reforms were enacted in government administration, in the army, and in Irish affairs. Civil service examinations were made compulsory for most government positions. Education was extended by the creation of tax-supported public schools divorced from religion, in keeping with the ideas of the Liberals. The Trades Union Act (1871) legalized labor unions. The secret ballot was provided by law in 1872.

Gladstone served as prime minister at four different times between the years 1868 and 1894. During this time the Conservative, Benjamin Disraeli (1804-1881), was Gladstone's leading political opponent. Gladstone and the Liberals supported some working-class measures, but they served primarily as spokesmen for the laissez-faire principles that enabled business interests to increase profits and exploit labor. In foreign affairs the Liberals promoted peace and avoided aggressive policies. The Liberals also drew support from religious dissenters and advocates of free trade and civil liberties.

Gladstone and Ireland. The chronic friction that persisted between Ireland and England for centuries since the middle ages still irritated relations between the two islands. Irish Catholics had to pay taxes to support the Church of Ireland, which was only a branch of the Anglican Church. Many Irish had to pay exorbitant rents to absentee landlords, many of whom were Englishmen whose ancestors had confiscated estates in the course of the suppression of innumerable Irish rebellions. The nationalist aspirations elsewhere in the world in the 1860's encouraged Irish demands for Home Rule. Poverty and discriminatory laws aggravated Irish discontent. An Irish rebellion in 1848 had failed. Under Gladstone the Disestablishment Act in 1869 relieved the Irish of the burden of paying taxes for the support of the Anglican Church. Some small protection was given the Irish tenants but the law fell far short of solving the problems of Irish tenancy.

In 1886 Gladstone sponsored the Home Rule Bill; it did not pass, yet it split the Liberal Party and returned the Conservatives to power. The problem of Home Rule was complicated by the Irish Protestants in Ulster who wished to remain under English rule. In 1914 Home Rule was finally enacted, but the outbreak of war caused Parliament to suspend its application until peace returned.

Disraeli and the Conservative Party. Disraeli served twice as a Conservative prime minister between 1867 and 1880. Disraeli did much to make the Conservative Party more attractive to the masses and actually passed more legislation, through his Tory Democracy, to improve conditions for the working class than did the Liberals. The Conservative Party drew its support from the country landowners; it favored the monarchy and the Anglican Church; it favored the principle of gradual change and stood for a more aggressive and imperialistic foreign policy than did the Liberals. Patriotic appeals were made to the electorate for support of the monarchy and the empire. In legislation, the Conservatives removed legal obstacles against striking and picketing; health and education acts were passed. The Disraeli government fought colonial wars against the Zulus and Afghans, proclaimed Victoria Empress of India, bought stock in the Suez Canal, and acquired Cyprus.

The extension of democracy. In 1884 Gladstone secured the passage of the Third Reform Bill that extended the suffrage to agricultural laborers by reducing the property qualifications for voting. Now almost all adult males could vote. In 1885 seats in the Commons were again redistributed so that all constituencies were of the same size in population. The Commons now represented England fairly well, but the House of Lords, which often assented to popular measures, could still block critical measures and assert the interests of the upper classes. The opposition of the Lords to Liberal reforms brought on a crisis in 1909 when the Lords fought fiercely against a budget prepared by the Lloyd George ministry; the budget bill taxed the rich heavily for the betterment of the poor. To break the opposition of the Lords, the Liberals and the new Labor Party combined to secure the passage of the Parliamentary Act of 1911. This important measure deprived the Lords of their veto power; money bills passed by the Commons could be only delayed by the Lords for a couple of months. Over other bills the Lords held only the power to delay passage for two years. The Lords assented to this loss of their power only after Prime Minister Herbert Asquith had King George V agree to create enough new peers to insure its passage. The threat sufficed. In the acts of 1918 and 1928 women were given the right to vote. An act in 1919 gave women legal equality with men.

The Labor Party and social reform. When Gladstone's support of Home Rule split the Liberal Party, the Conservatives returned to power from 1895 to 1905, but now gave less attention to social reform than under Disraeli's leadership. In 1901 the Taff Vale decision by the House of Lords, functioning as a final court of appeal, made a large award to the Taff Vale Railway Company for losses incurred during a strike. When this decision threatened to break the power of the trade unions, they decided to make themselves active in politics. The beginnings of the Labor Party, however, go back to 1893 when the Independent Labor Party was organized. The present Labor Party was soon formed after the Independent Labor Party gained the support of the Fabians and of the Social Democratic Federation. In 1906 Labor members helped the Liberal Party organize the Commons under Prime Minister Herbert Asquith (1908-1917). This coalition of Liberals and Labor members now passed a series of laws similar to the legislation of the American New Deal a generation later. The Trades-Disputes Act (1906) protected union funds. The Workingmen's Compensation Act (1906) protected workers and their families against losses from industrial accidents. Other acts brought various forms of social security and increased spending for education. Further social reform ceased with the outbreak of war in 1914.

FRANCE

France's defeat and humiliation in 1870 introduced an era of bitter political strife, strife that ended with further gains for republicanism and democracy. The attention given to France's weaknesses and political stresses should not be allowed to conceal the fact of her international renown for her art, science, and literature. France led the world in the production of fine luxury goods and in fashions. In a sense Paris remained the "capital of civilization."

**The Paris Commune (1871). At the end of the Franco-Prussian War, there occurred an uprising known as the Paris Commune. A combination of Parisian Republicans, Socialists, and other radical elements repudiated the authority of the National Assembly with its majority of rural, royalist, and bourgeois members. The Communards opposed the humiliating peace terms with Germany and feared the conservative outlook of the Assembly. Paris was put under siege by the forces of the National Assembly. The radical Communards seized control of the city and killed their hostages; both sides were guilty of terrorism. The national troops after several weeks regained control of Paris after about 15,000 persons had been killed. The National Assembly in the succeeding years could not agree whether France would be a republic or a monarchy. The main difficulty was the disagreement among the monarchists, who were split between Legitimists, Orleanists, and Bonapartists. The republican leader of France since the downfall of Napoleon, Adolphe Thiers, served as president but in 1873 was replaced by the royalist Marshall MacMahon.

The Third Republic. The Republicans gradually gained control of France under the vigorous leadership of Leon Gambetta and in 1875 the Assembly passed five laws which served as the constitution of the Third French Republic. Republican control of all branches of government became certain in the election of 1879. This Third Republic remained in effect until overthrown in World War II. It provided a Chamber of Deputies elected by universal manhood suffrage and a Senate chosen indirectly. The president was chosen by the senators and deputies jointly, but the real executive power was entrusted to a ministry composed of members of whatever party or coalition controlled the legislature. The multi-party system in France, as in other countries on the continent, usually meant that governments were formed by reshuffling coalitions in parliament more than by calling general elections as in Britain. Moderate Republicans controlled the Third Republic throughout most of its existence.

**Achievements and problems of the Republic.* The Third Republic quickly paid the indemnity to Germany, built extensive public works, and created a system of state-supported compulsory elementary schools. In 1884 trade unions were legalized.

The Republic after the mid-eighties suffered from various government scandals and factionalism. Opposing the middle-class government for the control of France were the clericals and royalists. Disillusionment with scandals and the desire for victory against Germany turned the eyes of many to the glamorous General Georges Boulanger, who seemed to be a man of destiny, but when the time for action came he lacked the nerve to stage a coup d'etat. He escaped to Belgium when the Republic prepared to bring treason charges against him.

Cases of sordid graft involving officials of the Republic Canal Company discredited politicians and ruined financiers. Ferdinand de Lesseps, who had built the Suez Canal, failed in Panama, because of yellow fever and unforseen construction difficulties.

The Dreyfus Affair (*1894-1906*). The attempts of the monarchists, militarists, and clericals to discredit the Republic came to a focus beginning in 1894 in the celebrated case of Captain Alfred Dreyfus, a Jewish army officer. A military court found Dreyfus guilty of selling secrets to the enemy, but the real culprit was a nobleman, Major Esterhazy. Dreyfus was sentenced to Devil's Island in French Guiana. He was convicted by reactionaries who sought to discredit the Republic. Evidence that Esterhazy was guilty was withheld to preserve the prestige of the army. Dreyfus was returned to France for re-trial in 1899 due to efforts initiated by the novelist Emile Zola, but Dreyfus's guilt was sustained by dishonest judges. The president pardoned him, but not until 1906 was he completely exonerated when his case was reviewed by the highest French court. The case backfired against such reactionaries as the militarists and clericals; socialists and republicans controlled France until 1914.

Church and state in France. The conflict between clericals and anticlericals in France persisted throughout this period. The extremist Catholics in France deplored the pope's loss of Rome to the Italian state and wanted a crusade to free the "prisoner" in the Vatican. The declaration of papal infallibility reinforced Catholic opposition to liberalism and republicanism. As loyal Catholics listened to Rome for guidance, they aroused the antagonism of nationalists in France, Germany, and elsewhere. Many Catholics adhered firmly to monarchism and tradition, and some of their brilliant writers became spokesmen for conservatism. The anticlerical opposition worked to separate Church and state, especially Church control of schools. Pope Leo XIII in 1892 sought to minimize the opposition of Catholics to the French government, but Catholic extremists still wanted the destruction of the Republic. After 1900 anti-clericals enacted several laws to restrict the influence of the clergy. In 1901 most of the religious orders engaged in educational and charitable work were dissolved. In 1905 France repealed the Concordat reached between Napoleon I and the pope in 1801. The state ceased to pay salaries of the clergy but gave up its right to regulate religious organizations.

Socialism and Labor Legislation. The defeat of the Communards weakened French socialists for some time, but the right to organize unions and go on strike remained, and the socialist following grew as time passed. In 1895 the unions, or *syndicats,* combined in a General Confederation of Labor (CGT). Syndicalism became a quite active force; several times large strikes were called and minor gains made. In 1905 a Socialist Party was organized; the party combined with the Republicans and soon passed a program of social security measures similar to the Labor program in Britain and the early measures in Germany. Prime Minister Aristide Briand, a former socialist, did not hesitate to break a general railway strike in 1910. He used the existing compulsory military service law to force trainmen to keep railroads in operation and avert a national breakdown. The French labor movement remained split between the Socialist Party and the CGT. Both organizations advocated pacifism, but both supported the nation when it entered World War I.

GERMANY

The German government from 1871 to the abdication of Kaiser William II in 1918 is known as the Second Reich (Empire). It was governed under constitutional forms, but actually dominated by Bismarck and King William II. This government conceded the demands of Socialists for social security, which was adopted earlier in Germany than elsewhere. The membership and power of the democratic elements increased greatly up to 1914, paralleling socialist gains in Britain and France. During this period Germany's great military and industrial power and her assertiveness in world affairs aroused an anxiety that contributed importantly to the causes of World War I.

*The German imperial government. The government of the German Empire as established in 1871 was a federal union of twenty-six states, among which were kingdoms, grand duchies and duchies, seven principalities, and three free cities. The king of Prussia, William II, was also emperor, or kaiser, of all Germany. The upper house, *Bundesrat,* represented the various states. The lower house, Reichstag, was made up of 382 deputies. This legislature differed critically from the typical British ministerial plan—the president of the Bundesrat served as imperial chancellor (head of the government) at the pleasure of the emperor and was not responsible to the legislature. Bismarck exercised his power by holding the office of chancellor. The Reichstag had little actual power and the chancellor could ignore its displeasure. The Bundesrat was so organized as to be controlled by Prussia, as was true of the whole empire. The various component states retained their ruling families, but the creation of improved machinery of government effectively united and efficiently administered the empire.

**The Kulturkampf. This is the name applied to the conflict that occurred between the German government and the Catholic Church during the 1870's. It was both a nationalistic and an anti-clerical movement. Bismarck viewed the Catholic Church as a threat to German nationalism and to the hegemony of Prussia in Germany. In 1870 the Centrist (Catholic) Party organized itself and in the same year the Vatican council declared the infallibility of the pope in matters of morals and

faith. Bismarck wished to win the support of German liberals who were anti-clerical and also wished to keep under control various national minorities who were Catholic in religion. By various laws Prussia assumed control over the church and the clergy. In 1872 the Jesuits were expelled. Many Catholic teaching orders were suppressed and various provisions enacted to regulate Catholic schools. Catholic disobedience to these laws resulted in exile and imprisonment. The Center Party actually gained such strength by 1878 that Bismarck abandoned the *Kulturkampf* and sought the cooperation of the Center Party in his opposition to the growing socialists. The anti-Catholic laws were gradually abandoned and the fear of Church interference also vanished.

**The government and social legislation. Two outstanding leaders in organizing the German working classes were Ferdinand Lasalle, who organized associations of workingmen after 1863, and Wilhelm Liebknecht, a Marxian who organized socialist parties. A fusion of the socialist parties in 1875 created the Social Democratic Party opposed to Bismarck's conception of the states. In 1878 Bismarck responded with harshly repressive measures against meetings and publications of the Social Democrats. At about the same time the Chancellor secured the passage of laws to satisfy the working class. Beginning in 1883 social insurance (security) laws were passed to give security against sickness, accident, and old age. Employers, workers, and the government made compulsory contributions to a fund to establish old age pensions. Thus, Germany provided the kinds of social insurance that Britain and France legislated twenty years later. Other laws were enacted for the special benefit and protection of labor, and the well-being of the working classes was greatly improved. William II withdrew the repressive measures against socialists, and their representation in the Reichstag steadily increased up to 1914.

Beginning in the days of the Old Regime, Germany had made more progress in education than any other nation of Europe. Under Bismarck vocational schools, high schools, and universities flourished. Scholarship enjoyed a higher prestige in Germany than in any other country. Foreign students went there to complete their advanced studies. The educational system contributed greatly to Germany's industrial growth.

Political parties in Germany. Germany's multiparty system included five important political parties. Only by forming coalitions did they control a majority vote in the Reichstag. The National Liberal Party of big business interests at first was Bismarck's strongest supporter, but he usually had the backing of the Free Conservative Party dominated by the Prussian landed nobility. The Center Party favored preservation of Catholic liberties and functions from state interference but supported social insurance. The Progressive Party represented small business and professional classes and advocated political democracy. The leftist Social Democratic Party representing workers grew less radical as it increased its membership by adding middle class reformers. The increasing assertiveness of the liberal parties had taken Germany well along on the road to parliamentary democracy when World War I broke out.

*Bismarck's resignation (1890). Kaiser William I (1797-1888), who had generally left Bismarck free to govern Germany, died in 1888. His successor, Frederick III, lived only three months and the young William II came to the throne in 1888. William wanted to rule in his own right. When he disagreed with Bismarck over social and foreign policy, Bismarck offered his resignation as he had often done before. To the Chancellor's surprise, William accepted. William II ceased to repress socialists but changed the defensive and peaceful foreign policy of Bismarck to one of militarism, imperialism, and tactless sabre-rattling. William did not wish to limit Germany's leadership to Europe but sought the larger role of world politics.

ITALY, SPAIN, AND PORTUGAL

The lack of experience in parliamentary government and illiteracy retarded the growth of democracy in Italy. Lack of natural resources held back industrial growth except in the North. Before 1914 Italy had developed a spirit of aggressive nationalism toward Africa and the Balkans.

The government and politics of Italy. Italy was united under the government of Piedmont whose constitution of 1848 was extended to the rest of Italy to create a centralized state. Only three kings held the throne from 1861 to 1946. Victor Emmanuel II held the throne until 1878 when his son, Humbert I, followed and reigned until 1900. He was succeeded by Victor Emmanuel II, a sincere liberal who reigned to the end of the monarchy in 1946. The kings were largely figureheads except in times of crisis. In 1870 only two percent of the population qualified to vote because of restrictive property and educational qualifications, but by 1912 universal manhood suffrage had been attained by the efforts of socialists and liberals. The Parliament of Great Britain served as a model for Italy as it had for other governments. The lower house of parliament was an elective Chamber of Deputies. Members of the upper house, the Senate, were appointed for life by the crown. The Chamber stayed under the control of either a coalition of the Left or of the Right. Both sides were so eager to retain office that they compromised on political issues. The chiefs of ministry followed a policy called *trasformismo* by which deals were made with deputies of the opposition so as to retain a parliamentary majority. Considerable corruption was perpetuated by prime ministers seeking to stay in power. After 1900 liberals and socialists combined to secure better working conditions, social insurance, compulsory education (to remedy Italy's great problem of illiteracy), and freedom of the press. Railways and insurance companies were nationalized. Provisions were made for the Church after the formation of the unified government of Italy. The Vatican was recognized as a separate state and given a subsidy for the loss of the papal estates. Church and state were separated, but Catholicism was recognized as the national religion. But the pope remained a prisoner in the Vatican by his own choice. The pope's advice to Italian Catholics not to vote or hold office weakened Italy to some extent. A *modus vivendi* was worked out with the "prisoner of the Vatican" around 1900, but friendly relations were not fully restored until 1929.

Economic problems. Italy lacked the basic natural resources of coal and iron to achieve the industrial progress of Germany or France. Her industry developed in the north. Southern Italy remained a problem because of poverty and illiteracy. The burden of past reactionary and corrupt governments added to the backwardness of at least the southern half of Italy. The development of hydroelectric power helped overcome Italy's power shortage. The high rate of illiteracy handicapped the nation economically as well as in its political life. Heavy immigration of young Italians to the United States and South America drained her of energetic laborers. Italian governments tried penetration of the Balkans with the objective of securing raw materials, but Austria-Hungary was too well-established there. Italy then turned to Africa and acquired some colonies. Italy began to show considerable economic progress by 1914.

Spain and Portugal. After 1815 the loss of nearly all of the American colonies left Spain weaker than ever. She no longer drew income from the colonies and remained in chronic bankruptcy. Spain failed to develop a class of landowning peasants. Nor did she develop her potentialities for industry. No progressive middle class existed to strive for democracy. Civil war weakened the nation from time to time. Spain retained her Bourbon line of kings. In 1898 the loss of Cuba, Puerto Rico, Guam, and the Philippines stripped Spain of her last distant colonies.

Spain's sister Iberian state, Portugal, continued to parallel Spain's political changes. Misgovernment and autocratic government bred various forms of extremism. Portugal, unlike Spain, retained a large empire in her colonies in Asia and Africa. During most of the nineteenth century Portugal retained close economic and diplomatic ties to Britain. The Revolution of 1910 produced a republic under bourgeois control but similar to that of France.

REVIEW QUESTIONS

Multiple-choice:

1. Which British Reform Bill gave the vote to agricultural workers and thereby established almost universal manhood suffrage? 1) Reform Bill of 1832   2) Reform Bill of 1867   3) the reform law of 1911   4) Third Reform Bill.

2. Which was the most influential in British politics from 1865 to 1900? 1) Disraeli   2) Gladstone   3) Queen Victoria   4) Joseph Chamberlain.

3. Disraeli introduced the Reform Bill of 1867 to   1) win the support of workers for the Conservative Party   2) steal the thunder of the radical socialists   3) win the loyalty of workers for the Liberal Party   4) create a system of social security for Italy.

4. Reform legislation passed by the party of Gladstone in the early 1870's included all *except*   1) the secret ballot   2) tax-supported public schools   3) social insurance to protect the working class   4) legalization of labor unions.

5. Which was *not* one of the nationalist movements of the 1860's? 1) Irish Home Rule   2) the unification of Italy   3) the Polish insurrection   4) agitation in Ulster.

6. The Parliamentary Act of 1911 1) broke the power of the House of Lords as a legislative body 2) permitted all British subjects to vote 3) recognized the independence of the Dominions 4) brought a comprehensive social insurance system to Britain.

7. The first western European nation to pass a program of social insurance was 1) France 2) Germany 3) Britain 4) Switzerland.

8. These names are all associated with the scandals and troubles of the Third French Republic *except* which one? 1) Panama Canal 2) Boulanger 3) Suez Canal 4) Dreyfus.

9. A Dreyfus sympathizer probably would not have belonged to any of these French political factions *except* which one? 1) Clericals 2) Republicans 3) monarchists 4) militarists.

10. The most frequent point of conflict between Church and state from 1870 to 1910 was over 1) education 2) the appointment of bishops 3) education of the clergy 4) payment of salaries of the clergy.

11. Bismarck waged the Kulturkampf for all reasons *except* 1) to win support of the anti-clerical German liberals 2) to weaken the power of the socialists 3) to weaken the influence of minorities in Germany 4) he thought the Church was a threat to German nationalism.

12. The political party in Germany that corresponded to the Labor Party in Britain was named the 1) Social Democrats 2) Centrist Party 3) National Liberals 4) Progressive Party.

13. Bismarck's power in Germany ended when 1) he was assassinated 2) he was forced to retire 3) he offered his resignation thinking it would not be accepted 4) he lost his majority in the Bundesrat.

14. Democracy made little progress in Italy because of all these *except* 1) illiteracy 2) corruption and intimidation 3) the opposition of the popes to the government 4) the opposition of the kings.

Completion:

15. Which followed the more aggressive policy in foreign affairs, Disraeli or Gladstone? . . . . .

16. A Parisian political group that revolted against the French

National Assembly after the surrender to Prussia was known as
the . . . . . .

17. France established a republic during the 1870's, because
the . . . . . could not agree upon the choice of a royal family.

18. The small state governed by the popes after 1870 is known
as the . . . . . .

19. The policy of Italian ministers of retaining office by political deals with the opposition is known by the Italian term . . . . . .

Matching:

20. Lloyd George	a. A leader in the defense of Dreyfus
21. Herbert Asquith	b. Former socialist who broke a railroad
22. Adolphe Thiers	strike in France
23. Emile Zola	c. Helped break power of the House
24. Aristide Briand	of Lords
25. Bismarck	d. Sent to Devil's Island
26. Dreyfus	e. Took over the reins of government
27. William II	when Bismarck resigned
28. Ferdinand de Lesseps	f. First president of the Third French
29. Georges Boulanger	Republic
	g. First emperor of the Second German Reich
	h. The "man of destiny" who fled France
	i. Held the office of chancellor
	j. Was made prime minister in 1906 with support of Labor Party
	k. Built the Suez Canal

FOR FURTHER READING

HARDBOUND:

Brogan, Denis W., *France Under the Republic: The Development
of Modern France, 1870-1939* (1940). Well written narrative.
Bourgeois, Emile, *History of Modern France* (1919).
Curtis, E., *History of Ireland* (6th ed., 1950).
Dawson, William H., *The Evolution of Modern Germany* (1915).
Emphasizes economic growth.

———, *The German Empire 1867-1914.* 2 vols. (1919).

Ensor, Robert, *England 1870-1914* (1949). Oxford History of England series. Solid information.

Halperin, Samuel, *The Separation of Church and State in Italian Thought from Cavour to Mussolini* (1937).

Lynd, Helen, *England in the Eighteen Eighties: Toward a Social Basis for Freedom* (1945).

Medlicott, W. N., *Bismarck, Gladstone and the Concert of Europe* (1956).

Slater, Gilbert, *The Growth of Modern England* (1939).

Somervell, David C., *Disraeli and Gladstone: A Duo-Biographical Sketch* (1926).

Strachey, Lytton, *Eminent Victorians* (1933). A witty classic.

———, *Queen Victoria* (1938). Popular.

Wright, Charles H. *History of the Third French Republic* (1916).

Young, C. M., *Victorian England: Portrait of an Age* (2nd ed., 1953). General coverage.

PAPERBOUND:

Albrecht-Carrié, R., *Italy from Napoleon to Mussolini* (Columbia).

Brinton, Crane, *English Political Thought in the Nineteenth Century* (Torchbooks).

Bruun, Geoffrey, *Nineteenth Century European Civilization* (Galaxy).

Halasz, Nicholas, *Captain Dreyfus: The Story of Mass Hysteria* (Evergreen).

Jackson, J. Hampden, *Clemenceau and the Third Republic* (Collier).

Rosenberg, Arthur, *Imperial Germany* (Beacon).

Schuyler, Robert L., and Weston, Corinne C., *British Constitutional History since 1832* (Anvil). Interpretation and documents.

Thompson, David, *England in the Nineteenth Century* (Penguin). Short history.

*1789	*The United States began as a federal government*
1789-1801	*Federalist Party in power*
1801	*Jefferson inaugurated*
*1803	*Louisiana purchased*
*1812-1814	*War of 1812*
1819	*Florida acquired from Spain*
1829	*Jackson and the Democratic Party came into power*
1836	*Texas won independence*
1840	*Whig Party elected its first president, Harrison*
*1845	*Republic of Texas annexed*
*1846	*Oregon Treaty won the Oregon territory for the United States*
*1846-1848	*Mexican War; Mexican Cession won*
*1850	*Compromise of 1850 briefly settled slavery controversy*
1854	*Republican Party organized*
*1860	*Lincoln elected president; Southern states secede*
*1861-1865	*Civil War; business interests gain control of federal government*
1865-1877	*Reconstruction Period in the South*
	Rise of new industries in the North
1867	*Alaska purchased from Russia*
1870's	*Farmers and workers from national organizations*
1890's	*Decade of Populism*
1896	*McKinley elected*
1901-1914	*Era of Progressivism and political reform*

9. Rise of the United States, 1789-1914

The civilization of the independent nations of North America and South America was borrowed mainly from Europe. Since their discovery, the Americas have always been inseparable from the patterns of Western Civilization.

The early role of America in perspective. The American aborigines' most advanced cultures offered almost nothing unless they are credited with valuable indigenous plant life such as Indian corn and tobacco. Both the extermination of the natives in some areas and their absorption in others influenced the cultural development in America. The greatest influence in America upon her own development and that of Europe has been the enormous wealth of natural resources that have been harvested and developed. For example, Spanish military power in Europe for long was dependent upon American gold and silver. In the long run it was the soil and its produce that offered the most to the increase in the wealth of America and Europe. Politically, America was no determining factor in the Western World until the United States won its independence. Then its main influence was that of setting the powerful example of a democratic government and society.

Ever since the American Revolution, the United States attracted much curious attention as a novel social and political system and as a vision to submerged masses in the Old World. The United States did not importantly affect the military balance in Europe until World War I. The United States, first, because of its smaller population and, later, its isolation policy did not act as a powerful factor in the Atlantic civilization until after 1890. The other American states, much smaller and less developed, had little influence and remained in a kind of colonial status, economically and culturally, to the great powers.

Political parties of the United States. While European countries underwent frequent changes in their forms of government, the adoption of the Constitution in 1788 was the last such change in the United States. With the exception of the Civil War, American political battles were conducted in the form of election campaigns. An outstanding feature of the United States government has been its adherence to a system of two major political parties. In this it resembles the British system and not the multi-party system of Europe, which usually requires a coalition of parties to maintain an administration in office. The first administration, that of President Washington (1789-1797), was under the Federalist Party, the party of Alexander Hamilton and one which represented the reactionary upper classes, commercial interests, and government by an aristocracy of wealth and education. The more democratic elements made up of smaller farmers, lower middle class elements, and workers soon asserted themselves under the leadership of Thomas Jefferson and organized the opposition party which was called the Republicans. This economic and social division of classes represented by the two political opponents, Hamilton and Jefferson, has been continued, generally speaking, as the basis of the two major parties since about 1793. After Andrew Jackson headed the Jeffersonian party it came to be called the Democratic Party. The Federalists lost control of the federal government in 1801 when Jefferson was inaugurated as president. Jefferson's election in 1800 introduced such important changes in the character of the government that it has been referred to as the "Revolution of 1800." The change gave the planters of the South and the agrarian elements the predominant voice at the nation's capital in Washington. The Federalist Party soon disintegrated.

In 1828 the presidential election brought another sharp liberal turn with the election victory of the Democratic Party and President Jackson, who gave a greater voice in government to smaller farmers in the West and to urban workers. The Democratic victory paralleled the European revolutions of 1830. In the 1830's the Whig Party arose as a successor to the defunct Federalists. The Whigs managed to come to power briefly in the 1840's with the election of two frontier military heroes as presidents. In the shifting political alignments of the 1850's, the Whigs emerged as the Republican Party, a sectional party which at first represented the antislavery elements in the North and West but which quickly came under the control of business interests of the North. The crisis of the Civil War and Reconstruction enabled the nationalist Republican Party to entrench itself and maintain, often precariously, a control of the presidency most of the time until 1932.

Territorial expansion and population growth. The United States in the nineteenth century experienced great increases in population and growth in territory. In 1803 the Louisiana Territory was purchased from France and doubled the size of the United States. In 1819 Florida was acquired from Spain by treaty agreement. In 1821 American settlers were invited to Texas by the Mexican government, but numerous quarrels led to rebellion by the Texans and the establishment of the Republic of Texas. Under an expansionist enthusiasm called Manifest Destiny, three great territorial additions carried American boundaries all the way across the continent to the Pacific. In 1845 Texas was annexed. In 1846 the Oregon Treaty provided for the division of the Oregon country between the United States and Great Britain. In the same year the Mexican War broke out and ended in 1848 with the acquisition of the Mexican Cession. The Gadsden Purchase from Mexico in 1853 added territory to the southern part of Arizona and New Mexico and completed the boundaries of the present mainland. Alaska was purchased from Russia in 1867, partly as a return favor for her friendship to the Union cause during the Civil War. The Spanish-American War in 1898 added the Philippines, and the independent Hawaiian Islands were annexed. Guam and Puerto Rico were taken from Spain in 1898. In 1902 the United States helped Panama win its independence from Colombia and acquired the Panama Canal Zone. Cuba and Panama became American protectorates. In 1916 the Virgin Islands were purchased from Denmark.

Rapid growth of population helped make the territorial expansion possible. American families were large, and a steady stream of immigrants came in. The main attraction of America was the opportunity to make a better living than in Europe, but there were always many who came to escape persecution or to enjoy more freedom. They came from England, Ireland, Scotland, and Germany mainly. After 1870 a great number began to immigrate from eastern and southern Europe. More Catholics and Jews entered, but America remained a predominantly Protestant nation. In the 1870's the first restrictions were placed on immigration, first against the Chinese and then laws to exclude undesirable persons. In 1921 the United States passed an immigration act which for the first time severely restricted the hitherto unlimited flow of the Old World's hungry people. There was little problem of assimilation as most were glad to identify themselves as Americans.

Economic development. The seemingly unlimited extent of fertile soil and favorable temperate climate kept the United States primarily agricultural in its economy. Other resources of furs, fish, timber, and minerals maintained the economy as a producer of raw materials. After Eli Whitney invented the cotton gin in 1793 the main export staple came to be raw cotton. After 1800 the profits of cotton farming rapidly drew both small farmers and large planters westward to clear the virgin soils. In the North, the Ohio Valley also filled quickly by farmers who produced meat and grain for export. The growth of industry was fostered by tariff protection; otherwise, the economic policy was one of laissez-faire. Both agriculture and industry benefited from the American flair for invention impelled by a constant shortage of labor and stimulated by opportunities for profit. The invention of the steamboat and rapid improvements in railroads helped settle the continent much faster than Jefferson had dreamed in 1800. The invention of the reaper (1830's) and steam threshers vastly increased grain production in the nineteenth century. Invention of sewing machines gave rise to the factory production of ready-made shoes and clothing. The telegraph (1846) speeded communications. After the Civil War the typewriter and the telephone brought still better business communications. The most fundamental of all inventions was the principle of interchangeable parts, put into application by Eli Whitney. It became the basis of America's mass production and assembly-line production of the twentieth century. By 1900 the automobile began to transform American life and economy. The great industrial development in the United States came after the Civil War when the Republican Party provided greater tariff protection and a favorable political climate.

Slavery and sectionalism. The shortage of labor in the colonies caused Americans to import African slaves as early as 1619. The practice increased after 1715 as slaves were brought in to produce rice, tobacco, and indigo in the South. The concern for human rights during the American Revolution produced much sentiment against slavery, and soon after independence, most slaves were freed in the North. But the rise of the textile industry and the invention of the cotton gin caused upland cotton farming to spread and made slavery decidedly profitable in the South. Antislavery societies began to rise by 1820, and in 1831 William Lloyd Garrison became active as a radical advocate of abolition of slaves without compensation to the owners. The accusations and lawless methods of abolitionists antagonized Southerners, put them on the defensive, and made them vigorously cling to their "peculiar institution." Meanwhile, the growing population of the North increased the congressional strength of the free states until the balance threatened to be permanently upset in favor of the states favoring abolition. The application for statehood by California under a free-state constitution created a crisis in which the slave states threatened secession. The United States was in grave danger of disintegration as the legality of secession was asserted by the states'-rights philosophy of Southern leaders. Civil War might have occurred between the two sections, but, fortunately for American nationalism, the Compromise of 1850 postponed secession until the North was strong enough to preserve the Union in the crisis of the Civil War.

The Civil War (1861-1865). The Compromise of 1850 settled the quarrel for only four years. It was renewed in 1854 by the Kansas-Nebraska Act which repealed the previous compromises. The earlier compromise of 1820 had confined the spread of slavery to the region south of the parallel of latitude of 36°-30'. By 1850 antislavery sentiment had become widespread in the North, where it had increased because of the efforts of humanitarian agitators. Northerners were alarmed that Kansas, north of the earlier limits of slavery, might become a slave state as a result of the Kansas-Nebraska Act. Now the realignment of political parties took place and the sectional antislavery Republican Party of the North soon took the place of the earlier national Whig Party. Several events followed and made the slavery quarrel irreconcilable. The election of Abraham Lincoln (1860), a Northern Republican pledged to oppose the further expansion of slavery, became the occasion for the threatened secession. The eleven secession states of the South organized the Confederate States of America. War was inevitable, since Northern sentiment was strong for the preservation of the Union. In spite of the great resources of the North, the American Civil War (1861-1865) lasted four years. It is sometimes called the first modern war because both sides employed devices widely used in subsequent wars—telegraphy, railroads, trenches, machine guns, ironclad warships, and the submarine. Over 600,000 lives were lost. The slaves were all freed by constitutional amendment. Two additional amendments during the postwar Reconstruction Period gave the freedmen citizenship and sought to give them equal civil rights, including the suffrage. But a conservative reaction set in and by the unofficial compromise of 1877 the Southern whites were left undisturbed in their determination to keep the Negro in a subordinate status. The Civil War brought nominal equality to the Negro, but its greater significance is in the economic revolution brought by the shift of political control to the aggressive and burgeoning corporate business interests of the North.

**The supremacy of big business. Industrialism proceeded much more rapidly now that the Southern agrarians had been dethroned. "Big business" interests, such as railroad builders, bankers, and manufacturers, used their money power to gain control of state and national politics. Political corruption was rampant and became the most prominent characteristic of the administration of President Grant. The laissez-faire economic philosophy was interpreted to leave business free from regulation but distorted to provide subsidies in the form of land grants to railroads and indirectly to industry through protective tariffs. Monopolies made a mockery of free enterprise. Unhindered corporations exploited natural resources such as timber, land, and water power. A deflationary monetary policy implemented by the gold standard favored the creditor class to the detriment of debtor farmers in the South and West. Protests arose on the part of farmers and workers but were slow in bringing any change.

***Reaction against the domination of big business.** The tradition of free enterprise and weak government and the opportunities afforded by the abundance of free land and economic growth prevented the rise of the radical Marxian political parties such as arose in Europe at this time. But farmers and workers in America did protest and organized on a national scale for the first time. In the 1870's farmers organized the National Grange to oppose the railroads and business trusts. Farmers and workers organized Greenback third parties to demand a regulated currency of silver and paper in the place of the deflationary gold standard.

In the 1880's farmers joined the Alliance movement, which after 1890 transformed itself into the Populist Party. The Populists had great hopes of victory in the national election of 1896 with their candidate William J. Bryan, who was also the nominee of the Democrats. It was the hardest fought election in American politics, but the Republican Party elected William McKinley as president. The Populist Party faded away, but the two major parties now gave heed to the agrarian protests and began to turn more liberal.

Workers organized too. The National Labor Union was succeeded by the Knights of Labor, which in turn was superseded by the present American Federation of Labor. These labor organizations followed moderate policies like British labor unions. A nationwide railroad strike conducted in 1877 was accompanied by much destruction of property. In the 1890's the Homestead steel strike and the Pullman railroad strike resulted in loss of life and much property destruction. The courts and government officials invariably took the side of employers in such conflicts. Some European anarchist influence resulted in bombings in labor's conflict with industry. The most violent of American labor movements was the syndicalist International Workers of the World (I.W.W.) whose members were involved in numerous incidents of violence after 1900.

The Progressive movement. After 1900 the Progressive movement absorbed the earlier reform movements and benefited from the exposures of business evils by the Muckrakers, a group of crusading journalists. The Progressive movement enjoyed a broader base and the prestige of great leaders like Robert M. La Follette and President Theodore Roosevelt. Its chief objective was political reforms by which the stranglehold of corporate business might be broken. The Progressives enacted more legislation in the states and cities than at the national level. Three presidents belonged to the Progressive Era: Roosevelt, Taft, and Wilson. Each of the three brought the enactment of measures of political and economic reform. The nearest parallel in Europe was the Social Democratic parties which now had also begun to attract middle-class liberals in Europe as the Progressives did in America.

REVIEW QUESTIONS

Multiple-choice:

1. Which American political party did *not* serve as the voice of the business interests and advocate a stronger national government? 1) Whigs 2) Democrats 3) Federalists 4) Republicans.

2. The political philosophies of which two political leaders have served most to polarize politics in the United States? 1) Washington and Jefferson 2) Jackson and Harrison 3) Lincoln and Bryan 4) Hamilton and Jefferson.

3. Which was *not* a major feature of American development from 1800 to 1914? 1) Intervention in European international politics 2) westward expansion 3) the absorption of millions of

immigrants from Europe   4) the growth of democratic institutions.

4. The expansion of the United States was at the greatest cost of territory to which country?   1) Spain   2) Mexico   3) France   4) Britain.

5. Which was the earliest and most notable departure from laissez-faire economic policy in the United States?   1) Regulation of business monopolies   2) regulation of the railroads   3) protective tariffs   4) aid to agriculture.

6. Which was the most important cause of the Civil War? 1) States' rights   2) business interests against Southern planters 3) quarrel over slavery   4) the right of secession.

7. That reform movement in America that most nearly corresponded to the Labor and Social Democratic parties of Europe was the   1) Democratic Party   2) the International Workers of the World   3) the Populists   4) the Progressives.

8. Which was a most significant outcome of the Civil War? 1) The political control of the nation by the North 2) improvement in the status of the Negro   3) the beginning of the industrial revolution   4) the rise of the Republican Party.

9. Which cause of strife in Europe caused the least contention in the United States?   1) Religion   2) differences between economic groups   3) nationalism   4) racial minorities.

FOR FURTHER READING

HARDBOUND:

Beard, Charles A., *The Rise of American Civilization* (1927). A famous economic interpretation.

Gabriel, Ralph H., *The Course of American Democratic Thought: An Intellectual History since 1815* (1940).

Hacker, Louis M., *The Triumph of American Capitalism* (1947). An economic history up to 1900 and the relation of economics to politics.

Kelly, Alfred H., and Harbison, Winifred A., *The American Constitution: Its Origins and Development* (Two vols., 1948). Shows changes in interpretation of the basic document.

Morison, Samuel E., and Commager, Henry S., *The Growth of the*

American Republic (1937). One of the best textbook surveys.

Savelle, Max, *The Foundations of American Civilization* (1942). Unusually good on American cultural developments.

PAPERBOUND:

Charles, Joseph, *Origins of the American Party System* (Torchbooks). Brief.

Cunliffe, Marcus, *The Nation Takes Shape, 1789-1837* (Chicago History of American Civilization). The early years of the United States told in a brief account for students.

De Tocqueville, Alexis, *Democracy in America* (Two vols, Vintage and other editions). A classic by a keen observer.

Dunning, W. A., *Reconstruction, Political and Economic* (Torchbooks). A standard history of the post-Civil War period.

Goldman, Eric, *Rendezvous with Destiny* (Vintage). Stimulating reading on the reform movements in the United States.

Handlin, Oscar, *The Uprooted* (Universal). Excellent account of the peoples who emigrated to America after 1800.

Hansen, Harry, *Civil War: A New One-Volume History* (Mentor). Helpful survey.

Hansen, Marcus L., *The Immigrant in American History* (Torchbooks).

Hicks, John D., *The Populist Revolt: A History of the Farmers' Alliance and the Peoples' Party* (Bison).

Hofstadter, Richard, *The American Political Tradition and the Men Who Made It* (Vintage). Discusses the American presidents and their leadership.

Klose, Nelson, *American History* (Two vols, BES). Concise survey for college students.

————, *The American Frontier* (Bison). Interpretive, concise survey.

Miller, John A., *The Federalist Era, 1789-1801* (Torchbooks).

Schlesinger, Arthur M., Jr., *The Age of Jackson* (NAL). Favorable interpretation of Jackson and readable account of the period.

Tocqueville, Alexis de, *Democracy in America* (2 vols., Vintage).

* 1848-1916   *Emperor Francis Joseph, emperor of the Dual Monarchy*
1880   *Industrialization began to proceed more rapidly in Russia*
1881   *Tsar Alexander II assassinated*
1894-1917   *Nicholas II, tsar of Russia*
1898   *Lenin organized Social Democratic Party*
* 1904-1905   *Russo-Japanese War*
* 1905   *Revolution of 1905; October Manifesto promised a Duma*
1906   *First Duma met*
1907   *Universal manhood suffrage in Austria-Hungary*
1912   *Fourth Duma met*
* 1914   *World War I began; Russian forces defeated before end of the year*
* 1917   *Russian Revolution began*

10. Russia and the Dual Monarchy

Russia and Austria-Hungary continued as the two great powers of eastern Europe. In 1870 Russia's great political and economic potential remained stunted under the dead weight of autocracy, illiteracy, and undeveloped economic resources. In Austria-Hungary the conglomeration of subject nationalities grew more and more restless under the continued frustration of their desire for freedom from their German and Hungarian rulers.

RUSSIAN AUTOCRACY

At a time when most of Europe had established at least constitutional monarchies, Russia remained under the autocratic tsars. A constitutional system was provided in 1905 but never effectively functioned as such.

Russia's progress after 1870. Russia had made some industrial progress by 1870, particularly in the textile and metallurgical industries. Industrialization accelerated after 1880. Considerable railway mileage was constructed in the 1870's and in itself accounts for the rise of a coal and iron industry. The government subsidized railway building and gave contracts to the metallurgical industry and tariff protection also. During the 1890's, the minister of finance, Court Serge Witte, by means of tariffs and the adoption of the gold standard, attracted investment capital to Russia to build industry and develop mineral deposits. A large urban working class appeared. Workers toiled under miserable conditions in these new factories as few regulations existed to safeguard employees. Workers were kept at subsistence wage levels.

Russian agriculture suffered from the preservation of the communes (*mirs*) and the ancient three-field system by which a third of the cultivated land remained idle each year. Lack of knowledge of modern agricultural technology left agriculture in a backward state. Suffering of the peasants on the overcrowded land led to frequent uprisings.

Russia by 1914 had made considerable cultural progress. Russia was on the way to providing elementary education for every child. She had flourishing universities. Great contributions had been made by famous Russians to literature, music, and science.

Labor. Workers were forbidden to organize any kind of society that would give employees any advantages in dealing with employers; even benevolent societies could not be set up by the workers. The government cooperated with employers to suppress unions, for labor organizations were regarded as dangerous to both the state and to the employers. Spies were kept in factories. The government tried in 1901 to divert workers by organizing them into patriotic societies. But workers organized and strikes were conducted in spite of all the precautions, and, after 1900, demonstrations were conducted against the political regime as well as against employers.

**Anarchists, nihilists, terrorists. Resentment against the tsarist autocracy found expression in the activities of three types of opponents: anarchists, nihilists, and terrorists. The anarchism of Proudhon influenced Bakunin of Russia to spread his ideas of revolutionary anarchism and terrorism against what he considered the tyranny of state and church. The selfish despotism of the tsar bred resentment of government. Nihilism arose among those intellectuals who were completely disgusted with the traditional authoritarian Russian institutions. Their rebellion took the form of philosophical debate, but some were willing to go to any length to vent their hatred.

The terrorists resorted to direct action, especially by the use of bombs and other explosives and by assassination to frighten the tsars and the ruling class into making reforms. The terrorists organized themselves, held secret meetings, and carefully planned their acts of violence. But the tsars were vigilant and thousands of persons were arrested and imprisoned or sent to Siberia.

**Alexander III (1881-1894) and Pobedonostsev. When Alexander II died by a terrorist bomb in 1881, his son succeeded him as Tsar Alexander III. Twenty-five years of harsh reaction followed until Alexander III and his successor succeeded in crushing the terrorist organizations. Little attempt was made to quiet the agitators by introducing reforms. The tsar supported the Orthodox Church as a defense against subversion, defended the prerogatives of the throne, and pursued a policy of Russian nationalism against the subject nationalities. By now the extension of the Russian empire had taken in more people of alien nationalities than there were of the Great Russians. Poles, Finns, and Jews suffered in the crusades of Russification. In 1897 the Finns were deprived of their constitution. Jews were persecuted by murderous drives called pogroms which were permitted and encouraged by the police. Alexander's agents in enforcing his reactionary program were Pobedonostsev, the Procurator of the Holy Synod, and Plehve, the police minister, who led the state police against revolutionaries.

*Nicholas II (1894-1917). Alexander's son, Nicholas II, continued the same policies of repression. Nicholas, weak in will-power, fell under the domination of the tsarina, who encouraged him to resist reform. Other persons also easily influenced Nicholas; the worst of these was the monk Rasputin whose evil genius dominated the tsarina. Moderate and revolutionary reformers both became more active after Nicholas took the throne.

***Political parties.** Liberals among the bourgeoisie expressed themselves very early as the zemstvos were created. 1] The more aggressive factions of the bourgeois liberals, who were called Cadets or Constitutional Democrats, advocated revolution as a means of achieving a constitutional monarchy along English parliamentary lines. 2] Right-wing liberals, called Octobrists, split off from the Cadets in 1905. Octobrists wanted constitutional government but not necessarily by revolution. 3] Another party, the Social Revolutionaries (S-R Party) not a Marxist party, represented the peasants' desires for seizure and division of lands belonging to the nobles. This radical party did not hesitate to resort to terrorism and assassination even though the tsars took some steps to improve the conditions of the peasants. 4] Marxian socialists began to organize secretly during the 1880's, and in 1898 Lenin and a few others organized the Social Democratic Party. In 1903 they held a conference in London and made plans for a socialist revolution. The Social Democratic Party soon split into two wings, one moderate and the other radical. The radicals, in the minority, were named the Bolsheviks and the moderates, in the majority, were named the Mensheviks. The Mensheviks favored more gradual reform and cooperation with middle-class groups. Lenin led the extremist Bolsheviks, who sought the cooperation of the peasants and favored revolution and control by force.

The Russo-Japanese War (1904-1905). The vast expansion of Russia in the nineteenth century carried her boundaries to the Pacific Ocean. Her desire to maintain control in Manchuria led to war with the rising empire of Japan in 1904. The same inefficiency and corruption that had caused defeat in the Crimean War again kept Russia from winning even a single victory against the Japanese. The incompetency of the government and defeat in war brought disorder and violence in various parts of Russia. Moderates drafted petitions asking for civil liberty, the creation of a national parliament, and religious toleration.

***The Revolution of 1905.** The massacre of hundreds of unarmed workers in St. Petersburg during a peaceful demonstration at the capital led by Father Gapon started the Revolution. This attack came to be called Bloody Sunday (January, 1905). It aroused the masses to begin a general strike that spread until Russia's government and economic life became paralyzed. In October, 1905, Nicholas II issued the October Manifesto that offered various democratic freedoms and promised to establish a parliament or Duma.

*The Dumas.** The first Duma met early in 1906, but much of the revolutionary fervor by then had dissipated itself in quarrels among the revolutionaries. When the Duma censured the government and demanded a responsible ministry, it was dissolved by the tsar, but revolutionary leaders could not arouse the people to reassert themselves. In 1906 Tsar Nicholas appointed Peter Stolypin as prime minister. Stolypin, a conservative, tried to improve the lot of workers and peasants but at the same time renewed the policy of arrests and hangings of revolutionists. Stolypin, like many other leading Russian officials, died at the hands of assassins. The lack of agreement and cooperation among the various revolutionary factions prevented them from consolidating their victory. The army, for the most part, remained loyal and suppressed strikes and riots.

A second Duma, which included many of Lenin's socialist followers, was dissolved in 1907 for its independent stance. A third Duma that lasted until 1912 was chosen in such a manner as to favor conservatives and exclude most representatives of workers but was allowed to act mainly as an advisory body. The fourth Duma (1912), also conservative, carried on the work of the third. Together the last two Dumas did introduce numerous reforms to improve the condition of peasants and workers and promote education and public services. But after World War I broke out, further reform was halted. Tsarist failure in the war provided the occasion for the great Russian Revolution of 1917.

THE DUAL MONARCHY

Austria-Hungary, like Russia, maintained an undemocratic system and ruled numerous restless nationalities. In spite of the loss of territories in Italy and of the control of Germany, the Dual Monarchy remained a powerful state. The Ausgleich in 1867 satisfied Hungarian nationalism at the expense of other minorities. Austrians and Hungarians themselves were minorities; the subject peoples under these Germans and Magyars were nearly all Slavs. Bitter discontent of the Slavs precipitated World War I by causing the assassination of the Austrian Archduke Ferdinand.

Austria. The respected Hapsburg Emperor Francis Joseph I succeeded to the throne in 1848 and ruled throughout this period and until 1916. The prestige of the emperor, as well as the strength of the army, did much to hold the empire together. The kindly emperor headed a state predominantly of Slavs. In the northern part of the Dual Monarchy were Czechs, Slovaks and Poles; in the south were Serbs, Croats, and Slovenes. The two-house parliament of Austria was chosen so as to keep control of the state in the hands of German upper middle classes and the landed aristocracy. The coming of universal manhood suffrage in 1907 failed to introduce truly popular government. Political parties represented nationalities rather than political principles. Though the subject nationalities disliked German rule, they also disliked each other. This situation permitted Austrian officials to play the nationalities against each other. No proposal could satisfy the conflicting minorities.

The growth of substantial industry in Austria, Silesia, and Bohemia produced a middle-class Liberal Party and opposing socialist groups as in other industrialized parts of Europe. Christian Socialists represented both the clerical and liberal influence, but Social Democrats were of Marxist origin. From 1880 to 1910 a program of social legislation, similar to such legislation in Germany and France, brought protection and security to workers. But still the Social Democrats greatly increased their number in the lower house. Economically, if not politically, the Dual Monarchy constituted a workable balance of agriculture and industry, but agriculture remained backward. Vienna served as the great financial, commercial and cultural center, a kind of "Paris" for central Europe. Nationalism of the various minorities was to destroy this economic unity.

Hungary. Hungary, the other part of the Dual Monarchy, with its own capital at Budapest, was less democratic in government than Austria. Hungary repressed minority nationalities, while Austria had tried to make satisfactory concessions. Hungary never permitted general manhood suffrage but limited the vote to a small minority. Her Parliament was almost entirely Magyar. Hungary remained agricultural, a nation of peasants and nobles. The followers of Kossuth continued to demand complete independence from Austria.

REVIEW QUESTIONS

Multiple-choice:

1. Russian progress in industrialization became pronounced 1) at the time of the American Civil War 2) not until after World War I 3) soon after 1900 4) between 1880 and 1900.

2. In which area had Russia made the *least* progress up to 1905? 1) In the sciences and arts 2) the suppression of revolutionary activity 3) development of democratic institutions 4) industry.

3. Which group was made up especially of intellectuals who rejected Russian institutions? 1) Anarchists 2) nihilists 3) Cadets 4) terrorists.

4. Which was the first event of the following in 1905? 1) Russia's defeat in the Russo-Japanese War 2) a massacre of peaceful demonstrators 3) a general strike 4) the October Manifesto.

5. The Russian Dumas failed to achieve adequate reforms chiefly because of 1) failure of the members to agree 2) dissolution and interference by the tsar 3) failure to raise adequate revenues.

6. A majority of the subject peoples of Austria-Hungary belonged to which of the following groups? 1) Italians 2) Finns 3) Slavs 4) Rumanians.

7. Which statement about Austria-Hungary is *not* true? 1) Hungary's government was less democratic than Austria's 2) some political parties represented national minorities instead of social classes 3) the Industrial Revolution had made no progress in the Dual Monarchy 4) the Dual Monarchy constituted a balance between agriculture and industry.

Matching:

8. Count Witte	a. Police minister who fought revolutionaries
9. Bakunin	
10. Pobedonostsev	b. Exerted evil influence over the tsarina
11. Plehve	c. Killed by terrorist bomb in 1881
12. Alexander II	d. Finance minister who attracted capital
13. Rasputin	e. Anarchist and terrorist

14. Lenin   f. Procurator of the Holy Synod
15. Stolypin   g. Organized the Social Democratic Party
     h. Prime minister in Russia after 1906
     i. Tsar during the Revolution of 1905

Matching:

16. Cadets
17. S-R Party
18. Social Democrats
19. Octobrists
20. Bolsheviks
21. Mensheviks

a. Party of the peasants who wanted land of the nobles
b. Moderate majority wing of Social Democrats
c. Wanted to achieve constitutional monarchy by revolution
d. Original Marxist party of Lenin
e. Right-wing liberals who disavowed necessity of revolution
f. Moderate party of the nobles and bourgeoisie
g. Radical minority of the Social Democrats

FOR FURTHER READING

HARDBOUND:

Aleksinsky, G., *Modern Russia* (1915).

Drage, Geoffrey, *Austria-Hungary* (1909).

Gayda, V., *Modern Austria* (1915).

Knatchbull-Hugesson, C. M., *Political Evolution of the Hungarian Nation* (1908).

Kornilov, A., *Modern Russian History* (1924).

Mazour, Anatole, *The First Russian Revolution: The December Movement, Its Origin, Development and Significance* (1937). A detailed study.

Pares, Bernard, *History of Russia* (1937).

Redlich, Joseph, *Emperor Francis Joseph of Austria* (1929).

Steed, Huey W., *The Hapsburg Monarchy* (1919). By a British journalist.

Taylor, A. J. P., *The Hapsburg Monarchy, 1809-1918* (Rev., 1948).

Vernadsky, G., *A History of Russia* (4th ed., 1954). A standard history.

PAPERBOUND:

Gourfinkel, Nina, *Lenin* (Evergreen).

Jaszi, Oscar, *The Dissolution of the Hapsburg Monarchy* (Phoenix).

Kohn, Hans, ed., *Mind of Modern Russia: Historical and Political Thought of Russia's Great Age* (Torchbooks).

Meyer, Alfred G., *Leninism* (Praeger).

Seton-Watson, Hugh, *The Decline of Imperial Russia, 1855-1914* (Praeger).

1863-1906	*King Christian IX ruled in Denmark*
1864	*Denmark lost Schleswig-Holstein*
*1869	*Suez Canal constructed*
1877	*Russo-Turkish War ended by the Treaty of San Stefano*
*1878	**Congress of Berlin dealt with the "Eastern Question"*
1905	*Norway successfully asserted independence of Sweden*
1907	*Norway gave vote to women*
1908	*"Young Turks," nationalists, gained control of Turkey*
1910-1920	*Decade of democratic growth in Scandinavia*
1914	*Albania won independence*

11. Southeastern Europe and the Smaller States

Sharply contrasting political and economic conditions prevailed in the remaining states of Europe. The Balkans suffered from poverty and backwardness dating far back to their conquest by the Turks. Holland, Belgium, Switzerland, and the Scandinavian states generally shared the economic and political progress of their larger neighbors.

TURKEY AND THE BALKAN STATES

The story of Turkey, the Ottoman Empire, is one of continued decline and dissolution. The Balkan states gained their independence and added Turkish territory as Turkey, the "sick man of Europe," failed to solve the internal weaknesses of the empire. The mountainous geography of the Balkan region predetermined its division into several separate states. After becoming independent, these turbulent nations turned against each other in quarrels over territory.

Turkey. The Ottoman Empire became so weak that statesmen of Europe from time to time discussed the partitioning of her lands. Turkey, like the Dual Monarchy, still controlled numerous subject nationalities but under a particularly cruel despotism headed by the sultan. Turkey's history is mainly an account of the loss of these subject peoples in Europe, Asia, and Africa from 1699 to 1918. Turkey was able to some extent to turn the Balkan nationalities against each other. The strong nationalism of the Balkans helped prevent any single major power from controlling this part of Europe. Also, the rivalry of the great powers, Britain, Russia, and France, would not permit any one of themselves to dominate the Balkans. Thus, Turkey was able to survive.

*Great power interests in the Near East. Since the time of Peter the Great, Russia's need for warm water seaports accounted for her drive, toward the Black Sea, into the Balkans, and toward the Mediterranean Sea. Great Britain's rivalry with Russia after 1820 helped keep Russia bottled up in the Black Sea. Great Britain's policy of controlling important sea routes gave her a special interest in the passage to India created by the opening of the Suez Canal in 1869. France had long since developed special relations with Turkey and was now trading in the Levant. In 1888 Germany entered the Balkan complex by gaining a concession to build the Berlin-to-Bagdad railway. The Holy Lands, under Turkey's rule, gave several nations an interest in Turkey.

**The Congress of Berlin (1878). The great powers gave their attention to the Balkans once again in 1866 when the Bulgars asserted their political independence from Turkey. Horrified at the massacres perpetrated there, Russia on behalf of the Christian Bulgarians, declared war on Turkey in 1877. Britain and Austria mobilized to save Turkey from Russian conquest, but in 1878 Russia quickly concluded the Treaty of San Stefano. This treaty recognized the independence of Bulgaria and reaffirmed the independence of Serbia, Rumania, and Montenegro. Great Britain and Austria were dissatisfied with Russian influence in Bulgaria, and, therefore, forced Russia in 1898 to revise the San Stefano agreements at the Congress of Berlin. Here Russia was checked but Austria now gained increased influence there. Under the Treaty of Berlin 1] Austria-Hungary won the right to occupy Bosnia-Herzego-

vina;   2] Russia received southern Bessarabia from Rumania and certain districts of Armenia. 3] Rumania received Dobruja; 4] Britain took Cyprus as a reward for her aid to Turkey; 5] Bulgaria was reduced in size;   6] Greece was awarded additional territory. 7] The independence of Montenegro, Serbia, and Rumania was again endorsed, and each won bits of territory.

*The Young Turks.   The name "Young Turks" is given to the nationalist movement to modernize and westernize the decadent Turkish empire. It was more of a nationalist than a liberal movement. In 1908 these patriotic and reforming Turks, with the aid of the army, seized control and restored the constitution of 1876 which had been discarded by Sultan Abdul Hamid II soon after its promulgation. The Young Turks established a constitutional monarchy, reformed the educational system and the army, and generally set about modernizing Turkey. These Turkish nationalists aroused the subject people to resistance and brought on the Balkan wars in 1912 and in 1913.

*The Balkans.   We have seen that Greece won recognition of her independence in 1829, and the independence of Montenegro, Rumania, Serbia, and Bulgaria was confirmed at Berlin in 1878. The great powers won independence for Albania in 1914. The independence of the five Balkan states created an extremely dangerous situation; each was extremely nationalistic and eager to add territory of its neighbors; and the great powers could not ignore any change that would open the Balkans to control by a rival. Nobles and peasants represented social classes of these backward agricultural states. All the states suffered from backwardness due to centuries of Turkish oppression.

THE SCANDINAVIAN AND OTHER
SMALLER STATES

The Scandinavian states of Denmark, Sweden, and Norway had given up their pretensions to great power status since about 1715. They progressed in cultural and economic development along with the larger countries.

Scandinavia. The Scandinavian countries devoted themselves mainly to agriculture and shipping. Agricultural cooperatives helped to establish a kind of economic democracy. These countries managed to avoid civil and foreign war after 1815, except for the Prussian-Austrian attack on Denmark in 1864.

Denmark was stripped of most of her possessions by the loss of Norway in 1815 and the loss of Schleswig and Holstein to Prussia in 1864. In Denmark King Christian IX (1863-1906) resisted the coming of real parliamentary government by his opposition to the lower house. Danish political struggles resembled those of Prussia. Not until 1915 was universal manhood suffrage won and real constitutional reforms made. Women were given the vote at the same time and also gained the suffrage in Sweden. Sweden had been reduced to a third-rate power by 1715. Sweden allowed Norway to become independent in 1905. The Bernadotte family continued to occupy the throne in Sweden. Norway had previously had a democratic government, as compared with the autocratic and feudal system of Sweden, and always resisted Swedish control. After 1870 Sweden developed considerable industry. After gaining independence, Norway made greater progress toward democracy by giving the vote to women (1907) and by establishing compulsory education and social insurance.

*The low countries and Switzerland. The two low countries, the Netherlands and Belgium, are partly protected by Great

Britain's desire to see them remain free of control by any large continental power. The Dutch benefited from their colonial empire in Asia, her commerce, and her own economic progress; Belgium acquired the Congo in 1908. Belgium's independence, won in 1830, was guaranteed by the major powers in 1839. She became a constitutional monarchy. Belgium, partly because of her endowment of minerals, became a thickly populated and highly industrialized nation. The political and social progress of Belgium and Holland kept pace with that of the most advanced nations of Europe.

Switzerland is the prime example of the small federal state. In the nineteenth century the Swiss advanced in political democracy ahead of the rest of Europe. Three main language groups comprise the Swiss nation. Germans are the most numerous, the French are second, and the Italians, third. Farming and manufacturing were the bases of the Swiss economy.

REVIEW QUESTIONS

Multiple-choice:

1. The Ottoman Empire survived mainly because 1) of the revival of its military power 2) the Balkan subject nationalities were turned against each other 3) the great powers would not permit any one of themselves to dominate the Balkans.

2. Which nation had long maintained a more friendly relationship with Turkey than the others? 1) Russia 2) Great Britain 3) Austria-Hungary 4) Finns 5) France.

3. Russia's main cause of friction with Turkey arose from 1) the tsars' desire for an outlet to the Mediterranean 2) differences of religion 3) Pan-slavism of Russia 4) differences in form of government.

4. The Congress of Berlin was held to reduce the gains made by which of these powers? 1) Russia 2) Turkey 3) Austria-Hungary 4) Bulgaria.

5. Which was *not* an outcome of the Treaty of Berlin?

1) Bulgaria received additional territory   2) Britain took Cyprus   3) Greece added more territory   4) the independence of Montenegro, Serbia, and Rumania was reaffirmed.

6. The "Young Turks" revolution won the greatest victory for which?   1) Democracy   2) Christians   3) freedom of the Balkans   4) nationalism (Turkish).

7. The independence of which represented a peaceful victory for nationalism?   1) Sweden   2) Norway   3) Denmark   4) Finland.

8. An important factor in the continued independence of Belgium and the Netherlands has been   1) military alliances between them   2) the possession of overseas colonies   3) Britain's long-standing policy of opposing their domination by any strong continental power   4) the economic poverty of each nation.

9. Which is the smallest language group in Switzerland?   1) Italian   2) French   3) German.

FOR FURTHER READING

HARDBOUND:

Bain, Robert, *Scandinavia: A Political History of Denmark, Norway and Sweden from 1513 to 1900* (1905).

Barnouw, Adrian, *The Dutch: A Portrait Study of the People of Holland* (1940).

Croce, Benedetto, *A History of Italy, 1871-1915* (1929). By the liberal philosopher.

Eversley, G. J. S. L., *The Turkish Empire: Its Growth and Decay* (1917).

Forbes, N., *et al.*, *The Balkans* (1915). Each nation is taken up by a specialist.

Goris, Johannes, ed., *Belgium* (1945).

Gewehr, W. M., *The Rise of Nationalism in the Balkans, 1800-1930* (1931). Brief study.

Marriott, John A. R., *The Eastern Question: An Historical Study in European Diplomacy* (1940).

Martin, William, *History of Switzerland* (1931).

Miller, William, *The Ottoman Empire and Its Successors* (1923).

Rappard, William, *The Government of Switzerland* (1936).
Schevill, Ferdinand, *The History of the Balkan Peninsula from the Earliest Times to the Present Day* (1933). A standard history.
Tyler, Mason, *The European Powers and the Near East* (1925).
Young, George, *Portugal Old and Young* (1917).

1783	*End of the Old Imperialism*
*1839-1842	*First Opium War*
1850-1864	*Taiping Rebellion in China*
*1854	*Perry opened ports in Japan*
1856	*Second British war against China*
1857	*Sepoy Mutiny in India*
1867	*Dominion of Canada became a self-governing confederated state*
1868	*Japan began Westernization*
*1870	*Beginning of the New Imperialism*
1876	*International African Association organized by Leopold II of Belgium*
*1884	*Germany and Britain began annexing colonies in Africa*
	International Conference on Africa held in Berlin
1889	*First Pan-American Conference met*
1895-1896	*Sino-Japanese War*
	Jameson Raid in the Transvaal
1896	*Italy suffered defeat at Adowa, Abyssinia*
*1898	*Spanish-American War began*
	Fashoda Incident
*1899	*Open-Door policy*
1899-1902	*Boer War*
*1900-1901	*Boxer Rebellion*
1900	*Commonwealth of Australia gained self-government*
*1902	*Japanese-British alliance formed*
*1904-1905	*Russo-Japanese War*
1907	*Union of South Africa organized*
*1912	*Republic of China established by Sun Yat-sen*

12. The New Imperialism

Beginning about 1870 the world's leading nations showed a renewed interest in annexing colonies in undeveloped or backward areas of the world. This expansionism is called the "new imperialism."

NATURE OF THE NEW IMPERIALISM

A distinction needs to be made between the "old imperialism" and the "new imperialism." This distinction and a study of the motives and forms of empire building will help reveal the nature of the new imperialism itself.

**The old imperialism and the new. The word *imperialism* has taken on different meanings. Basically, it is the domination in some form by one country of people of a different nationality. Its motives help to reveal its nature. The economic motive is the strongest but national defense and prestige are other motives. More technologically advanced and vigorous people have always read in the weakness of other people an invitation to rule them.

The earlier interest in acquiring overseas colonies ended in the years after 1783. Great Britain, in the best position to annex colonies, showed little interest in expanding her empire after she lost the American Thirteen Colonies. The French had lost most of their colonies in 1763. Spain and Portugal lost most of their American colonies as a consequence of the Napoleonic Wars. Other potential colonizing powers were busy with domestic problems or concerned about relations with their immediate neighbors.

144

The European humanitarians caused Parliament to abolish slavery in the British colonies. Colonies became less profitable when slave labor ceased; consequently, there were fewer interests to argue the benefits of colonial expansion after the abolition of slavery. Colonies were viewed as a burden to taxpayers by "Little Englanders" and others. The beginnings of freer world trade obviated the need to control colonies in order to monopolize their trade. The new imperialism is usually dated from about 1870, a date that calls attention to the new industrialism as a cause of renewed interest in the control of other parts of the world. Sometimes the change is dated from 1871 because the consolidation of Germany created an aggressive state whose later interest in overseas lands may have excited others to re-enter the competition for colonies. However, Germany under Bismarck avoided the acquisition of colonies until 1884. Germany did not begin an aggressive colonial policy until after 1890 when Bismarck resigned.

***The motives of the new imperialism.** Some motives in the old imperialism perhaps played a less important role in the new imperialism. Basically, the motives were very similar but expressed themselves in different forms. 1] Colonization of surplus population, a strong motive of earlier imperialism, was not so prominent in the new. There were arguments for encouraging emigration but not for the founding of trading colonies, such as those of the seventeenth century. Life in the industrialized countries became so attractive that people lost interest in emigrating to colonies that were distant, undeveloped, or in tropical climates. Migrants moved instead to developed lands and to temperate climates, as in the United States and South America. 2] There were several powerful economic motives. Perhaps the search for markets was the strongest of these. Control of overseas areas assured a market for the manufactured goods of the industrialized nations. The great expansion of world trade became possible with the extension of railroads, steamship lines, and communication facilities. These same technological developments made it possible to administer and exploit far away lands. 3] Raw materials from overseas lands were needed to keep the factories humming in Europe and to furnish foodstuffs for large urban industrial populations. Fibers, minerals, and foodstuffs had to be imported. 4] An outlet for the profitable investment of surplus capital motivated control of undeveloped lands. Various forms of control served as a means of keeping out competitors, protecting investments, and insuring returns. Mines, land, railways, utilities, loans to foreign governments were the prime outlets of investment capital. Foreign investments offered higher returns on capital than under more competitive conditions in satiated home markets. 5] National pride in territorial expansion became a powerful factor. The British took great pride in saying that the sun never set on their empire. 6] Kipling glorified the "white man's burden" of governing and enlightening benighted peoples. Racial pride in Germany and England was cultivated by certain propagandists who held that the superiority of the Anglo-Saxons and Nordics entitled them to guide other races less fortunately endowed with vigor and intelligence. The "white man's burden" calls attention to the motives of humanitarian and missionary activities. These motives, like national pride, appealed to the masses who had become enfranchised in the western world. 7] The military motive accounts for the acquisition of strategic areas. British acquisition of strategic points on world trade routes, such as her "life line" to Asia, operated as a motive in the nineteenth century when colonies were not acquired for other reasons. Colonies were taken to create buffer states to protect lands already held. In relation to the motives above it should be noted that there were popular motives for imperialism, possibly as important as the selfish motives of industrialism or finance capitalism.

Dependent relationships to imperial nations. Imperialism imposed itself upon alien lands through the form of various dependent relationships. The most familiar form was the *colony*, a term that covers many kinds of subordinate states. The term *colony* suggests possession and various degrees of subjection to control of the imperial power. *Concessions*, special business privileges to develop mines and invest capital, were secured in highly populated countries having weak or corrupt governments. *"Spheres of influence"* were used by rivals to divide weak countries, such as China, into regions monopolized by the business interests of imperialist nations. Under *protectorates* and *dependencies*, weak and small countries were forced to accept the control or "advice" of the great power, particularly in military and diplomatic matters. *Leaseholds* granted economic and other rights for a fixed term of years. These forms of imperialism may also be thought of as stages in the extension or relaxation of imperial control. In more recent years the term *satellite* has been used to designate economic and military dependence of weaker countries not necessarily thought of as of subordinate status. The economic dependence of poorer countries and the assertion of economic power over them is often described as *economic imperialism*.

****The benefits and evils of imperialism.*** Imperialism needs to be evaluated from the viewpoints of both subject and ruling peoples. The defenders of imperialism point out that it introduced the many benefits of Europe's advanced civilization. Internal law and order and protection against external aggression in the forms of piracy, slave raiding, and cannibalism were provided. Democracy, humanitarianism, sanitation, medicine, education, religion, technology, and material improvements of all sorts, such as transportation and better food and clothing, were introduced. The imperial powers benefited, or thought they did, by accomplishing the various goals that brought about their intervention. Without the benefits introduced to them the primitive and backward areas would never have been able to throw out their masters.

On the debit side, the subject peoples were often so cruelly exploited that they were often worse off than before the coming of the white man. Some of the fine qualities of other cultures were lost in the adoption of Western culture with its vices and aggressiveness. The missionary motives were not entirely separated from the desire to open new markets by developing among foreign people a taste for Western goods. The white man brought epidemics of his diseases that killed people who had no hereditary immunity to such maladies as measles and smallpox. Economic exploitation or forced labor superseded slavery. Lack of respect for the cultures of subject or "backward" people brought a violent reaction against Europeans. The imperial powers became embroiled in costly wars with natives and with each other and had to maintain costly military establishments. In most countries, the colonies benefited only a few groups, such as traders and militarists, while they imposed an extra burden of taxation on the nation. Investment overseas drained the imperialist countries of capital. Many of the benefits of trade might have been enjoyed without the possession of colonies.

IMPERIALISM IN ASIA AND THE PACIFIC

The great land mass of Asia and its outlying islands experienced earlier and more extensive imperialistic activity than Africa, the other main field of operation for the new imperialists.

***British India.** The year 1857 witnessed important change in the government of British India. The Sepoy Mutiny disclosed abuses of power by the East India Company and caused Britain to deprive the Company of its powers of government.

India now became a crown dominion and the government of India was reorganized. Indian members were permitted to sit in certain legislative councils. Trained Britishers were put in civil service positions. Railroads were built and efforts made to combat famine. Britain's own high regard for democratic institutions transmitted itself to the Indians. In 1885 the Indian National Congress, the political party of Indian nationalism, was organized and the move for independence quickly spread. The British extended many humanitarian reforms there but prepared too many Indians for white collar government jobs. When thousands went unemployed they became engaged in revolutionary activities and some resorted to assassinations. Another reorganization of government was permitted by the British after 1907. Indians were given majority representation in provincial legislatures but not in the central legislature. Radical nationalists were demanding full independence by 1914.

China and the West.   China, content with her own ancient civilization, for centuries remained aloof toward foreigners and expected them to approach China as inferiors rather than as equals. The trade of foreign merchants for a long time had been confined to the single city of Canton. It was the British who were responsible for the opening of new ports in China outside the city of Canton, and it came about because of the so-called "Opium War." To meet the problem of paying for imports of tea, silks, and china, the British shipped furs and other Western products, but also, in cooperation with Chinese merchants, shipped opium into China. Other westerners also took up the opium trade. In a clash resulting from Chinese attempts to stop this trade, there occurred the First Opium War lasting from 1839 to 1842. The war, ended by the Treaty of Nanking, forced China to open four additional ports to Great Britain and provided for the cession of Hong Kong. China soon opened these same ports peacefully to other nations. As a result of a second British war against China, beginning in 1856, other ports were opened to foreign traders, and China agreed to limit tariff rates on British goods. Among privileges granted by the Chinese was the right of extraterritoriality by which China permitted foreigners accused of crime to be tried by their own courts and not by Chinese courts—a humiliating relinquishment of Chinese sovereignty.

Foreign privileges in China. The loss of prestige by the weakening Manchu rulers of China brought on a long Chinese civil war called the Taiping Rebellion (1850-1864). The rebellion was put down with the aid of foreign military adventurers who gained further privileges in China. China now began to lose territory and had to give up cities and provinces to foreign control, a process that threatened eventually to lead to the dismemberment of the Celestial Empire. By 1860 Russia had absorbed the region north of the Amur River and Britain had gained Hong Kong. France took Indo-China and Britain advanced from India to take over Burma. Portugal took Macao. In the Sino-Japanese War of 1895-1896 Japan forced China to give independence to Korea—preparatory to absorbing it herself. Japan also took a large indemnity and the island of Formosa. The Liaotung Peninsula was taken but Japan was soon forced to give it up. Britain, France, Germany, and Russia now followed Japan and forced China to grant leaseholds in various areas. Russia demanded Manchuria and Mongolia and Germany the Shantung area.

***The Open-Door Policy.** The danger that China would soon be taken over by various imperialists to the exclusion of the large trade of the United States and of other American business interests aroused Secretary of State John Hay to initiate what became known as the Open Door Policy. Stated in its simplest terms the policy sought to preserve respect for the laws of China and to assure equality of business opportunity to all countries in all parts of China, but its provisions were stated in more specific terms. The United States secured the grudging assent of other powers to this policy, but the full intent of the "open door" was never actually realized.

China herself soon reacted against foreign aggression. The strong-minded Dowager Empress Tzu Hsi encouraged the Boxers, a patriotic nationalist society, to attempt to expel all foreigners from China. Many European official representatives were killed in the Boxer Rebellion of 1900. An international army fought its way to Peking and restored order in 1901. China was forced to pay a huge indemnity. Soon afterward, other nationalists who wished to modernize China led a rebellion against and overthrew the Manchu rulers. In 1912 the successful revolution established the Republic of China with a constitution, and Sun Yat-sen became its president. But China's immense problems were not solved. The central government was unable to bring all of the provinces under its control. Civil war and disunity prevailed, and China made little economic and social progress. The interference of foreign powers, as well as China's own backwardness and inertia, kept her from dealing with her problems successfully.

***Japan, Korea, and the West.** For centuries Japan permitted foreign trade to be conducted only by the Dutch at the harbor of Nagasaki. When Christianity began to spread rapidly in Japan, the *shogun* (ruler), backed up by feudal lords and their warriors, tried to stamp out what was regarded as subversion and took other measures to insulate Japan against foreign influences.

Soon after Great Britain had taken the lead in opening China to the world, the United States similarly opened Japan. In 1853 Commodore Matthew Perry, at the head of a large naval force, sailed to Japan to win trading privileges there. By a display of modern naval weapons, dignity, and tact he impressed the Japanese leaders with the seriousness of his mission. After giving the rulers ample time to consider the American demands, Perry and the Japanese signed the Treaty of Kanagawa by which two ports were opened and hospitable treatment promised for shipwrecked sailors. A revolution in Japan in 1868 introduced a deliberate policy of Westernization, including the creation of a modern military establishment and the machinery of government modelled along Western lines. The business institutions, industrial technology, and the other paraphernalia of Western progress were absorbed.

Some time after the opening of Japan, Korea was opened in a similar fashion and Western religion and civilization, as well as Western goods, were introduced.

***The Russo-Japanese War (1904-1905).** Japan's adoption of modern military techniques, its victory over China in 1895, and Japanese effectiveness in the Boxer intervention won Western admiration. In 1902 Great Britain and Japan formed a defensive alliance. Japan soon turned the alliance to her advantage in her rivalry with Russia. Russian determination to take over Manchuria and Korea, both of which Japan also coveted, led to a Japanese attack and war against Russia in 1904. Japan soon won a series of victories over Russia. President Theodore Roosevelt intervened in 1905 and helped both belligerents agree to the Treaty of Portsmouth. Japan secured the southern half of Sakhalin and took over the Russian leaseholds in Liaotung, Port Arthur, and in Manchuria. Japan's suzerainty over Korea was recognized; she soon absorbed Korea completely. Japan's defeat of Russia, a Western power, assumed great significance. It brought further recognition of Japan's military power and enhanced Japanese pride; it stiffened the resistance of Asians to foreign domination. In a determination to dominate China, Japan challenged America's Open Door policy from time to time in a hostility that eventually brought war between the United States and Japan in 1941.

Southeast Asia. In addition to Burma, which was annexed by Great Britain between 1823 and 1885, and Tibet, which became a British protectorate, Britain extended her control of Malayan ports into the interior. The acquisition of Singapore gave Britain a port of great strategic importance. France took Indo-China. Thailand (Siam) retained her independence as a buffer state by her shrewdness in turning her would-be captors against each other but lost Laos and Cambodia to France and certain Malayan territories to the British. In 1802 the British took Ceylon from the Dutch.

As for the extensive Dutch holdings in the East Indies, the Dutch East India Company in 1798 was abolished and its possessions taken over by the Dutch crown. In the 1830's the Dutch introduced the "culture system" by which a fifth of the land was set aside to grow crops for the Dutch; the natives were required to spend a fifth of their time working government crops. This system was abandoned after having been exposed by Dutch humanitarians. The Netherlands did not prepare her colonial subjects for self-government.

**The United States in Asia and the Pacific. In taking the Philippines from Spain in 1898 the United States participated in the new imperialism along with European powers. The Spanish had managed to hold the Philippines after their discovery by Magellan in 1521. The land was Christianized but the Filipinos resented Spanish political control. The Filipinos were in revolt when the United States declared war on Spain in 1898. In the Spanish-American War the United States sank the Spanish fleets in the Philippines and in Cuba, won Spanish colonial possessions in Asia and in the Caribbean, and gave Cuba her freedom. In taking the Philippines and Guam the United States became a leading imperialist nation in the Pacific and gained in world prestige as a military power. American rule brought more benefits to the Philippines than to the

United States, but the Filipinos still longed for national independence as they had earlier from Spain. American industry had expanded after the Civil War and by 1890 the United States was impelled to act under the same motives of imperialism that affected the governments of Europe.

Russia in Asia.   Russia, as an imperialist power, did not establish overseas colonies but annexed adjoining lands. Russia had no secure ports to the oceans of the world and had not become a strong naval power. Russia's expansion began from its center, the Grand Duchy of Moscow, and she continued to expand during the middle ages and in the centuries following. Russia grew by occupying vacant lands, conquering neighboring civilized lands, and by absorbing lands held by primitive tribes in Asia. Her expansion toward the Baltic, the Black Sea, and to Port Arthur in Manchuria was carried out in quest of outlets leading to the oceans. Her expansion took over vast areas of Siberia and moved into the region east of the Caspian Sea and into parts of northern China. In 1741 her expansion carried her across the Bering Sea to Alaska whence she enlarged her colony southward. In 1867 Russia sold Alaska to the United States. Russia completed a 4000-mile Trans-Siberian railroad in 1903 to the port of Vladivostok. On her southern borders, Russia expanded into the Caucasus at the expense of Turkey and Persia and took the Turkestan from its native tribes.

**Russian-British rivalry in Asia.*   During the nineteenth century Russian and British colonial expansion brought them into conflict at many points and created an ever-present danger of war. In taking the Turkestan, Russia stood on the borders of Afghanistan as did Great Britain in the possession of India. Both became rivals for control of the Afghans as well as of the Tibetans. The Russian push into the Middle East had as an object the acquisition of a warm water port on the Persian Gulf. Russia developed various ties with the weak Persian shahs. The British, who feared the Russian approach to their lifeline to India, established economic and financial interests in Persia also. In 1907 Britain and Russia reached an agreement because of the greater danger each felt from the growing power of Germany. They agreed to British hegemony in an independent Afghanistan. Persia was divided into a Russian sphere of interest in the north, a British zone in the south, and a neutral zone in the center. But a touchy situation remained there. Previously we have noted Anglo-Russian rivalry over Turkish lands in Asia and Europe.

THE PARTITION OF AFRICA

The vast continent of Africa remained unexplored and, except at various fringes, of little importance to Europe. The Portuguese in the fifteenth century had developed trading interests on the west coast. By 1870 they held the colonies of Portuguese East and West Africa and Guinea. From Cape Colony in the South, the Boers had moved northward and established the republics of Orange Free State and Transvaal. Great Britain held the Cape Colony and Natal. France held Algeria.

**Livingstone and Stanley. The work of the sincere humanitarian and medical missionary David Livingstone led to the opening of Africa. Livingstone began working in Africa in 1841 and in time devoted himself entirely to exploration there. Henry Morton Stanley, a British journalist and explorer, located Livingstone in the jungle in 1871 and published newspaper articles that called the world's attention to Africa. Livingstone conducted explorations over much of the continent, and, later, Stanley made other explorations. These explorers revealed much about Africa's resources. When Belgium, France, Great Britain, and Portugal began to lay claim to the Congo region, other powers protested. An international conference was held in Berlin in 1884. A large part of central and western Africa was parcelled out among the powers. A pattern was established for future claims to protectorates. It was agreed that the powers would notify each other when establishing a claim and would cooperate to abolish the slave trade and to introduce civilization to Africa.

Belgium in Africa. Leopold II of Belgium took an interest in Africa in 1876 and organized the International African Association of scientists and explorers. One achievement of Leopold's organization was the suppression of the Arab slave hunting that had shocked both Livingston and Stanley. Leopold appointed Stanley to make treaties with African chiefs to secure territories. These ceded territories became the Congo Free State under the personal rule of Leopold II, who proceeded to exploit the colony and cruelly work the natives in order to build his private fortune. Reaction to Leopold's outrages against humanity forced him to hand the Free State over to the Belgian government in 1908.

Egypt. In 1875 the financial difficulties of the spendthrift Egyptian ruler (the khedive) forced him to sell his shares in the Suez Canal. Because of the strategic value of the canal, Disraeli purchased the shares for the British government. In 1876 Great Britain and France assumed joint control over Egypt's bankrupt finances. A revolt in 1882 led to the appointment in 1883 of a British administrator who ruled the country until 1907. His rule brought Egypt one of the most enlightened colonial administrations on record, but Egypt increasingly demanded self-government.

Germany in Africa. After negotiations with natives, German Southwest Africa was founded as a protectorate in 1884. The German Togoland and the Cameroons also had their beginnings in 1884, when a German protectorate was declared there. Germany's most important acquisition was made on the east coast—German East Africa. Carl Peters, a student of British colonization methods, negotiated treaties with local chiefs. Bismarck in 1885 proclaimed German East Africa as a German colony.

Britain in Africa. In 1885 the British organized the British East Africa Company north of the German claim. Conflicting claims of Germany and Great Britain were settled amicably in 1886 and in 1890. By way of compensation Germany acquired the strategic island of Helgoland in the North Sea and recognition of her protectorate over East Africa (Tanganyika). The British took Uganda, British East Africa (Kenya), Zanzibar, and Nyasaland. In 1884 Britain acquired the strategic protectorate of Somaliland on the Gulf of Aden and conquered the Anglo-Egyptian Sudan in 1898. In 1900 Nigeria became a British colony as well as Gambia, Sierra Leone, and the Gold Coast. By 1890 Cecil Rhodes, the British empire builder in Africa, had founded Rhodesia. Only German East Africa prevented Great Britain from building a Cape-to-Cairo railroad through the Dark Continent.

The Boer War (1899-1902). From Capetown, Dutch colonists had moved northward, since 1815. Friction developed early between the British and the earlier Dutch Boer settlers. Further trouble arose when gold and diamonds were discovered in 1886 in the Transvaal, a republic set up by the Boers north of the British Cape Colony. The ensuing conflict of British and Boers led to a raid engineered by Cecil Rhodes, who sent a Dr. Jameson into the Transvaal at the head of a small armed force. When Paul Kruger, the Boer leader, captured Dr. Jameson's force in 1895, Emperor William II sent a telegram of congratulations. The Boer War broke out in 1899.

By 1902 the Boers were finally defeated and British rule was extended over their republics. In 1909 the provinces of Cape Colony, Natal, Orange Free State, and Transvaal were united in the Union of South Africa; the local parliament was generally dominated by the Boers who were given political rights under the British crown.

**The French in Africa. In 1881 Tunis and Algeria became French protectorates, in spite of Turkish protests. From Algeria the French pushed southward. From the colony of Senegal they pushed to the east, hoping to extend French holdings entirely across Africa to the sea. Other French possessions, taken in earlier times, included Dahomey, the Ivory Coast, French Guinea, and the French Congo. The whole region of the Sahara Desert became French West Africa.

The Fashoda incident (1898) occurred as the French challenged British plans to link their colonies in Africa from north to south. A great danger of military engagement between French and British forces, whose paths crossed at the town of Fashoda in the Sudan, subsided when the French forces backed away. France was not prepared militarily and felt a need to support Britain against Germany. Between 1899 and 1904 the British and French settled their differences in Africa by negotiation. The French were permitted to establish a protectorate in Morocco by way of compensation. France also had acquired the French Somaliland and the island of Madagascar by 1914.

The Italians in Africa. In 1885 Italy established a colony in Eritrea on the Red Sea and in a few years took another in Somaliland. Subsequently, the Italians tried to conquer the independent kingdom of Abyssinia (Ethiopia) but in 1896 suffered a catastrophic defeat at Adowa. Abyssinia retained her independence. Italy's colonies in Africa in 1914 also included Libya which was taken in 1911 from Turkey.

CANADA, AUSTRALIA, AND NEW ZEALAND

Outside the main areas of colonial exploitation already treated in the foregoing discussions there are the British possessions of Canada, Australia, and New Zealand.

**Canada. A rebellion in Canada in 1837 was easily suppressed, but the British government made an investigation of the unrest. Lord Durham's famous report of 1839 caused Britain to grant local self-government to each province, in 1840. In 1867, under the British North American Act, Canada became a confederated state known as the Dominion of Canada. Self-government was achieved through a Canadian parliament; a governor-general served to provide the main tie with the British crown. A source of unrest in Canada since its acquisition by Great Britain has been the conflict of interests between Catholic Quebec and the English population. The act of 1867 allowed enough local self-government in the provinces to ease this problem considerably by allowing cultural and religious freedom to the French dissidents of Quebec.

Australia. Captain Cook visited Australia in 1770. In 1788, after North America was no longer available as a dumping ground for convicts, Australia had its beginnings with the founding of penal colonies there. Free settlers coming in soon objected to the practice and Australia ceased to serve in its initial role. After 1800 five separate colonies were formed as well as the settlement on the island of Tasmania. Gold and sheep-raising provided stimulus to Australian growth after 1850 and immigration increased. In 1900 the Commonwealth of Australia was formed and self-government similar to Canada's was gained.

New Zealand. The islands of New Zealand, twelve hundred miles to the east of Australia, were colonized and settled during the nineteenth century. New Zealand achieved dominion status in 1907. The Maori, a native race of considerable ability, delayed the colony's early growth. New Zealand before 1900 achieved fame for her democracy, social insurance, and socialistic projects.

LATIN AMERICA

The same causes of unrest that operated in Latin America after these states had gained their independence remain in effect at the present day. Latin-American economic well-being came to be based too much upon the production of specialized commodities for export. A decline in the price of a particular crop, such as coffee or sugar, brought severe economic depression and often led to political unrest. Plantations, mines, land, petroleum, and shipping came under the control of European and American investors. Loans were made to governments by foreign investors in return for rich concessions. When the loans could not be repaid or if irresponsible Latin politicians refused to pay them, foreign intervention followed. The influence and power of the United States was felt more and more after 1850. In 1902 Germany, Great Britain, and Italy intervened in Venezuela to force payment of defaulted debts. Theodore Roosevelt forced the creditors to accept arbitration. To preclude European interests, Roosevelt in 1904 announced the Roosevelt Corollary to the Monroe Doctrine. This corollary asserted the right of the United States to police Latin-American nations who failed to honor their obligations. Subsequently, the United States intervened in several instances in the Caribbean area. There were various other instances of armed intervention by the United States. Roosevelt helped Panama win independence in order to obtain rights for the United States to dig the Panama Canal. The Mexican Revolution, beginning in 1910, brought American troops into Mexico at three different times. Beginning in 1889 the Pan-American Union was organized, but the application of the "Big Stick" policy and of "Dollar Diplomacy" made Latin America take a cynical view of Pan-Americanism and continue to fear the "Colossus of the North."

REVIEW QUESTIONS

Multiple-choice:

1. Which is *least* relevant to the decline of the old imperialism? 1) The independence movements in America 2) the concern of nations with European international and domestic problems 3) a century of peace after the Vienna settlements 4) decreased profits from colonial enterprises 5) abolition of slavery.

2. On balance the effects of imperialism on both colonies and mother country were 1) beneficial 2) harmful 3) both beneficial and harmful 4) difficult to determine and subject to inconclusive discussion.

3. The change in British rule in India in 1857 resulted from 1) the tragedy of the "Black Hole" of Calcutta 2) the election of Gladstone as prime minister 3) the Sepoy Mutiny 4) the succession of Queen Victoria.

4. The first of these leaders to actually seek overseas possessions for his country was 1) Bismarck 2) Theodore Roosevelt 3) Cecil Rhodes 4) Napoleon III 5) Count Cavour.

5. The rule of the British East India Company in India was terminated as a result of 1) the Crimean War 2) reorganization of the British Empire 3) the ambitions of Queen Victoria 4) the Sepoy Mutiny.

6. The leading motives of imperialism in the Far East were 1) trade and investment 2) missionary work and military bases 3) prestige and glory 4) humanitarianism and good government.

7. Great Britain exported opium to China in order to 1) demoralize Chinese resistance to conquest 2) find a means of paying for imports from China 3) goad the Chinese into war 4) overcome trade rivals.

8. The most friendly power in supporting China against foreign aggression around 1900 was 1) Germany 2) the United States 3) Great Britain 4) Russia

9. Which of these parts in China was taken by France
1) Formosa   2) Indo-China   3) Macao   4) Hong Kong.

10. The American who opened Japan to the West was
1) Theodore Roosevelt   2) William McKinley   3) Commodore
Perry   4) Commodore Dewey.

11. Which was *not* a result of the Russo-Japanese War?
1) the Westernization of Japan   2) Japanese gains of Russian territories   3) an underlying hostility of Japan to the United States
4) resistance of Asians to imperialism.

12. Which imperialist power did the most to prepare her colonies for eventual self-rule?   1) Russia   2) Great Britain
3) France   4) the Netherlands   5) Portugal.

13. Which imperialist nation was first to lose all her possessions in the Pacific and Asiatic areas?   1) France   2) the Netherlands   3) Spain   4) Japan   5) Germany.

14. The main country that kept Russia from gaining outlets
to the sea from 1800 to 1900 was   1) Great Britain   2) Japan
3) Turkey   4) France.

15. The first person to call attention to Africa and bring about
its colonization was   1) Henry M. Stanley   2) Cecil Rhodes
3) David Livingstone   4) King Leopold

16. The United States became deeply involved in Asiatic affairs as a result of   1) the Russo-Japanese War   2) the Spanish-
American War   3) World War I   4) the Burlingame Treaty.

17. The two imperialist powers that clashed most often in Asia
in the nineteenth century were   1) Great Britain and France
2) Japan and Russia   3) France and Germany   4) Russia and
Britain.

18. The Fashoda incident brought   1) French victory in the
Sudan   2) opened the way for an East-West African railway by
Germany   3) defeat and compensation elsewhere for France
4) defeat and compensation elsewhere for Germany.

19. Which imperialist nation in Africa gave up a colonial ambition after suffering defeat at the hands of the natives?   1) Germany   2) Italy   3) Portugal   4) Austria.

20. A nation which went unchallenged in her control of Egypt
after 1875 was   1) Britain   2) France   3) Germany   4) Turkey.

21. Which British dominion first achieved self-government?
1) Australia   2) New Zealand   3) India   4) Canada.

Completion:

22. A political organization favoring independence for India was known as the Indian National . . . . . .

23. Trade of foreigners in China for a long time was limited to the port of a) . . . . . . The ruling dynasty in China in modern times was the b) . . . . . family. A long civil war in China after 1850 is known as the c) . . . . . Rebellion. The American policy of supporting equal opportunity for all in China was known as the d) . . . . . policy. Chinese reaction against foreign intervention resulted in the e) . . . . . Rebellion in 1901.

24. The colonizers of South Africa whose lands were eventually organized as the Union of South Africa were Dutchmen known as the a) . . . . . . Their first prominent leader was b) . . . . . .

25. The United States asserted its right to intervene in the affairs of Latin American nations in the a) . . . . . to the Monroe Doctrine. United States interest in the Caribbean arose from her ownership of the b) . . . . . . The promotion of American commercial and financial interests in Latin America came to be called c) . . . . . .

FOR FURTHER READING

HARDBOUND:

Burt, Alfred P., *The Evolution of the British Empire and Commonwealth from the American Revolution* (1956). A general text on the history of the Commonwealth and their governments.

Cloete, Stuart, *Against These Three* (1945). Rivalry of the British, Boers, and natives in Africa.

Fairbank, John K., *The United States and China* (1948). Survey.

Dulles, Foster, *America in the Pacific: A Century of Expansion* (1938).

Furnivall, John S., *Colonial Policy and Practice* (1948). Deals with the subject of Burma and East Indies; the best study of colonial administration.

Hayes, Carlton J. H., *The Historical Evolution of Modern Nationalism* (1931). A widely used introduction to this subject.

Hobson, John. *Imperialism: A Study* (5th ed., 1952). A classic indictment of imperialism.

Hyma, A., *The Dutch in the Far East* (1942).

Langer, William L., *The Diplomacy of Imperialism* (2nd ed., 1951). Deals with the period 1890-1902.

Latourette, Kenneth S., *A Short History of the Far East* (1946). Good survey.

Moon, Parker T., *Imperialism and World Politics* (1926). A standard work that deals with early new imperialism.

Muir, Ramsey, *The Expansion of Europe* (1939).

Roberts, Stephen H., *History of French Colonial Policy* (1929).

Robinson, R. E., and J. Gallagher, *Africa and the Victorians* (1962). Deals with policy making.

Seeley, John R., *The Expansion of England* (1883). A classic on imperialism. A series of lectures in defense of imperialism.

Strauss, William, *Joseph Chamberlain and the Theory of Imperialism.*

Vinacke, Harold M., *A History of the Far East in Modern Times* (1941).

*1871	*France lost Alsace-Lorraine in Treaty of Frankfurt*
1872, 1881	*Three Emperors' League (Germany, Russia, Austria-Hungary)*
1879-1882	*Dual Alliance (Germany, Austria-Hungary)*
1881-1887	*Three Emperors' League renewed*
*1882-1914	*Triple Alliance (Germany, Italy, Austria-Hungary)*
1882-1890	*Reinsurance Treaty (Germany, Russia)*
*1891	*Dual Alliance (France, Russia) formed*
1899	*First Hague Conference met*
*1902	*British-Japanese Alliance formed*
	German-Turkish agreement to the Berlin-Bagdad railway
*1904	*Entente Cordiale (France, Great Britain)*
1905	*First Moroccan crisis*
1906	*Algeciras Conference*
*1907	*Anglo-Russian Entente formed*
1908	*Second Moroccan crisis*
	Austria annexed Bosnia (First Balkan crisis)
1911	*Third Moroccan crisis (Agadir)*
1911-1912	*Turco-Italian War*
1912-1913	*First Balkan War*
1913	*Second Balkan War*
1914	*Outbreak of World War I*

13. The Background of World War I

The national tensions that developed into war in Europe in 1914 date back to 1871 when German unification introduced a great change in European politics. Up to 1870 peace had been preserved in Europe since 1815 except for the Crimean War and the brief wars of unification. The nations had busied themselves with internal social struggles. But the German victory in the Franco-Prussian War left France so humiliated in the loss of Alsace-Lorraine and of her long-held hegemony on the continent that she would never be satisfied without an attempt to regain her lost territory and prestige. Germany vibrated with the fervor characteristic of a new and victorious nationalist movement. At this same time, the new industrialism introduced worldwide economic competition between Germany and Britain. Britain after 1895 also became conscious of the upset in the European balance of power caused by the unification of Germany. Why this led to World War I may be understood better by observing the fundamental forces operating among the European nations and the conflict of international interests before 1914.

FUNDAMENTAL FORCES FOR WAR

On the basis of a mass of tangled events and developments in Europe preceding World War I certain fundamental causes of the war may be discerned. Areas and trouble spots where these underlying causes operated are noted.

**_Economic imperialism._ The rivalries among the large industrialized nations of Europe, as discussed in the preceding chapter, illustrate the nature of economic as well as of territorial imperialism. This competition for markets, fields of investment, and sources of raw materials caused almost numberless clashes between the great powers after 1870. Because of the development of worldwide transportation and communications, nations became more dependent economically upon other countries. The industrialized states sought to control less developed states or areas or to acquire colonies for economic reasons. The especially strong commercial rivalry of Britain and Germany led to military and diplomatic rivalry. Governments defended the property and promoted the interests of their own subjects in colonial areas, but in some places business interests often were used to justify political interests or to cloak political motives. Economic imperialism of Germany and Britain threatened war particularly over the Berlin-Bagdad railway. Actual conflicts, such as the Boer War and the Russo-Japanese War, originated from imperialism.

Nationalism. In the nineteenth century nationalism acted as an emotional drive to peoples over the world as religion did in the sixteenth century. Nationalism had become an ever-growing force since the Napoleonic Wars and more and more peoples became imbued with its spirit. Common schools and the popular press cultivated national sentiments. Nationalistic literature and historiography intensified national prejudices, patriotism, and prestige consciousness. Racist writings convinced nations of the superiority of their particular people and culture and bred a contempt for other people. This militant, boastful, and unreasoning patriotism is often referred to under the names of *chauvinism* and *jingoism*. New countries or minorities aspiring to independence were guilty of especially strident nationalism. Nations desired to annex lands which were deemed to belong to their own people. German nationalism was as assertive as any, and the French wished to avenge the national humiliation of 1871. The French wanted Alsace-Lorraine restored. The nationalism of the numerous Balkan states created a powder keg always in danger of being ignited. Russia, Turkey, and Austria-Hungary all ruled minorities aspiring to independence. Many nationalists welcomed war as a means of realizing their ambitions. Anti-semitism aroused national aspirations among the Jews, who began, about 1897, to look to Palestine as national home. Russia cultivated Pan-Slavism among Slavic minorities; this movement encouraged the Slavs to look to Russia for aid in case of trouble. Russia and Austria-Hungary clashed over Pan-Slavism. Pan-Germanism sought to unify all German-speaking people into the German Empire.

**The failure of diplomacy.   International anarchy prevailed rather than international law. Since each nation behaved as individuals might in a lawless state, war followed when diplomacy failed. In the absence of international law, nations strengthened themselves by forming alliances of mutual defense in case of attack. Because nations made alliances that sometimes conflicted with commitments to another ally or because commitments were made to compensate allies at the expense of another nation's territory, these agreements were made in secret.

Weakness of the forces for peace.   Peace societies had been organized after the Napoleonic Wars and increased in number and in membership as thoughtful persons realized the destruction that modern war might bring. International agreements, conferences, international societies, and Olympic games manifested cooperation among nations; many peace societies held international conferences. Philanthropists, such as Alfred Nobel and Andrew Carnegie, contributed funds to the cause of peace and worked to promote international arbitration of disputes and limitation of armaments. The First Hague Conference met in 1899 and established an international Hague Tribunal for the arbitration of disputes. A great many disputes were arbitrated. In 1907 the Second Hague Conference strengthened the Hague Tribunal. But nations were not ready to permit international courts to settle all disputes; they preferred reliance upon power and war if necessary to protect their major interests. International forces for peace were simply too weak and ineffective to offset the appeal of nationalism.

Military factors. The dependence upon military forces to uphold the prestige and defend a government forced the various nations to build great military and naval forces. After 1871 national compulsory military training for all males built up huge Prussian-type conscript armies prepared to answer the nation's call to arms in time of crisis. Nations accepted the burden of supporting large armies equipped with modern machines of war. Britain and Germany engaged in a naval race out of fear of each other. The defensive preparations of each nation were viewed as offensive in purpose by suspicious rivals who then increased their own strength still further.

Peacemaking factors were offset by militant psychology. The great powers of Britain, Germany, and Japan had become so by military strength. War was accepted as a historical fact and inevitable. Darwinism emphasized the struggle for existence as a condition of nature. Some writers glorified war, as Treitschke in Germany. Military leaders were necessarily entrusted with important decisions and otherwise exerted much influence. The extensive preparations for war made many nations feel confident of victory if it came.

Systems of alliances. Statesmen, beginning with Bismarck (who felt a need to protect Germany against French revenge), arranged protective alliances with nations of parallel interests. Rivals outside these alliances felt forced to create alliances of their own. A network of alliances, instead of preventing war, may have encouraged nations to follow more aggressive policies and assured that, in the event of war, all allied states would be drawn in. A threat against one member of an alliance constituted a threat against other members who, therefore, prepared to take action as if the threat had been made directly against themselves.

** *Areas of tension.* Certain trouble spots in Europe became chronic threats to peace or kept alive hateful animosity. Alsace-Lorraine, a borderland area of France and Germany taken by Germany in 1871, left France determined to regain it. A large part of the population there wished to return to the French flag, but much of the population was German.

Italia Irredenta, unredeemed Italy, was a name given to certain districts held by Austria; these areas were South Tyrol, Trieste, and a part of Dalmatia. Even though these lands were a part of the territory of her ally, Austria, Italy desired them because of their large Italian population.

The Balkan states all coveted the territory of one or more of their neighboring states. Bosnia, the Alsace-Lorraine of the Balkans, was coveted by Serbia. The subject nationalities in Austria-Hungary wished for independence. Russia, Austria-Hungary, Germany, and Great Britain were all ready to intervene to avoid any change in the balance of power among the Balkan states.

THE SYSTEM OF ALLIANCES

Nations hoped that alliances would prevent wars by isolating aggressors but if war came no nation wanted to be without allies. While serving as chancellor, Bismarck successfully built alliances to isolate France and prevent her from starting a war of revenge.

German Alliances. Bismarck knew that France would want to regain Alsace-Lorraine as soon as she felt strong enough and that Germany must protect herself with allies and isolate France at the same time. In 1873 he formed the Three Emperor's League (the Dreikaiserbund) of Germany, Austria-Hungary, and Russia; each of these three had a common interest in keeping its Polish subjects in hand. But rivalry between Germany and Russia over the Balkans in 1878 ended this alliance temporarily.

The secret, defensive Dual Alliance of Germany and Austria-Hungary was formed by Bismarck in 1879. In 1882 Italy was admitted and the Triple Alliance became effective. Italy joined because of her anger at France over the annexation of Tunis. The Triple Alliance remained in effect as a defensive combination until 1914. In 1881 the Three Emperors' League (Dreikaiserbund) was revived when Alexander III became tsar, but the alliance was terminated in 1887 after Austria and Russia clashed once again over the Balkans. When this League expired, Bismarck made a secret three-year Reinsurance Treaty with Russia. Essentially these alliances protected Germany from an attack by France. In 1912 the old Triple Alliance was renewed, but it was known that Italy would not back up her commitments unless it should serve her own interest to do so. Italy had been too long exploited in past centuries not to look out for her own interests first. By 1914 only a Dual Alliance with Austria actually remained to bring substantial aid to Germany in case of war.

French alliances. The rivalry of Austria and Russia caused Russia to join France in the Dual Alliance of 1891. In 1894, in a secret formal agreement, France and Russia further agreed that if either were attacked by Germany the other would enter the war against Germany. Resentment of British imperialism also helped to drive Russia and France together.

After the Fashoda incident the French foreign minister, Delcassé, worked to win British friendship. In 1904 France recognized British control of Egypt, and Britain recognized

French interests in Morocco. France and Britain agreed to support each other in North Africa. This *rapprochement* of the old-time enemies was called the *Entente Cordiale* since no formal treaty was made. Britain welcomed the alliance because of the colonial, commercial, and naval competition of Germany.

British alliances. The threat of German naval forces in Europe caused Britain to concentrate her warships in the North Sea, and she made agreements permitting her to withdraw her ships from Asia, the Caribbean, and the Mediterranean. In 1902 the British and Japanese alliance was formed, and Japan was left to look out for their joint interests in Asiatic waters. The Entente Cordiale with France in 1904 permitted the withdrawal of British ships in the Mediterranean. An understanding with the United States during the negotiations for the abrogation of the Clayton-Bulwer Treaty allowed Britain to withdraw ships from the Caribbean. By the abrogation of the Clayton-Bulwer Treaty, Britain conceded the right of the United States alone to build and fortify the Panama Canal.

The defeat of Russia in the Russo-Japanese War ended the long-standing rivalry of Britain and Russia, for it demonstrated to Britain that Russia was not a great threat. The war also convinced France that she needed a stronger ally than Russia. Thus, in 1907, the Anglo-Russian Entente was negotiated and quarrels between the two former rivals were settled. Now that Russia, France, and Britain were joined in a Triple Entente, Germany felt surrounded by enemies. The Entente proved to be more binding than the Triple Alliance of the Central Powers.

INTERNATIONAL CRISES

A series of international crises in the decade before 1914 threatened general war.

**Moroccan crisis (1904-1911). France and Italy settled their
differences over the Italian annexation of Tripoli (Libya) in
1900 with the understanding that France might assume supremacy in Tunis and Morocco. Agreements with Britain and
Spain cleared the way further for French dominance in Morocco. William II, feeling miffed that these arrangements had
left Germany out, demanded an international conference over
Morocco. In the Algeciras Conference in 1906, it was agreed
that Morocco would remain intact, but France and Spain were
granted the right to provide police protection for foreigners
there.

In 1907 the French landed troops in Morocco and in 1908
created trouble by invading the German consulate there. The
subsequent dispute submitted to the Hague Tribunal was
compromised.

In 1911 when the French occupied the leading Moroccan
city of Fez, Germany dispatched her warship the *Panther* to
the post of Agadir to prevent French annexation of Moroccan
territory. Another compromise settled a dangerous crisis. The
French established a protectorate over Morocco, and Germany
was compensated by two strips of the French Congo. But
other issues kept strong French and German animosities alive.

**The Balkan crises. Like Austria, Germany too became interested in the Balkans. In 1902 Germany concluded an agreement with Turkey by which Germany would extend a German
and Austrian railroad to Bagdad and to the Persian Gulf. Such
a railroad would enable Germany to expand her trade with the
Orient by fast transportation—faster than that of Britain and
France through the Suez Canal. This German *Drang nach
Osten* (drive to the East), reinforced by Germany's other
friendly cooperation with Turkey, aroused the fears of Britain,
France, and Russia.

In 1908 Austria annexed the two Balkan provinces of

Bosnia-Herzegovina. The stormy Serbs were outraged at this, since it blocked their plans for a future state (such as was formed subsequently in Yugoslavia). The Serbs prepared for war in expectation of Russian aid, but France and Britain advised caution and Serbia had to yield. Bitterness of the Serbs against Austria was intensified by other clashes.

The Turco-Italian War of 1911-1912 was followed by another crisis. Italy had easily taken Tripoli and thereby had demonstrated the weakness of Turkey. The second Near-Eastern Crisis (1912-1913) resulted in what is designated as the First Balkan War. Greece, Serbia, Montenegro, and Bulgaria in a joint effort attacked Turkey and reconquered most of the European part of the Ottoman Empire.

The Second Balkan War followed in 1913 when Bulgaria attacked her late allies. Bulgaria suffered overwhelming defeat as Turkey and Rumania joined the attack against her. In the peace negotiations the great powers intervened and Austria blocked any provision that would permit Serbian aggrandizement. Austria won the recognition of Albania as an independent state and thereby blocked Serbia's desire for an outlet to the Adriatic Sea. The great powers watched anxiously to see that changes in the Balkan puzzle did not benefit rivals. Austria thwarted Serbia who wished to create a strong Slavic state. Serbian propaganda encouraged restlessness of the subject Slavs of Austria. The quarrel between Austria and Serbia led to the outbreak of World War I.

REVIEW QUESTIONS

Multiple-choice:

1. Which nation did *not* rule a restless national minority? 1) Austria-Hungary 2) Germany 3) France 4) Great Britain.

2. The First Hague Conference resulted in 1) settlement of the conflict over Morocco 2) a step toward peaceful settlement

of disputes   3) abolition of secret treaties   4) compulsory arbitration of disputes among small nations.

3. The most important military development after 1870 was 1) the adoption of the practice of compulsory military service 2) the construction of tanks   3) preparations for offensive rather than defensive war   4) the growth of pacifism.

4. Which of these nationalistic movements did the most to worsen the danger of war in the Balkans? 1) Pan-Germanism 2) Pan-Slavism   3) the Young Turks   4) the Celtic revival.

5. The alliance system had all of these effects *except* which one?   1) Assured that if war broke out many nations would be drawn in   2) encouraged members of alliances to take more aggressive stands in disputes   3) forced nations to seek additional allies   4) a tendency to isolate wars.

6. Which was *not* the cause of a dispute over a border area? 1) *Italia Irredenta*   2) Alsace-Lorraine   3) Bosnia   4) Morocco.

7. What area of conflict caused the break-up of the Three Kaiser's League? 1) Balkans   2) Turkey   3) Persia   4) *Italia Irredenta*.

8. Italian rivalry with France over what country caused Italy to join the Triple Alliance? 1) Morocco   2) Cyprus   3) Tunis 4) Algeria.

9. Which is the only alliance that proved completely effective in World War I? 1) The Reinsurance Treaty   2) Triple Entente 3) Triple Alliance.

10. Which nation was *least* successful in isolating her rivals by diplomacy before World War I? 1) Britain   2) Germany 3) France   4) Russia.

11. Germany finally received compensation in satisfaction of her claims in Morocco by a grant of territory in   1) British East Africa   2) French Congo   3) a small strip of Morocco   4) recognition of her special rights in Turkey.

12. The ambitions of which of the Balkan states did the most to cause World War I?   1) Bulgaria   2) Greece   3) Serbia   4) Rumania.

13. Which was of *least* importance in causing Anglo-German rivalry before World War I?   1) The naval race   2) German diplomatic successes   3) commercial competition   4) colonial rivalry.

FOR FURTHER READING

HARDBOUND:

Benns, F. Lee, *European History since 1870* (1950). Detailed and general.

Fay, Sidney B., *Origins of the World War* (2nd ed., 1943). Objective, comprehensive.

Langer, William L., *European Alliances and Alignments* (1931).

Mendenhall, T., *et al.*, *The Quest for a Principle of Authority in Europe, 1715 to the Present* (1948). Study of effects of nationalism.

Schmitt, Bernadotte E., *Triple Alliance and Triple Entente* (1934). Brief.

Schurman, Jacob G., *The Balkan Wars* (1916).

Shafer, Boyd C., *Nationalism: Myth and Reality* (1955). Recent study.

Sontag, Raymond J., *European Diplomatic History, 1871-1932* (1933).

Taylor, A. J. P., *Struggle for the Mastery of Europe, 1848-1914* (1955).

PAPERBOUND:

Hayes, Carlton J. H., *Generation of Materialism, 1871-1900* (Torchbooks).

ESSAY TYPE REVIEW QUESTIONS FOR MID-TERM AND FINAL EXAMINATIONS

1. What change characterized the New Industrialism after 1870?

2. What were some of the manifestations of revisionist socialism and who were some of its leaders?

3. Discuss the progress of the labor movement after 1870 and illustrate by citing various gains made for the benefit of the working class in different countries.

4. What was each: syndicalism, Fabian socialism, Christian socialism?

5. How did organized religion meet the challenges of Marxism, Darwinism, and science?

6. Explain the Darwinian theory? What influence did it have outside of natural science?

7. Characterize the philosophy of Nietzsche.

8. What were the main trends of political and social legislation in the western world from 1870 to 1914?

9. Characterize the nature of the rising political parties after 1900 in the more democratic countries.

10. Discuss the differences between the political parties of Gladstone and Disraeli.

11. Discuss the significance of the Dreyfus Affair.

12. What real success, if any, did Bismarck gain in his battles against the Church and against socialism? Explain.

13. What economic problems and political factors retarded progress in Italy.

14. What is the significance of the political changes made in the United States as a result of the elections of 1800, 1828, and 1860?

15. Sketch the territorial expansion of the United States.

16. What were the causes and state the significance of the American Civil War?

17. What reaction did the domination of big business bring in the United States?

18. Identify: anarchists, nihilists, terrorists, Slavophils.

19. Identify the main political parties in Russia up to 1914.

20. What success did the Russian Dumas encounter in their attempts to introduce reforms?

21. What was the cause and significance of the Congress of Berlin in 1878?

22. Explain fully the motives of the New Imperialism. Compare the New and the Old imperialisms. What brought an end to the Old Imperialism?

23. Defend and criticize the effects of the New Imperialism on both the subject peoples and dominant nations.

24. Explain how China and Japan were opened to the West.

25. What was the significance of the Russo-Japanese War?

26. What role did each play in the opening of Africa: Livingstone, Stanley, and Leopold II? What nations took part in the partition of Africa?

27. What nations clashed and where in the rivalry over colonial areas?

28. What changes took place in the evolution of self-government in Canada, Australia, and New Zealand?

29. Explain the nature of each: the Boer War and the Fashoda incident.

30. Discuss the role of the United States in relation to Latin America.

31. What alliances and other developments brought the diplomatic isolation of Germany before 1914?

32. What international crises threatened war from 1904 to 1914?

33. Write an essay on the fundamental forces for war and peace before 1914.

WORLD WAR I AND

ITS AFTERMATH

1914-1939

The great changes caused by World War I, changes which became especially evident during the postwar years, introduced a new era in the history of Europe. The old era of European dominance of the world had ended. The crucial role of the United States in bringing the war to an end, because of American manpower and economic resources, demonstrated that Europe's world leadership had passed. From the role of creditor, Europe emerged as a debtor to the United States. The postwar years revealed the extent of Europe's economic decline and of her political demoralization. Because democracy seemed inadequate to meet the needs of the nations that lost the war, the new totalitarian political systems of communism and fascism went into operation in countries that emerged with the greatest war losses. The war did not solve Europe's problems but created new ones. One great legacy of the war was world depression. The failure of collective security opened the way for calculating aggressor nations. A new era of tension and crisis produced the Second World War, beginning in 1939.

*1914   *World War I began

June 28, assassination of Archduke Ferdinand at Sarajevo

July 23, Austrian ultimatum issued to Serbia

July 28, Austria declared war on Serbia

July 29, Russia ordered mobilization

Aug. 1, Germany declared war on Russia

Aug. 3, Germany declared war on France and invaded Belgium

Aug. 4, Britain declared war on Germany

Aug. 26, Russians defeated in battle of Tannenberg on the Eastern Front

October, Turkey entered war by attacking Russia

1915   Disastrous British campaign in the Dardanelles

Italy joined Allies in the war

Bulgaria entered war on side of Central Powers

Lusitania sunk

1916   Naval battle of Jutland

Battle of Verdun; Allied offensive on the Somme

Rumania entered on Allied side

*1917   Germany resumed unrestricted submarine warfare around British Isles

March, Russian Revolution began

*April, United States declared war on Germany

November, Bolsheviks took control of Russian Revolution

*1918   *March, Treaty of Brest-Litovsk

Ludendorff's drive on Western Front failed

Successful counterattack of Foch in second battle of the Marne

*Nov. 11, Armistice signed

14. World War I

A century without major war in Europe and the passing of various crises in the decade before 1914 left Europe optimistic that universal war might not occur again. When some diplomats in early August, 1914, were crushed at their failure to prevent war, crowds in holiday gaiety in the larger countries cheered mobilizing troops. A quick victory was expected to vanquish the enemy and end the past years of tension. No one foresaw the long stalemate and grinding death and destruction during the four years from 1914 to 1918 and the aftermath of wars and starvation in eastern Europe. No such total war that commandeered and destroyed so many millions of soldiers and billions of dollars of resources had been recorded.

THE BEGINNING AND NATURE OF THE WAR

The intense nationalism of the Balkans ignited the conflict. The system of alliances rapidly drew the major nations and their smaller allies into the struggle. Trench warfare perpetuated the deadly stalemate that prolonged the war. New weapons technology made the was especially destructive.

The assassination of Archduke Ferdinand. The heir to the Austrian throne, Archduke Francis Ferdinand, and his wife were shot and killed on June 28, 1914, in the streets of Sarajevo, the little capital of Bosnia. This precipitated the last of the Balkan crises and a month later brought a declaration of war by the major nations of Europe.

Serbian nationalists planned the murder to destroy the

heir to the throne of the aged Emperor Francis Joseph. Ferdinand was known to favor reconciliation of his southern Slav subjects by concessions which were intended to quiet their unrest. Ferdinand's plans might thwart Serbian nationalists who hoped to capitalize upon the unrest and unite by force Austrian Slavs to a greater Serbia. The plan of the assassination was drawn up by a leader of the Serbian general staff. The Serbian government had no official part in the plot but knew if it and took no step to interfere in it.

Europe reacted with shock and sympathy for Austria. Austria now decided to punish Serbia and destroy this center of anti-Austrian agitation. Austria deliberately prepared for war and ascertained that the German Kaiser and Chancellor Bethmann-Hollweg would support her. Since Germany could not abandon her only strong ally, she gave a "blank check" to Austria to proceed. Germany thought the war would remain a local one.

The ultimatum to Serbia. With Germany's backing Austria's foreign minister, Count Berchtold, issued a harsh, sweeping ultimatum to Serbia to stop all anti-Austrian activities and punish persons involved in the assassination of the Archduke. Austria demanded a reply in forty-eight hours. The Serbian reply was evasive but conciliatory, but Austria wanted to punish Serbia and accordingly declared war on Serbia on July 28, 1914.

Outbreak of war. Britain and Germany had had no success in trying to settle the quarrel by mediation. Russia's action was crucial; she was the first great power to mobilize. Russia did not wish to lose face with the Slavs by permitting Austria to crush Serbia. Britain gave no clear indication of what she would do. Russia's mobilization forced Germany to act. Diplomats and militarists worked under great strain, because vital decisions had to be made quickly by the powers obligated to each other under the terms of the alliances. Delay would give an attacking enemy crucial advantage. Attempts by Great Britain and Germany to win Austria's consent to mediation were refused. Germany replied to Russia's mobilization by an ultimatum to stop mobilizing or face war. Receiving no reply after twelve hours, Germany declared war on Russia on August 1. France mobilized to be ready to fulfill her alliance with Russia. Germany did not wish to permit France to gain the advantage of the initial attack and on August 3 declared war on France. Germany's plan of attack in event of war, the Schlieffen Plan, called for a quick strike against France across the weakly protected Belgian frontier. When Germany marched into Belgium, England declared war on August 4. Germany's attack on Belgium violated Belgian neutrality as guaranteed in the treaty of 1839. Besides, Britain could not permit a strategic area of such importance, directly across the English Channel, to be occupied by a strong power. Thus were the major powers pulled into the Austrian war against Serbia. The two governments that really wanted war were Austria and Serbia and both expected to benefit from it. None of the other nations were solely responsible for the outbreak, but all were involved in the conditions that caused it to spread.

Further spread of the war. Turkey entered the war as one of the Central Powers in October, 1914, by bombarding Russian ports in the Black Sea. Japan declared war on the Central Powers (Austria-Hungary, Germany, and Turkey) in August, 1914, and seized German leaseholds in China and the German-held islands in the Pacific. Italy declared her neutrality at first but after allied promises of generous spoils of territory Italy took the side of the Allies (Great Britain, France, and Russia) in 1915. Italy began war by an attack on Austria. Bulgaria joined the Central Powers in 1915. Greece, Rumania, Montenegro took the side of the Allies and so did Portugal. Nations that remained neutral throughout the war were Spain, Switzerland, the Netherlands, Denmark, Norway, and Sweden. The United States of America did not enter until 1917.

**Strategy of the belligerents. Germany's great power made her the obvious Allied target and her location in Central Europe made her especially vulnerable. Her strategy called for a quick war, first to knock out France and later to deal with the slower-moving Russians. Germany planned to cross Belgium quickly and flank French fortifications along the German border and march to the south to strike at Paris. England landed troops to defend Belgium and France. Britain and France began a naval blockade to prevent the importation of foodstuffs and war supplies. When Belgium was attacked, the French shifted troops to that frontier to block the German advance. Germany could hope to win only by a quick victory, because time would favor the British who used their greater naval power to deny Germany access to world resources. Britain herself, having control of the seas and greater wealth, could command the resources of her colonies and the world.

*Weapons, methods, and propaganda. The belligerents employed new weapons or improved weapons not previously used on a large scale—submarines, poisonous gasses, armored tanks, faster machine guns, greater explosives, long-range cannon, airplanes, and zeppelins.

The fighting on the six hundred mile Western Front within a few weeks settled down to trench fighting. These trenches, about six feet deep, extended all along the Western Front. It was extremely difficult to conduct an offensive across several parallel trenches. Behind the lines, civilians worked as in no previous war to produce the vast amount of equipment, weapons, ammunition, and foodstuffs needed.

The literacy of large populations made propaganda a useful weapon. The Allies used propaganda more effectively than did the Central Powers. Much was made of the blundering German reference to the treaty guaranteeing Belgian independence and neutrality as a "scrap of paper." Germans were accused of the vilest atrocities and of causing the war.

MILITARY ACTION UP TO 1918

The decisive action of the war occurred on the Western Front, but action on the Eastern Front and the war at sea greatly affected the ability of the belligerents to bring overseas men and resources into action.

***The Western Front.** The German Schlieffen plan did not succeed, because too many troops had to be diverted to oppose the Russian armies in the east. The German drive to Paris lost its momentum, partly because of the unexpected vigor of Belgian resistance, as well as British resistance to the Germans. The Germans lost the first great crucial battle of the Marne. Otherwise, they might have quickly taken Paris and secured a French surrender as had been done in 1870. The Western Front settled down to one of trench warfare that lasted throughout most of the war. The opposing lines of trenches had changed little when armistice came. Regularly, assaults were launched to break enemy lines, but only a little space could be gained. The largest action was the battle of Verdun in 1916; each side lost a half million soldiers in this six months' engagement, but neither gained any advantage.

The war to the East. Millions of troops were engaged on the Eastern Front. The crucial battle of Tannenberg, a Russian defeat, came in August, 1914. The Russian attacks had the effect of diverting large German forces that were needed in the West. In 1915 the Germans and Austrians inflicted heavy losses on the Russians and drove them back. The Russian economy and morale deteriorated as the war continued. In March, 1917, revolution in Russia practically took that country out of the war; in November, 1917, the Bolsheviks began peace negotiations with the Central Powers. A costly and disastrous campaign was waged by Britain and France early in 1915 to take the Dardanelles Straits and force Turkey out of the war. The campaign was abandoned before the end of the year.

The war at sea. The only great naval engagement of the war was the gigantic battle of Jutland in mid-1916 in the North Sea. The Germans fought more expertly than the British and British losses were greater. For practical purposes, however, the battle was a German defeat, since the German navy retired and never risked another such fleet engagement.

The blockade by the British fleet greatly helped to bring victory by cutting off supplies for Germany and by protecting troop transports from Allied overseas countries. Germany's best hope of winning the war at sea was the submarine; she used it to blockade the British Isles by sinking merchant shipping into British coastal waters. The weapon was very effective until the Allies used its own submarines, destroyers, depth bombs, airplanes, and mines to sink them and used convoys and other methods of evasion.

THE END OF THE WAR

In 1917 neither side saw any prospect of near victory. The British and French sacrificed hundreds of thousands of men in desperate efforts to break the stalemate. Demoralized troops were on the verge of wholesale mutiny. Early in 1917 Germany's desperation caused her to resort to unrestricted submarine warfare in the waters surrounding the British Isles. She did so at the risk of bringing the United States into war against her.

***The United States in the war.** President Wilson of the United States at the opening of the war called upon all Americans to remain neutral. The English background of a majority of Americans predisposed the United States to favor an Allied victory. At first the British blockade and rules of war offended America and brought protests. But Germany's unrestricted submarine warfare, with its disregard for loss of life, brought more serious protests and warnings. The sinking of the *Lusitania* and the *Sussex* brought an American ultimatum to abandon unrestricted submarine warfare and Germany agreed. For a time Germany abandoned her submarine campaign against *all* shipping around the British Isles. But resumption of such sinkings early in 1917 brought an American declaration of war against Germany in April. British propaganda, the high idealism of President Wilson, the Anglophilism of the administration, and the future danger in a German victory were other causes of American entry.

The great resources and manpower of America came just in time to turn the tide for an Allied victory. The victory of the Bolshevik revolution brought the collapse of the Russian war effort and permitted Germany to concentrate additional forces on the Western Front early in 1917. Since America desired an Allied victory it was imperative now that she enter the war. The American war spirit was aroused at the same time by the release of the Zimmermann note by which Germany had invited Mexico to enter the war against the United States if the United States should declare war on Germany. The moral effect of American entry was immediate, but it took many months to bring her military power to bear on the Western Front. American entry lifted the spirits of the Allies as it depressed morale of the Germans.

Victory in 1918. Early in 1918 the enlarged German forces on the Western Front made three great attempts to overwhelm the Allied lines. Substantial gains were made but there was no decisive breakthrough. American forces helped defeat General Ludendorff's last desperate drive in mid-1918. Marshall Foch, at the head of all Allied troops, launched a counter-attack in July in the second battle of the Marne. The Germans were now forced back, later retreated, and by October had abandoned most of French soil. Allied propaganda, especially Wilson's Fourteen Points for peace, helped break civilian morale in Germany. The Kaiser was forced to abdicate in a revolution against the monarchy. Bulgaria surrendered in September and Turkey soon afterward. Early in November, Austria abandoned the struggle and soon disintegrated when her minorities revolted. On November 11, 1918, the Germans signed the Armistice by which defeat was admitted and her military equipment surrendered.

REVIEW QUESTIONS

Multiple-choice:

1. Archduke Ferdinand was assassinated by Serbian nationalists, because 1) he planned to annex Bosnia 2) he planned to crush all Serbian opposition to Austria 3) the concessions he planned to make to the Slavs would have frustrated the extreme ambitions of the nationalists 4) the Serbs hoped to provoke Germany into attacking Russia.

2. The general agreement of historians places the blame for the fundamental causes of the war 1) upon the Balkan nations 2) upon the capitalistic nations 3) upon the Central Powers 4) equally upon all the nations involved 5) upon the Allied Powers.

3. As for the immediate cause of general war, the blame must be borne by 1) Britain for not making her position clear 2) Germany for giving Austria a carte blanche 3) Serbia for plotting the assassination 4) Russia for mobilizing 5) no single nation.

4. Which nation opposed the others in World War I? 1) Italy 2) Britain 3) Russia 4) Turkey 5) Rumania.

5. Germany's main plan for a quick victory led to 1) the invasion of Belgium 2) submarine warfare 3) promoting revolution in Russia 4) concentration of troops on the Eastern Front.

6. Which statement is *not* true? 1) Italy switched her support to the Allies in order to gain territory 2) Japan fought on the side of Germany 3) Britain's immediate reason for declaring war on Germany was Germany's invasion of Belgium 4) All the Scandinavian countries remained neutral.

7. The first major nation to suffer crushing defeat was 1) Russia 2) Germany 3) Italy 4) Austria-Hungary 5) Turkey.

8. Germany surrendered sooner than she might have because of the effect of the 1) failure of her submarine offensive 2) the defeat of Austria-Hungary 3) the Fourteen Points 4) starvation on the home front.

9. The main immediate and avowed cause of the entry of the United States in the war was 1) Russia had ceased to effectively oppose Germany 2) Germany's submarine warfare 3) Wilson's desire to win Allied support for organizing the League of Nations 4) England was on the verge of collapse.

10. Before the war was over 1) the Central Powers gained the most allies 2) fewer countries were still at war than at the beginning 3) Britain and France added the most allies.

Completion:

11. Germany's plan for the capture of Paris is known as the . . . . . plan.

12. The great fleet engagement of the war was the battle of . . . . . .

13. A weapon used prominently in World War I but not used extensively before or since was a) . . . . . . The main cause of the stalemate on the Western Front throughout the war was that the opposing armies defended their lines by b) . . . . . fighting.

14. When Italy entered the war she attacked what country? . . . . . .

15. A non-military weapon used by the belligerents because of the literacy of large populations was . . . . . .

FOR FURTHER READING

HARDBOUND:

Churchill, Winston, *The World Crisis* (1931). Brilliant, in a one-volume edition.

Cruttwell, Charles, *A History of the Great War, 1914-1918* (2nd ed., 1936).

Falls, Agnes, *The Great War, 1914-1918* (1960).

Hayes, Carlton J. H., *Brief History of the Great War* (1920).

Liddell-Hart, Basil H., *A History of the World War* (1935).

————, *The War in Outline, 1914-1918* (1938). By a British military authority.

Pollard, A. F., *Short History of the Great War* (1920).

Remak, J., *Sarajevo* (1959).

Zeman, Z. A. B., *The Breakup of the Hapsburg Empire* (1961).

*1914   *World War I began
*1917   March, Russian Revolution began
*1918   November 11, Armistice signed
 1918   Lloyd George won "khaki election" in Britain
*1919   January-June, Paris Peace Conference met to
             draft peace terms for Germany. Communist-
             inspired riots and other violence in eastern
             Europe underlined urgency of speedy peace
             settlement

15. The Paris Peace Settlements, 1919

Many important changes in the map of Europe were made as a consequence of the war and the peace conferences. The task of the diplomats was immense, greater than the similar settlements at Vienna or at Utrecht at the conclusion of earlier general wars. Representatives of the Allied nations met at Paris to draw up separate treaties dealing with the defeated nations.

Aftermath of the war. The settlements made at Paris were conditioned by various current factors which help to explain why these various provisions were made. The war losses of the Allied nations in dead, maimed, and wounded and of property destruction in France and Belgium left them filled with a craving for vengeance. Diplomats were sent to Paris who were determined to make the Germans pay the full cost of the war in so far as that would be possible. The conference was held in Paris where these feelings of hate were already concentrated. One of the most prominent of these factors was the spread of communism and the fear of it. Bolsheviks grasped control of the Russian Revolution late in 1918. The Allies dispatched troops to several points in Russia, hoping to deter the Bolshevists. Communist riots in Germany followed the Revolution there. There were communist movements in other parts of Europe. In 1919 the Greeks made war against the Turks. Arab subjects of Turkey soon made trouble for their new French and British masters. The Italians and Yugoslavs quarrelled over the port of Fiume on the Adriatic.

***Difficulty of making peace terms.** In the end the terms of the Treaty of Versailles were decided by the Big Four: Woodrow Wilson of the United States, Lloyd George of Great Britain, Clemenceau of France, and Orlando of Italy; Orlando really played only a minor part. The delegates met in Paris from January to June, 1919, to draw up the treaty with Germany. The work of drafting the treaties with the other powers came afterwards. All except Wilson were practical politicians, self-seeking realists who were tuned, not to the unselfish principles of Wilson, but to the vengeful and grasping demands of their own constituents. Secret treaties made by the Allies contradicted Wilson's Fourteen Points. Wilson's decision to meet the Allied diplomats at Paris in face-to-face conferences was a mistake. It put him under direct pressure to compromise, which he did in order to win approval for the League of Nations. Clemenceau, the "Tiger of France," wanted revenge and wanted to weaken Germany to assure French security. In the preceding election campaigns, the "khaki election" of 1918, Lloyd George in England promised to make the "Huns" pay the full cost of the war. The danger of the spread of Bolshevism made it necessary to reach agreements quickly.

***The Fourteen Points.** Wilson's Fourteen Points were carried into Germany during the war and offered as a basis for peace. The terms were so reasonable that they influenced the German people to give up the struggle. The provisions were important, therefore, as a basis for peace and for their influence on the terms of the peace treaty. They are summarized as follows, with parenthetical comments as to the extent of fulfillment by the Allies.

1] Peace treaties openly arrived at and an end to secret diplomacy. (The treaties were made in secret with Wilson's assent.)

2] Freedom of the seas in peace and war. (British opposition prevailed; never discussed at the conference.)

3] Pursuit of the goal of free trade and the establishment of equality of trade. (Violated by the creation of many new nations each with its trade barriers and by general adoption of protective principles in the United States and elsewhere.)

4] Disarmament of forces that might be used for offensive purposes. (Applied only to the defeated nations.)

5] The settlement of colonial claims on the basis of the interest of colonial populations as well as claims of outside governments. (In effect, the victors divided the spoils, since the colonies were mandated to the victors and treated as parts of their colonial empires.)

6] To evacuate Russia and permit her to determine her own political future. (Allies intervened with military forces to overthrow or hamper the Bolsheviks.)

7] Restoration of Belgium. (This was done.)

8] Restoration of France's boundaries, including Alsace-Lorraine. (This was fulfilled.)

9] To readjust the boundaries of Italy so as to include bordering Italian districts. (Overdone by awarding German and Yugoslav districts to Italy.)

10] Self-government for the people of Austria-Hungary. (Executed but Slavs favored over Germans and Magyars in cases of disputes.)

11] Restoration and evacuation of the Balkan states and guaranty of independence and boundaries. (Realized.)

12] Independence for subject peoples of Turkey; opening of the Dardanelles to all nations. (Subject peoples not really left free under the mandate system.)

13] Independence for Poland and access to the sea. (Realized.)

14] A League of Nations to guarantee independence and territorial integrity to all nations. (Return of Republicans to power caused the United States to renounce membership in the League; American absence proved to be a fatal weakness.)

Terms of the peace treaties. In the suburbs of Paris, the terms of the various peace treaties were drawn up and applied to the defeated nations. The names of the treaties for each of the defeated powers were: Versailles with Germany, St. Germain with Austria, Neuilly with Bulgaria, Trianon with Hungary, Sevres with Turkey. The settlements resulting from these treaties follows.

In Europe, Germany lost territories as follows: 1] Alsace-Lorraine was returned to France. 2] The Saar region was placed under the supervision of the League, but the coal mines were transferred to France in compensation for the retreating German army's deliberate destruction of French mines. Provisions for a plebiscite brought a return of the Saar to Germany in 1935. 3] Germany lost a bit of territory to Belgium; 4] in the east she lost territory to reconstructed Poland, including the "Polish Corridor" which severed East Prussia from Germany. 5] Danzig was made a free state 6] Germany lost Memel to Lithuania; 7] part of Silesia went to Czechoslovakia; 8] Schleswig-Holstein was returned to Denmark by plebiscite; 9] the Rhineland was demilitarized as security for France. Germany's various military services were drastically limited in size. The treaty included a war guilt clause by which Germany was forced to admit sole guilt for the war. The purpose of this clause was to justify a requirement that Germany would pay an unstated reparations bill for all war damage. But Germany was stripped of her merchant marine, her colonies, and other resources for meeting the reparations bill. An army of occupation was to be stationed on the left bank of the Rhine for fifteen years.

Austria was reduced to a small state of German-speaking people, and Hungary lost two thirds of her territory populated by the subject nationalities. Russia gained Transylvania from Hungary. Bulgaria lost much territory, part to Yugoslavia and some to Greece.

Other results of the settlements were the restoration of Belgium and the re-creation of Poland. New states created were Czechoslovakia and Yugoslavia (which absorbed Serbia and Montenegro). Gaining independence at the expense of Russia were Finland, Estonia, Latvia, and Lithuania. Russia also lost Bessarabia to Rumania.

Germany lost all her overseas colonies. In Africa, the colonies as "mandates" were transferred to Great Britain, France, and Belgium. (Mandated territories were entrusted to the victors for supervision until the subject people became ready for self-determination. In practice they became colonies.) The German islands in the Pacific went to Japan, New Zealand, Australia, and the British Empire.

The Ottoman Empire's subject nationalities were assigned to Great Britain (Iraq and Palestine) and France (Syria) or became independent (Hejaz). The Dardanelles Straits and their approaches were demilitarized.

A *dictated peace*.   The Treaty of Versailles was a dictated peace (*diktat,* the Germans complained). Contrary to precedent, Germany had no representative at the conference table but was presented with the completed treaty and required to sign it. The terms of the treaty were more severe than any previously imposed in European wars. The treaty was additionally severe in that it stripped Germany completely of her colonies. The unlimited reparations were based on the false assumption that Germany was solely guilty of starting the war and therefore for the damage caused by it. Historians since have pointed out that the blame, for various reasons, must be shared by all. The burden of reparations and the impossibility of payment proved to be unwise and contributed to the war debt problem of the 1920's. The Allies desired a democratic government in Germany, but the onus of signing the treaty left the postwar German republic discredited with its citizens. The harsh terms gave Hitler an argument for popular support of the Nazis and permitted him to rationalize for disregard for the terms of the treaty. In defense of the harsh treaty it is pointed out that France needed security against the revival of a strong Germany. The terms that Germany imposed on Russia in the Treaty of Brest-Litovsk supposedly indicate that Germany would have imposed equally harsh terms upon the Allies if she had defeated them. The treaties awarded independence to several subject nationalities.

In the elections in 1918 and 1920 Wilson's party, the Democratic, was defeated. The United States Senate never approved the Treaty of Versailles, which Wilson brought back from Paris, but later made separate peace with Germany.

The League of Nations. The League of Nations was the special project of President Wilson. He compromised other points to win support of the League, because he believed such an international organization would remedy any mistakes made in the peace treaties. It was intended to prevent future wars by requiring peaceful settlement of disputes and by requiring the use of sanctions against any aggressor that might threaten peace.

The governmental structure of the League Covenant (constitution) provided, at the top, for a Council composed of the representatives of the great powers; the Council had authority to act in case of dangerous disputes. The Assembly, made up of representatives of all member nations, could deliberate but not legislate. The Secretariat was a permanent staff of civil servants created to carry on the continuous work of the League. A World Court was created as a successor to the Hague Court. The International Labor Organization was created to work closely with the League.

The League never had the effectiveness it might have had

if the United States had joined it. Wilson himself must share the responsibility for the defeat of the League, since he was unwilling to compromise the terms of the Treaty of Versailles—as the United States Senate wished. The election of Wilson's opponents, the Republicans, in the 1920 presidential election, seemed to indicate that Americans wanted to avoid involvement in European disputes. Wilson's foresight and idealism have since been vindicated by the general willingness of America and other nations to create and support the United Nations. Although Germany entered the League in 1926 and Russia in 1934, the League never became effective in the preservation of world peace. The League never became a truly international organization but served to enforce the terms of the Allied peace settlements at Paris.

REVIEW QUESTIONS

Multiple-choice:

1. The desires of which nation at the peace conference differed the most from the demands of the others? 1) The United States 2) Great Britain 3) France 4) Italy.

2. As regards the Fourteen Points and the adherence of the peacemakers to its promises 1) None of its provisions were observed 2) only the general provisions were fulfilled 3) it was mainly the provisions relating to the separate nations which were carried out.

3. Which was the *least* factor affecting the peace terms drawn up at Versailles? 1) Secret agreements made at the beginning of the war 2) the danger of communism spreading in Europe 3) the outcome of the elections in Allied countries at the end of the war 4) a Republican congressional victory in the 1918 elections in the United States.

4. The most important gain fought for by Wilson at the Peace Conference was 1) the organization of the League of Nations 2) the establishment of new nations 3) the restoration of Belgium 4) freedom of the seas.

5. The provision of the Treaty of Versailles most resented by Germany was   1) the return of Alsace-Lorraine   2) the war guilt clause   3) compulsory membership in the League   4) loss of her colonies.

6. The most prominent and largest new nation to regain independence was   1) Czechoslovakia   2) Serbia   3) Poland   4) Hungary.

7. The German islands in the Pacific were awarded mainly to 1) the United States   2) Great Britain   3) Japan   4) Australia.

8. The most unusual feature of the procedure in arriving at the terms of peace was   1) the exclusion of German representatives from the conference table   2) the hurry in which the terms were arrived at   3) the careful consultation of experts in arriving at the terms   4) the site of the proceedings.

9. The most prominent justification of the harsh terms imposed upon Germany was   1) the harsh terms imposed by Germany in the Treaty of Brest-Litovsk   2) Germany's unconditional surrender   3) the avowed war aims of Germany   4) the length of the war.

10. The United States did not join the League of Nations, because   1) the Republicans won the election in 1918   2) Wilson was unwilling to compromise with Republicans in the Senate   3) its terms did not recognize the Monroe Doctrine   4) Japan was permitted to join.

11. Who was least prominent among these delegates at Versailles?   1) Clemenceau   2) Orlando   3) Lloyd George   4) Wilson

FOR FURTHER READING

HARDBOUND:

Bailey, Thomas A., *Wilson and the Peacemakers* (1947). Critical of Wilson's efforts after World War I.

Birdsall, P., *Versailles Twenty Years After* (1941).

Bonsal, Stephen, *Suitors and Suppliants* (1946).

———, *Unfinished Business* (1944). Bonsal's books are written by an eyewitness at the peace conference and are for the general reader.

Cobban, Alfred, *National Self-Determination* (1945). Helpful treatment of the postwar settlement.

Gathorne-Hardy, Geoffrey, *The Fourteen Points and the Treaty of Versailles* (1940).

Nicholson, Harold, *Peacemaking, 1919* (1939). A first-hand account of one who attended the peace conference.

Nowak, K. F., *Versailles* (1929). A German viewpoint.

Sontag, Raymond, *European Diplomatic History, 1871-1932* (1933). Good short survey.

Tardieu, André, *The Truth About the Treaty* (1921). French view.

*1917   *Russian Revolution began*
March, strikes broke out in the capital, Petrograd.
July, Kerensky assumed leadership of the Revolution
November, Bolshevists in Petrograd took control of the Revolution and Kerensky went into exile

*1918   *March, Treaty of Brest-Litovsk signed*
July, Royal family executed

*1919   *"Red Terror" began*

*1921   *New Economic Policy began. Lenin went into semi-retirement*

1921-1922   *Drouth and famine*

*1924   *Lenin died; power struggle began between Stalin and Trotsky*

1928   *First Five-Year Plan began; kulaks forced into collectives*

1929   *Trotsky driven into exile*

1933   *United States recognized Soviet Russia*

1936   *Soviet constitution revised*

16. The Russian Revolution and the Soviet Government

In the Crimean War, the Russo-Japanese War, and again in World War I the Russian tsarist government with its graft and inefficiency proved incompetent to meet the war crises. The pent-up resentment of the people against decades of harsh rule by the tsars broke out in riots and in other violence. As in the French Revolution in 1789, the long-suppressed need for reform and desire for popular government broke forth with a vigor that matched the extent of earlier repression.

Causes of the Russian Revolution. At the opening of World War I the Russian armies had considerably more success than had been expected. But the Russians were soon forced to pull back, and subsequent offensives were mainly gestures. Shortages of guns and ammunition caused enormous losses of men killed, wounded, and taken prisoner. The prospect of further frightful war losses, shortages of necessities in the cities, the evil influence of Rasputin over the royal family, the refusal of the tsar to concede power to the Duma—these and other evidences of incompetence and of evil tyranny brought criticism and demands for change.

Outbreak of revolution. In early March, 1917, strikes broke out in the capital of Petrograd (formerly St. Petersburg, Leningrad today). The tsar, pursuing the old repressive measures, ordered troops to suppress the riots and dissolved the Duma. The Duma refused to dissolve, strikers defied the government by holding mass meetings, and the army sided with the people. The Revolution had begun.

The Duma created a provisional and liberal government headed by Prince Lvov. This middle-class revolutionary regime came under the leadership of Alexander Kerensky in July. The purpose of these liberals was to create a constitutional democracy, honor Russia's obligations, introduce reforms, and continue the war. In opposition to the liberal government, the radical Bolsheviks at Petrograd organized a soviet (local council) of workers and soldiers to carry out a Marxist revolution. The Bolsheviks cooperated at first with the Kerensky government while organizing their own soviets. The Germans took Lenin out of exile in Switzerland and helped him to return to Russia to lead the revolution. The Germans did so to weaken Russia, still at war on the Eastern Front. Lenin quickly established his leadership over the Bolshevists and helped them win control of the powerful soviets of Petrograd and Moscow.

The Kerensky government. The provisional government of Kerensky under the Duma accepted the responsibilities of government. The soviets controlled the military forces but permitted the Kerensky government to function until November, 1917. The provisional government busied itself with the prosecution of the war but suffered military defeats while the Bolsheviks, just released from prisons, gained control of the soviets. The provisional government under Kerensky failed to heed the wishes of the workers and peasants; it continued the war against their wishes; it did not immediately agree to the peasants' demand for land nor provide food for the hungry workers. Reactionary military leaders, as well as the Bolshevists, opposed the Kerensky provisional government.

**The Bolshevik Revolution.* Early in November, 1917, Lenin took advantage of a hunger crisis in Petrograd to lead an uprising among the sailors of the Baltic fleet and among local troops. He took control of the capital and Kerensky fled. In other large cities the soviets assumed control, and Lenin headed a new Council of the People's Commissars. In two months a Constituent Assembly was elected. When the Bolshevists failed to win control of the Assembly, they dissolved it by force. A dictatorship of the proletariat was established; Lenin, Trotsky, and Stalin all became leaders in the new government. One of the first acts of the Bolsheviks was to initiate peace negotiations with Germany. The Treaty of Brest-Litovsk was signed in March 3, 1918.

**Early Bolshevist rule.   Once in full power, the Bolshevists under Lenin put their extreme program of "War Communism" in effect. The great estates were confiscated by the peasants' soviets, and private ownership of land abolished. Factories were taken over by local workers' soviets. Banks, railways, mines, and church property were confiscated. Tsarist debts were all repudiated. The royal family, after several months of detention, were murdered by the Communists in July, 1918.

After March, 1918, civil war began in Russia. The Bolshevists (Reds) were opposed by anti-Bolshevist elements (Whites). Trotsky organized the Red Army which defeated the White armies one by one. Russia's former allies sent in troops to salvage Allied munition dumps and aid the enemies of the Bolshevists, but these troops were soon withdrawn. In 1919 the Red army reoccupied the Ukraine.

During the civil war the Bolshevists instituted a severe program of repression in order to crush the opposition. During a reign of terror, authorities estimate, millions were executed or died. Workers were forbidden to strike and the press was censored. A phase called the "Red Terror" was instituted in 1919. The Cheka, or secret police, to maintain the Bolshevists in power, searched out and executed counter-revolutionaries.

*Treaty of Brest-Litovsk.   The failure of Russia's military offensives, and the imminence of civil war caused Lenin to appeal to all the belligerents to conclude a *de facto* peace. Between

December 22 and March 3, 1918, Russia withdrew while the terms of the Treaty of Brest-Litovsk were being drawn up. Russia gave up her claim to Finland, Latvia, Esthonia, Lithuania, Poland, and the Ukraine.

***Lenin's New Economic Policy.** The task of quickly converting Russia to a thoroughgoing socialist regime proved too difficult. Production fell in industry; the peasants balked at surrendering their crops to feed the factory workers and began producing only what they needed for themselves. Drought and famine took the lives of about four million Russians in 1921-1922. Lenin, therefore, began a compromise program employing capitalistic incentives to motivate greater production, but it was made clear that the retreat was only temporary. The program was called the New Economic Policy (NEP). Private trade and foreign investment were encouraged.

*Socialist leaders.** Alexander Kerensky, the earliest prominent revolutionary leader, belonged to the Socialist Revolutionary Party. He was overthrown as prime minister of the second provisional government, because the policies of his weak bourgeois government were too moderate for Lenin. Kerensky went into exile when the Bolshevists captured Petrograd in November, 1919.

Nikolai Lenin succeeded Kerensky and practically became dictator. Lenin had become a revolutionary after his older brother had been executed for taking part in the plot against Tsar Alexander III. Lenin as early as 1903 became the strong intellectual and practical leader of the Bolshevist faction. Lenin led the revolutionary program from 1919 to 1921 along with two other of the most prominent Bolshevists, Trotsky and Stalin. From 1921 until his death in 1924 Lenin retired from active leadership, but until his death his prestige prevented a quarrel among the others who wished to succeed him.

Leon Trotsky, the son of a Jewish farmer, became a revolutionist in 1896. His activities brought numerous arrests and imprisonment in Siberia. He spent most of the years from 1902 to 1917 in exile but busied himself with socialist journalism. His main role in the Revolution was that of organizing the Red Army of which he became the commander-in-chief. In 1924 the struggle with Stalin for power began. Trotsky favored world revolution, but Stalin favored the tactic of creating a successful communist regime in Russia first. Trotsky was demoted in 1926, exiled in 1929, and murdered in Mexico in 1940.

Joseph Stalin, born in the Caucasus, became a Bolshevist in 1903. Stalin remained in Russia as an underground conspirator during the years preceding the Revolution. He served in various roles in the early years of Communist government. He strengthened himself by becoming a strong leader of the Communist Party. From 1924 to 1932 he intrigued and eliminated various competitors for power. By purges he consolidated his power by destroying nearly all the old Bolsheviks who might be able to overthrow him. In a series of publicized trials many of these "Trotskyists" made confessions and were executed. No one knows how the confessions were obtained from these hard-boiled revolutionaries.

Soviet economic planning.   In 1928 Stalin, now the leader of the Soviet government, with his advisers decided to resume the advance of socialism. The first Five-Year Plan, calling for the rapid industrialization of Russia, was put in effect. This kind of overall planning of the economy became the main feature of Soviet economic life thereafter as one economic plan succeeded another. Goals were set for the whole nation and quotas assigned to various production units, which were praised, investigated, or punished according to their fulfillment of these goals. This overall planning contrasted with the production of goods in capitalistic countries where production was determined by market demand. The great emphasis upon capital investment in such projects or factories and power projects limited the production of consumer goods and necessitated great sacrifices on the part of the people. Foreign engineers were hired to direct projects. Through this economic planning Russia was industrialized quickly but at great cost. Workers were encouraged but many punished or sent to Siberia for lack of cooperation.

Collectivization of agriculture. Lenin's ideal state was an industrialized one; only industrial states could produce the machines necessary for the survival of a great nation. Stalin's economic planning subordinated the peasants and agriculture to the needs of the state. The peasants had been permitted to own land and sell its produce in the free market, and the landowning peasants, called *kulaks,* prospered. Stalin, whose special interest was agricultural planning, began to liquidate the kulaks, who comprised a stronghold of private enterprise. The kulaks were forced to turn their land over to the collective farms; by the hundreds of thousands those who resisted were either killed or sent to Siberia. Mechanization made agriculture more efficient; government tractor stations furnished machinery to the collective farms and helped make the farms dependent upon the government.

Soviet government. The Union of Soviet Socialist Republics is one of autonomous republics. The different nationalities are represented in a Council of Nationalities and their special cultures are encouraged or at least tolerated. In 1936 the revised constitution provided a bicameral legislature called the Supreme Soviet; the Supreme Council was the upper house and the Council of Nationalities the lower house. Corresponding to an executive cabinet is the Council of People's Commissars, whose members are chosen in joint session by the Supreme Soviet. The Supreme Soviet is chosen by the provincial soviets who in turn are chosen by the local soviets in the towns. This structure is somewhat of a facade, for the decisions of state are determined by the Communist Party.

The Communist Party.   The Communist Party, the only political party permitted, runs the Soviet government. Whoever controls the party controls the government; Stalin's career illustrates this, since he achieved power not by holding government position but through control of the party. The party represents industrial workers primarily. The membership of the party is highly selective; only three percent or less of the Russian population have been members at any time.

At the local level the party is organized as cells; higher levels of organization culminate in the powerful central committee. The general secretary of the party, a Praesidium member, is the top party official; Stalin ruled as dictator by holding this position, as did Khrushchev. Above this is the Praesidium, an oligarchy which determines party policy and communicates policy decisions down into the lower levels of the hierarchy. Political police, the MVD, deal with party deviationists. A party-controlled press conducts propaganda and denounces opponents of party policy.

Soviet foreign policy.   At first the Soviet government concentrated upon building a strong communist system and avoiding foreign entanglements. The capitalistic nations of the West tried to insulate themselves against communist influence. A string of states from Finland to Rumania served as a *cordon sanitaire* to insulate the West against Russia. Russian changes in foreign policy were dictated by expediency. In the 1930's Communists were told to join "popular fronts" and cooperate with other socialist parties in the West.

From the beginning, the ultimate goal of the Russian

Communists was world revolution. Other nations, therefore, opposed the Reds in Russia. At first the Soviets worked to convert China to communism. Repudiation of foreign debts, the publication of the secret treaties, and the announced goal of working to promote class revolution all antagonized the nations of the West, who opposed the Reds and withheld recognition. During the later 1920's Russia renounced the Third International and won European recognition of the Soviet government and United States' recognition in 1933. Danger from Germany and Japan in the 1930's caused Russia to cooperate with the West and to support collective security by joining the League of Nations and by signing defensive treaties with France and Czechoslovakia.

After Russia was left out of the Munich pact, which abandoned Czechoslovakia to Hitler's Germany, Russia in 1939 cooperated with Germany in the non-aggression pact by which the two nations partitioned Poland. At the same time Russia began an attempt to conquer Finland and succeeded in reannexing the Baltic states in the same year.

Education and culture under the Soviets. The great achievement of Russian education was the abolition of illiteracy. Adult education, including indoctrination in Communist doctrine, was emphasized. Soviet schools prepare the individual primarily for his economic role in Russian society.

Cultural achievement of various kinds is encouraged by granting special privileges to individuals. Literature, art, and even science are expected to at least follow, if not actively support, party doctrine. Scientific theory is sometimes condemned as capitalistic or bourgeois if it contradicts Communist doctrine. Religion of any kind is discouraged as the opiate of the people. Religious property of all kinds was confiscated during the Revolution. However, policy toward religion has varied according to what party interests seem to require.

REVIEW QUESTIONS

Multiple-choice:

1. If Kerensky had remained in power Russia would have 1) dropped out of the war earlier   2) become a constitutional democracy   3) carried out no reforms.

2. The New Economic Policy mainly reflected the   1) Soviets' desire to attract investment capital   2) desire to soften foreign opposition to communism   3) need to make concessions to private initiative   4) importance of communizing agriculture.

3. Russian economic planning in the thirties emphasized the need to   1) increase agricultural production   2) prepare for war   3) become more aggressive with propaganda   4) develop industry.

4. During the period of "War Communism" the Soviets did all *except*   1) confiscate all large estates   2) conclude peace with Germany   3) murder the royal family   4) permit workers to strike.

5. An important difference between Trotsky and Stalin is that Trotsky   1) wanted to promote world revolution and Stalin wanted to make communism successful in Russia first   2) wanted to collectivize agriculture but Stalin did not   3) wished to spare the royal family but Stalin did not.

6. The most important decisions in Soviet government are made by   1) the local soviets   2) the Supreme Soviet   3) the Communist Party   4) national referendums.

7. The Communists antagonized other nations by all *except* 1) publishing the secret treaties of World War I   2) their avowed purpose of world revolution   3) building heavy industry   4) repudiating foreign debts.

Completion:

8. The Russian Revolution broke out first in the capital then known as the city of a) ..... . The legislative body of Russia known as the b) ..... refused to dissolve when ordered to do so by Tsar c) ..... .

9. The most prominent of the middle-class revolutionary leaders at the head of the Mensheviks was a) ..... . When he was forced to flee, the Revolution came under the leadership of the long-time Bolshevist leader b) ..... who shared leadership with the commander of the Red armies whose name was c) ...... After Lenin died Trotsky's power was gradually undermined by his rival named d) ......

10. The local councils that conducted the Revolution were called a) ...... The most extreme phase of the Revolution is known as the period of b) ..... Communism. It was followed by a period of compromise with capitalistic motivations known as the c) ......

11. Counter-revolutionary armies that opposed the Red armies were known as the a) ..... armies. The "Red Terror" was carried out by secret police known as the b) ......

12. The landowning peasants who were liquidated by Stalin were known as the ......

FOR FURTHER READING

HARDBOUND:

Deutscher, Isaac, *Stalin, A Political Biography* (1948).

Duranty, W., *U.S.S.R.: The Story of Soviet Russia* (1944).

Florinsky, M. T., *Toward an Understanding of the U.S.S.R.* (1939).

Kennan, George, *Russia Leaves the War* (1956). The Russian Revolution and the attitude of the Western nations toward it.

Pares, B., *Russia* (1941).

Vernadsky, G., *Lenin, Red Dictator* (1931).

PAPERBOUND:

Bauer, Raymond A., *et al.*, *How the Soviet System Works: Cultural, Psychological, and Social Themes* (Harvard). Based on interviews.

Brinton, Crane, *The Anatomy of Revolution* (Vintage). The best study of its kind; on the nature of three of the greatest modern revolutions.

Deutscher, Isaac, *Stalin: A Political Biography* (Vintage). Best biography of Stalin.

Fischer, Louis, *The Soviets in World Affairs* (2nd ed., abridged in Vintage edition).

Moorhead, Alan, *The Russian Revolution* (Bantam). Popular account.

Rauch, George van, *A History of Soviet Russia* (2nd ed., Praeger.)

Rostow, W. W., *et al.*, *The Dynamics of Soviet Society* (NAL). Attempt to analyze the Soviets' behavior.

Shub, David, *Lenin* (NAL abridgment). Excellent biography of Lenin.

Trotsky, Leon, *The Russian Revolution* (Abridged, Anchor and Universal.) Strong on early events of the Bolshevist period.

———, *Stalin* (Universal). By Stalin's exiled rival.

Wolfe, Bertram, *Three Who Made a Revolution* (Beacon). Very helpful classic.

1919   *Self-government extended in India. Home Rule granted to Ireland*

1920   *Republican election victory in the United States, a decision against the Treaty of Versailles and the League of Nations*

1921   *Reparations Commission assessed war damage claims at $33 billions against Germany*

1921-1922   *Washington Naval Conference*

1922-1925   *French troops occupied the Ruhr Valley when Germany failed to pay reparations installments*

1924   *Dawes Plan*
            Labor Party won its first election in Britain

1925   *Locarno Pacts began a few years of better relations in Europe*

1926   *Critical general strike in Great Britain*

1927   *Geneva Conference failed*

*1928   *Pact of Paris renounced war*

1929   *Young Plan*
            Worldwide Great Depression began

1931   *Hoover moratorium*
            British Statute of Westminster recognized independence of the Dominions

1932   *Lausanne Agreement drastically reduced debt payments. Allies made token payments to the United States and defaulted completely afterward*
            Franklin D. Roosevelt elected president

*1933   *Nazis came to power and began the rearmament of Germany*

213

Large program of New Deal legislation enacted

1935   Self-government further extended by the Government of India Act

1936   King George V died. Edward VIII abdicated and George VI became king

Popular Front government came to power in France under Leon Blum, Socialist

17. The Western Nations from 1919 to 1939

The war that had been fought "to make the world safe for democracy" left the United States disillusioned. By 1939 dictatorships had sprung up over eastern Europe. The only remaining democracies were Britain, France, Belgium, the Netherlands, Switzerland, Finland, Norway, Denmark, and Sweden. The United States failed to provide the leadership that the West needed to preserve the peace.

In this chapter we review first the significant developments in the postwar readjustment of international relations and then the developments relating to particular nations. The revolutionary governments of Russia, Germany, and Italy are discussed in other chapters. In the 1930's international problems and crises dominated domestic life of the separate countries, as well as the international scene, and are accordingly discussed together in Chapter 19.

INTERNATIONAL RELATIONS

Among the European democracies in the twenties, the international problems deserve more attention than those of a purely domestic nature. The first problem to dominate international relations was that of the inter-governmental debts. Another was the search for peace and security.

Nature of the war debts problem. Relation between participants in World War I, whether allies or enemies, were bedeviled by the complex problem of inter-governmental debts. These debts were of two kinds: 1] the inter-allied debts resulting from loans made to the Allies by the United States and 2] the reparations assessed against the defeated nations, mainly against Germany. The attempts to collect the obligations fostered antagonisms among all nations concerned. France and Great Britain revengefully sought full payment from Germany for the full cost of the war, and the United States regarded the complex problem of repayment to it of wartime credits as a simple obligation that honest debtors ought to meet.

All the debtors found it difficult to pay because of the wartime damage to their economies and the unwillingness of the United States to lower her tariffs and accept payment in goods. The debts had been created by the sale of American goods, but America wished to be paid in gold. But the United States already held the larger part of the world's monetary gold. The payments problem caused not only ill-feeling but contributed to economic breakdown and world depression.

In several steps the burden of the debts was reduced through American negotiation. When Germany became defiant enough and the world depression struck, she stopped making payments. Britain and France insisted that payment of obligations to the United States was dependent upon collecting from Germany. Eventually all debtor nations except Finland practically repudiated the obligations. The United States recognized the evil effects of such postwar debts by avoiding the problem in the Second World War. The steps by which the nations attempted to solve these problems now need to be traced.

Attempted solution of the reparations problem. In 1921 the reparations commission assessed the damage payments due from Germany at 33 billions of dollars. The indemnity was out of all proportion to such indemnities in the past, and economists said it could never be collected. But Allied politicians had promised to make Germany pay and, under the Versailles settlement, gave themselves the right to take punitive action if Germany failed to pay. In 1922 Germany fell far short of meeting the annual installment then due. Poincaré of France responded by sending French troops to seize Germany's industrial Ruhr Valley. The credit of the German government collapsed, and the mark rapidly lost its value in a wild inflation.

The Dawes Plan was drawn up and put in effect in 1924 by an international committee headed by the American banker, Charles G. Dawes. A loan was made to stabilize the German currency and to aid the recovery of German industry. The Dawes Plan arranged to reduce the annual payments temporarily. The French evacuated the Ruhr Valley in 1925.

The Young Plan in 1929, drawn up under the advice of another American banker, Owed D. Young, limited the total reparations bill against Germany to nine billions of dollars and amortized the debt over a period of fifty-nine years. The remaining Allied troops were withdrawn from the Rhineland and Germany made further payments.

The "Hoover Moratorium" in 1931 was put in effect by the American president, Herbert Hoover, because of the severity of the Great Depression. It allowed all debtors to postpone payments for one year in order to aid their recovery. The Lausanne Agreement the next year drastically reduced Germany's bill to two billions of dollars. But Hitler came to power in 1933 and repudiated the Versailles settlement.

The Allied debts to America.   The Allies, Britain, France, and Belgium, insisted that the whole inter-governmental debts problem was interrelated and expected the United States to reduce or cancel Allied obligations as the Allies had done for Germany. At Lausanne the United States government had reduced the debts from eleven billions of dollars to seven billions by 1932. The United States refused further reductions, but in 1932 the former Allies made only token payments and thereafter defaulted completely. Finland, the exception, paid because she owed less and enjoyed a favorable balance of trade with the United States. In World War II the United States aided the Allies by lend-lease instead of credit sales of wartime supplies.

The Allies' difficulties in paying the debts was due to American tariffs that prevented the export of goods to the United States. Only by earning American gold could the Allies earn money to apply to debt repayment. The Allies could not reduce their own gold reserves further without wrecking their currencies and economies.

The problem of peace and security.   American failure to join the League left that agency weak. France's great fear that Germany might recover and seek revenge caused her to seek allies for security. In 1920 France made a secret defensive alliance with Belgium and in 1921 with Poland. Other states that had benefited from or had been created by the war also had an interest in protecting themselves against a resurgent Germany. Czechoslovakia, Rumania, and Yugoslavia formed a defensive alliance in 1920, and Poland soon joined them. France concluded treaties with Czechoslovakia in 1924 and with Yugoslavia in 1927 and thus tied all the foregoing states together in an alliance. French support of the eastern European states served to block the expansion of Communist Russia by creating the *"cordon sanitaire"* of buffer states. France assumed great armaments burdens of maintaining the largest army and airforce in Western Europe. France built the Maginot Line along the German border, an immensely costly and elaborate defense system of barriers above ground and interconnected fortifications underground.

The Locarno Pacts (1925).   At Locarno, Switzerland, five treaties were drawn up to settle controversies that might cause war. Aristide Briand of France and Gustav Stresemann of Germany, seeking mutual reconciliation, called the conference, which was attended also by Great Britain, Italy, Belgium, Poland, and Czechoslovakia. France, Germany, and Belgium agreed to accept their borders as drawn by the Versailles Treaty, and Britain and Italy undertook to guarantee these agreements. France, Germany, and Belgium sought further to prevent war by agreeing to submit future disputes to arbitration. Other agreements made were similar to those just outlined. In 1926 Germany was admitted to the League as a result of the "spirit of Locarno."

The Pact of Paris (1928). Briand next drew up a pledge renouncing war as a solution for quarrels. The pact was also called the Kellogg-Briand Pact, because the American Secretary of State Kellogg participated in drafting it. The Pact was signed by fifteen nations, and later others signed until the total increased to nearly fifty nations. The right to make war for self-defense and and the absence of means for the enforcement of the pact against violators or enemies of the League of Nations practically nullified the agreement.

Naval disarmament. In 1921 the United States invited the leading naval powers to a conference in Washington to consider the reduction of naval armaments and cessation of a naval armaments race. The ratio of capital ships of 5:5:3:1.7:1.7 was accepted by the United States, Great Britain, Japan, France, and Italy respectively. A ten-year holiday in the construction of capital ships was also accepted. The other treaties signed sought to preserve peace in the Far East and Pacific.

Several subsequent naval disarmament conferences failed to achieve further success. In Geneva, Britain and the United States failed to agree in 1927. At London in 1930, the United States, Britain, and Japan agreed to extend the naval holiday and the 5:5:3 ratio to cruisers and submarines. The Geneva Disarmament Conference in 1932-1934 failed, because Japan and Germany had begun their defiant attitudes. Rearmament began in 1933 in Germany.

The League of Nations. The League began to operate in 1920 and met regularly at Geneva. Although it ultimately failed, as did other efforts to preserve international law and order, its contribution to preserving peace and the experience gained by this predecessor of the United Nations deserve to be mentioned to its credit. The League did help to settle incidents that might have caused war.

THE UNITED STATES

After World War I the United States played a role of half-hearted cooperation in European affairs. Americans cynically wished to avoid involvement in Europe's quarrels and shrank from the role of leadership which its great power status had thrust upon it. It failed also to recognize that during the war it had shifted from a debtor to a creditor nation.

The conservatism and prosperity of the twenties. In the election of 1920 the United States overwhelmingly rejected Wilson, the Democratic Party, and the League of Nations. Harding won the election and was succeeded by the equally conservative administrations of Coolidge and Hoover. Prewar Progressivism was forgotten. A wave of anti-foreignism manifested itself in such developments as the rise of the Ku Klux Klan, immigration restriction, and the Sacco-Vanzetti case. Big business took credit for the great prosperity that most Americans enjoyed, except the farmers. Manufacturers received the benefits of higher protective tariff rates, but farmers received no material government aid and prices of commodities fell under mounting surpluses. A great wave of speculation in the stock market resulted in the Great Crash of 1929 which precipitated the prolonged Great Depression of the thirties. The depression was caused by the overexpansion of agriculture and industry, the high tariff policy which reduced foreign trade, and the failure to share the profits of industry with farmers and workers. The length and severity of the depression were not anticipated. President Hoover took more steps to fight the depression than any president had ever taken before, but he condemned any measures that might lead to socialism. His "rugged individualism" came to be called "ragged individualism" as more people blamed the lack of government action for the severity of the depression.

***The New Deal.** In the election of 1932 the Democratic Party was assured of victory. The election of Franklin D. Roosevelt began a major effort to bring relief, recovery, and reform. In the "Hundred Days" beginning in March, 1933, a great program of domestic legislation ushered in the New Deal. Up to 1939 a large number of reform laws were enacted and brought in permanent changes of revolutionary proportions. Their effect, however, was to modify and preserve the free enterprise system and democratic institutions which in other countries had been swept away by the effects of the depression. Farmers benefited from fixed prices and government payments. Labor was encouraged to organize unions for collective bargaining, and they did so with alacrity. The Social Security Act of 1935 affected more people than any other measure and brought various benefits that similar legislation had begun in Europe as early as the 1880's. For the protection of the public, financial legislation brought reform and regulation of banking, public utilities, and the securities markets. The gold standard was modified and reflation undertaken to correct the deflation that had lasted from 1921 to 1933. The most stubborn problem that defied solution was that of unemployment. In spite of all the measures to restore prosperity, only a limited recovery was achieved. Unemployment remained about as high as ever until World War II took men into the armed services and into war industries.

THE BRITISH EMPIRE AND COMMONWEALTH

Great Britain's problems after World War I arose mainly from and reflected her decline in economic affluence. (It should be understood that in most historical discussion the word "decline" in reference to nations or to various changes may mean a relative decline and not necessarily an absolute one.)

***The economic decline of Great Britain.** The decline of Britain's pre-war economic strength relative to that of other nations revealed itself in several difficulties during the twenties and thirties. After 1919 her foreign trade dropped, she suffered from severe unemployment, and found herself burdened with a heavy postwar debt. Britain had been forced to sell her foreign investments to finance the war against Germany and no longer retained her creditor position and the flow of income from investments abroad. The United States now assumed the creditor role of banker and financier to the world. Britain lost her large export market for coal because other nations produced more. Britain's mines produced only at high cost, and petroleum (which she did not possess) replaced coal as fuel in many places. Britain lost the income from much of her shipping, which had been sunk by German submarines. These were the problems that politicians had to deal with.

Labor and Conservative Governments. In 1918 the Conservatives became the strongest party in Britain, but they permitted the Liberal David Lloyd George to continue as prime minister until 1922. The Liberals declined to a third party status, and the Labor Party in 1922 became the leading opposition to the Conservatives who now returned to power. Stanley Baldwin became prime minister in 1923 and proposed a return to protective tariffs but suffered defeat on the issue in 1924.

The Labor Party first attained control of the British government in 1924 under Prime Minister Ramsay MacDonald, a moderate socialist. MacDonald's ministry was broadly based and included many small businessmen and professional people, since it depended upon the Liberals for support. Under MacDonald, Britain recognized Soviet Russia.

Baldwin and the Conservatives returned to office in 1924. In 1926 he faced a critical general strike that began with coal miners who opposed a cut in wages and a lengthened work day. The Trades Union Congress called a general strike in support of the miners. Volunteers and labor opponents ran essential industries and after nine days the crippling strike was called off by the trades unionists. Parliament reacted by passing the anti-labor Trades Disputes Act in 1927.

The Labor Party under MacDonald returned to power again in 1929, but was restrained by its dependence upon Liberal support. MacDonald's failure to appease the radical Laborites brought a new election in which MacDonald was retained in office with the support of a coalition of large factions of all three parties. But this was essentially a conservative government, a remarkable political switch for MacDonald. He proceeded to deal with the problems of the depression. Britain went off the gold standard and devalued the pound, social services were reduced; protective tariffs and imperial preference tariffs were passed. The abandonment of the gold standard and of free trade finally gave recognition to the weakened economic position of Britain.

A crisis over the British crown arose in 1936 when George V died. His son, Edward, inherited the throne. Edward VIII had fallen in love with a twice-divorced American, Mrs. Wallis Warfield Simpson, and soon announced his decision to marry her. The Church of England and conservative English opinion throughout the Commonwealth opposed the marriage. Edward abdicated rather than give up his plans. Edward's younger brother took the throne as George VI.

FRANCE AND THE OTHER DEMOCRACIES

After the war France busied herself with reconstruction at home and at making herself diplomatically and militarily secure against Germany.

France in the 1920's. Most of the fighting on the Western Front had been on French soil. The enormous destruction left France with a major task of physical reconstruction after the return of peace. Heavy losses of manpower—French dead numbered 1,385,000 and the wounded were many more—and property destruction during the war crippled her resources for recovery. Nevertheless, the French set to work with energy and repaired the war damage in less than a decade. French dreams that German reparations would pay for the reconstruction proved a delusion. France herself had to assume the great burden of financing the reconstruction, since Germany was unable to make full reparations.

The French government in 1919 came under the control of a conservative coalition under Premier Poincaré, who concerned himself with the task of reconstruction and the implementation of a vindictive policy of making Germany pay the whole cost of the war. In 1924, the Left Cartel began two years in power. They were unsuccessful in increasing income taxes and could not preserve the value of the fast-eroding franc. In 1926 the National Union coalition took control under Poincaré. Drastic measures of taxation saved the franc, but not until it had lost eighty percent of its value. French bondholders involuntarily paid most of the war debt by suffering heavy depreciation in the value of their holdings. Workmen's insurance was passed and reconstruction completed.

France in the 1930's. France failed to recover from the effects of the Great Depression as other countries had done. The paralysis of her multiparty system and financial corruption in government left France almost helpless. Fascist organizations arose during the depression. In 1936 a Popular Front government came into power under the Socialist Leon Blum; legislation was passed to aid farmers and workers and to restore government finances. Edouard Daladier succeeded to power in 1937. France was torn between her Right and Left factions during this decade. She felt compelled to maintain heavy expenditures on a huge armaments and defense establishment.

THE BRITISH COMMONWEALTH AND EMPIRE

The self-governing Dominions of the British Empire had voluntarily come to England's aid in the war, but at the peace conference and during the twenties they displayed a concern for their own interests.

Status of the Dominions defined. The Dominions—Canada, Australia, the Union of South Africa, and New Zealand—had their relationship with Great Britain clarified at the Imperial Conference of 1926. The conference recognized that the Dominions were "autonomous communities within the British Empire equal in status, in no way subordinate one to another . . . though united by a common allegiance to the Crown, and freely associated as members of the British Commonwealth of Nations."

The Statute of Westminster in 1931 provided that the British Parliament could no longer pass laws for the Dominions nor void the acts of a Dominion parliament. The Dominions became independent, but sentiments of loyalty to the British Crown, common language, customs, cultural heritage, and mutual economic interests still held the Dominions to England.

The British Empire, apart from the Commonwealth, consisted of outright possessions, such as India and the Crown colonies. Still other lands were held as mandates, protectorates, leaseholds, and under other dependent relationships.

Ireland. War had interrupted Irish Home Rule in 1914. Irish extremists rebelled in 1916 in the "Easter Rebellion." In 1918 the radical republican Sinn Fein party won control of Ireland and refused to send its members to the British Parliament. A guerrilla war began with Britain that lasted until 1923. In 1920 a new law gave Ireland Home Rule and provided a separate parliament for Ulster (Northern Ireland). In 1922 the Sinn Feiners accepted the Irish Free State and Dominion status. In 1923 Irish violence quieted down as Eamon De Valera, the radical leader who wanted complete separation, changed his strategy. Ireland joined the League of Nations in 1923. In 1932 De Valera gained power and continued his effort to break all ties with Great Britain. The new state was renamed *Eire.* In World War II Eire did not join Britain but remained neutral and unfriendly. In 1949 the name was changed to the Republic of Ireland, and Ireland declared complete independence, an already accomplished fact. Ulster remained a part of the United Kingdom.

*India. The Indian (Hindu) National Congress and the Moslem League expected Britain to concede Indian self-government in return for cooperation in World War I, but Britain found it difficult to give up India. 1] Many Englishmen opposed the surrender of a land that had long yielded such large profits. 2] India was almost certain to relapse into complex civil war among its many antagonistic peoples. 3] Russia or Japan might step in and take over India.

The Government of India Act in 1919 increased native self-government further. The Indian National Congress Party under the great Mohandas K. Gandhi refused to cooperate except under complete home rule. Gandhi encouraged nonviolence or passive resistance to the British government. In 1935 another Government of India Act provided for increased self-government but fell far short of the goals of the radical National Congress under Jawaharlal Nehru. The Moslem League under Mohammed Ali Jinnah wanted India divided between Moslems and Hindus. World War II helped India gain freedom.

Egypt. Egypt, though nominally under Turkish suzerainty, was actually ruled by Britain and occupied by British forces since 1882. After World War I Egypt became a British protectorate, but the extreme nationalism of the Egyptians won independence under a constitutional monarchy headed by King Feisal. Egypt still resisted British control of both the Suez Canal and the Egyptian Sudan to the south. The nationalist Wafd party demanded complete evacuation of British forces from the Suez and the Sudan.

Palestine and Iraq. Of the territories mandated to Britain by the League of Nations, Palestine and Iraq proved to be the most troublesome. During World War I the British promised Palestine would be set aside as a homeland for the Jews. Britain granted Iraq independence in return for a treaty of alliance in 1932. Iraq became an Arab kingdom and a member of the League. The Arab Mohammedan majority there wanted independence and Britain set aside a region east of the Jordan River as Trans-Jordan (now Jordan) and granted it independence in 1928. The conflict between Jews and Arabs delayed the settlement of the Palestine question until after World War II.

REVIEW QUESTIONS

Multiple-choice:
1. The United States took the lead in working out arrangements to facilitate payment of international war debts because she

1) was the largest creditor nation   2) wished to keep Germany weak   3) needed gold   4) wished to prevent Communism from spreading.

2. The credit of Germany collapsed and the *mark* lost its value when   1) France occupied the Ruhr Valley   2) the Dawes Plan went into effect   3) the depression struck   4) Hitler came into power.

3. Which did *not* reduce the burden of international debt obligations in some way?   1) The Young Plan   2) the Dawes Plan   3) the Hoover Moratorium   4) the Locarno treaties.

4. Which nation *never* joined the League of Nations?   1) France   2) the United States   3) Germany   4) Russia   5) Japan.

5. The strongest military power on land in Europe after World War I was presumed to be   1) Russia   2) Britain   3) France   4) Turkey.

6. To protect herself against German aggression during the 1920's France did all *except*   1) build the Maginot Line   2) voluntarily return the Saar to Germany   3) make treaties of alliance with several small countries on Germany's borders   4) maintain a large standing army.

7. The New Deal in the United States brought   1) only slight changes in American government and society   2) only temporary changes   3) permanent changes of great significance   4) a return of economic prosperity.

8. In the 1920's Great Britain experienced all *except*   1) a return of the Labor Party to power   2) regaining her former creditor status   3) abandonment of the gold standard   4) suffering from great unemployment.

Completion:

9. The independence of the British Dominions was recognized in 1931 by the parliamentary Statute of a) ...... The freely associated nations became known as b) ...... The British king who resigned in 1936 was c) ......

10. The nationalist party which gained independence for Ireland was the a) ..... party. The name of its most prominent leader was b) ......

11. The notable leader of the Indian independence movement in the 1920's and 1930's was a) ...... His great weapon was b) ..... resistance.

Matching:

12. Herbert Hoover	a. Labor prime minister in Great Britain
13. Aristide Briand	
14. Franklin D. Roosevelt	b. Moslem leader in India
15. Ramsay MacDonald	c. American president during the worst of the Great Depression
16. Ali Jinnah	
17. Nehru	d. Took vigorous steps to end the American depression
18. Poincaré	
19. Leon Blum	e. Author of a famous peace pact
	f. Popular Front premier in the thirties
	g. Conservative premier in France
	h. Radical National Congress leader

FOR FURTHER READING

HARDBOUND:

Benns, Frank, *Europe Since 1914 in Its World Setting* (6th ed., 1946). A textbook survey.

Black, Cyril E., and Helmreich, E. C., *Twentieth Century Europe* (1950).

Buell, R. L., The Washington Conference (1922).

Carr, Edward H., *A History of Soviet Russia* (4 vols., 1950-1954). Detailed account of the Revolution.

Gulick, Charles, *Austria from Habsburg to Hitler* (2 vols., 1948).

Halperin, Sidney, *Germany Tried Democracy* (1946). On the Weimar Republic.

Keynes, John M., *The Economic Consequences of the Peace* (1920). A famous book by one who foresaw the economic effects of the Allied demands for reparations.

Langsam, W. C., *The World since 1914* (1948). Survey.

Martins, J. P. de Oliveira, *A History of Iberian Civilization* (1930). The best general work on Spain and Portugal.

May, Arthur, *Europe and Two World Wars* (1947).

Miller, D. H., *The Peace Pact of Paris* (1928).

Moulton, H. G. and Pasvolsky, L., *War Debts and World Prosperity* (1932).

Mowat, Charles L., *Britain between the Wars, 1918-1940* (1953).

Vlekke, B. H. M., *The Evolution of the Dutch Nation* (1945).

Wilson, F., *The Origins of the League Covenant* (1928).

PAPERBOUND:

Allen, Frederick Lewis, *Only Yesterday* (Bantam). Scholarly and popular account of the United States during the 1920's.

Bailey, Sydney D., *British Parliamentary Democracy* (Houghton Mifflin).

Bury, J. P. T., *France, 1814-1940* (Perpetua).

Carr, E. H., *Twenty Years' Crisis, 1919-1939* (Torchbooks).

Gandhi, Mohandas K., *Autobiography* (Beacon).

Kennan, George F., *American Diplomacy, 1900-1950* (NAL). Critical of American foreign policies.

Knapton, Ernest J., *France Since Versailles* (Berkshire). Short account for students.

Leuchtenburg, William E., *The Perils of Prosperity, 1914-1932.* Useful survey of the United States in the period, written for college students.

Leuthy, Herbert, *France Against Herself* (Meridian). Problems of France in recent times.

Nanda, B. R., *Mahatma Gandhi* (Barron's Educational Series, Inc.).

1900-1946	*Victor Immanuel III, king of Italy*
*1918	*The German Empire (Second Reich) overthrown*
1919	*Weimar constitution adopted in Germany*
1920	*Allies forced Italy to abandon Fiume*
1923	*Germany suffered disastrous inflation*
	Dictatorship of Primero de Rivera
1924	*Fascists murdered the Socialist leader Matteotti*
	Dawes Plan put in effect in Germany
*1925	*Mussolini proclaimed his dictatorship*
	Hindenburg elected president of Germany
1929	*Lateran Treaty settled quarrel between the Papacy and the Italian government*
1931	*Spanish Republic set up*
*1933	*Hitler came to power in Germany*
	Germany withdrew from the League of Nations
1935	*Hitler repudiated the Versailles Treaty restrictions on Germany*
1936	*Germany reoccupied the Rhineland*
*1936-1939	*Spanish Civil War results in victory of General Franco*

18. The Rise of Fascism

A lack of confidence in political democracy and dissatisfaction with the capitalistic, free enterprise economic system caused two new totalitarian systems to challenge the parliamentary democracies of Western Europe. The first of these, the communist system in Russia, has been discussed. Fascism, the other system, arose first in Italy, then in Germany, and under dictatorships spread in varying degrees to other countries.

FASCISM IN ITALY

Italy suffered from unusually great political confusion, economic breakdown, and disillusionment after World War I. This environment was conducive to the rise of the fascist state in Italy, the first fascist government in postwar Europe.

Background of Italian fascism. After unification, Italy failed to gain a satisfying role in international affairs; after World War I she was further disappointed at not receiving more of the promised spoils of victory. In her political life, Italy had never developed a workable democracy. Bribery, fixed elections, and numerous splinter parties characterized her politics. Overpopulation and lack of natural resources kept the country in poverty.

After the war, Italy suffered from unemployment, strikes, industrial anarchy, and frequent changes in government. The histrionic poet Gabriele D'Annunzio had taken Fiume and established a semi-fascist regime there soon after the war, but

Italy was forced by the Allies to make a humiliating retreat in 1920. Radical Socialists made political gains, and active Communists hoped to create a proletarian state.

**Mussolini takes control. Before Mussolini, D'Annunzio had led his right-wing nationalist followers into Fiume. This faction adopted a distinctive black shirt and adopted the ancient Roman arm salute as Mussolini did later. Benito Mussolini, son of a blacksmith and himself the publisher of Socialist newspapers, had advocated an Italian alliance with Britain and France when World War I broke out. He entered the army and was wounded in the war. After the war he formed a fascist organization among the war veterans and socialists and began to advocate a political program that appealed to patriotic sentiments for a stronger Italy. The fascists advocated a program to aid workers, offered assurances to capitalists who feared communism, and promised to restore order and stability.

The fascist groups engaged in physical attacks on political opponents, especially communists, and broke up their meetings. Mussolini's black-shirted troops broke strikes and tortured and intimidated political opponents. In 1921 the fascists won thirty-five seats in parliament and had a following of over 200,000 persons, mostly from the middle class. In October, 1922, Mussolini made preparation for his famous "March on Rome." King Victor Emmanuel invited him to form a new government. At first he had only emergency powers, but he abolished most of the other political parties and worked to gain further control over the Italian government and to repress opposition; it required several years to achieve these goals. In 1924 the socialist leader, Giacomo Matteotti, was murdered by Mussolini's men. Shocked public opinion reacted against the fascists, but Mussolini discovered the weakness of his opponents; in 1925 he formally proclaimed his dictatorship.

**The fascist state.   The fascists had no well-formulated program but one took shape gradually as problems came up. Unlike communism, fascism has no definite program prepared for application everywhere but adapts itself to the particular national circumstances where it takes root.

The Italian Senate was retained but dominated by fascists. Victor Emmanuel III (1900-1946) retained the throne but only as a figurehead. The Chamber of Deputies lost its power and was replaced later by an appointive Chamber of Fasces and Corporations. The fascists established the "corporate state" by organizing various parts of the economy as syndicates or corporations and basing representation in government upon such economic groupings. Geographical representation was replaced by representation from economic groups—at least on the surface.

The real power of government, however, resided in *Il Duce,* as Mussolini was called, and in the Fascist Party's Grand Council, the members of which held all important government posts. Mussolini himself held as many as eight ministerial posts at one time. Fascist Party members filled most government posts everywhere. Local government was brought under the highly centralized control of Rome.

Fascist economic program.   Much attention was given to strengthening Italy's economic life. In agriculture, irrigation and drainage projects and improved practices helped increase production. The fuel shortage of Italy was offset by construction of hydroelectric power projects. Industry failed to develop as Mussolini planned and unemployment remained a chronic problem. Debt harassed the government and taxes remained high. Heavy rearmament expenses and the need to import foodstuffs and various raw materials kept Italy economically weak.

Accord with the Papacy. In 1927 Pius XI condemned fascist theories regarding the supremacy of the state. But in 1929 the Lateran Treaty settled the quarrel that had persisted since 1870 between the Papacy and the state. Catholic teaching was restored in the schools. Vatican City was recognized as a sovereign state, Roman Catholicism as the official religion, and a large sum paid to the Church to give up its claims against the state. The Holy See in return recognized the Kingdom of Italy. Papal pronouncements in the thirties denounced militarism and extremist patriots and suggested that money spent for armaments be used for humane services.

Totalitarian aspects of fascism. Fascism as a political doctrine emphasizes the primacy of unity and of obedience by the people to the state. The individual is subordinated to the state. All organizations are either used, subordinated, or affected by the centralizing power of government. Force was exalted in foreign affairs and war glorified. Labor lost its right to strike and industrial disputes were usually settled by Fascist advisers in the interest of employers. Private property was protected but regulated more and more in the interest of the state. A high birth rate was encouraged. Public buildings and other large projects gave Italian Fascism a progressive face.

NAZI GERMANY

In 1918 Germany overthrew the Second Reich and subsequently established the Weimar Republic which in turn was discarded by the Nazis who established the Third Reich.

***The Weimar Republic. Friedrich Ebert, leader of the Social Democrats, the majority party, assumed authority as soon as Emperor William II abdicated. Communists, called "Spartacists," failed in their attempts to gain control. The moderate parties elected a majority of delegates to the constitutional convention; among them the Social Democrats was the leading party. At Weimar, Germany's cultural center, an exceptionally liberal constitution was written in 1919. It provided that the president and a chancellor share the executive power. Proportional representation created a system of splinter parties. The president had the extraordinary power of issuing emergency decrees.

The Republic was discredited from the beginning by having to sign the humiliating Treaty of Versailles. In 1923 Germany suffered a disastrous inflation when the French occupied the Ruhr region; the middle class saw their savings melt away with the inflation of paper money. The Dawes Plan (1924) arrangements revived the German economy, however, and there followed a period of considerable progress and recovery. During this period Gustav Stresemann, who was in charge of foreign affairs, did much to restore good will toward Germany by his cooperation with the former enemy powers. The dignified old Field Marshal Paul von Hindenburg was elected president in 1925 and reelected in 1932. He disappointed those nationalists who wanted more concessions wrung from the Allies, concessions that would have increased the prestige of the Republic with the people of Germany.

Hitler's rise to power. After Germany began to suffer the effects of the worldwide depression beginning in 1929, the National Socialist Party under Adolf Hitler began its rapid rise to power. In January, 1933, President Hindenburg was pressured into inviting Hitler to organize a cabinet, and Hitler became chancellor at a time when his party still lacked a majority in the Reichstag. In March, 1933, Hitler called a new election to increase his following in the Reichstag. On the eve of the election the Reichstag building was set on fire by Nazis, but communists were blamed for the clandestine act. The emergency clause of the Weimar constitution was invoked to suppress Hitler's opponents, but he still won only forty-four percent of the national vote. But by combining with another smaller party Hitler secured a parliamentary majority, and, with the support of the Catholic Center Party, an Enabling Act was passed awarding dictatorial powers to the government. Opposition parties were now dissolved and the National Socialists (abbreviated NAZIS) began a one-party rule, a regime that lasted until Hitler lost the war and committed suicide in 1945). Hitler appointed more Nazis to his cabinet. After President Hindenburg died in 1934, Hitler merged the office of president with his own office of chancellor. Hitler rose to power by democratic means and took advantage of the power of office and the support of other parties to make himself dictator. After becoming dictator it was easy enough to consolidate his power over the nation. A revolution had been won by the Nazis.

**Background of Nazi success. This fateful overthrow of the Weimar Republic occurred for several reasons. 1] Like Italy, Germany had not developed a tradition of democratic government after 1870. The Weimar Republic was viewed as a discredit to democracy. Furthermore, influences in Germany's past created a reverence for authoritarianism. 2] Germans felt humiliated and offended by what they regarded as the betrayal of the Treaty of Versailles with its war guilt clause, impossible reparations, and other severe terms. They called it a *diktat;* they had expected a negotiated peace adhering to the Fourteen Points. In 1919 Hitler chose to make a career of restoring Germany's former power. He began his career by agitation—appealing to others and convincing them that Germany had not lost the war but had been stabbed by "pacifist traitors." 3] Middle classes supported Hitler because of his nationalism, his campaign against communists, and because they had been ruined by the inflation in 1923. 4] The coming of the depression and the failure of successive cabinets to deal successfully with the problems of unemployment and other depression-caused sufferings helped Hitler gain votes rapidly after 1928. 5] The emergency clause of the Weimar constitution not only permitted Hitler to win power but its use had discredited democratic processes earlier.

Hitler and his followers watched Mussolini's rise to power, imitated Italian Fascist methods of agitation, made about the same appeals to the disillusioned, and achieved office and consolidated their power along the same lines. Both received financial aid from wealthy industrialists, both appealed to the middle-class fears of communism, and both made appeals to socialists and the nationalists. Similarities in these expressions of fascism could be extended indefinitely.

***Nazi policies.* In government Nazis effected their rule without sweeping aside the existing machinery, but it was operated in a different way. The Reichstag remained but met less often and acted as a rubber stamp for the Nazi Party. Elections were held to allow the people to approve Nazi acts. The federal states were brought under centralized control. The legal system changed to place the welfare of the state above that of the individual. The Gestapo, secret police, made secret arrests, and concentration camps received thousands of political dissenters.

In economic policy the government kept its promise to provide jobs for all by planning a public works program. Labor unions lost the right to strike and were brought under control of a "Labor Front." Owners of industrial property had to adhere to government regulations of all kinds; in fact, the whole economy was subject to controls similar to emergency or wartime regulations. Farmers were more favored than workers. National economic independence became a leading Nazi goal. In the absence of a German gold-based currency, Dr. Hjalmar Schacht, a financial genius, devised a system of special currencies and barter deals to extend Germany's foreign trade.

In foreign policy Hitler kept his promise to repudiate the limitations on armaments and other restrictions of the Versailles Treaty. Germany withdrew from the League (1933). Rearmament was begun in 1935. The next year the Rhineland was reoccupied in defiance of the Allies. His territorial annexations are a part of the account of the origins of World War II.

Fascist characteristics. Certain beliefs and conduct are characteristic of fascism. Prominent among these are theories of racial superiority. This may involve the persecution of "inferior" or "enemy" people. Extreme nationalism repudiates international cooperation in favor of belligerent independence. The cult of the strongman (*Der Fuehrer, Il Duce*) exalts the dictator as a primitive folk leader in a modern setting. Government is totalitarian in that it touches every aspect of the national life and subordinates individuals to the state. All dissent is crushed by the one-party system, by overwhelming propaganda, by fear, and by secret police. Detailed planning and self-sufficiency are characteristic of the economic life.

FASCIST AND OTHER DICTATORSHIPS

Most of the European countries abandoned democracy and chose dictatorships of one kind or another.

Spain. Troubles in Spain similar to those in Italy led to a dictatorship in 1923 under General Primero de Rivera and with the approval of King Alphonso XIII. Reaction against the dictator in 1931 introduced a brief trial of democracy with typical republican principles of separation of church and state, religious freedom, secularization of education, and nationalization of church property. The Republic did not succeed in preventing strikes and insurrections. In 1936 a bloody three-year Civil War began and ended after General Francisco Franco won control and made himself dictator; his regime continued in control and remains in control at the present time.

Eastern Europe. Dictatorships sprang up all over eastern Europe at different times after World War I because of a lack of democratic traditions, economic problems, and dissatisfied minorities. The Baltic states of Latvia, Lithuania, Estonia, and Poland became dictatorships. Austria, Hungary, Rumania, Bulgaria, Yugoslavia, and Albania accepted dictators. Czechoslovakia remained democratic until it was partitioned by Germany and its other neighbors in 1939. The Danube countries copied the fascist system of Italy. Greece in 1936 established the dictatorship under General Metaxas.

In the Near East the Republic of Turkey was established under the firm leadership of Mustapha Kemal as president (1924-1938), and it carried out extensive reforms to modernize the country.

REVIEW QUESTIONS

Multiple-choice

1. Which nation was the first to adopt fascism after World War I?   1) Spain   2) Germany   3) Italy   4) Portugal.

2. Which is *not* characteristic of fascist nations?   1) International cooperation   2) worshipful attitude toward a strong leader   3) regimentation of the national economy   4) suppression of opposition political parties.

3. The following features of fascism differ from communism *except* in   1) protection of private property   2) the suppression of opposition political parties   3) an emphasis upon racism   4) lack of an international revolutionary organization.

4. One of the strongest appeals of fascism in Germany and Italy was   1) opposition to the Church   2) dislike of racial minorities   3) fear of communism   4) hatred of capitalism.

5. All of these helped Hitler come into power *except* which?

1) A strong parliamentary majority for the National Socialist Party 2) Germans felt humiliated at the terms of the Treaty of Versailles 3) unemployment during the Great Depression 4) the emergency clause of the Weimar constitution.

6. The last nation to avoid a dictatorship in eastern Europe was 1) Poland 2) Czechoslovakia 3) Yugoslavia 4) Austria.

7. In which nation did fascism come to power after a bloody civil war? 1) Spain 2) Italy 3) Germany 4) Poland.

8. The fascist dictator who described his government as a "corporate state" was 1) Hitler 2) Mussolini 3) Franco 4) Pilsudski.

9. Just before the Civil War broke out Spain had become a 1) dictatorship 2) communist state 3) republic 4) federation.

FOR FURTHER READING

HARDBOUND:

Ebenstein, W., *Fascist Italy* (1939).

Fermi, Lauri, *Mussolini* (1960). Biography.

Fromm, Erich, *Escape from Freedom* (1941). Why Germans accepted fascism.

Halperin, S. W., *Germany Tried Democracy: A Political History of the Reich from 1918 to 1933* (1946). An objective and clear survey.

Hitler, Adolf, *Mein Kampf* (1939).

Neumann, Franz L., *Behemoth: The Structure and Practice of National Socialism* (1942). Nazi government.

Salvemini, Gaetano, *Under the Axe of Fascism* (1936). An attack on Italian fascism.

Veit, Valentine, *The German People: Their History and Civilization from the Holy Roman Empire to the Third Reich* (1946).

PAPERBOUND:

Arendt, Hannah, *The Origins of Totalitarianism* (Meridian).

Bullock, Alan, *Hitler, A Study in Tyranny* (Bantam). Abridgment of the leading biography of *Der Fuehrer*.

Halperin, S. William, *Mussolini and Italian Fascism* (Anvil).

Talmon, J. L., *Origins of Totalitarian Democracy* (Praeger).

*1931   *Japan invaded Manchuria*
 1933   *Japan withdrew from the League of Nations*
*1935   *Italy invaded Ethiopia*
*1936   *Japan entered anti-Communist pact with Germany and Italy*
        Germany reoccupied the Rhineland
*1936   *Spanish Civil War began*
*1937   *Japan began war against China*
        Italy entered the "Anti-Comintern Pact"
*1938   *Germany annexed Austria*
        Sudeten crisis ended with the Munich surrender to Hitler's demands
*1939   *Germany annexed most of Czechoslovakia*
        Mussolini annexed Albania
        German-Russian nonaggression pact
        **Sept. 1, German invasion of Poland precipitated World War II*

19. The Background of World War II

Most of the more prosperous allied nations of World War I and other democracies pursued policies of preserving the peace. These nations, the "Haves," with colonies and their own wealth of natural resources, were largely satisfied with the status quo. One of the former allies, Russia, abandoned its beginnings of parliamentary government, partly because of defeat in the war; another, Italy, dissatisfied, poor, and disturbed by disorder after the war, adopted fascism in hope of improving its condition. These two latter nations were classified as "Have-nots" along with defeated Germany and overcrowded Japan. The "Have-nots" took the road of aggression in order to gain a larger share of the world's resources and trade.

The deprivation caused by world depression contributed to the beginning of aggression by the "Have-nots." Unpreparedness, lack of cooperation, and appeasement by the democracies permitted the aggressors to take with impunity the route of aggression and of expansion. The background of World War II is a record of the successive acts of aggression of the "Have-not" nations.

**_Japanese in Manchuria_ (1931). Of the aggressors, Japan was the first to test the resolution of the League and discover the weakness of the Western nations. On pretext of suppressing banditry the Japanese army occupied all of Manchuria. The League appointed a commission to study the occupation, and in 1933 the League Assembly condemned Japan's action. Japan in February, 1933, withdrew from the League. Secretary of State Stimson informed Japan that the United States would not recognize the Japanese puppet regime in Manchukuo. The League failed to take legal sanctions against Japan. Since the

United States was not a member of the League, there was no cooperation from her. The depths of the depression had weakened the democracies, and Germany had just come under the defiant regime of Hitler.

Japan's War on China (1937). By 1937 Japan had grown more warlike and had fallen under a military dictatorship of army and navy officers, a kind of fascist regime. Japan converted her mandated islands in the Pacific into fortified naval bases. In 1934 she had denounced the naval limitations of the Washington Conference and later began a naval race with other powers and in 1936 entered an anti-communist pact with Germany.

In 1937 Japan began a major war against China. League condemnation again did not deter Japan from continuing the war. In 1937 Japanese sinking of the American gunboat *Panay* in China proved that the United States would not go to war. Britain was intimidated by the growing threat in Europe.

Hitler's early defiance. Soon after coming to power in 1933, Hitler took steps to repudiate the settlements of World War I. He demonstrated the new defiance of Germany by withdrawing from the League. The former Allies again adopted a policy of "collective security." France and Russia drew together, and Russia joined the League of Nations. In 1935 Hitler began the rearmament of Germany and introduced compulsory military service. In 1936 the German army reoccupied Germany's Rhineland, and Hitler began to refortify it in defiance of the Treaty of Versailles.

Through propaganda that harped on the injustices of the Treaty of Versailles, Hitler won considerable acceptance from world opinion of his actions. Hitler disguised his aggressions against neighbors as a single desire to unite Germans to the fatherland. At the same time, he confused Europe by reassuring gestures and by promises which he broke as soon as Germany became stronger. After a time his stand against communism won him defenders among certain groups in the democratic countries. His enemies hoped that his aggression might be turned against Russia and that the two totalitarian states might exhaust themselves in a struggle that would leave the democracies standing aside as happy spectators.

*Italy against Ethiopia (1935). The defiant actions of Germany and Japan showed Mussolini that Italy might avail herself of the weakness of Britain and France to build an empire. Ethiopia (formerly Abyssinia) offered a logical target; it lay next to Italy's Somaliland, and there Mussolini might redeem the defeat of the Italian army at Adowa in 1896. A frontier fight became the pretext for Italian demands against the independent African monarchy. The League failed to act resolutely, and Mussolini avoided a compromise of the dispute. The war began in 1935 with an invasion by Italy. The League adopted such weak sanctions against Italy that the war effort was not halted but frightened Mussolini into entering an alliance with Hitler. Ethiopia, unprepared to withstand modern war machines, was soon occupied and wholly annexed.

**Formation of the Rome-Berlin-Tokyo axis (1937). Germany and Italy came together in October, 1936, during the Ethiopian crisis and formed what Mussolini referred to as an "axis" around which other European states might collaborate to preserve peace. In November, Germany and Japan drew together in an "Anti-Comintern Pact" purportedly against international Communism. Italy joined the pact in 1937 and thus completed the formation of a union against the League powers. The alliances were confirmed by treaty agreement in 1939 and 1940, after which the union was joined by Hungary, Rumania, Bulgaria, Slovakia, and Croatia. The latter two were German puppet states formed out of Czechoslovakia.

The failure of the former allies to effectively resist defiance encouraged aggression, and the aggressors became mutually supporting and acknowledged by formal alliances. British distrust of Russia and the apathetic accord of France and Russia showed that the old Triple Entente would be hard to revive.

*The Spanish Civil War (1936-1939). The Spanish Civil War that broke out in July, 1936, also demonstrated the lack of resolution on the part of the democracies. It was known early that fascist forces from Germany and Italy were supporting the revolt begun by General Francisco Franco against the Spanish Republican government. Russian aid to the Republican forces, who were supported by Spanish communists, confused the issues in the war and weakened the will of the democracies to come to the aid of the Republican government of Spain. German technicians, pilots, and aircraft and Italian troops enabled Franco's fascist forces to win Spain against the most determined resistance of the liberal and radical elements during the long and bloody struggle. The war is spoken of as a testing ground for German techniques of war to be applied in the Second World War. British and French policy of non-intervention was a farce that further encouraged the Axis partners.

*German annexation of Austria (1938). The first Nazi annexation of territory, the Saar Basin, was accomplished legally by plebiscite in 1935. Austria, however, became the first target of annexation by aggression. Propaganda to justify the *Anschluss,* or union, of German-speaking Austria with greater Germany preceded a bloodless invasion by armed force in March, 1938. Another violation of the Versailles treaty had succeeded here.

***The Munich surrender (1938). Examination of the map of Europe in 1938 will show that the annexation of Austria left Czechoslovakia gripped by two prongs of German territory. Hitler next moved against Czechoslovakia by launching a propaganda offensive for the "redemption" of the German-speaking Sudeten people living in the mountain borders of Czechoslovakia. Britain and France by now were more likely to and did offer diplomatic resistance. Prime Minister Neville Chamberlain of Britain worked to appease Hitler who demanded the annexation of the Sudetenland. Czechoslovakia prepared to defend herself and Russia sought to win an agreement to aid her. A grave crisis developed and threatened war. Leaders of the democracies were joined by Mussolini in a plea for a negotiated settlement. The leaders met at Munich and consented to Hitler's annexation of the Sudeten regions. In a policy of appeasement the democracies had sacrificed Czechoslovakia to Hitler's demands in return for a pledge of respect for the remainder of Czechoslovakia's territory. Russia was not allowed to participate in the Munich conference; after this rebuff she felt it best to pursue her interests in her own way.

Annexation of Czechoslovakia (1939). The surrender of Czechoslovakia doomed the only democratic government in eastern Europe. Czechoslovakia soon began to fall apart; Slovakia demanded independence and Hitler offered German protection to her. Next, Bohemia and Moravia were made German "protectorates" but were in effect annexed. Hitler by these moves made it clear that his aggressions were imperialistic and not purely nationalistic as he had represented them. Next the territory of Memel was annexed (taken from Lithuania). Britain now was convinced that its trust had been misplaced and prepared by both alliance and rearmament to resist further aggression by Hitler. British assurances of support were made to Poland, Greece, Rumania, and Turkey.

Mussolini in April took advantage of the situation to win acclaim for himself in Italy by stepping across the Adriatic to invade and annex Albania.

**German-Russian accord (August, 1939). After Hitler's success in March, 1939, Russia began diplomatic negotiations with both sides. Britain and France both were reluctant to join the Soviets inasmuch as Stalin demanded Russian primacy in eastern Europe, and there were doubts as to the effectiveness of a Red army that had suffered from Stalin's purges. But Hitler, desiring to pursue conquests in the West, agreed to a nonaggression pact with Russia. The pact included a division of eastern Europe into German and Russian spheres of influence. The pact was mutually advantageous; Russia was free to absorb her former lands in eastern Europe and Germany was free to pursue her aggression in western Europe. This "diplomatic revolution" naturally came as a great shock to the West and raised doubts as to whether Britain and France would come to Poland's aid in case of the attack that now threatened there.

***The Polish crisis of 1939. Immediately after the pact was concluded with Russia, Hitler made military preparations to invade Poland and demanded that Poland surrender her rights to the free city of Danzig. After failing to win appeasement in another conference with Great Britain, Hitler invaded Poland on September 1, 1939. Britain and France declared war on Germany on September 3. The Second World War had begun. Poland was soon swamped by German forces in a blitzkrieg.

REVIEW QUESTIONS

Multiple-choice:

1. The first aggressor nation to challenge the ability of the League of Nations to prevent aggression was 1) Germany 2) Japan 3) Italy 4) Russia.

2. Japanese aggression in Asia in the 1930's was first directed

against   1) China proper   2) Korea   3) Formosa   4) Manchuria.

3. Germany's first act of defiance of the League of Nations was   1) the annexation of the Saar   2) the occupation of the Rhineland   3) the annexation of Austria   4) annexation of Czechoslovakia.

4. Hitler justified his aggression before world opinion by explaining that he wanted to   1) gain more defensible boundaries for Germany   2) unite Germans with the fatherland   3) suppress communism among his neighbors.

5. In his war with Ethiopia, Mussolini   1) suffered overwhelming defeat   2) gained a substantial proportion of the kingdom   3) annexed all of Ethiopia   4) abandoned the war when the League imposed sanctions.

6. The "Anti-Comintern Pact" included all *except*   1) Spain   2) Italy   3) Germany   4) Japan.

7. The aid of which country was *least* effective in determining the outcome of the Civil War in Spain?   1) Italy   2) Germany   3) Russia.

8. Which nation worked to help Czechoslovakia resist German aggression?   1) The United States   2) France   3) Britain   4) Russia.

Completion:

9. The union of Austria and Germany is spoken of as the . . . . . .

10. The surrender of Czechoslovakia to Hitler occurred at a) . . . . . . The British prime minister who agreed to the surrender there was b) . . . . . . Hitler demanded the return of Czechoslovakian border lands inhabited by a German minority called the c) . . . . . . The policy of the democracies of satisfying the aggressors was described by the word d) . . . . . .

11. Germany and Russia agreed to a non-aggression pact in the year a) . . . . . . The Russian leader at the time was b) . . . . .; the agreement was soon followed by a joint attack upon what country? c) . . . . . . That nation was quickly defeated by the German armies in a kind of quick attack known by the term d) . . . . . .

FOR FURTHER READING

HARDBOUND:

Brenan, Gerald, *Spanish Labyrinth: An Account of the Social and Political Background of the Civil War* (2nd ed., 1950). An analysis.

Carr, Edward H., *International Relations, 1919-1939* (1947).

————, *Twenty Years' Crisis, 1919-1939* (2nd ed., 1946).

Gedye, G. E. R., *Betrayal in Central Europe* (1939). An attack on the abandonment of the Czechs at Munich.

Jarman, T. L., *The Rise and Fall of Nazi Germany* (1956). A survey.

Lewis, W. Arthur, *Economic Survey, 1919-1939* (1949). The depression as a background for unrest.

Millis, Walter, *Why Europe Fights* (1940).

Schacht, H. H. G., *Autobiography* (1956). By Hitler's economic expert.

Schuman, Frederick L., *Europe on the Eve—The Crisis of Diplomacy* (1939). Angry history of the appeasement policies of the democracies.

Walters, F. P., *A History of the League of Nations* (2 vols, new ed., 1961). The most comprehensive account.

Werth, Alexander, *The Twilight of France, 1933-1940* (1942). Pessimistic views of a journalist but informative.

PAPERBOUND:

Allen, Frederick L., *Since Yesterday* (Bantam). Popular but accurate history.

Bullock, Alan, *Hitler: A Study in Tyranny* (Bantam).

Crankshaw, Edward, *Gestapo: Instrument of Tyranny* (Pyramid).

Feis, Herbert, *The Road to Pearl Harbor* (Atheneum).

Fischer, Louis, *The Soviets in World Affairs* (Vintage, abridged).

Graves, Robert, and Hodge, Alan, *The Long Weekend: A Social History of Great Britain, 1918-1939* (1941).

Orwell, George, *Homage to Catalonia* (Beacon). On the Spanish Civil War.

Perkins, Dexter, *The New Age of Franklin D. Roosevelt, 1932-1945* (University of Chicago). A helpful short survey.

ESSAY TYPE REVIEW QUESTIONS FOR MID-TERM AND FINAL EXAMINATIONS

1. Explain how each of the major nations was drawn into war in July and August of 1914. Discuss the responsibility of each for causing the outbreak and spread of hostilities.

2. What was the German plan for winning the war? Why did it fail and what were the consequences?

3. Why did the United States enter World War I?

4. What were the causes of the failure of the victorious powers to make satisfactory peace settlements after World War I?

5. What were the general provisions of the Fourteen Points? What were the provisions relating to the various nations taken separately?

6. What provisions of the Treaty of Versailles relating to Germany were considered especially severe and unjust?

7. What were the new states created after the war?

8. Outline the structure of the League of Nations.

9. Explain the more immediate causes and the early events of the Russian Revolution.

10. How did the Bolshevists gain control of the Russian Revolution?

11. What were the consequences of the Bolshevist rule under "War Communism"?

12. What were the changes and significance of New Economic Policy?

13. What was the role of each leader in the Russian Revolution: Kerensky, Lenin, Trotsky, Stalin?

14. How did Communist planning affect industry and agriculture in Russia?

15. Discuss Soviet foreign policy from 1918 to 1940.

16. Explain the nature of the war debts problem and the failure of the debtors to meet their full obligations.

17. What attempts did the leading nations make to preserve peace from 1921 to 1934?

18. Discuss the causes and effects of the Great Depression and the solutions sought in the various leading countries.

19. What was the nature of the New Deal reforms in the United States?

20. What were the causes of the economic decline of Great Britain? What is the significance of the Statute of Westminster?

21. What were the causes of French weakness during the 1920's and 1930's?

22. Sketch the achievement of Irish independence. What progress did India make toward self-government?

23. Explain the rise of fascism in Italy. What changes did Mussolini bring to Italy?

24. Explain Hitler's rise to power in Germany. What changes did the Nazis bring to Germany?

25. What are some of the leading characteristics of fascism?

26. Sketch the various aggressive acts of the Axis powers during the 1930's.

27. What was the significance of the Civil War in Spain?

WORLD WAR II TO THE PRESENT

The greatest war of all time proved that peace could not be preserved without organized effort and not without risk of war. America neglected to risk her power to prevent World War II, but used it to win the victory when forced to go to war. She took the lead in international collaboration to preserve peace afterwards. Western Europe now definitely had lost its leadership in world affairs to the United States and Russia. Asia and Africa found the times ripe to stage successful revolts against the imperial nations of Europe.

1935-1937	*Neutrality laws enacted by the United States in order to avoid war*
1937	*Roosevelt took stand against Axis aggressors*
*1939	**Sept. 1, World War II began with German invasion of Poland. Russia took eastern Poland* *November, Russia attacked Finland*
1939	*American neutrality acts modified to permit sale of munitions to Great Britain and France*
1939-1940	*Winter, Sitzkrieg on the Western front*
*1940	*March, Finland surrendered to Russia* *April, Denmark and Norway occupied by Nazis* **May-June, Germany occupied the Low Countries and France* *Winston Churchill organized the war cabinet in Britain* *August, Russo-German non-aggression pact signed* *September, Germans occupied Rumania* *October, Mussolini invaded Greece*
*1941	*Bulgaria joined Germany in the war* *April, Germany sent Rommel to Libya* *May, Yugoslavia fell to the Germans* **June, Germany attacked Russia* *August, Atlantic Charter announced* **December 7, Japan attack at Pearl Harbor brought the United States into the war. Japan overran Southeast Asia in the next four months*
*1942	*May, Battle of the Coral Sea, an American victory over Japan*

*August, United States made landings in Solomon Islands

*November, American and British forces made landings in North Africa

*1943   *January, Germans defeated at Stalingrad

May, Axis forces driven out of North Africa

September, Italy surrendered. Americans established beachheads in Italy

*1944   *June 6, Allied "D-Day" invasions in Normandy. Other Allied landings soon made on French Mediterranean coast.

October, 1944, American landings made in Philippines

*1944-1945 December-January, Battle of the Bulge, the failure of the Germans last great effort

*1945   *February, Yalta Conference; U. N. O. organized at San Francisco

April, Roosevelt died and Truman became president

*May 8, proclaimed V-E Day

*August 15, V-J Day

20. World War II

World War II by any measure was both the worst and the most extensive war the world had ever seen. The use of massive air power and fast-moving ground forces brought an entirely different kind of war from that of World War I. The atomic bomb was employed only twice but brought a speedy end to the war against Japan. Historians agree on the causes of the war, which are readily apparent in the ambitions of the fascist powers, in the initial unwillingness of the peace-loving nations to organize to prevent aggression, and tardiness in resisting the initial steps of aggressor nations. Other causes originated in dissatisfaction with the settlements after World War I and the effects of the Great Depression.

AXIS SUCCESSES

The aggressors had planned and prepared for war and won a long succession of victories before the United States as a belligerent brought its full resources into action on the side of the Allies.

The fall of Poland and the Baltic states. Poland was crushed within the month of September, 1939. Nazi blitzkrieg (lightning war) tactics were carried out by a motorized army and mass air attacks. As the Nazis occupied western Poland the Soviet Union occupied the eastern half of Poland, in accordance with the nonaggression pact with Germany. A Polish government-in-exile was set up in London by leaders who had escaped. The Germans employed the Poles as forced labor and exterminated three million Polish Jews during their occupation of eastern Europe.

After Poland the Baltic states fell to Russia; Estonia, Latvia, and Lithuania were forced to join the Soviet Union as republics. When the Finns refused to meet Soviet demands for bases and territory, Russia attacked her in November, 1939, but met unexpected resistance. The League expelled Russia as an aggressor, but Finland fell in March, 1948, and surrendered territory and made other concessions. Later, when Germany invaded Russia, Finland took the side of Nazi Germany. Russia also occupied Bessarabia in this stage of the war.

The "Sitzkrieg." In the West a strange lull, nicknamed the "Sitzkrieg," followed the downfall of Poland and continued through the winter of 1939. Only insignificant fighting occurred along the German and French border, and it seemed that Germany did not wish to advance against the French Maginot Line nor the French against the Siegfried Line. But the Nazis were preparing for the spring offensive.

The occupation of Denmark and Normay. In April, 1940, Hitler suddenly fell upon Denmark and Norway. Denmark, unable to resist, surrendered without fighting. Norway was attacked by sea and her ports seized by German landing forces. Other forces were flown in and seized Norway's airports. A fifth column aided the downfall. A puppet regime under the Norwegian traitor Quisling was established. Norway provided the Nazis with important naval and air bases. Sweden was not occupied but was effectively isolated by the fall of Denmark and Norway.

***The conquest of the low countries and France. Immediately after the occupation of Norway, German forces overwhelmed the Netherlands, Belgium, and Luxemburg. Again, the invasion of Belgium enabled Germany to advance quickly into France, since the Maginot Line had not been extended along France's Belgian border. Within a week the German troops had entered France. The rapidity of German movement was achieved through the use of dive bomber attacks, parachute troops, and motorized armies. The Germans quickly broke through to the sea and drove a wedge that cut off large British and French forces in Belgium. In the "miracle of Dunkirk" the British pressed into service hundreds of sea craft of all kinds and under cover of aircraft succeeded in saving 300,000 men to fight another day.

The rapid penetration of France by overwhelming German forces surrounded French troops and cut them off from supplies. Paris was quickly taken. Armistice terms of the French surrender permitted Germany to occupy more than half of France. The French national government continued under the aged Petain and his ally, Pierre Laval. The capital was removed to Vichy. The Petain government collaborated with the Germans. Toward the end of the fall of France the Italians entered the war by declaring war on France, but Italian forces occupied very little of French soil. General Charles de Gaulle escaped to England to become the recognized leader of the French government in exile.

The battle of Britain. The defeat of British forces in Norway brought criticism of the Chamberlain government and forced Prime Minister Chamberlain to resign. Winston Churchill then organized the war cabinet and made Anthony Eden War Secretary. Hitler, unprepared to cross the channel and invade England, attacked the island from the air and sent submarines against her shipping. Britain sustained tremendous shipping losses. The British airforce, prepared primarily for defensive warfare, took a heavy toll of German bombing planes. Notable bombing targets of the Germans were the motor manufacturing center of Coventry and the financial district of London. Bombing did not destroy British morale and the British were able to carry their own bombing raids to German industrial targets.

The war in the Balkans. Rumania was occupied by Germany in September, 1940. In October, Mussolini invaded Greece. Like the Finns, the Greeks offered unexpected resistance. Italy in the spring, 1941, began driving into the Balkans. Bulgaria joined Germany in the war in March. By May, Yugoslavia fell to the Germans who then drove into Greece to rescue the Italians and to occupy Greece themselves. The Germans next struck at the island of Crete in a spectacular paratroop invasion, but the Germans suffered heavy losses.

**The war in North Africa. Italian forces landed in North Africa and attacked Egypt from Libya, but British troops in Egypt defeated the Italians. Germany sent General Rommel into Libya in April, 1941, and pushed the British back toward Cairo but they held at El Alamein. It was essential for the British to hold Egypt in order to keep the Germans from taking the Suez Canal and gaining control of the Mediterranean Sea. There would be grave danger also in permitting the Axis to invade the Middle East and gain control of its great oil fields. The North African fighting ended in May, 1943, after the United States had entered the war. American landings in North Africa coordinated with the British in Egypt cleared the Axis out of North Africa.

**The German invasion of Russia. Neither Hitler nor Stalin trusted the other after their non-aggression pact of August, 1940. The decision of Germany to attack Russia, an attack that came in June, 1941, is explained by 1] the expansionist plans of each in eastern Europe and southeast Europe and Hitler's long-standing intention of driving eastward into Russia for *Lebensraum* (living space). 2] Germany's truce with

Communist Russia was only a temporary expedient. 3] If Hitler could defeat Russia, he hoped that Britain, without Russia as an ally, could be induced to make peace.

The Germans advanced deep into Russia in the initial thrust. Kiev was taken in the fall of the year and the Germans soon threatened Moscow and Leningrad. The attack immediately brought British and American aid to Russia. The climax of the German-Russian war came in the long and terrific battle of Stalingrad which ended in German defeat in January, 1943.

The German invasion of Russia and subsequent defeat resembled the disaster of Napoleon's Grand Army in 1812. The Germans were not prepared for such cold winter weather as they encountered. The Russian masses showed determined resistance and accepted losses of millions of troops and civilian lives. Instead of coming as a liberator, Hitler treated the Russians with contempt and cruelty. Hitler directed the war himself and forced his generals to overextend themselves at times when strategic withdrawals would have been advisable.

The Role of the United States. During the thirties when the Axis powers pursued their successive steps of conquest of Europe, the United States reacted by enacting a series of neutrality laws which forbade aid to the belligerents. America's action is explained by her disillusionment with the consequences of World War I and the belief that her entry had been a mistake. The neutrality laws of the thirties were designed to keep America from becoming embroiled once again in Europe's wars. However, President Franklin D. Roosevelt in 1937 condemned the Axis powers and began to lead the nation in the direction of aid to the Allies. In 1939 he succeeded in getting Congress to modify the neutrality acts to permit the sale of munitions to belligerents on a "cash and carry" basis, knowing that this could only favor Britain and France. After such sales were permitted in November, 1939, large quantities of war materials were shipped to Britain and to Russia when Germany invaded that country. It was the American Lend-Lease Act of 1941 that made the billions of dollars of American goods available to friendly nations even before the United States entered the war in December of that year. Various other measures were also taken by the American government to aid the Allies. America began to act as the "arsenal of democracy," but still expected to avoid war until the Japanese attacked the American navy at Pearl Harbor.

AMERICA TURNS THE TIDE OF WAR

The uninterrupted expansion of the Axis nations and their successive victories ended within several months after the United States entered the war. The pledge to fight until the Axis Powers were brought to an unconditional surrender meant that the Axis would have to be completely broken before peace could be restored and that the war would not end in compromise and armistice.

***Japanese-American tension and Pearl Harbor.** Japanese disregard for the Open Door in China had antagonized the United States at various times since the Russo-Japanese War ended in 1905. Japan had long dreamed of dominating Asia in a more aggressive way than the United States had asserted its power in the Americas or Great Britain had in Europe. Axis successes in Europe by 1940 offered the opportunity for which Japan had apparently been waiting. Japan continued the war against China, occupied coastal areas to shut out American aid, and occupied Indo-China in 1941. The United States had placed embargoes on the export of scrap iron and petroleum by August, 1941. The Japanese war effort had depended upon these supplies, and Japan now became desperate. Negotiations between the United States and Japan were pursued, but American terms, calling for Japanese withdrawal from China, seemed like surrender to the war lords who controlled Japan. On December 7 the Japanese made the surprise attack on the American naval base at Pearl Harbor, Hawaii. In the few days the United States and the remaining Axis Powers had declared war on each other. America now mobilized her great strength of manpower and industry and rapidly expanded her military forces. America had to fight to resist Japan, but priority was given to winning the war in Europe.

Japanese victories in Asia. The Japanese attack on Pearl Harbor was designed to destroy the effectiveness of the American navy so as to permit Japan to take over the great resources of oil, rubber, and other raw materials in the Dutch East Indies. A nonaggression pact with Russia had freed Japan from that source of potential danger. The Japanese, under their wartime leader Premier Tojo, soon defeated Allied sea power in Asia and occupied the Philippines, the East Indies, the Malay Peninsula, the islands of the central Pacific, and, later, Burma.

Fall of Italy. In November, 1942, combined American and British forces landed at various points in North Africa. As already noted, these forces drove the Axis out of North Africa by May, 1943. Next, the Allied forces jumped from Africa to Sicily and quickly occupied that island. On September 3, 1943, Italy forced Mussolini to resign and signed an armistice with the Allies. But the Germans then took control of Italy so that there was no change in the military situation. Americans landed in Italy in September and took Naples. But German resistance behind mountain defense positions held up the Allied northward advance. In 1945 Mussolini was killed by anti-fascist Italians. Instead of a major attack in Italy the Allies saved their main forces for the "D-Day" assault on German-held France.

***The Second Front: the war against "Festung Europa."**
It required many long months for the Allies to gather supplies
and train troops for the Second Front, the massive assault that
would have to be made to defeat German forces that could
be sent to any Allied invasion point in "Festung Europa" as
the Germans referred to their defenses of the continent. On
June 6, 1944, General Dwight D. Eisenhower, the supreme
commander of the Allied invasion forces, began the attack
against the Fortress of Europe with the "D-Day" landings in
Normandy. In three weeks two million men had been landed.
The Germans had been weakened by continuous day and
night bombing raids, almost since the war began, on the factories and transportation facilities of the homeland. The Germans had also suffered heavy losses in the war against Russia
and were still engaged there as fiercely as ever. The landings
in France on the Mediterranean coast as well as in Normandy,
forced the Germans to fight on two great fronts. The Allies
steadily pushed the Germans back. In the winter of 1944-1945
Germany made and lost a great counterattack known as the
"Battle of the Bulge" in the Ardennes Forest. In the east the
Russians had driven the Germans out of Russian territory. In
April, Hitler and some of his leaders committed suicide. May
8 was proclaimed V-E (Victory in Europe) Day as the war
officially ended in Europe.

The conquest of Japan. The first defeat of Japan by American forces in the Pacific occurred in the battle of the Coral
Sea in May, 1942; it was a naval engagement fought by car-
rier-based planes. The opposing ships never sighted each
other. In June, in a Japanese offensive against Midway Island,
Japan's navy was decisively defeated. Next, the United States
took her first important offensive action by landing in the
Solomon Islands in August, 1942. After six months the Americans won the battle of Guadalcanal, one of the hardest-fought
campaigns of the war. Various Japanese-held island fortresses

in the central Pacific were taken by Admiral Nimitz's naval forces in later campaigns. General MacArthur led the American forces in the Southwest Pacific up the north coast of New Guinea and on to the Philippines, where landings were made in October, 1944. In the greatest naval battle ever fought, the battle of Leyte Gulf, the Japanese suffered losses that practically took her navy out of the war. The two atomic bombs dropped at Hiroshima and at Nagasaki in early August soon brought surrender. August 15 was declared V-J Day.

ALLIED DIPLOMACY IN THE WAR

The wartime conferences between the Allied leaders served to state general war aims, to plan the strategy for victory, and to plan the postwar settlement. The grand coalition of the Allies proved more effective than any such alliance had ever been; the Axis Powers by contrast did not coordinate their strategy or arrange conferences of government heads for other planning. The Soviets made various moves to win good will among the democracies; for example, the Third International was abolished in 1943, and the Patriarch of the Russian Church was restored in Moscow.

**The Atlantic Charter. In August, 1941, even before the United States had officially entered the war, Roosevelt and Churchill met and agreed upon a general statement of the kind of postwar world they were fighting for. This Atlantic Charter was soon signed by twenty-six Allied nations and later by many others; together they became known as the United Nations. The Atlantic Charter was comparable to Wilson's Fourteen Points but was stated in more general terms. The motive of territorial gain was renounced; people would be free to choose their own form of government; economic equality for all nations and disarmament were promised.

**The wartime conferences. At the conference in Casablanca (January, 1943) the Allies announced their agreement to fight for "unconditional surrender" of the Axis Powers and also planned military strategy to achieve this goal. At Quebec (August, 1943) Roosevelt and Churchill met and planned for the subsequent meeting at Moscow (November, 1943) with Stalin where joint agreements were made for the prosecution of the war and for the establishment of the United Nations. In November, 1943, the Big Three met again at Teheran and reached agreements on the postwar settlements. In December, 1943, Roosevelt and Churchill met with Chiang Kai-shek of China to discuss the war against Japan. In October, 1944, the Allies met at Dumbarton Oaks, in Washington, D. C., and drew up plans for the charter of the United Nations Organization.

***The Yalta and Potsdam Conferences. The greatest of all the conferences was held in February, 1945, at Yalta (Russia) on the Black Sea. Here the United States wished to secure Russia's aid in concluding the war against Japan and her agreement to the UNO charter that had been drafted.

Russia was awarded eastern Poland and agreed to permit the Polish government in exile in London to share in the postwar Polish government. This agreement was never observed by the Russians. The states of central and eastern Europe were to be restored under democratic governments. Germany was to be divided into occupation zones and required to pay reparations to the Allies.

At Potsdam (July, 1945) the Allied leaders met and agreed to disarm, denazify, and democratize Germany and made other plans for the postwar peace treaties.

***The United Nations organized. In February, 1945, the representatives of fifty-one Allied nations met at San Francisco to approve the charter for the United Nations Organization. It was agreed that each nation would have one vote in the General Assembly, except Russia which was given three.

The structure of the United Nations resembled that of the League of Nations. 1] The great powers were represented in the Security Council. The five permanent members were the United States, Great Britain, Soviet Russia, France, and China —any one of these might exercise the veto in the Council. Six non-permanent members were to be chosen for two-year terms by the General Assembly. 2] The General Assembly included all nations admitted to membership in the United Nations. 3] The International Court of Justice was made up of fifteen jurists chosen by the Security Council and the General Assembly. 4] The Secretariat was created as the administrative organization. An especially important agency placed under the authority of the Assembly was the Economic and Social Council for supervising various broad humanitarian agencies (such as the World Health Organization (WHO) and the Food and Agriculture Organization (FAO). The Trusteeship Council was created to supervise the "trust territories."

***The postwar settlements.** A council of foreign ministers of the great powers meeting at different cities, drafted (1946) peace treaties with the defeated German satellites. Treaties were made with the small countries first. All had to pay reparations.

Italy had to 1] surrender bits of territory to France, Yugoslavia, Greece, and Albania. 2] Italy was required to surrender her colonies, all of which were in Africa, but was allowed to keep a trusteeship over Somaliland. Libya became independent and Eritrea joined Ethiopia.

Romania 1] lost Bessarabia and part of Bukovina to Russia. 2] Romania also lost part of Dobruja to Bulgaria but 3] regained Transylvania from Hungary.

Bulgaria regained Dobruja but had to pay reparations to Greece and Yugoslavia.

Hungary lost some territory to Czechoslovakia and the eastern half of Transylvania to Romania.

Yugoslavia and Albania came under the rule of local Communists.

Czechoslovakia was restored as a nation, but in 1948 its government fell into the hands of local Communists.

Finland lost bits of territory to Russia. Russia kept Estonia, Latvia, and Lithuania which had been organized as Soviet republics after their occupation by Soviet troops in 1940.

Poland was restored; she was compensated for territory east of the Curzon Line that was lost to Russia by gaining Danzig and parts of East Prussia, Silesia, and Pomerania, all of which were German in population.

Austria was not restored until a peace treaty was signed by the major powers in 1955. Until then Austria was jointly occupied by Russia, Great Britain, France, and the United States.

**Allied occupation of Germany.   Russia and the other Allies have yet to agree upon a peace treaty for Germany and the prospect for an agreement seems as remote as ever. Germany, therefore, remains divided between East Germany and West Germany. However, Russia and the Allies did reach agreements with that part of Germany under the occupation of each. At Potsdam immediately after the war the Allies agreed upon the disposition to be made of Germany. Germany was divided into four zones that were occupied by France, Britain, the United States, and Russia; the capital, Berlin, similarly was divided into occupation zones. Russia later established the Communist East German government in her zone. The Allies ended the state of war with Germany in 1950 and in 1952 by treaty restored sovereignty to the West German government. Nazi war criminals were tried and punished by the military tribunal at Nuremberg beginning in 1946; others, as apprehended were later tried by German courts. Reparations were collected, Germany was disarmed, and denazification was carried out.

American occupation of Japan. In 1945 Japan was permitted to retain her Emperor and continued to govern her own local affairs, but General MacArthur at the head of American occupation forces became the real power there. Russia regained the territories she had lost to Japan in 1905. Japan was demilitarized and her war criminals tried and punished. The United States drew up a peace treaty in 1951 and secured its approval by other nations in 1952. By the treaty Japan regained her sovereignty, lost all territory except for her four main islands, and accepted American military occupation for an indefinite time. Korea became independent but was divided along the 38th parallel into two occupation zones. American troops occupied the southern zone and Russian troops the northern zone. Japan's Pacific islands were assigned by the United Nations to the United States as trustee.

REVIEW QUESTIONS

Multiple-choice:

1. Which group of nations was *last* to be overrun by Germany in World War II? 1) France and the Low Countries 2) Scandinavia   3) the Balkans.

2. Italy entered World War II 1) when Germany attacked Poland 2) after Hitler attacked Russia 3) when Germany occupied Norway 4) after Hitler had succeeded in overrunning western Europe.

3. The turning point in the war between Germany and Russia occurred in 1943 at 1) Leningrad 2) Moscow 3) Stalingrad 4) in Finland.

4. The chief objective of the German-Italian campaign in North Africa was 1) to acquire colonies 2) to take the Suez Canal 3) to close the gateway to the Mediterranean at Gibraltar 4) to prevent an invasion of southern Europe.

5. The first American offensive in the European theater was in 1) North Africa 2) southern France 3) Sicily 4) Italy.

6. In the Pacific, the first defeats inflicted upon Japan occurred 1) in Guadacanal 2) in New Guinea 3) in the battles of Midway and Coral Sea 4) in the Philippines.

7. Italy attacked the Allies in all areas *except* 1) Albania 2) Yugoslavia 3) Greece 4) North Africa.

8. During the approach and early months of World War II, the United States government 1) did not hesitate in extending aid to the British and French 2) gave no aid until it was forced into war by Japan 3) enacted a series of neutrality laws in order to avoid war and later began several measures to aid Britain and Russia.

9. The most important and widely used weapon in World War II was 1) the submarine 2) the airplane 3) tanks 4) motorized infantry 5) bazookas.

10. The main change affecting the countries of eastern Europe after the war were 1) the establishment of communist regimes and reannexation of former possessions by Russia 2) the creation of new independent states 3) heavy losses of territory to Russia 4) division into Russian and Allied occupation zones.

11. Which country was not divided into occupation zones by the victorious powers? 1) Germany 2) Austria 3) Korea 4) Japan.

12. In the postwar settlement, Germany experienced all *except* 1) a peace treaty agreed to by the victorious powers 2) division into occupation zones 3) restoration of sovereignty to West Germany 4) payment of reparations.

13. Italy's main loss in the war was 1) border territories 2) her colonies 3) reparations 4) division into occupation zones.

14. With which country did the United States conclude peace without Russian assent? 1) Austria 2) Italy 3) Japan 4) Czechoslovakia.

Completion:

15. Opposite each of the following nations in World War II place the name of the wartime head of state, the year each nation was drawn into the war, and the date of surrender of the nations that did so at any time during the war.

United States   a) ....

Great Britain   b) ....

Free France   c) ....

Vichy France   d) ....

Russia   e) ....

Italy   f) ....

Germany   g) ....

Japan   h) ....

China   i) ....

16. A lull in the war in the winter of 1939-1940 was spoken of as the a) ..... during which the French remained behind their defense line called the b) ..... Line and the Germans behind the c) ..... Line.

17. The United States placed a priority upon winning the war first in which, Europe or Asia? ......

18. Japan attacked the United States at Pearl Harbor after the failure of negotiations related to Japan's activities in what country? ......

19. Supreme commander of the "D-Day" landing forces in Normandy was ......

20. In the war against Japan the United States first took the offensive in a campaign in what group of Pacific islands? ......

21. The first atomic bomb dropped on Japan was at ......

22. The American and British war aims were stated in what document? ......

23. The most comprehensive of wartime conferences of the Allies was held at ......

24. The United Nations was organized in the city of a) ..... in the year b) ......

25. In charge of the American occupation of Japan was General ......

26. In Asia the United States and Russia agreed to separate occupation zones in the country of ......

FOR FURTHER READING

HARDBOUND:

Aron, Robert, *History of Vichy* (1958). Fair and objective.

Borsody, Stephen, *The Triumph of Tyranny: The Nazi and Soviet Conquest of Central Europe* (1960). Unusually objective account of the works of the two conquerers.

Churchill, Winston S., *The Gathering Storm* (1948); *Their Finest Hour* (1949); *The Grand Alliance* (1950); *The Hinge of Fate* (1950).

Davis, F., and Lindley, E. K., *How the War Came* (1942). By two American journalists.

Eisenhower, Dwight D., *Crusade in Europe* (1948). Readable and popular.

Jungk, Robert, *Brighter Than a Thousand Suns* (1958). Excellent book on atomic weapons.

Liebling, A. J., ed., *The Republic of Silence* (1947). Selections on the French Resistance movement.

May, A. J., *Europe and Two World Wars* (1947).

Snyder, Louis L., *The War: A Concise History, 1939-1945* (1960). A readable narrative that covers the whole war.

PAPERBOUND:

Buchanan, A. Russell, *United States and World War II* (2 vols., Torchbooks).

Hersey, John, *Hiroshima* (Bantam). The effects of the atomic bomb.

Liddell-Hart, Basil H., *The German Generals Talk* (Berkley). Views of German generals after the war.

Reitlinger, Gerald, *The Final Solution* (Perpetua). On non-military side of the war.

Shirer, William L., *The Rise and Fall of the Third Reich: A History of Nazi Germany* (Crest). Readable, popular, journalistic, by a foreign correspondent.

Taylor, Robert L., *Winston Churchill* (Pocket Books). An excellent biography, friendly to its subject.

1945   *Dutch monarchs returned to the Netherlands*
       Austrian Republic organized
       Conservatives and Churchill lose office; Labor Party victory brought large program of welfare legislation to Britain
       Germany divided into occupation zones by the Allies

1946   *Fourth French Republic established. Collaborators with the Germans punished*
       Italy abolished its monarchy

1947   *Israel established*

1947   *Organization of the American States succeeded the Pan-American Union*

1948   *Czechoslovakia taken over by Communist regime*
       Berlin blockade and airlift

1949   *Russians established a separate government in East Germany*
       West German Republic established with capital at Bonn
       Indonesia won independence from the Netherlands

1951   *Baudouin I became king of Belgium*

1952   *Eisenhower elected president and Republicans returned to power*
       George VI died; Elizabeth II became queen

*1953 *Stalin died*

1954   *German sovereignty recognized by Western powers*

1955   *Peace treaty with Austria signed*

1956   *Revolts in East Germany, Poland, and Hungary*

*1958 *French army in Algeria seized control there and demanded return of De Gaulle to power. Fifth French Republic established with De Gaulle as president*

*1960 *Castro won control of Cuba*

1961   *Democrats returned to power with election of Kennedy as president*

21.   The Nations after the War

Much of Europe faced the same problems of physical reconstruction and economic recovery as after World War I. Loss of life, however, was less than in the earlier war, because highly mobile military campaigns decided the issue quickly. Russia was the only large nation to suffer greater loss of life than in World War I. In the United States after the war, domestic problems were overshadowed by the Cold War and by the reality of America's role as the leader of the Free World. In most of the countries of Western Europe, Catholic and socialist parties won control and enacted measures to extend social security. After several years, some countries began to elect more conservative governments to office. But in eastern Europe, many countries fell under the "Iron Curtain" of Communist rule.

THE NON-COMMUNIST NATIONS

The nations of western Europe recovered rather quickly, a recovery that was reflected in the statistics of production. Economic and military aid from the United States was a most effective factor in bringing about this recovery. The political strength of the communists in the European nations diminished as recovery took hold.

***The United States.** The United States had almost completed its demobilization in 1947 when it became apparent that a return to normalcy would not be possible. A Full Employment Act was enacted to bring the power of the federal government into action to deal with a return to depression conditions which were generally expected. But the rearmament program, the European Recovery Program, the Korean War, and various forms of foreign aid kept the economy going strongly without any major postwar depression. Peacetime conscription, high taxes, American leadership in world affairs, and recurring crises in foreign affairs reminded Americans that isolationism had been abandoned. The national debt rose almost steadily year after year, but the dollar generally continued as the world's strongest currency.

In 1945, shortly before the war ended in Europe, President Roosevelt died early in his fourth term. Harry S. Truman succeeded to the presidency and in 1948 won reelection, to everyone's surprise. He worked energetically to extend New Deal reforms in what was called the Fair Deal. In foreign affairs he pursued a vigorous policy of American leadership and cooperation in the early Cold War crisis. The loss of China as an ally and the outbreak of the unpopular Korean War left many Americans angry and confused. In 1952 the popular war leader, General Dwight D. Eisenhower, brought the Republicans into office for the first time since 1933. Other than a marked predilection for businessmen in government, there was no really great change in either domestic or foreign policy. The Democrats returned to power in 1961 when John F. Kennedy won by a narrow margin. The major change toward political democracy and social equality occurred in the various steps taken by the federal government to extend to the Negro full civil and political rights.

Great Britain and the welfare state.   Prime Minister Churchill and the Conservative Party lost the parliamentary election in 1945 to Clement Attlee and the Labor Party. The change was not meant to discredit the wartime leader but reflected voters' belief that in peacetime, domestic problems could be best managed under the philosophy of the Labor Party. The Laborites enacted a limited socialist program. Certain parts of the economy were nationalized: coal mining, certain public utilities, the steel industry, the Bank of England, railways, motor transport, and aviation. Agriculture was regulated. Important social insurance legislation designed to provide "cradle to grave" security was passed and included free national health service, so-called "socialized medicine." This all-inclusive medical program proved quite popular and on the whole, workable. National health improved remarkably. Altogether, a moderate revolution had taken place that created in Britain the most elaborate social welfare system of any among the Western nations. When minor benefits under the health program were curtailed, the more radical Labor politician, Aneurin Bevan, registered his protest by resigning and heading a minor protest faction. An Education Act in 1944 began to open equal opportunity for all to obtain high school and college education; the educational benefits were enlarged in succeeding years.

In 1951 Churchill and the Conservatives returned to power, but there was no significant reversal of the socialist program enacted by the Labor Party. The steel and motor transport industries were returned to private enterprise. Sir Anthony Eden, Conservative, succeeded as prime minister in 1955 when Churchill retired. In 1957 Harold Macmillan, also a Conservative, became prime minister when Eden resigned over the Suez crisis. King George VI died in 1952 and his daughter Elizabeth II became queen. Great Britain had spent all its foreign assets in fighting the war. Many of her dependencies achieved independence or became self-governing. Britain was forced to undergo a period of years of sacrifice to regain her economic vigor. In effect, the war had reduced Britain to a second-rate power, an unaccustomed situation that the British found most difficult to reconcile with their past.

**The Fourth and Fifth French Republics.   The Third French Republic was destroyed by the German occupation. General

Charles de Gaulle, leader of the wartime Free French Movement, headed the postwar provisional government of France. Marshal Pétain, who had headed the Vichy regime, was tried for treason and condemned to death, but the sentence was commuted to life imprisonment. His closest colleague, Pierre Laval was executed. Thousands of French who had collaborated with the Germans had been marked for punishment by the underground and after the liberation of France were mobbed, imprisoned, and executed. De Gaulle's government began several measures that aided the economic recovery of France.

The Fourth French Republic came into being in 1946 when an elected constituent National Assembly drafted a new constitution. The weak executive of the earlier republic was restored against the objection of De Gaulle. A strong Communist movement after the war grew weaker as France grew stronger economically. The French birth rate increased also. Coalitions of leftist parties nationalized industries and passed social welfare legislation similar to that of Britain.

The French government underwent rapid cabinet changes as new coalitions were formed on an average of one every eight months during the twelve-year life of the Fourth French Republic. This instability destroyed confidence in the government at home and among foreign nations. France suffered from costly colonial revolts which she attempted unsuccessfully to put down.

In 1958 the French army in Algeria seized control and demanded the return of De Gaulle to power and reconstruction of stronger government. The Assembly gave in and De Gaulle assumed control. The constitution for the Fifth French Republic, strongly ratified by the voters, created a government with a powerful chief executive. De Gaulle won election as president and became the strongest leader in France since Napoleon III.

**The division of Germany. The Yalta agreements provided for a four-power occupation of Germany. Russia, Britain, France, and the United States each governed its separate zone. An Allied Council in Berlin was set up to coordinate the government of the four zones. Here arose the strongest early evidence of Soviet determination not to adhere to the Potsdam agreements but to govern in Russia's interest alone and to seek to communize Germany. Russia collected reparations in a move designed to depress Germany economically and create an environment suitable to the growth of communism there and in the rest of Europe. All of Europe's economy had long since become interrelated with Germany's industry and dependent upon it.

The friction with Russia caused the Western powers to merge their zones and sponsor the growth of a separate government that might eventually include eastern Germany. Toward Germany, the Western powers changed their policy from one of punishment and weakening the nation to the goal of building Germany as a strong ally. In 1948 a Soviet blockade of Berlin designed to cut off access from the western zones showed that the Russians wished to gain control of the capital for themselves. An "Airlift" of the Western powers forced the Russians to lift the blockade the next year. In 1949 the Soviet government completed the creation of the separate Democratic Republic of East Germany.

In 1949 the German Federal Republic with its capital at Bonn was created in West Germany. Konrad Adenauer, a Christian Democrat, was made chancellor by a coalition of moderate and conservative parties. In 1954 this Republic was recognized as a sovereign state by the Western powers. This republic provided for a bicameral legislature; the executive power was entrusted to the chancellor and the cabinet. Adenauer won the continued support of Germans and the respect of the Western powers; Germany became a trusted ally. Adenauer cooperated with France and in various European international economic and defense projects. Germany was allowed to re-arm and was given military aid when she became a member of the North Atlantic Treaty Organization. Germany experienced remarkable economic recovery and her prosperity soon surpassed that of prewar years.

In the Soviet zone of East Germany the German Democratic Republic was proclaimed in 1949. Wilhelm Pieck, the German Communist Party head became its president. The effective control of government resided in the hands of Walther Ulbricht, head of the East German Politburo. This repressive regime, subordinated as it was to Russian interests, was briefly threatened by outbreaks of angry rioting in the summer of 1953. The Western powers refused to recognize the East German government; Russia insisted that unification must come by negotiation between the two German republics. It appeared that Germany would be divided indefinitely. Berlin, in East Germany, continued to pose the worst threat to world peace, for Russia sought to force the Western occupation authorities out of the city. The danger was heightened by Russia's threats to withdraw and leave East Germany under its own government, one which the Western powers refused to recognize.

Italy.   The Italians abolished their monarchy in 1946. A middle-of-the-road coalition led by Christian Democrats under Alcide de Gasperi governed. The possibility that a communist government might take power subsided as economic recovery set in. Italy became a loyal member of the Western bloc in the East-West Cold War.

Austria.   The Allies agreed to treat Austria not as a defeated enemy but as a liberated nation; her boundaries and her independence were restored. The Austrian Republic was organized in 1945 and the peace treaty of 1955 brought a withdrawal of troops of the four occupying powers.

Belgium. Since King Leopold III of Belgium lost favor with his subjects for having surrendered too readily to the Germans, the regency held the throne until 1951. His son then succeeded as Baudouin I. Belgium resumed her former place among the European nations and cooperated closely with the other Western powers.

The Netherlands. Queen Wilhelmina returned in 1945 from exile in London, and in 1948 her daughter Juliana succeeded to the throne. The Dutch rebuilt their cities destroyed in the German invasion and reclaimed lands flooded when the dikes were opened to the invaders. The Dutch East Indies asserted their independence after the Japanese forces were driven out. In 1949 the United States of Indonesia was established.

Finland. Communists seemed likely to take over the government of Finland until 1948, after which time the communists were kept out of coalition governments. Finland remained subordinated to Russia by the provisions of the Soviet-Finnish Mutual Aid Treaty of 1948 and by the postwar peace with Russia, but Finland never accepted a communist regime as did other European countries bordering Russia.

The smaller non-communist states. In Norway the Labor Party gained control of the postwar government. The monarchy under King Haakon VII remained in power as before.

Denmark retained her monarchy. In Greece the monarchy was restored, but its authority was challenged by communist enemies. American aid to sustain the government replaced the aid that Britain could no longer provide. Turkey also received American economic and military aid to protect her against pressure from Russia.

The five European nations that maintained their neutrality during the war naturally underwent fewer changes in government. A moderate socialist government remained in power under the nominal monarchy in Sweden. Switzerland's traditional neutrality enabled her to trade her manufactures and enjoy wartime and great postwar prosperity. Ireland remained neutral. In Spain Francisco Franco remained in power at the head of the prewar fascist regime. Portugal's fascist government under Dr. Salazar also survived the war years.

Israel. The Republic of Israel was established in Palestine in 1948 after Britain withdrew the year before. The Balfour Declaration in 1917 had promised the Zionists a national homeland for the Jews. Chaim Weizmann was elected president. The surrounding Arab states waged an unsuccessful war upon Israel until a United Nation's mission restored peace in a truce by which Israel's territory was somewhat enlarged.

Latin America. In 1933 in the "Good Neighbor" policy of Roosevelt the United States renounced its previously asserted rights of unilateral intervention in the affairs of Latin America. The protectorates in Cuba and Panama were abrogated, and the last troops stationed in the Caribbean states were withdrawn. Frequent Pan-American conferences were held as the threat of war in Europe increased, and agreements were made for mutual cooperation. Latin America prospered during the war, but afterwards suffered from a decline in the price of many of its raw materials. In 1948 the Organization of American States superseded the Pan-American Union. Dictatorships and democracies both attempted to deal with or suppress the chronic problem of poverty. In 1960, revolution in Cuba brought into power the communistic regime of Fidel Castro. The United States stepped up its economic aid to Latin America in 1961 in a program which was called the Alliance for Progress.

RUSSIA AND THE COMMUNIST STATES

World War II enabled Russia to win control of the governments of eastern Europe and take them behind the "Iron Curtain" by establishing communist regimes.

***Russia.** Russia suffered far greater physical damage and loss of life than any other belligerent in World War II. Loss of military and civilian population was estimated to run from twenty to thirty millions. Under Stalin the five-year plans of 1946 and 1951 brought economic recovery and growth. But many consumer needs went unsatisfied as Russia directed resources into the improvement of weapons and began the race for nuclear supremacy with the United States. The productive capacity of basic industries was greatly increased. Controls over agriculture were tightened, but efficiency did not increase sufficiently, and low productivity in agriculture remained a serious problem of the Soviet economy.

Stalin died in 1953; most of his power was assumed by Georgi M. Malenkov in association wtih Beria, Molotov, and Nikita S. Khrushchev. During an interregnum before Khrushchev succeeded in undermining the others, the government relaxed and permitted an increase in the production of consumer goods. Malenkov's successor, Bulganin, was really under Khrushchev's influence. Khrushchev emphasized economic achievement in a peaceful contest by which the Soviets would prove their system superior to that of the United States. Khrushchev ruled by holding the office of Secretary of the Communist Party and the office of prime minister in the government. In 1956 Khrushchev began a systematic program of denouncing Stalin's rule and downgrading the former tyrant.

****Eastern Europe.** The accomplished fact of military occupation by the Soviets toward the end of World War II

brought most of eastern Europe under communist governments or "people's democracies." These were established in
Albania, Bulgaria, Rumania, Poland, Hungary, and Yugoslavia. East Germany was given a communist government in
1948, and Czechoslovakia at the same time accepted a communist regime. Allied acceptance of the predominant influence of Russia in most of these countries recognized what the
Soviets had already accomplished by arms. The governments
of Albania and Czechoslovakia were taken over by native
communists. Communists gained full control by political
maneuvering, removed the opposition leaders, and liquidated
other political parties. Presence of Russian troops aided the
political takeovers. The Communist regime in Poland and
Hungary showed up in 1947.

Czechoslovakia came under Communist control when
President Benes and other democratic leaders resigned under
Soviet pressure. Czechoslovakia's resistance to Russia had
been weakened by a distrust of the Western nations that had
abandoned her at Munich. Czechoslovakia's liberation by the
Soviets, the presence of Soviet troops, and the exhaustion of
war were other factors that made her accept communism.

The Soviets entered into various agreements with the
satellite states to the advantage of Russia. The subordination
of these states closely resembled colonial imperialism at its
worst. The exploitation caused native revolts which were
crushed in East Germany, Poland, and, worst of all, in Hungary. In Hungary the Soviets demonstrated that the states of
eastern Europe were held by force. The same was evident in
Russia's unsuccessful attempt to control the shape of communism in Yugoslavia. Here Marshal Tito, a partisan leader
in the war, organized the postwar heretical, deviationist communist regime along lines adapted to Yugoslav nationalism.
Tito's communism differed in being more decentralized, in
the decision not to collectivize agriculture, and in various
profit-sharing industrial enterprises. Yugoslavia's real posi-

tion in the communist-Free World struggle was so unclear and changeful that there was much opposition in the United States to the aid given the Yugoslav government. Russia also vacillated in its attitude toward the independent stance of Tito.

REVIEW QUESTIONS

Multiple-choice:

1. The most critical problem of the United States government after 1946 was   1) high taxes   2) depression   3) the containment of Russia's aggression   4) inflation.

2. Least among important developments in Great Britain after the war was   1) the nationalization of important industries   2) the defeat of Churchill as prime minister   3) the loss of British colonies   4) danger of communist subversion.

3. One nation that did not suffer any loss of territory as a result of the war was   1) Italy   2) Finland   3) Austria   4) Poland.

4. Two nations where strong communist parties seemed likely to win election victories after 1946 were   1) Belgium and France   2) Denmark and Italy   3) Portugal and Italy   4) Italy and France.

5. The outstanding feature of French government since World War I has been   1) its instability   2) threat of communist control   3) threat of dictatorship   4) size of the pro-fascist element.

6. After the war, West Germany   1) suffered from prolonged depression   2) refused to cooperate with occupation authorities   3) developed a stable and successful democratic government   4) suffered disastrous inflation.

7. After 1950 armed resistance to communist regimes was crushed in all of the following *except*   1) Czechoslovakia   2) Poland   3) West Germany   4) Hungary.

Completion:

8. The socialization of important industries in Great Britain was carried out by the a) . . . . . Party which later lost power when b) . . . . . regained the office of prime minister.

9. The main change in French government since World War II has been the strengthening of the ..... branch.

10. A great democratic leader of Czechoslovakia who was forced to give way to a communist regime was President ......

11. A communist country that offended Russia by pursuing its own national brand of communism was ......

Matching:

12. Franklin D. Roosevelt
13. Dwight D. Eisenhower
14. Winston Churchill
15. Charles de Gaulle
16. Konrad Adenauer
17. Walther Ulbricht
18. Dr. Salazar
19. Malenkov
20. Marshal Tito
21. Nikita Khrushchev

a. Followed Truman as president
b. Strongest French leader since Napoleon III
c. Effective head of the East German Republic
d. Dictator of Portugal
e. A non-conformist communist leader
f. Defeated by Attlee in 1945 election
g. Head of the Christian Democrat Party
h. First of the war leaders to die
i. Headed Russian secret police
j. Immediate successor to a degraded dictator
k. Leader in denouncing Stalin

FOR FURTHER READING

HARDBOUND:

Andersson, Ingvar, *A History of Sweden* (1956).

Feis, Herbert, *Between War and Peace* (1901).

————, *Churchill-Roosevelt-Stalin: The War They Waged and the Peace They Sought* (1957). Objective, informative, detailed.

Larsen, Karen, *A History of Norway* (1948).

Lukacs, John A., *The Great Powers and Eastern Europe* (1953).

Ripka, H., *Eastern Europe in the Postwar World* (1961). On the Russian satellites.

Salvatorelli, Luigi, *A Concise History of Italy* (1940).

Schwartz, Harry, *Russia's Soviet Economy* (2nd ed., 1954). Accurate and comprehensive.

Valentin, Veit, *The German People* (1946). A standard survey.

Wilgus, A. Curtis, *The Development of Hispanic America* (1941). Comprehensive, expert survey.

Wolff, Robert L., *The Balkans in Our Time* (1956).

PAPERBOUND:

Agar, Herbert, *The Price of Power: America Since 1945* (University of Chicago).

Aron, Raymond, *France, the New Republic* (Oceana).

————, *The Century of Total War* (Beacon).

Borsody, Stephen, *Tragedy of Central Europe* (Collier).

Brzyezinski, Z. K., *The Soviet Bloc: Unity and Conflict* (Praeger). Recommended.

Hand, Learned, *The Spirit of Liberty* (Vintage). The ideals of America.

Mercy, T., *Thirteen Days that Shook the Kremlin* (Praeger). On the revolt in Hungary in 1956.

*1945   *Truman became president of the United States*
*1947   **Beginning of the Cold War*
        Cominform organized by Russia
        United States began "containment" policy toward Russia
        Truman Doctrine applied for first time, in Greece and Turkey
        Organization of American States formed
        **Marshall Plan first proposed*
*1949   *NATO formed*
*1950   **Korean War began*
        Red China and Russia signed mutual assistance pact
        European Coal and Steel Community formed
 1952   *ANZUS Treaty*
*1953   *Stalin's death brought relaxation in the Cold War*
 1954   *Defense pact signed between the United States and Formosa*
 1955   *SEATO formed*
        "Summit Conference" met at Geneva
*1958   **Common Market (EEC) went into effect*
        Euratom organized
 1959   *Khrushchev visited the United States*

22. Conflict and Cooperation in the Cold War Period

The "Cold War" that developed between the United States and Russia soon after the end of World War II dominated international relations and made international problems of more importance than the domestic affairs of the nations. The United States and Russia were the only two first-rate powers to emerge from the war; other nations polarized about these two or were forced to take an avowed "neutralist" position. Essentially the differences between Russia and the United States may be reduced to two opposing philosophies of social organization. The United States represented the Western liberal traditions of individual freedom. Except where the fulfillment of individual lives could be best achieved by social action, the realization of the individual personality retained primacy over the aggrandizement of the state. The communist philosophy gives first place to the interests of society, as represented by the state; this presumably requires the drastic curtailment of individual freedom, particularly in economic matters. The agencies of individual expression, such as the press, the arts, and so on, are employed to express and indoctrinate the views of the state, and individuals may not question official views except at the invitation of the state.

Europe's affairs became so closely related to those of the rest of the world that they could no longer be considered without substantial reference to worldwide developments. The term "Cold War" came to be used in reference to the power struggle between the two great blocs, one headed by the United States and the other by Russia. Attempts of communists to make new political gains created an environment of almost perpetual crisis as the West resisted such aggressions.

This chapter deals first with the employment of military power and the systems of alliances and later with organizations created to bring about international economic aid and cooperation.

THE COLD WAR AND MILITARY ALLIANCES

Efforts of the Soviet Union to gain control of Germany soon made it clear that strong and concerted measures of resistance were necessary to save the free governments and institutions of Central and western Europe. The turning point in relations between the United States and Russia came in 1947 when the United States and western Europe were compelled to face the intransigeance of Russia. The United States took the lead in rearming Europe and integrating its defenses under the North Atlantic Treaty Organization (NATO).

**Beginnings of the Cold War. The activities of Russia to promote the Communist goal of world revolution were accelerated after the defeat of Germany. At first Russia's subversion of eastern Europe was excused as the action of a nation seeking to protect herself in the future from the horrible suffering Russia had experienced from the German invasion. In 1947 the communist countries revived the dissolved Comintern under the new name "Cominform." The Cominform coordinates the various activities of communist regimes of eastern Europe. Numerous obstructive actions in Germany, the subversion of Czechoslovakia and the Berlin blockade, all revealed clearly the shape of aggression. The outstanding act of Soviet aggression was the blockade of Berlin by which Russia sought to stop America and Britain from sending supplies into the city by rail or truck. The "Berlin Airlift" in 1948-1949 flew in food and coal by airplane until the blockade was lifted. In 1947 the United States under President Harry S. Truman initiated its policy of "containment."

***The Truman Doctrine (1947).** The American containment policy went into effect in Greece and Turkey first. When Communist guerrilla forces from Yugoslavia and Russia infiltrated to give aid to native communists in Greece and threatened to take that nation behind the Iron Curtain, President Truman asked Congress to vote economic and military aid for Greece and Turkey. Great Britain, the traditional protector of Greece, had announced that she did not have the resources to support the Greek government in its fight against subversion. Russia at this same time was exerting pressure in Turkey and making demands that would have entirely subordinated Turkey to the Soviet Union. Control of Greece and Turkey would have given Russia control of the eastern Mediterranean. The Truman Doctrine declared it to be the policy of the United States to support "free peoples who are resisting attempted subjugation by armed minorities" within or from the outside. The menace of communist subjugation soon subsided in these countries. President Truman introduced the "Point Four" program in 1949 as a measure to blunt the appeal of communism in underdeveloped countries by giving them technical aid.

***The North Atlantic Treaty Organization (1949).** This military alliance between the United States and the countries of Western Europe was formed in 1949 by the North Atlantic Pact. For the first time since winning her independence, the United States entered a peacetime military alliance with European nations. Danger of Russian aggression, which could not be prevented by the UNO, could now be met by the army of a firm military alliance. The United States spent billions of dollars to re-arm and to integrate the military forces of member nations; all stood prepared to resist aggression against any member. Members included the United States, Canada, Great Britain, France, Belgium, the Netherlands, Luxemburg, Italy, Denmark, Norway, Iceland, and Portugal; later Greece, Turkey, and West Germany joined. Later, Spain consented to the building of military bases on her soil in return for economic aid from the United States. To NATO Russia and her satellites immediately replied with a series of military alliances which were confirmed by the Warsaw Pact in 1955.

***The Korean War (1950-1953).* A communist test of the willingness of the anti-communist nations to check aggression came in Korea in June, 1950. Korea was freed from Japan at the end of World War II. The nation was divided for occupation purposes along the 38th parallel pending the formation of a national government. North Korea was occupied by Russia and South Korea by the United States. The Communist regime in the north established by Russia invaded South Korea in 1950, following the withdrawal of American forces the year before. The UN Security Council immediately met and declared North Korea an aggressor and called for the restoration of peace. At that time Russia had boycotted the Security Council in protest against the presence of a representative of the Chinese Nationalist government of Formosa and, therefore, did not veto the resolution. When Russia returned to block action in the Security Council, the General Assembly recommended continued defense of South Korea. The United States provided nine-tenths of the military personnel other than that given by the South Koreans.

The early reverses of the UN forces were overcome and the invaders forced back into North Korea. As the UN forces approached the Chinese border to the North, Chinese Communist "volunteers" that had crossed the border from Manchuria staged a massive attack against the UN troops and drove them far back into South Korea. Again the UN forces recovered and eventually established a frontier just north of the 38th parallel. UN negotiations then brought a truce three years after the war began. The large-scale and bloody conflict settled nothing in Korea, but it demonstrated that the United States would resist Communist military intervention wherever it occurred.

Military alliances. Besides NATO, other Free World alliances were formed in the continuing Cold War. Regional alliances for mutual security were permitted by the UN Charter. The Organization of American States was formed in 1947 as a successor to the Pan-American Union and at the same time provided for an alliance among the American states. In Western Europe the Brussels Treaty in 1948 provided for military and other cooperation between Great Britain, Belgium, France, Luxembourg, and the Netherlands. In 1949 these countries were absorbed into the NATO. In 1952 Australia, New Zealand, and the United States signed the ANZUS Treaty to provide mutual defense. In 1954 the United States signed a similar pact with Nationalist China for the defense of Formosa and the Pescadores. In 1955 the Southeast Asia Treaty Organization (SEATO) was formed by Britain, France, Australia, New Zealand, Pakistan, the Philippine Republic, and Thailand to provide for mutual defense. In the Middle East the Bagdad Pact (1955) joined Great Britain, Turkey, Iraq, Iran, and Pakistan in a defense of that region against Russian expansion; in 1959 Iraq withdrew and the organization was renamed the Central Treaty Organization (CENTO).

Russia made similar alliances with her satellites and with Communist China. In 1950 Red China and Russia signed their mutual assistance pact.

Peaceful coexistence. Relations between Russia and the West improved after the death of Stalin in 1953. The peace treaty with Austria was signed; Russia welcomed tourists from the United States and established diplomatic relations with West Germany.

In 1955 the Big Four held a "Summit Conference" at Geneva, the first such meeting between heads of state since Potsdam in 1945. No important agreements resulted, but more friendly relations between the leaders followed. In 1959 Khrushchev visited the United States. In 1960 a Paris summit meeting was planned but called off by Khrushchev after President Eisenhower officially admitted that an American U-2 reconnaissance plane had been forced down on Russian soil. Generally, Khrushchev called for peaceful coexistence, renounced the inevitability of war with the West, and called upon Communists to pursue economic and cultural competition by which (he asserted) the West would eventually be buried.

ECONOMIC COOPERATION IN EUROPE

The United States recognized the importance of restoring Europe's economic life and increasing the production of foodstuffs and consumer goods so that Europeans could live better. In the long run communist dictatorships are more effectively prevented by flourishing economies than by military force.

The remarkable efforts at economic cooperation of the nations of Europe after the war may be attributed to 1] American aid and encouragement and 2] to the economic thought of John Maynard Keynes which recognized the necessity of government intervention in a nation's economic life. 3] Another factor was European desire to assert itself against domination of Russia and to achieve more independence from American pressure. 4] A great similarity in the domestic, constitutional governments and in political parties in power in the various countries made cooperation easier. All the nations of western Europe opposed extreme nationalism.

***The Marshall Plan** (1947).* The United Nations Relief and Rehabilitation Administration formed in Washington in 1943 sustained Europe over the immediate economic suffering of the war. Great Britain received a large postwar loan from the United States when lend-lease aid ceased after the Axis had surrendered.

The United States recognized the need for better planning of economic aid than UNRRA provided. In 1947, soon after the American Congress voted military aid to Greece and Turkey, Congress also appropriated billions of dollars for the so-called Marshall Plan, officially known as the European Recovery Plan. The plan was designed to promote European economic recovery by encouraging these nations to cooperate in helping each other. Prosperity in Europe would discourage communism. Among other things the plan called for reduction of trade barriers, sound currencies, and balanced budgets. The Marshall Plan was effective in bringing about a startling recovery and various organizations for economic integration among the European free nations.

The earliest consequence of this movement toward European unity was the customs union known as Benelux (1947) entered into by Belgium, the Netherlands, and Luxembourg; after a period of trial a full customs union was created.

In 1950 the European Payments Union was established by the Organization for European Economic Cooperation (the name of the organization created by the Marshall Plan). The EPU extended credit to businessmen and member nations who needed to borrow money to pay for foreign imports. Eurofina in 1953 set up a European railway authority to coordinate transportation facilities.

The European Coal and Steel Community (1950). This agreement among the Benelux nations and France, Italy, and Germany integrated their production and marketing of coal and steel. The agreement, called the Schuman Plan from the

French foreign minister, created a government with an executive, assembly, and court; members are chosen by the governments of the participating nations. The great success of this effort encouraged still another and greater organization for the economic integration of Europe, the Common Market.

Euratom, an organization created by treaty agreements in 1958, provided for European cooperation in the regulation and development of atomic energy.

**The European Common Market. The six members of the Coal and Steel Community began negotiations in 1955 that led to the Treaty of Rome in 1957. This treaty provided for the creation, beginning in 1958, of the Common Market, or European Economic Community (EEC). This organization began to eliminate tariff duties and other trade barriers among its members and their overseas colonies. The EEC made great strides toward the unification of Europe. It created several legislative, executive, and judicial bodies to provide the machinery of its government, the Executive Commission, the Council of Ministers, the Court of Justice, and the Assembly (a kind of European parliament). It created various funds, including a Development Fund to aid economic development in overseas areas. Other European countries were invited to join it. Its capital was at Brussels. Its creation was the work of three prominent economists and political leaders, Jean Monnet of France, Walter Hallstein of Germany, and Paul-Henri Spaak of Belgium.

Great Britain at first did not wish to join the Common Market and organized (1959) a similar customs union called the Outer Seven (European Free Trade Association) made up of Britain, Sweden, Denmark, Norway, Switzerland, Portugal, and Austria; these countries for one reason or another did not wish to join the Common Market. The possibility of a union of the Common Market and the Outer Seven might create what De Gaulle envisioned, a European third force between the United States and Russia.

REVIEW QUESTIONS

Multiple-choice:

1. Which event occurred first? 1) Bagdad Pact signed 2) organization of NATO   3) election of Eisenhower as president   4) the Korean War.

2. Which development in the postwar period bears the closest resemblance to earlier history? 1) The abandonment of isolation by the United States   2) the emergence of the United States and Russia as the only two first-rate powers   3) the steps toward the economic integration of Europe   4) cooperation of the European nations against a strong aggressive nation   5) the entrance of the United States into a peacetime military alliance.

3. In what country did Russia's policy of trying to communize a people lead to the most serious disagreement with the Allies? 1) Italy   2) Japan   3) Germany   4) France.

4. Russia exerted pressure against Turkey and Greece in 1947 to 1) extend Soviet control into the eastern Mediterranean 2) to take advantage of the unpopularity of the Allies   3) simply to add territory.

5. Which was not a member of NATO?   1) Finland   2) Denmark   3) Norway   4) France.

6. The Korean War ended   1) with a substantial victory for South Korea   2) with only a slight change in the boundary and one that favored South Korea   3) with no change at all 4) slight change in favor of North Korea.

7. The economic integration of Europe resulted primarily from 1) Europe's fear of Russia   2) the similarity in political regions there   3) the stimulus of the Marshall Plan   4) a desire to resist strong American leadership.

Completion:

8. The communist international organization of Europe is now known by the abbreviated name . . . . . .

9. The leading military organization of the Western allied nations is known by the initials a) ...... The communist counterpart organization was created by the ..... Pact.

10. The United States policy of limiting Russian expansion begun under Truman is called the policy of ......

11. The Truman Doctrine originated in a move to aid what two countries against communist aggression? ......

12. North and South Korea were divided along the a) ..... parallel. The Korean War broke out in the year b) ..... when c) ..... Korea began an invasion of the other zone of Korea.

13. Three mutual defense organizations in Asia are designated by the alphabetic names ....., ..., ...

14. The first meeting of the former Allies in World War II convened in 1955 at a) .....; a second planned to meet at Paris in 1960 was called off because Premier Khrushchev was offended by the b) ..... incident.

15. The popular name of the ERP was the ..... Plan?

16. Name the Benelux countries. The Schuman Plan included these countries plus three others, namely a) ....., ..., ... The same six nations organized a more comprehensive economic union in 1957 by the Treaty of b) ..... and became known by the popular name c) ......

FOR FURTHER READING

HARDBOUND:

Beck, F., and Godin, W., *Russian Purge and the Extractions of Confession* (1951).

Davenport, Russel W., *The Dignity of Man* (1955). Comparison of Soviet and American goals.

Gulick, Edward V., *Europe's Classical Balance of Power* (1955).

Haas, Ernest, *The Uniting of Europe* (1960).

Jasny, N., *Soviet Industrialization, 1928-1952* (1961).

Kennan, George F., *Russia, the Atom, and the West* (1958). By a brilliant analyst.

Moore, Ben T., *NATO and the Future of Europe* (1958). On international cooperation in Europe.

Niebuhr, Reinhold, *The Irony of American History* (1952). Criticism of American judgments of foreigners.

Seton-Watson, Hugh, *From Lenin to Malenkov: The History of World Communism* (1953).

————, *Neither War nor Peace* (1960).

Shapiro, L. P., *The Communist Party of the Soviet Union* (1960).

PAPERBOUND:

Aron, Raymond, *The Century of Cold War* (Beacon).

Coyle, David Cushman, *The United Nations and How It Works* (NAL). Useful brief introduction.

Crossman, R. H. S., *The God That Failed* (Bantam). The disillusionment of the intellectuals with Communism.

Goldman, Eric, *Crucial Decade* (Vintage). Excellent history of the decade after World War II.

Millis, Walter, *Arms and Men* (NAL). Earlier warfare and nuclear war.

Nystrom, J. Warren, and Malof, Peter, *Common Market: The European Community in Action* (Searchlight).

Roberts, H. L., *Russia and America: Dangers and Prospects* (NAL).

Salvadori, Massimo, *The Rise of Modern Communism* (Berkshire).

Sethe, Paul, *A Short History of Russia* (Gateway). Very brief introduction.

1925   *Chiang Kai-shek succeeded Dr. Sun as head of the Kuomintang in China*

1945   *Nationalists in Indo-China under Ho Chi Minh resist return of French rule*

Indonesia began war against return of Dutch rule

1946   *Philippines granted independence*

*1947   *Independence granted to India. India (Hindu) and Pakistan (Moslem) became separate republics and remained in the British Commonwealth*

1948   *Burma granted independence*

1949   *Indonesia won independence as result of truce arranged by the UN*

1950   *Kuomintang government confined to Formosa as Reds completed conquest of mainland China*

1953   *Egypt ousted King Farouk and established a republic*

1954   *North Vietnam became independent*

Nasser took control of Egypt

1956   *Egypt seized the Suez Canal; Israel invaded Egypt*

1957   *Eisenhower doctrine announced for the Middle East*

Ghana became independent, the first African Negro state to win independence after the war

1959   *Communist China crushed Tibet*

1960   *Twenty-two independent states created in Africa since 1950*

Independence in Belgian Congo followed by anarchy

1961   *Union of South Africa withdrew from the Commonwealth*

1963   *Algeria won independence*

23. The Revolt Against Imperialism

In the decade following World War II most of the colonies, as well as other areas governed or dominated by the European nations, won independence or otherwise broke away from their subordination. In most cases the break was made peacefully; in other instances only armed violence won independence. The weakening of the mother countries by World War II helped make independence possible just as the occupation of Spain and Portugal during the Napoleonic Wars enabled Latin America to gain independence at that time. The rivalry between the free and communist worlds encouraged the independence movements. Suicidal wars by now had destroyed Europe's domination of the rest of the world.

The "uncommitted nations" of Asia and Africa recognized the threat of communist domination as they also remembered the imperialism of the Western nations. Many, therefore, steered clear of joining either great bloc in the Cold War. The smaller nations also benefited from the rivalry just as the United States and the other American nations had in their early years profited from the rivalries of Europe.

THE FAR EAST AND THE MIDDLE EAST

The older civilizations of Asia resented especially the colonial status imposed by the white man of Europe and decisively broke his rule in the postwar years. However, the nationalism of Asia will always be indebted to Europe for much of the inspiration for the ideals of democracy and self-government. The science, technology, and even the culture of Europe are being blended into the ancient heritages of the East and of Africa.

**Communist China.   The father of the Chinese Revolution, Dr. Sun Yat-sen, at the head of the Kuomintang, or National Revolutionary Party, ruled China until he died in 1925. Under Dr. Sun, China failed to achieve a strong, unified government, and a Chinese Communist Party became active in opposing the rule of the Kuomintang. After 1925 General Chiang Kai-shek made himself the strong man of China. He continued a war against the Chinese Communists who were driven into the northwest. Efforts to strengthen Chinese control over her own affairs were opposed by Japan. Japan's desire to dominate Asia caused her to seek a weak China that she could exploit. After 1931 China's main problem was the war with Japan, first in Manchuria and then in China proper, but the Communists also waged war against Chiang's nationalist regime at Nanking.

At the end of World War II the Chinese people had lost confidence in the Nationalist government; it had not brought progress or prosperity to China but instead gave it a selfish and corrupt officialdom. Nor was Chiang's government democratic. Landlords exploited the masses who longed for reform.

Mao Tse-tung and Chou En-lai, energetic Communist revolutionary leaders, had promised to end the evils of corruption, inflation, and exploitation of the people. After 1947 the Communists rapidly took control over China and set up a "People's Republic" at Peiping. Chiang and the Kuomintang fled to Formosa and established the Nationalist Chinese government there, hoping that some day they might be able to return to power on the mainland. Communist China in 1950 won recognition of a number of European governments and made an alliance with Russia. The Communists, who had earlier represented themselves as agrarian reformers, carried out a merciless war against enemies of their new order. Foreigners, businessmen, and missionaries were forced out of China. The violent revolution was partly a reaction against long years of domination by foreigners; it was both a communist revolution and a patriotic movement. By 1962 China was challenging Russia's leadership of world communism; specifically, China disagreed with Khrushchev's policy of peaceful coexistence with the capitalistic democracies of the West. Red China absorbed Tibet in 1959 in an expansion move and later took a border strip of northern India.

Indo-China. A militant Communist China now wished to reassert the ancient Chinese leadership in Asia. The Chinese Communists engaged the U. N. forces in Korea and afterward became more active in infiltrating French Indo-China to the South and the neighboring lands of Thailand (Siam), Burma, and Malaya. After 1945 Nationalists in Indo-China resisted the French until they won a large measure of self-rule within the French Union for the provinces of Vietnam, Laos, and Cambodia. Ho Chi Minh continued to resist the French and demanded complete independence for a communist state in Vietnam. Russia and China sent munitions to aid the Vietnam nationalists. In 1954 North Vietnam became independent, but the followers of Ho Chi Minh continued to conduct guerrilla warfare in Indo-China in a move to win all of southeast Asia for communism.

India and Burma. The Labor Party kept Britain's promise to grant independence to India at the end of World War II and did not quibble as to how it should be done. The Independence of India Act of 1947 left India to determine her future ties with Britain. Both India and Pakistan became republics and chose membership in the Commonwealth. India was divided between Hindus and Moslems, India being the Hindu state and Pakistan the Moslem state. The Republic of Pakistan was divided into two parts, the larger to the northwest of India and the other in Bengal to the east of India. Civil war followed upon the independence and separation of India; Moslems fled India for Pakistan and vice versa. Tens of thousands of persons were slain. The state of Kashmir was claimed by both new nations, and the dispute over it remains unsettled. Nehru became India's prime minister. In 1958 General Ayub Khan became practical but benevolent dictator of Pakistan. India adopted a neutral role in the Cold War while Pakistan allied herself with the West.

Burma, a region east of India was given independence by Britain in 1948 and chose, like Ireland, not to remain in the Commonwealth. Burma suffers from frequent internal political disturbances.

Indonesia. When Indonesia secured its freedom from Japanese occupation in 1945, it did not wish to retain the rule of the Netherlands. Fighting continued until 1949 when the UN helped arrange a truce. The Dutch recognized the independence in the same year. Sukarno became president of this large state composed of Java, Sumatra, Borneo, and other islands of the East Indies. In the early sixties the expansion-minded republic won the eastern (Netherlands) part of New Guinea.

The Philippines. The United States had provided for Philippine independence in 1934. Independence was to be granted after a ten-year transition period, which was interrupted by the war. In 1946 the Philippine Republic was established by treaty agreement which permitted the United States to retain military bases. The Philippine government was troubled by much corruption. American aid helped restore her economy and repair the destruction caused by the Japanese conquest and the American reconquest of the islands in World War II.

The Middle East. The break-up of the Ottoman Empire eventually brought complete independence, but not until after World War II, to several new states in the Middle East. Several conditions tend to maintain instability in the Middle East.

The great oil deposits are of crucial importance to Europe. The Arab states—Egypt, Jordan, Syria, Lebanon, Iraq, and Iran— are extremely nationalistic but remained feudal in their economic and social life. The establishment of the state of Israel deeply antagonized all the neighboring Arab states. Great power rivalries complicate international relations in this area. In 1957 President Eisenhower issued a statement of policy that came to be known as the Eisenhower Doctrine. He stated that the United States would send military and economic aid to any Middle Eastern nation resisting the aggression of "any nation controlled by international Communism."

Egypt and the Suez crisis (1956). Egypt, after ejecting King Farouk, established a republic in 1953. Egypt's dispute with Britain over the Sudan was settled by provisions for a plebiscite, and in 1955 the Sudan became an independent state. The strongman Gamal Abdel Nasser assumed control of Egypt in 1954 and aspired to unite the Arab states of the Near East. In July, 1956, Egypt seized the Suez Canal in order to use its revenues for construction of the Aswan High Dam. Britain and France, as owners of the Suez Canal, greatly resented the seizure of the canal, as did Israel. Israel's ships were forbidden the use of the canal.

The Suez crisis was precipitated in October, 1956, when Israeli troops invaded the disputed Gaza Strip and moved into Egypt. France and Britain entered the war presumably to protect the canal. The United States abandoned its allies and joined Russia in demanding a withdrawal from Egypt and submission of the dispute to the U. N. The invaders submitted and U. N. forces occupied the Suez.

AFRICA

From only four independent states in Africa in 1950, the number increased to twenty-six in 1960. It appeared that almost all of Africa would soon become independent. The term "Black Africa" is often used to distinguish the Negro states from the North African states and parts of Africa occupied by Europeans. The new African nations were promptly admitted to the UN and rapidly swelled its membership. The African states chose to avoid taking sides in the Cold War.

African problems. Certain conditions in Africa present serious political and economic difficulties. The nations are primitive and illiterate, and population already exceeds the production of foodstuffs. The natives speak about seven hundred dialects. Africans are lacking in sufficient educated leadership for successful self-government, but with freedom and assistance they are rapidly adopting the techniques of European civilization.

North Africa. France successfully repressed independence movements in Tunisia and Morocco until 1954. Habib Bourguiba, exiled Tunisian nationalist, was permitted to return in 1955. In 1956 Tunisia won practical independence. In the same year Morocco was granted independence after two years of disorder and violence.

Algeria began war for independence in 1954 with nationalists receiving direction from Egyptian and Iraqui leaders. In 1958 the French army led an uprising of the European colonists who feared Algeria would go the way of Tunisia and Morocco. Savage warfare followed; the native rebels received aid from the communist world. Algeria won its independence by 1963.

*The Union of South Africa. This former member of the Commonwealth shares with the United States, Ireland, and Burma the fact of having made a complete break with Great Britain, instead of retaining Commonwealth status. South

Africa in 1961 withdrew because the other Commonwealth states were critical of her policy of *apartheid* (apartness, segregation). This policy, adopted in 1948, calls for racial segregation and subordination of the natives. The system, designed partly to protect lower class whites from native economic competition, led to bloody clashes between police and native demonstrators. South Africa's racial elements also include Indians, who held a status between whites and Africans.

*Ghana and Guinea. Ghana, formerly the British Gold Coast, peacefully achieved independence in 1957. There were no white settlers there to complicate the problem of granting independence. Except for Liberia, Ghana was the first African Negro state to gain independence. Ghana by 1960 showed noteworthy progress in its economic and social development. Its leader, Kwame Nkrumah, therefore, became a leader of African nationalism elsewhere on the continent.

Guinea, formerly a French colony, shares with Ghana a similar leadership among the Africans. In 1958 De Gaulle permitted French colonies to choose either autonomy in the French Union or independence. Only Guinea chose complete independence. President Toure of Guinea joined Nkrumah in promoting a pan-African movement and a union of the independent African states.

Reaction against white rule. In 1959 Belgian Congo demanded independence and forced Belgian officials and leaders to abandon the Congo. When independence was granted in 1960 the Congo entered a state of anarchy; it had not been prepared for self-government. In particular, Katanga Province, rich in minerals, made trouble by an armed secession movement. U. N. troops intervened to restore and preserve order. The Congo rivalry presented another crisis in the Cold War when the Soviet Union took sides in the Congo dispute.

REVIEW QUESTIONS

Multiple-choice:

1. The revolt against imperialism resulted from all *except*
1) the rivalry of the Russians with the nations of Western Europe
2) the complete readiness for independence among all the colonies
3) the weakness of the imperialist nations following World War II
4) influence of Japanese victories in Asia.

2. In the Cold War most of the newly independent nations of Asia and Africa 1) joined Russia 2) drifted into the non-communist orbit 3) chose neutrality 4) shifted erratically.

3. The most obvious cause of disagreement between Red China and Russia is 1) territorial aggression of China 2) the Russian policy of peaceful coexistence 3) China's bid for leadership of the communist world 4) competition in Cuba.

4. Which of these nations did not gain its independence from Britain? 1) Indonesia 2) Burma 3) Pakistan 4) Palestine.

5. Which nation granted independence to its colonies with the least resistance? 1) Britain 2) France 3) Portugal 4) the Netherlands.

6. The Suez crisis in 1956 was settled by 1) the surrender of Egypt 2) the defeat of Palestine 3) intervention of Britain and France 4) intervention of Russia and the United States against the aggressors.

7. In what area have the most new nations been created after World War II? 1) Southeast Asia 2) the Middle East 3) Africa 4) the Far East.

Completion:

8. The nationalist party of Dr. Sun is named the . . . . . .

9. The nationalist government of China is now located on the island of . . . . . .

10. Red China disagrees with the policy of Khrushchev which is summed up by the expression . . . . . .

11. The largest area absorbed by resurgent China has been the neighboring land of . . . . . .

12. What is the name of the Moslem republic in the region of India? a) ...... A disputed borderland between India and her Moslem neighbor is the region of b) ......

13. An Asian land which won complete independence of Britain without remaining in the Commonwealth is ......

14. The nation which won its independence from the Netherlands in southeast Asia is called the Republic of ......

15. The United States granted independence to the Philippines in the year ......

16. Segregation policy in South Africa is known by the term ......

Matching:

17. Sun Yat-sen	a.	Benevolent dictator of Pakistan
18. Chiang Kai-shek	b.	Strong man successor to Dr. Sun
19. Mao Tse-tung	c.	Leading associate of Mao Tse-tung
20. Chou En-lai	d.	Father of the Chinese Revolution
21. Ho Chi Minh	e.	Egyptian nationalist leader
22. Sukarno	f.	Main leader of the People's Republic of
23. Ayub Khan	g.	China
24. General Nasser	h.	Leader of Indonesia
25. Kwame Nkrumah	i.	Thailand communist leader
	j.	Communist leader in Vietnam
		Leader of Ghana

FOR FURTHER READING

HARDBOUND:

Gillespie, Jean, *Algeria: Rebellion and Revolution* (1961).

Lancaster, D., *The Emancipation of French Indo-China* (1961). An important study.

Laquer, W. Z., ed., *The Middle East in Transition* (1958).

Menon, V. P., *The Transfer of Power in India* (1957).

Murdock, George P., *Africa: Its People and Their Culture History* (1959). By an anthropologist.

Nuseibeh, H. Z., *Ideas of Arab Nationalism* (1946). About the Arab League and its aims.

Rostow, W. W., *et al., The Prospects for Communist China* (1954).

Thornton, A. P., *The Imperial Idea and Its Enemies* (1959). Sympathetic to more recent imperialism.

PAPERBOUND:

Adams, Thomas R., *Government and Politics in Africa South of the Sahara* (Random House). On the most recent developments in Africa.

――――, *Modern Colonialism: Institutions and Policies* (Random House). Brief.

Carter, M., *Independence for Africa* (Praeger).

Dean, Vera M., *The Nature of the Non-Western World* (NAL). Life among non-European peoples.

Harrison, Selig S., *India: The Most Dangerous Decades* (1960). India's present and future.

Latourette, Kenneth S., *A History of Modern China* (Penguin). Brief account by a leading historian of China.

Smith, Wilfred Cantwell, *Islam in Modern History* (NAL).

1842-1910	*William James, philosopher*
1856-1939	*Freud, introduced the new psychology*
1859-1952	*John Dewey, philosopher of pragmatism and educator*
1861-1947	*Whitehead, English philosopher*
1883-1946	*Lord Keynes, business cycle economist*
1895	*Roentgen discovered the X-ray*
1896	*Becquerel discovered radioactivity of uranium*
1900	*Planck propounded quantum theory*
*1905	*Einstein developed theory of relativity*
1920	*Rutherford converted nitrogen atoms into hydrogen and oxygen atoms*
1940's	*Rocket propulsion made practical by German scientists*
*1945	*First atomic bomb exploded in New Mexico and two others soon dropped on Japanese cities*
*1957	*First earth satellite launched into space by Russia*
*1961	*First manned spacecraft placed in orbit by Russia*

24. Science and Thought Since 1900

Only a few developments recognized as of the greatest significance can be selected for treatment in the brief chapter of a survey history such as this. Western civilization accelerates its scientific discoveries and technological changes rather than exhausting such possibilities. Western thought attempts to keep abreast of the new knowledge of the universe and Western art attempts to interpret their significance to man.

***The New Physics and the atom.** The "New Physics" around the opening of the twentieth century began making discoveries that carried physicists beyond the discoveries of Newton and gave answers that Newton had been unable to supply. These various discoveries and many technological innovations culminated in man's ability to control atomic reactions.

In 1895 Roentgen (1845-1923) discovered the X-ray which showed that a ray could penetrate solid matter and still register on photographic film. In 1896 Becquerel discovered the phenomenon of radioactivity of uranium by which particles are emitted by disintegrating matter. Then Pierre and Marie Curie discovered radium (in the mineral pitchblende). These discoveries led to a better understanding of the nature of the atom which had been postulated by the ancient Greek philosophers.

Max Planck, a German physicist in studies of heat and light showed (1900) that radiant energy is given off not continually but in particles or bundles called *quanta,* hence, the *quantum* theory. Further questions were raised by these studies about the nature and behavior of matter.

***Einstein's work.*   Albert Einstein (1879-1955), a young German physicist, in 1905 next developed his theory of relativity by which he contradicted Newton's physics and showed that time and space are not absolute but relative to the observer. He extended his findings to explain gravitation and motion. He developed a formula to explain that matter and energy are the same, that disintegrating matter produces energy by radiation. The theory showed that a small amount of matter undergoing atomic changes would produce an enormous amount of energy. There was still much to be done before this theory could be applied in the construction of an atomic bomb.

In 1920 the English physicist Ernest Rutherford converted nitrogen atoms into hydrogen and oxygen atoms. Through the work of others it was discovered that the bombardment of the nucleus of uranium would cause it to split and release enormous amounts of energy. The rapid breakdown of the nucleus of one form of uranium sets off a chain reaction somewhat as a fire spreads through combustible material. The application of this knowledge was the work of the American wartime Manhattan Project which produced the first atomic bomb that was tested in New Mexico in 1945. Within weeks the two atomic bombs dropped on the Japanese cities brought the end of World War II. Since the war, the reading public has become familiar with many peacetime applications of atomic energy.

**Weapons development and space research.*   Toward the latter part of World War II the Germans began to bombard the southeast coast of England with frightful rocket-propelled explosives. German scientists who produced these weapons were captured by both Americans and Russians and put to work on further weapons research and development. Both countries produced a large array of rocket-propelled missiles for various kinds of tactical use in offensive and defensive warfare. Enormous intercontinental ballistic missiles (ICBM's) rendered the large cities of the whole world vulnerable to destruction in case the Cold War should become an all-out military struggle. A kind of frightful balance of power had been produced that made both nations less eager to avenge the misdeeds of the other. Some commentators asserted that the certain loss of millions of lives in large-scale atomic attacks had made a major war obsolete.

Rocket propulsion was soon harnessed to unmanned and to manned craft equipped with instruments for space exploration. In 1957 Russia put the first earth satellite (Sputnik) in orbit. Space research was spurred by defense requirements as well as by the search for scientific information. National prestige came to be the most important factor of all in Soviet and American appropriations for orbiting manned spaceships. Shots of unmanned spacecraft into orbit by both nations produced data that made the orbiting of the numerous manned spacecraft possible. In 1961 the Soviets orbited the first two manned craft; the United States and Russia both followed with other such flights.

Sigmund Freud (1856-1939) and the new psychology. As important as the material progress of physical science is the new understanding of man's behavior which psychology and the social sciences are providing. Corresponding in significance to the theory of biological evolution and to the new physics are the findings of psychologists relating to man's mind and behavior. Of the most significance here is the work of Freud and other psychologists who came after him.

Sigmund Freud, an Austrian physician and psychiatrist, developed the method of psychoanalysis as a means of therapy for mental patients. By helping the patient to recall early experiences buried in the unconscious, psychoanalysis helps the patient to effect his own cure. Freud taught that civilized society requires people to suppress normal animal sex drives, but that such motives, affecting individuals below the conscious level, causes fears and abnormal behavior. Scientific analysis of dreams, he thought, helps to understand mental ailments.

Keynesian economics. Since about 1920 the works of John Maynard Keynes (1883-1946) have exerted an influence on economic thought comparable to that of Adam Smith a century earlier. Lord Keynes specialized in the study of the business cycle; his theories were widely applied by governments during the Great Depression and after World War II. Keynes stressed the need for government measures to offset deflationary forces. His countermeasures were designed to encourage investment and discourage oversaving. Their effect was to increase the money supply, reduce interest rates, and promote a certain degree of inflation. He advocated liberal government spending, including spending for welfare programs. His ideas increased the influence of those who favored government intervention in economic matters.

Philosophy. American influence on thought exerted itself through the writings of thinkers who developed the philosophy known as Pragmatism. The new philosophy was founded by Charles Peirce but was elaborated by William James (1842-1910) and John Dewey (1859-1952). Pragmatism teaches that the test of truth is whether or not a thing give practical results, i.e., the pragmatic test. Truth is not absolute but relative; what is good in one place and time may not be in another. Pragmatists had no interest in metaphysics as a way of discovering the nature of reality. Pragmatic philosophy recognized man's freedom to choose his own destiny. John Dewey, also an educational authority, stressed the value of education in helping man to operate intelligently his governments and rule himself under democratic institutions.

Alfred North Whitehead (1861-1947) son of an Anglican clergyman and a professor of philosophy at Harvard, offered another optimistic philosophy. He sought to harmonize thought with the new findings of science; he was strongly influenced by Plato, Kant, and Einstein. Whitehead believed in God, benevolent but not all-powerful, who aided man in his struggle against evil.

Existentialism, the new leading postwar philosophy, was founded by Jean-Paul Sartre, a French philosophy teacher and Resistance leader against the Germans in World War II. This pessimistic philosophy teaches that man exists as a free individual who is morally responsible. Sartre's type of existentialism denied the existence of God or purpose in the universe or in man's life but held that man's best hope of escape from the predicament of life is in "involvement" in life around him. Man's highest virtue is being true to the demands of his own nature. An earlier, Christian form of existentialist philosophy was originated in the teachings of Soren Kierkegaard, a Danish theologian; he, too, held that man's loneliness and terror originate in his freedom. To escape, man must make the "leap" of faith and find God. Existentialists urge man to free himself and his personality from the dehumanization of industrial society and the pressure of convention.

History: Spengler and Toynbee.   The German, Oswald Spengler (1880-1936), wrote the *Decline of the West*, an interpretation of the history of the Western World. In the cycle of history corresponding to man's life cycle, Spengler wrote, Western Civilization had entered a decadent phase. Spengler was anti-intellectual, contemptuous of the masses, and denied the possibility of democracy. An admirer of ruthlessness and power, he wrote from a Nazi mentality. Spengler attempted prophecy more than the production of scientific history.

Arnold J. Toynbee (1889-   ), the English historian, is the best known of his profession today. Toynbee, the author of *A Study of History*, dealt with the rise and fall of civilizations. Toynbee says civilization begins with man's "response" to some kind of "challenge" in his environment. He condemned nationalism as the villain of modern times. He places Western society in the downward phase of its life cycle but does not necessarily condemn it to continue on that path.

REVIEW QUESTIONS

Multiple-choice:

1. Albert Einstein's contribution to atomic development was 1) the theory of relativity   2) development of mathematical symbols   3) development of formula that showed that matter and energy are the same   4) his studies in the theory of light.

2. The most recent revolution in warfare which has not yet been effectively tested on large scale is   1) the development of the atomic bomb   2) displacement of the battleship by aircraft carriers   3) development of ICBM's   4) radar.

3. Keynesian theories of economic behavior relate especially to the problem of   1) war finance   2) repayment of international obligations and elimination of tariff barriers   3) depression   4) automation.

4. Pragmatic philosophy developed in   1) the United States   2) England   3) Russia   4) France.

5. Existentialism is a philosophy of   1) resignation   2) involvement   3) mainly concerned with the proofs of deity   4) escapism.

6. Toynbee's philosophy of history holds   1) that Western society is irrevocably doomed to eclipse by the East   2) that God will save the West   3) Western society could reverse the present downward phase of its life cycle   4) that democracy is really impossible.

Matching:

7. Roentgen   a. Theory of relativity
8. Becquerel   b. Discoverer of radioactivity of uranium
9. Marie Curie   c. Method of psychoanalysis
10. Max Planck   d. Philosopher and educator
11. Albert Einstein   e. Discoverer of X-ray

12. Ernest Rutherford   f. Quantum theory
13. Sigmund Freud   g. Co-discoverer of radium
14. J. M. Keynes   h. Converted nitrogen atoms to other
15. John Dewey   i.   atoms
16. A. N. Whitehead   j. Student of the business cycle
17. Jean-Paul Sartre   k. Originator of pragmatism
18. Arnold Toynbee   l. Existentialist philosophy
                           m. Best known contemporary historian
                             English philosopher

FOR FURTHER READING

HARDBOUND:

Ayer, A. J., *et al.*, *The Revolution in Philosophy* (1956).

Easton, Stewart C., *The Twilight of European Colonialism* (1960).
Deals with politics in the colonies of the major colonial powers
and the government of the new nations.

Levi, Albert W., *Philosophy and the Modern World* (1959). A
statement of the philosophy of twentieth century thinkers.

Magnus, Laurie, *A History of European Liberalism* (1934).

Macy, John A., *The Story of the World's Literature* (1925).

Spengler, Oswald, *The Decline of the West* (1932).

Von Rensh, Georg, *A History of Soviet Russia* (1957).

PAPERBOUND:

Allen, Frederick L., *The Big Change* (Bantam). Lively reading
in serious history of social changes in America.

Aron, Raymond, *The Dawn of Universal History* (Praeger). An
interpretation of the present age.

Blackham, H. J., *Six Existentialist Thinkers* (Torchbooks).

Broglie, Louis de, Physics and Microphysics (Torchbooks).

Carr, E. H., *The New Society* (Beacon). On the welfare state.

Eddington, Arthur, *The Nature of the Physical World* (Ann Arbor).
Popular.

Hayek, F. A., *The Road to Serfdom* (Phoenix). A conservative's
arguments.

Heilbroner, Richard L., *The Future as History* (Evergreen).

Huxley, Julian, *Man in the Modern World* (Mentor).

Jaspers, Karl, *Man in the Modern Age* (Anchor).

Jeans, Sir James, *The New Background of Science* (Ann Arbor).

Kirchner, Walter, *History of Russia* (Barnes and Noble).

Klose, Nelson, *American History* (2 vols, BES). Concise topical survey for college students.

Nelson, Benjamin, ed., *Freud and the Twentieth Century* (Meridian).

Riesman, David, *The Lonely Crowd* (Anchor). An abridgment of an effective sociological study.

Tillich, Paul, *The Religious Situation* (Meridian).

Toynbee, Arnold, *A Study of History* (2 vol. abridgment, 1946, 1957).

Whitehead, Alfred N., *Science and the Modern World* (NAL).

ESSAY TYPE QUESTIONS FOR MID-TERM AND FINAL EXAMINATIONS

1. Sketch the German victories in Europe from 1939 to 1942.

2. What were the causes of the German invasion of Russia?

3. What part did the United States play up to late 1941 in the developing war in Europe?

4. Sketch the Japanese expansion after Pearl Harbor.

5. What were the causes of German defeat in World War II?

6. Sketch the American campaigns for the conquest of Japan.

7. Discuss American diplomatic cooperation during World War II.

8. Describe the structure of the United Nations Organization.

9. Summarize the peace settlements after World War II.

10. What were the main changes in domestic politics from 1945 to 1960 in the United States, Great Britain, France, and Germany?

11. Sketch Allied relations with Germany from 1945 to 1954.

12. What changes in leadership occurred in Russia during the 1950's?

13. In what countries did the communist's win control after the war?

14. What measures did the United States take to contain Communist expansion after World War II?

15. What steps did western Europe take toward economic integration after World War II?

16. Sketch the spread of communism in Asia since 1945.

17. What new countries achieved independence in Asia after World War II?

18. What were the causes and results of the Suez Crisis in 1956?

19. Sketch the development of atomic physics from 1895 to 1945.

20. Explain the contributions of Freud, Keynes, John Dewey, and Arnold Toynbee. What is existentialism?

Answers

1. 2	*3.* 1	*5.* 2	*7.* 4	*9.* 2
2. 5	*4.* 3	*6.* 1	*8.* 3	

1. 1	*8.* a	*14.* 1	*18.* a) Scientific
2. 2	*9.* h	*15.* d	b) *Communist*
3. 1	*10.* k	*16.* Louis Blanc	*Manifesto*
4. 4	*11.* j	*17.* a) Robert Owen	c) *Das Kapital*
5. 3	*12.* b	b) New Harmony	d) Proletariat
6. c	*13.* e		e) Capitalism
7. f			*19.* a) Proudhon
			b) Bakunin

1. 2	*8.* 3	*15.* 1	*22.* j
2. 4	*9.* 2	*16.* d	*23.* f
3. 1	*10.* 3	*17.* e	*24.* i
4. 4	*11.* 3	*18.* h	*25.* a) Aristocracy
5. 2	*12.* 1	*19.* a	b) Bourgeoisie
6. 3	*13.* 3	*20.* b	*26.* Liberal
7. 4	*14.* 2	*21.* c	*27.* Clericals
			28. Olmutz

1. 1	*3.* 3	*5.* 4	*7.* 2	*9.* 1
2. 3	*4.* 1	*6.* 2	*8.* 2	*10.* 4

ANSWERS TO CHAPTER 5 *Page 63 to 64*

1. 1	*5.* 2	*9.* 4	*13.* 3
2. 1	*6.* 4	*10.* 1	*14.* 4
3. 3	*7.* 2	*11.* 2	*15.* 1
4. 3	*8.* 1	*12.* 2	*16.* 3

ANSWERS TO CHAPTER 6 *Page 72 to 73*

1. 3	*6.* 1	*11.* g	*16.* e
2. 3	*7.* 1	*12.* i	*17.* b
3. 2	*8.* 2	*13.* a	
4. 1	*9.* 1	*14.* d	
5. 1	*10.* c	*15.* h	

ANSWERS TO CHAPTER 7 *Page 88 to 89*

1. 3	*8.* 2	*15.* Lenin	*22.* j
2. 1	*9.* 1	*16.* Labor	*23.* f
3. 1	*10.* 4	*17.* c	*24.* b
4. 3	*11.* 2	*18.* g	*25.* h
5. 4	*12.* Malthus	*19.* i	*26.* d
6. 2	*13.* Cartel	*20.* a	
7. 3	*14.* Fabian	*21.* e	

ANSWERS TO CHAPTER 8 *Page 108 to 110*

1. 4	*8.* 3	*15.* Disraeli	*22.* f
2. 2	*9.* 2	*16.* Communards	*23.* a
3. 1	*10.* 1	*17.* Monarchists	*24.* b
4. 3	*11.* 2	*18.* Vatican	*25.* i
5. 4	*12.* 1	*19.* Trasformismo	*26.* d
6. 1	*13.* 3	*20.* c	*27.* g
7. 2	*14.* 4	*21.* j	*28.* k
			29. h

ANSWERS TO CHAPTER 9 *Page 121 to 122*

1. 2	4. 2	7. 4
2. 4	5. 3	8. 1
3. 1	6. 3	9. 1

ANSWERS TO CHAPTER 10 *Page 132 to 133*

1. 4	6. 3	11. a	16. c
2. 3	7. 3	12. c	17. a
3. 2	8. d	13. b	18. d
4. 1	9. e	14. g	19. d
5. 2	10. b	15. h	20. g
			21. b

ANSWERS TO CHAPTER 11 *Page 140 to 141*

1. 3	4. 1	7. 2
2. 5	5. 1	8. 3
3. 1	6. 4	9. 1

ANSWERS TO CHAPTER 12 *Page 161 to 163*

1. 3	9. 2	17. 4	c) Taiping
2. 4	10. 3	18. 3	d) Open Door
3. 3	11. 1	19. 2	e) Boxer
4. 4	12. 2	20. 1	24. a) Boers
5. 4	13. 3	21. 4	b) Paul Kruger
6. 1	14. 1	22. Congress	25. a) Roosevelt Corollary
7. 2	15. 3	23. a) Canton	b) Panama Canal
8. 2	16. 2	b) Manchu	c) Dollar Diplomacy

ANSWERS TO CHAPTER 13 *Page 174 to 175*

1. 3	5. 4	9. 2	13. 2
2. 2	6. 4	10. 2	
3. 1	7. 1	11. 2	
4. 2	8. 3	12. 3	

ANSWERS TO CHAPTER 14 *Page 188 to 189*

1. 3	*5.* 1	*9.* 2	*13.* a) Poison gas
2. 4	*6.* 2	*10.* 3	b) Trench
3. 5	*7.* 1	*11.* Schlieffen	*14.* Austria
4. 4	*8.* 3	*12.* Jutland	*15.* Propaganda

ANSWERS TO CHAPTER 15 *Page 198 to 199*

1. 1	*4.* 1	*7.* 3	*10.* 2
2. 3	*5.* 2	*8.* 1	*11.* 2
3. 4	*6.* 3	*9.* 1	

ANSWERS TO CHAPTER 16 *Page 210 to 211*

1. 2	*6.* 3	*9.* a) Kerensky	*10.* a) Soviets
2. 3	*7.* 3	b) Lenin	b) War
3. 4	*8.* a) Petrograd	c) Trotsky	c) NEP
4. 4	b) Duma	d) Stalin	*11.* a) White
5. 1	c) Nicholas II		b) Cheka
			12. Kulaks

ANSWERS TO CHAPTER 17 *Page 227 to 229*

1. 1	*7.* 3	*10.* a) Sinn Fein	*14.* d
2. 1	*8.* 2	b) De Valera	*15.* a
3. 4	*9.* a) Westminster	*11.* a) Gandhi	*16.* b
4. 2	b) the Commonwealth	b) Passive	*17.* h
5. 3	c) Edward VII	*12.* c	*18.* g
6. 2		*13.* e	*19.* f

ANSWERS TO CHAPTER 18 *Page 240 to 241*

1. 3	*4.* 3	*7.* 1
2. 1	*5.* 1	*8.* 2
3. 2	*6.* 2	*9.* 3

ANSWERS TO CHAPTER 19 *Page 248 to 249*

1. 2	*6.* 1	*10.* a) Munich	*11.* a) 1939
2. 4	*7.* 3	b) Chamberlain	b) Stalin
3. 2	*8.* 4	c) Sudetens	c) Poland
4. 2	*9.* Anschluss	d) appeasement	d) blitzkrieg
5. 3			

ANSWERS TO CHAPTER 20 *Page 268 to 270*

1. 3	*14.* 3	*17.* Europe
2. 4	*15.* a) Roosevelt, 1941	*18.* China
3. 3	b) Churchill, 1939	*19.* Eisenhower
4. 2	c) De Gaulle, 1939, 1939	*20.* Solomons
5. 1	d) Petain, 1939, 1945	*21.* Hiroshima
6. 3	e) Stalin, 1939	*22.* the Atlantic
7. 2	f) Mussolini, 1940, 1943	Charter
8. 3	g) Hitler, 1939, 1945	*23.* Yalta
9. 2	h) Tojo, 1941, 1945	*24.* a) San Francisco
10. 1	i) Chiang Kai-shek, 1941	b) 1945
11. 4	*16.* a) Sitzkrieg	*25.* MacArthur
12. 1	b) Maginot	*26.* Korea
13. 2	c) Siegfried	

ANSWERS TO CHAPTER 21 *Page 283 to 284*

1. 3	*7.* 1	*12.* h	*18.* d
2. 1	*8.* a) Labor	*13.* a	*19.* j
3. 3	b) Churchill	*14.* f	*20.* e
4. 4	*9.* Executive	*15.* b	*21.* k
5. 1	*10.* Benes	*16.* g	
6. 3	*11.* Yugoslavia	*17.* c	

ANSWERS TO CHAPTER 22 *Page 295 to 296*

1. 2	*7.* 3	*12.* a) 38th	*15.* Marshall
2. 4	*8.* Cominform	b) 1950	*16.* a) France,
3. 3	*9.* a) NATO	c) North	Italy,
4. 1	b) Warsaw	*13.* ANZUS,	Germany
5. 1	*10.* Containment	SEATO,	b) Rome
6. 2	*11.* Greece and	CENTO	c) European
	Turkey	*14.* a) Geneva	Common
		b) U-2	Market

ANSWERS TO CHAPTER 23 *Page 306 to 307*

1. 2	*8.* Kuomintang	*14.* Indonesia	*21.* i
2. 3	*9.* Formosa	*15.* 1946	*22.* g
3. 2	*10.* Peaceful coexistence	*16.* Apartheid	*23.* a
4. 1	*11.* Tibet	*17.* d	*24.* e
5. 1	*12.* a) Pakistan	*18.* b	*25.* j
6. 4	b) Kashmir	*19.* f	
7. 3	*13.* Burma	*20.* c	

ANSWERS TO CHAPTER 24 *Page 315 to 316*

1. 3	*6.* 3	*11.* a	*16.* m
2. 3	*7.* e	*12.* h	*17.* k
3. 3	*8.* b	*13.* c	*18.* l
4. 1	*9.* g	*14.* i	
5. 2	*10.* f	*15.* d	

Dictionary of Important and Difficult Terms

Hint to the Student: It would be helpful to study or at least read the vocabulary entries in this dictionary so that one may know the meaning of these terms when he encounters them in the textbook or lectures. However, this dictionary is intended mainly as a quick and convenient reference for identifying terms and defining words by giving their special meanings in the context of Modern Western Civilization. See the *Index* for persons, words, or terms not listed here.

ABC POWERS. Argentina, Brazil, and Chile, the three leading nations of South America.

absolutism. Form of government, such as absolute monarchy, in which the head of state rules without the limitations or advice of any legislative body or persons except as he chooses.

Algeciras Conference, 1906. A meeting at Algeciras, Morocco, of France, Germany, Great Britain, and Spain, called upon Germany's demand to review the international status of Morocco. On balance, its decisions favored France by giving her control over police in Morocco. British support enabled France in 1912 to annex all of Morocco except a small strip assigned to Spain.

alliance. An agreement between nations providing for military aid or cooperation under certain conditions or contingencies.

"Alliance for Progress," 1961. A program of economic assistance for Latin America begun by the Kennedy administration; had objectives of political and social reform as a means of combating Communist influence among impoverished peoples.

anarchism. Political theory opposed to government maintained by force; favors voluntary cooperation for social and economic purposes.

Ancien Regime. French for *Old Regime.*

Anglo-Japanese Alliance, 1902. Provided that Great Britain and Japan would give mutual support in case the interests of either were attacked in the Far East. Enabled Japan to attack Russia in 1904 and Britain to withdraw her main Far Eastern naval units to European waters.

Anschluss.   Political unification, used especially in reference to the union of Austria and Germany. Hitler accomplished the *Anschluss* in 1938.

anti-clericals.   Those opposed to the Catholic Church, especially to any special favored position in government for the Church.

Anti-Comintern Pact, 1936.   Agreement of Germany, Italy, and Japan to stand together against the Communist International or, actually, any enemy power.

anti-Semitism.   Hostility to the Jews.

ANZUS Pact, 1952.   A mutual security pact between Australia, New Zealand, and the United States, signed to allay fears of the possible military resurgence of Japan.

apartheid.   Literally, *apartness.* The policy of discrimination against non-whites practiced in the Union of South Africa.

appeasement.   Policy of concession to a dissatisfied opponent, used especially in reference to concessions to Axis Powers before World War II.

Arab League.   A diplomatic confederation of Egypt, the Sudan, Jordan, Lebanon, Syria, Saudi Arabia, Yemen, and Libya organized in 1945 with the ultimate goal of creating an Arab nation. The Arab League is neutral in the Cold War, opposes colonialism, and seeks the destruction of Israel.

aristocracy.   A privileged or superior class, or government by such a class.

Armada.   Spanish fleet gathered for the conquest of England in 1588; its defeat in the battle of the Armada marks the beginning of English naval supremacy.

armistice.   An agreement to cease fighting pending negotiation of a treaty of peace by which war is legally concluded.

assignats.   Paper money issued during the French Revolution; their value was based on land that had been confiscated from the Church. The *assignats* became worthless due to excessive issues. This case is often cited as a classical example of paper money inflation abuse.

Atlantic Charter, August, 1941.   A joint statement of war aims issued by Roosevelt and Churchill. Corresponded to the Fourteen

Points in World War I but was not as specific. Endorsed by other nations later in the year.

Ausgleich.   The agreement between Austria and Hungary in 1867; granted Hungary a separate government but joined Hungary to Austria under the same emperor.

autarchy.   A country under the rule of a despotic monarch.

authoritarian.   Government or other organization characterized by strong controls over the beliefs and actions of its subjects or members; a government without constitutional limits upon its powers.

autocracy.   A government of unlimited power exercised by a monarch or dictator.

autonomy.   Local self-government under the nominal rule of another country.

Axis Powers.   The alliance of Germany and Italy begun in 1936; by 1941 it had been joined by Japan, Finland, Hungary, Rumania, and Bulgaria.

"Babylonian Captivity," 1309-1378.   The time when the French government forced the pope to reside at Avignon in southern France. See *Great Schism.*

Bagdad Pact, 1955.   A defense pact formed by Iraq, Iran, Turkey, the United Kingdom, and Pakistan; it serves as a barrier to Soviet expansion in the Near East and is friendly to the United States which cooperates but is not a member. The neutralist Arab League has not felt friendly to the Pact. Iraq withdrew in 1959 and the name was then changed to Central Treaty Organization (CENTO).

balance of payments.   The difference in the value of goods and services bought and sold by a nation. An unfavorable balance represents payments in excess of receipts and ultimately has to be settled by payments of gold.

balance of power.   The equality of power among nations, or groups of nations, or the policy of uniting against any nation which becomes so powerful as to threaten the independence of the others.

Balfour Declaration, 1917.   A statement of the British government making an implied promise to create a national homeland for Jewish people in Palestine. It led to the formation of the state of Israel but not until 1948.

Benelux Nations. Belgium, Netherlands, and Luxemburg, members of a customs union formed in 1947.

Berlin Conference, 1884. First conference of nations providing general conditions for establishing claims to territories in Africa; followed by rapid partitioning of Africa by colonial powers.

Berlin, Congress of, 1878. Conference called to revise the Treaty of San Stefano, which Russia had imposed upon the Turks after the Russo-Turkish War of 1877. Austria-Hungary and Britain forced a revision of its terms, which were considered too favorable to Russia. The conference wrote a new settlement of the Eastern Question by the terms of the Treaty of Berlin.

bill of rights. Any list of the rights of individuals which a government is bound to respect; it also prohibits the exercise of certain powers by a government. The English Bill of Rights was granted by the king in 1689 upon the demand of Parliament. The United States Constitution added a Bill of Rights in the first ten amendments.

blockade. The isolation of an enemy by military forces, usually naval patrols, to cut off commerce with the rest of the world; a paper blockade is one not actually in effect in the vicinity of the enemy coastline or ports.

Bolsheviks, or *Bolsheviki.* The minority, radical faction of the Social Democratic Party in Russia. The majority faction, or Mensheviks, were more liberal and favored cooperation with middle class liberals. The Bolsheviks took control of the Russian Revolution in 1917 and established the present Communist state.

bourgeois. As a noun, singular and plural, refers to middle class town dwellers. As a class they were called the *bourgeoisie.* The adjective *bourgeois* means characteristic of a bourgeois or of the bourgeoisie; that is, middle class; thrifty, respectable, conventional, or commonplace.

bourse. Stock exchange, term used in Europe.

Boxer Uprising, 1900. Nationalist rebellion in China in which many foreigners were killed; led to intervention by an international expedition that included United States troops.

boycott. A concerted movement, as of labor or consumers, to refuse to buy or sell.

Bund. German word for the German Confederation created by

Napoleon in 1806 and dominated later by Austria. See *German Confederation*.

bureaucracy. A body of efficient professional administrative officials. Also a term often used invidiously in reference to a set of officials who follow fixed rules and cumbersome administrative procedures.

Burschenschaften. Student revolutionary societies organized in the German universities to promote German unification and nationalism.

Cadets. Name given to the liberal Constitutional Democratic Party in Russia in the Revolution of 1905.

Calvinism. The religious teachings of John Calvin; its most prominent feature was the doctrine of predestination which held that most persons, except for a few "elect," were predestined for eternal damnation.

capitalism. The private enterprise economic system, in which the means of production and decisions regarding investment and production and consumption are made by individual choice instead of by governing authorities; the profit system.

carbonari. An Italian secret society of revolutionists who worked for Italian nationalism after 1815. Literally, means *charcoal burners.*

Carlsbad Decrees, 1819. Decrees adopted by the Diet of the German Confederation to repress any liberal activities or publications in the German states.

center. See *left.*

Central Treaty Organization (CENTO). Middle East defense pact against Russia initiated by the United States in 1955 and known as the Bagdad Pact until the name was changed in 1959. The United States did not become a full member until 1958.

Chartist movement. Reform movement to extend political rights; conducted by working class leaders. Culminated in the presentation of a monster petition but failed in 1848 due to resistance of Parliament.

Christian Democratic Union. The coalition party of Dr. Konrad Adenauer formed after World War II. It included the Center Party, the Bavarian Catholic Party, and non-Marxist socialist parties; a moderate, pro-Western party that has controlled the West German government since World War II.

classical economists.   Those who opposed government regulation or the economy. Leading economists in Britain were Adam Smith, Robert Malthus, and David Ricardo; in France, Jean Baptiste Say; in Germany, Friedrich List. List favored protective tariffs, however.

clericals.   French political faction favoring the influence of the Church in government, particularly in schools and charitable functions.

coalition.   A temporary alliance of political parties or factions to create a ministry; or an alliance of nations in war against a common enemy.

Cold War.   A term widely used beginning in 1947 in reference to the hostility between the United States and Russia.

Colombo Plan, 1950.   A plan for economic cooperation established at Colombo, Ceylon. Its purpose is to develop the resources of a number of states of Southeast Asia. It is financed by the Commonwealth countries, the World Bank, and the United States.

colony.   See definitions of different types of dependencies on page 147, vol. II.

Cominform.   The key Communist information organization set up by Russia in 1947 to assure the loyalty of Communist parties in other countries. Replaced the Comintern which had been dissolved in 1943 as a gesture of cooperation to the Allies during World War II.

Commercial Revolution.   The rise of extensive commerce in Europe in the late middle ages and the introduction of modern business methods; included large scale merchandising and the use of money in transactions.

common law.   The unwritten law of England based on ancient Anglo-Saxon customs and handed down in court decisions which became precedents for the settlement of similar subsequent cases; differs from Roman law and statutory law.

Commonwealth Nations.   A term applied to the former dominions of the British Empire.

Communards.   Mixed revolutionary groups that joined the Paris

Commune in 1871 in the revolt against the conservative government of the National Assembly. They included socialists, anarchists, radical republicans, and utopians.

Communism. Basically, means common ownership of property used in production and equal distribution of goods produced. To use the word in this original sense is now confusing because *communism* has come to be identified with the Communist system, as practiced in Russia, China, or Yugoslavia, or with Marxian Socialism. See *socialism.*

Communist Manifesto, 1848. A pamphlet issued by Marx and Engels; became the "fundamental charter of socialism."

compact theory. A term used to designate both John Locke's theory of government and the states' rights theory of the relationship of the states to the federal government.

Concert of Europe. The cooperation of the members of the Quadruple Alliance in formulating uniform policies and preserving the peace of Europe for several decades after 1815.

Concordat of 1801. The agreement between the pope and Napoleon by which a reconciliation was reached between the papacy and the revolutionary government of France. The word *concordat* indicates any agreement made with the Roman papacy.

conservative. Favoring the preservation of established institutions and opposition to change.

constituent assembly. Any representative body which drafts a constitution as distinguished from a legislative assembly which enacts laws permitted under a constitution already in effect.

Consulate, 1799-1804. Period of Napoleon's joint rule with two other consuls, but Napoleon, as First Consul, actually ruled.

containment policy. A basic foreign policy followed by the United States since 1947 to prevent further expansion of Communist Russia.

Cordon sanitaire. A buffer zone to separate antagonistic nations; specifically, a string of states with which France made alliances in the 1920's in Eastern Europe between Communist Russia and Central Europe.

Cortes. Name of the parliamentary body of Spain.

coup d'etat. Literally, *stroke of state.* A sudden, forceful overthrow of a government.

Crusades. The series of seven successive religious wars from 1095-1291 waged by Europe against the Moslems in the regions bordering the eastern Mediterranean.

Curzon Line, 1919. A line suggested by Lord Curzon for the eastern boundary of Poland. The present eastern boundary of Poland follows the Curzon Line rather closely.

customs union. Any international agreement to create a free trade area by abolishing tariff duties between member nations; significant as a preliminary to possible political unification.

Dawes Plan, 1924. Arrangement for Germany's payment of reparations, drawn up under the leadership of the American banker, Charles G. Dawes.

Decembrists. Liberals who revolted against Nicholas I in December, 1825, at the time of his accession to the throne.

de facto. Meaning the actual situation existing as distinguished from what is legal or moral.

Deism. A religion or philosophy of free thinkers; flourished during the period of the American Revolution; denied the minute intervention of God in the lives of individuals and, therefore, considered as atheistic.

Demarcation Line. Global boundary drawn in 1492 and altered in 1493 in the Treaty of Tordesillas by the pope to separate Spanish and Portuguese spheres of trade and colonization.

demarche. A change of policy.

democracy. Government by a majority of the people providing equality of rights of all persons.

detente. A relaxation of strained relations between nations.

dictatorship. A form of government in which one man holds supreme political power without constitutional or legal limits.

diet. A name given to parliamentary, representative assemblies in some countries, as in Germany and Scandinavia.

Diplomatic Revolution. A change in allies made by the great powers in Europe before the Seven Years' War. The traditional enemies France and Austria became friends as did Great Britain and Prussia. We might say, France and Britain remained enemies but exchanged allies.

Directory, 1795-1797. The reactionary government established in France under the new constitution of 1795. Noted usually as a cynical, corrupt, selfish regime, but they maintained order in spite of extremists of both the right and the left.

doge.   The heads of the city-states of Venice and Genoa.

domestic system.   Under this system of production, raw materials were worked up into goods at home and outside the control of the craft gild.

Drang nach Osten.   Before 1914, a German drive into the Near East made by gaining concessions from Turkey. A source of conflict with Britain, since the occupation of the Near East threatened Britain's lifeline to India.

Dreikaiserbund, 1872, 1881.   Agreements of friendship between the rulers of Germany, Austria, and Russia under the leadership of Bismarck, but the agreements broke down due to conflicts of interest between Austria and Russia.

Dreyfus case.   The affair in France in the 1890's arising from false charges of treason brought against Captain Alfred Dreyfus, who was convicted of selling military secrets to Germany. The affair eventually turned against reactionary elements and strengthened the liberals after Dreyfus was exonerated.

Dual Alliance, 1891.   A defense alliance between France and Russia drawn up against the Triple Alliance of Germany, Austria-Hungary, and Italy.

Dual Monarchy.   Austria-Hungary after 1867 when Austria agreed to grant a separate (Ausgleich) parliament to Hungary.

Duma.   The Russian parliament granted by Nicholas II in 1905 after the revolution.

dynastic.   Having to do with a ruling family or house.

dynasty.   A family of rulers having hereditary right to reign over certain territory or territories which do not necessarily correspond to a particular nationality. Some European states had elective monarchs instead of hereditary.

Eastern Question.   Expression referring to the problem, before World War I, of what should be done about the territories belonging to the weak Ottoman Empire.

Edict of Nantes, 1598.   The grant of religious toleration made by Henry IV in France; was cancelled by Louis XIV in 1685 in the Revocation of the Edict of Nantes after which Huguenots were forcibly converted to Catholicism or driven into exile.

Eisenhower Doctrine, 1957.   A policy of the Eisenhower administration of using military and economic aid to support Middle Eastern nations in resisting aggression of "any nation controlled by international communism."

embargo.   Any government restriction of commerce; similar to boycott which results from private decisions.

emigres.   Noblemen and churchmen who left France following the Revolution of 1789.

Ems dispatch, 1870.   Bismarck's edition of a telegram from Kaiser William I of Prussia. Bismarck omitted certain words and released the telegram to the press. Its effect, as intended, was to antagonize French and Germans and help bring on the Franco-Prussian War.

enlightened despots.   Paternalistic absolute monarchs during the last years of the Old Regime. They read the philosophers and arbitrarily introduced reforms in the interest of their realms.

Entente Cordiale, 1904.   The establishment of friendly relations between Great Britain and France; in effect, it was an alliance that brought them together before World War I.

Estates.   The three social classes in most countries in medieval times—clergy, nobles, and commoners. The Estates were represented by separate bodies in the various medieval national assemblies, as in the Estates-General in France.

Euratom.   The European Atomic Energy Community composed of West Germany, France, Italy, Belgium, the Netherlands, and Luxemburg; their purpose is to cooperate in the development of atomic power.

European Cooperation Administration.   See *Marshall Plan.*

European Common Market.   A customs union of six nations— France, West Germany, Italy, the Netherlands, Belgium, and Luxemburg—officially known as the European Economic Community (EEC) and established by the Treaty of Rome in 1957. Its ultimate goal is economic and political unity for its present member nations and others that may be admitted later.

European Recovery Program (ERP).   See *Marshall Plan.*

Fabianism.   Fabian socialism was advocated by Sidney and Beatrice Webb in England. Instead of revolutionary action, they advocated educational methods of winning gradual acceptance of socialism; called *Fabian* because they wished to follow the strategy of the Roman general Fabius who avoided a head-on clash with the enemy.

factory system. The production of manufactured goods in factories instead of under the earlier gild system or domestic system.

fait accompli. An accomplished fact or deed that is likely to be accepted as the settlement of a question.

fascism. A totalitarian form of government which emphasizes above all the unity of a nation under a single political party dominated by a strong leader. No brief definition is possible, because fascism includes many features, which may vary from one country to another. It is an extreme form of militaristic nationalism that suppresses or persecutes racial or other minorities not considered characteristic of the national body. Fascist governments often arise where democratic traditions have not taken sufficient hold and where a people are fearful of communist or foreign influences. Fascism preserves private property but calls for whatever controls are necessary to subordinate a nation's economy to the needs of a strong state.

Fashoda incident, 1898. A meeting of French and British forces at the town of Fashoda in the Sudan (Africa). War threatened when the French claimed the town, but the French forces gave way and the French received compensation elsewhere.

feudalism. The economic and social organization of medieval Europe. In the absence of strong central government most government functions resided in the hands of local lords.

Fianna Fail. See *Sinn Fein.*

fifth column. Persons in a country ready to give aid to a foreign enemy.

Fourteen Points. A statement of American war aims as announced by President Wilson in January, 1918, and accepted by Germany as the basis of the Armistice in November, 1918. The Fourteenth Point called for the League of Nations.

franchise. Any special right granted by a governing body, such as the individual right to vote or the right of a corporation to operate a public utility.

Fronde, 1648-1653. The last rebellion of the nobles in France against the monarchy; it began in the Parlement of Paris which refused to register (approve) an edict imposing an increased tax against certain nobles. The civil war ended with an enhancement of the royal power.

Geographic Revolution. The widening knowledge of other lands among Europeans in the late middle ages and the shift in the center of the Western world from the Mediterranean to the Atlantic.

German Confederation. The central organization of German States, created by Napoleon and destroyed by Bismarck in 1867, at which time the North German Confederation was created.

gilds, or *guilds.* Medieval organizations of 1] merchants and 2] craftsmen for the mutual protection of members and to provide business, social, and religious functions. *Gild system* refers to the production of goods in shops under control of gild regulations.

Good Neighbor policy. Foreign policy of friendship toward Latin America adopted during the 1920's but given this name by Roosevelt.

Great Britain. Often called "Britain" for short. Great Britain includes England, Wales, and Scotland, political entities which share the island of Britain. Add northern Ireland and we have the United Kingdom. *England* is often used synonymously but loosely to mean Great Britain just as *Holland* is used in referring to the Netherlands. England and Scotland were united in 1707 to form the government of Great Britain. We should speak of the government as *English* before 1707 and *British* after 1707.

Great Schism, 1378-1417. The split in the Roman Church when it was headed by the pope in Rome and another in Avignon.

Hague Court. Organized in 1899 by the First Hague Peace Conference and is the predecessor to the Permanent Court of International Justice (World Court).

Hanseatic League, Hanse towns. A medieval league, mainly of North German towns, organized to protect and extend the trade of their merchants. Its chief function was mercantile rather than political, and it declined as modern nations increased their own controls over trade.

hegemony. The leadership or dominance of one government or state among others.

Holy Alliance, 1815. In its exact meaning was an agreement initiated by Tsar Alexander I, signed by Austria and Prussia, and others, providing that these nations would be guided by Christian principles in their relations. More loosely, the term refers to the cooperation of Austria, Russia, and Prussia in suppressing democratic revolutionary governments.

Huguenots. French Protestants, followers of Calvinist doctrines and contemporaries of English Puritans.

humanism. A cultural movement that emphasized the interests of man in the present world; originated with scholars who studied classical Greek and Latin literature during the late middle ages.

Hundred Days. A period of about three months after Napoleon's escape from Elba during which time he raised an army in France and attempted to restore himself to power. The battle of Waterloo ended his brief return to power.

Hundred Years' War. The first Hundred Years' War was fought between England and France from 1338-1453. The second was fought between the same two antagonists from 1689-1815. Each was a series of wars broken by long intervals of peace.

imperialism. Expansionist sentiment for rule over foreign people, as in colonial expansion.

Inquisition. A general term for an organ of the Roman Catholic Church that inquired into the purity of faith and morals of Christians. Its present day successor is the Holy Office which makes pronouncements upon Catholic faith and morals. The harsh Spanish Inquisition, reluctantly approved by the pope in 1478, was concerned mainly with the faith of converts from Islam and Judaism. The Inquisition was active also in Italy and other countries where it was also employed by civil governments to put down heresy.

International. Name given by Marxian Communists to three international movements to organize and promote Communism over the world. The First International was organized in 1864, the Second International in 1889, and the Third International in 1919.

"Iron Curtain." A term first used by Winston Churchill in 1946 in an address in Fulton, Missouri; it called attention to Russian

domination of the countries of Eastern Europe and the threat of Soviet aggression.

irredentism. The desire of a country to annex territory populated by the same nationality but belonging to another country. Used particularly in reference to Italy's desire to annex "Italia Irredenta," neighboring districts of Austria with Italian-speaking populations.

Islam. The Moslem or Mohammedan religion; the lands where the Moslem religion predominates.

Jacobins. The most radical group of the French revolutionists; they gained control of the Legislative Assembly after October, 1791, in opposition to the less radical Girondists.

joint-stock company. Trading company, forerunner of present day corporation, organized for single trading ventures by selling stock to members; used as organization for early colonies in America and elsewhere.

July Monarchy. The regime of Louis Philippe in France from 1830-1848; it came in power with the revolution of July, 1830.

Junkers. Landed nobility in Germany, used especially in reference to the Prussian ruling class.

Kellogg-Briand Pact, 1928. Also known as the Pact of Paris. American Secretary of State Kellogg and Aristide Briand, French foreign minister, took the lead in negotiating treaties by which most of the nations of the world renounced war as an instrument of national policy.

Keynesian economics. The economic recommendations of the most influential economist in recent times, John Maynard Keynes of Britain. He dealt especially with the problem of depression and advised deficit spending, mild inflation, and liberal welfare payments as countermeasures.

kulaks. Well-to-do, thrifty land-owning peasant class in Russia who generally resented being forced into the Soviet collective farms. Stalin liquidated them after 1928 in the drive to socialize agriculture.

Kulturkampf. Bismarck's campaign during the 1870's to reduce the power of the Church in Germany.

Kuomintang. The Chinese Nationalist Party which governed China under Sun Yat-sen and Chiang Kai-shek. The Kuomintang now governs Formosa.

laissez-faire. French for "let (people) do (as they please)." The doctrine of unregulated business enterprise advocated by nineteenth century liberals and identified with the economic philosophy of Adam Smith and free enterprise capitalism.

Lebensraum. An expression used by Germany to justify expansion in order to secure "living space."

left. Modern usage has fallen into the convenient practice of attempting to classify all political parties, factions, and philosophies according to where they stand relative to the existing political (social and economic) system. In the *center* are the conservatives who wish to preserve the existing laws, institutions, and distribution of political power. To the *right* are various degrees of reactionaries who wish to return to the arrangements of an earlier day when political power was exercised by fewer favored persons. The *left* is composed of various degrees of liberals (progressives) who wish to introduce changes to effect a still wider distribution of power. Usually most people are *moderates* or *middle-of-the-road* and desire only minor changes. One can imagine a political spectrum from *reactionaries* on the *extreme right* to *radicals* on the *extreme left* and all shades of opinion in between. This conventional classification began with the habit of radical deputies in the French Revolution who were in the habit of seating themselves on the left of the presiding officer.

legitimacy. The claim that some former ruling family should be restored to power.

Lend-lease Act, 1941. A measure won by President Roosevelt which permitted the President to lend or lease war materials to nations acting as American allies in World War II.

lettres de cachet. Orders by which the absolute monarchs of France could arbitrarily imprison a subject.

liberal. A *liberal* in the nineteenth century was one who favored freedom (*liber,* Latin, *free*) of business enterprise from government regulations and the extension of political democracy. Thus, the liberals stood for reform. Political reformers and progressives are still called *liberals,* but modern *liberals* favor government regulation of business in the interest of labor and consumers because it came to be recognized that liberty for business might mean oppression of workers and abuse of consumers. One has to discern from any context whether reference is made to nineteenth century or to contemporary liberalism. See *left*.

Liberal Party (British). After 1832 the British Whig Party became the spokesman for the liberal business elements which joined it, and its name was changed to "Liberal." The Liberal Party declined after 1920 but survived as a small third party.

Locarno Pact, 1925. A security and non-aggression agreement made between Germany, Britain, France, Belgium, and Italy recognizing existing boundaries and providing for peaceful settlement of disputes; marked beginning of a few years of better feeling on Germany's part.

Lusitania. A British passenger liner carrying troops and munitions as well as American civilians, sunk by German submarine attack in 1915. The sinking was used by pro-British propagandists to turn American opinion against Germany.

Low Countries. Refers to the Netherlands and Belgium.

Maginot Line. A series of interconnected forts of concrete and steel built by the French as a defense against German invasion. The Line was considered impregnable and gave the French a false sense of security. The Germans were able to break through it and pass around the western end, which was not extended along the Belgian frontier.

mandates. Colonies of the defeated powers, Germany and Turkey, awarded to Britain, France, and Japan by the League of Nations after World War I; similarly, former possessions of Japan were awarded to the United States by the UNO under the trusteeship system after World War II.

"March on Rome," 1922. Mussolini's concentration of Fascist Party members around Rome. The threat to use force to seize control of the Italian government caused King Victor Emmanuel to ask Mussolini to form a cabinet. Once in power Mussolini consolidated his position to create a dictatorship.

Marshall Plan, 1948. Also known as the European Recovery Program (ERP). An American plan to aid the economic recovery of Europe in order to combat Communism; prepared by Secretary of State George C. Marshall and President Truman, it went into effect in 1948; contributed much to Europe's recovery and prosperity.

mercantilism. The prevailing economic theory applied in Europe during the eighteenth century; called for the exercise of numerous economic regulations and controls by the state; contrasts with later economic philosophy of laissez-faire or free enterprise. Neo-mercantilism is the name given to the revival of similar regulations particularly in reference to foreign trade.

middle class. See *bourgeois.* As used in earlier European history, refers to business and professional classes in the towns; the class between the nobility and the workers and peasants.

Middle East. Iran and the surrounding lands.

Monroe Doctrine, 1823. The assertion of President Monroe in 1823 that European powers should refrain from any attempt to interfere in the governments of the American nations or to extend colonization over any new areas in America.

moratorium. A provision for delaying the repayment of debt.

Munich Conference, 1938. Reached agreement by Britain, France, Germany, and Italy that ceded the Czechoslovakian Sudetenland to Germany as part of an appeasement policy toward Germany.

nationalism. An intense loyalty to one's own nation. See discussion in text.

NATO, North Atlantic Treaty Organization, 1949. Military organization created by its members for mutual defense against Russian aggression; included the nations of Western Europe mainly and the United States.

Navigation Acts. A series of mercantilist laws enacted by Parliament from 1651 to the American Revolution to regulate or encourage shipping, trade, and industry in the colonies.

NAZIS. Abbreviation of the German spelling of the National Socialist Party of Adolf Hitler, pronounced nat'-zis.

Near East. Asia Minor and the surrounding region including the Balkans and part of Africa now or formerly under Turkish rule.

New Economic Policy (NEP). A relaxation of Communist controls over agriculture and industry in Russia in 1921; a compromise with capitalist principles in an effort to encourage production in agriculture and industry.

nihilism. The belief that all social institutions must be destroyed in order to create new institutions. Nihilists joined anarchists in terrorism and assassination against the Tsarist government before 1917.

noble.   Person possessing hereditary privileges according to various ranks and titles. Titles of nobility were conferred by monarchs upon persons who had rendered some special service to their country.

Nuremberg Trials.   Trials held at Nuremberg, Germany, to try Nazis accused of war crimes in World War II. The trials, begun in 1945, were conducted by a Four-Power International Tribunal and resulted in the conviction of hundreds of Nazi leaders who had committed crimes against humanity.

Old Regime.   The social and political system of Europe before the French Revolution of 1789. Used especially in reference to France, but may refer to society and politics in general in Europe for a century or two before 1789.

oligarchy.   Rule by a small number; the term is usually employed in a derogatory sense.

Open Door Policy, 1899.   The American foreign policy begun under Secretary of State Hay in order to promote equal rights of foreign nations in China and to uphold the rights of China against aggressive imperialist powers.

Opium War, 1840-1842.   War between Britain and China that resulted in the opening of additional ports to the Western nations.

Organization of American States (*OAS*).   A collective defense system organized in 1947 at Rio de Janeiro by the United States and twenty Latin American states under the Rio Treaty. The OAS absorbed the Pan-American Union.

Pact of Paris, 1928.   See *Kellogg-Briand Peace Pact.*

Pan-Americanism.   Movement for cooperation among the American nations. The first Pan-American Conference in 1889 organized the Pan-American Union with a membership of twenty-one republics of North and South America. Various conferences, usually named according to the cities where they met, adopted statements of policy to guide the American states before and after World War II.

Pan-Slavism.   A movement, chiefly led by Russia, for the cooperation and defense of Slavic peoples in Eastern Europe.

parlement. The Parlement of Paris or any of several provincial courts in France which retained the right to protest a royal edict by refusing to register it. If not registered, edicts were not binding upon the courts; was a kind of forehanded judicial review. By a royal appearance, called a *lit de justice* (literally, *bed of justice*) the king might personally require a parlement to register an edict.

parliament. Word originated from French *parler*, to speak. Originally used as name of the English representative assembly and came to be used as a general term to refer to any similar national legislative body regardless of its name in any given country. The following are names of various parliamentary bodies: Congress, Diet, Cortes, Estates, Parliament, Duma, Assembly, Legislature.

partisan. One who gives aid. The term was used in reference to persons, in the countries overrun by the Nazis, who resisted their conquerers and gave aid to the Allies in World War II.

peasant. Originated from French, *pays*, country; *paysan*, countryman, and referred to persons of various status who made their living cultivating the soil. Implies a close attachment to the land and often to indicate lower social status. Many peasants were and are well-to-do landowners and are, therefore, the equivalent of American farmers, but the term is not used in the United States and Britain. In Europe, peasants were sometimes more prosperous than impoverished noblemen.

Permanent Court of International Justice. See *World Court.*

Petition of Right, 1628. A famous charter, or written statement of prohibitions against the king's power forced upon Charles I by Parliament.

philosophes. In France, a popular group of philosophical writers (we would say social scientists today) who criticized the institutions of the Old Regime.

physiocrats. A group of French economists who opposed government regulation; were forerunners of Adam Smith and the "classical economists." The physiocrats stressed the importance of fostering agriculture.

plebiscite. An election or referendum held to determine the will of the people upon some important question, such as whether they wish to join one country or another or to ratify or reject acts of a dictator.

plurality. The votes polled by the leading candidate, not necessarily a majority of all votes cast.

Point Four Program, 1949. A program of technical assistance announced by President Truman in 1949 to give aid to underdeveloped nations. It went into effect the next year with a large appropriation from Congress. Hundreds of millions were appropriated in subsequent years to keep the program in effect. It was extended to thirty-three nations by 1953 and has often been praised as a most beneficial kind of American foreign aid.

Polish Corridor. A strip of territory between Germany and East Prussia awarded to Poland after World War I to give Poland an outlet to the Baltic Sea.

popular fronts. Liberal and socialist parties or a combination of such parties.

Potsdam Conference, 1945. Meeting of Truman, Churchill, Attlee, and Stalin in Potsdam, Germany, to determine policies for the occupation of Germany and the postwar settlement of Europe.

price revolution. A steady rise in prices in the sixteenth century due to the inflow of gold and silver from America and the consequent inflation of the money supply of Europe.

privateering. Waging war by privately owned, armed vessels commissioned to capture enemy ships, a kind of legalized piracy, outlawed by international agreement since 1856.

Progressive movement, 1901-1914. The American reform crusade to break the control of politics by corporate wealth and to enlarge political power of the people.

proletariat. Propertyless working classes who make their living by working for wages; the word often has Marxist connotations.

protectorate. A dependent state whose foreign affairs are controlled in the interest of its "protector."

Puritans. Religious dissenters in England who wished to extend the Reformation and purify the Anglican Church of elaborate ceremonies and forms; many Puritans came to America. Most Puritans remained within the Anglican Church, but some, such as the Separatists, established separate congregations and came to be called Congregationalists.

putsch. An attempt to seize control of a government.

Quadruple Alliance, 1815. Included Britain, Austria, Russia, and Prussia in an alliance to maintain the peace of Europe and preserve the Vienna settlement; became the Quintuple Alliance in 1818 when France joined it.

Quintuple Alliance, 1818. See *Quadruple Alliance.*

radical. Political views favoring drastic change in the direction of greater political, economic, or social equality. See *left.* Also used colloquially to mean any extreme view.

rapprochement. A reconciliation or steps taken in that direction by two nations.

reactionary. Political views favoring a return to earlier less democratic practices. See *left.*

reciprocity. Mutual concessions to reduce tariff rates made in trade agreements between two countries.

Reformation. The movement beginning in the sixteenth century to correct abuses and change doctrines in the Church. The Protestant Revolt is the outstanding development. The Catholic Reformation, or Counter-Reformation, occurred at approximately the same time.

regime. Any system or form of government; such as monarchical or republican regime. The term is not used to designate a change in a ministry or administration.

Renaissance. This term is used in different contexts and has no limited, fixed meaning except its literal definition, *rebirth.* A renaissance occurred in different countries at different times and each flowering differed in character. See discussion in text.

reparations. Payments assessed usually against a defeated nation held responsible for war damage.

republic. From the Latin, *res publica,* a public thing, meaning a government of the people created by elective representative officials, as distinguished from a direct democracy in which people in mass meetings made decisions. Most "democracies" are republican in form.

republicanism. Representative, constitutional government as opposed to one of a hereditary ruler.

revolution. In its narrowest usage refers to sudden and extensive political change, usually involving war or violence against a

regime seeking to retain authority. Counterrevolution designates
a return to authority by a government overthrown by revolution.
Rebellion is used to connote the failure of an armed attempt to
overthrow existing authority and *revolt* may be used in the same
sense or in reference to a successful movement. An *insurrection*
suggests a smaller rebellion. *Uprising* is a general term for small
movements or initial revolutionary movements. *Mutiny* is a defiant
movement of sailors or soldiers against their officers.

right. See *left.*

rump parliament or *assembly.*   Any active legislative body made
up of only a part of those originally chosen, because some members left voluntarily or were expelled. The "rump" faction are
those who remain sitting, in session.

"salutary neglect."   Description of the British colonial policy
toward the Thirteen Colonies during the ministry of Sir Robert
Walpole; the neglect proved beneficial as it left the colonies free
of burdensome regulation.

sanctions.   The application of an economic boycott against a nation to force it to obey international law; was applied briefly
against the export of arms and ammunition to Italy upon her
invasion of Ethiopia in 1935.

San Francisco Conference, 1945.   Meeting of most of the original
members of the United Nations to draft the terms of the United
Nations Organization Charter. Earlier agreements had only provided for such an organization and for its general outlines.

Schuman Plan, 1950.   The European Coal and Steel Community
agreed to by France, West Germany, Belgium, the Netherlands,
Luxemburg, and Italy for the control of coal, iron, and steel.

Scientific Socialism.   The type and theories of socialism originated
by Karl Marx and which became the basis of the leading socialist movements after 1850. Scientific socialism led to the organization of workmen themselves into political parties, whereas
previous theories of socialism had little appeal to workers but
mainly to philanthropists and theorists.

"Sick Man of Europe."   In a proposal during the nineteenth century for the division of feeble Turkey the Russians referred to
it by this expression.

Sinn Fein.   The Irish nationalist party which led the movement for Home Rule and, after World War I, for independence. De Valera was its leader, but in 1921 the radical De Valera at the head of the Fianna Fail went into opposition to the terms by which Britain granted independence in 1921. In 1932 De Valera came into power when his Fianna Fail Party won the Irish elections.

Slavophils. Russians who wished to cling to the old ways of Russia itself instead of adopting the modern institutions of Europe as advocated by the Westernizers.

social contract. Theory of government formulated by the English philosopher John Locke; became the philosophical basis of the American Revolution.

socialism. A general philosophy that advocates social (not private) ownership and control of the means of production of goods and services and the distribution of production according to need. There are such great differences in the kinds of socialism that one should always qualify the use of the term, as Marxist socialism, Christian socialism, state socialism, and so on. There are degrees as well as kinds of socialism. For example, conservative capitalist societies may recognize the need for social ownership and control of public schools, banking, or medicine.

Southeast Asia Treaty Organization (SEATO), 1954. A weak mutual defense organization was initiated by the United States and included Great Britain, France, Australia, New Zealand, Pakistan, Thailand, and the Philippines; does not commit members to go to war in case of attack of a member.

sovereignty. The independent authority of a government in its freedom from outside control. Also refers to the source of governmental authority, as the people in a democracy or the king in an absolute monarchy are *sovereign.*

Soviets. Councils organized in Russia to govern at the various levels.

Spartacists. Communist revolutionaries who made attempts to take over Germany in 1918-1919.

sphere of influence. An area over which an imperialist power claims special political or commercial rights or priority over rival powers.

state. The student must recognize different meanings of the word as he encounters it. In the study of history and government the *state* means a government *and* the territory under its rule.

status quo. As in "status quo anti bellum," meaning the restoration of an earlier condition; or preservation of an existing relationship.

Stimson Doctrine, 1931. The American policy of nonrecognition of the Japanese puppet government set up in Manchuria, called Manchukuo; was announced by Secretary of State Stimson under Hoover.

Suez Crisis, 1956. The threat of international war caused by Israeli invasion of Egypt in October, 1956. Britain and France joined Israel, but the United States and Russia, acting through the UN, secured a cease-fire.

suzerainty. The special, limited authority of one government over another, as the right to guide the foreign relations or veto the enactments of the subordinate government.

syndicalism. Radical trade union movement and philosophy advocating control of an industry by syndicates of workers and the employment of violent, direct action, such as general strikes and sabotage, in industrial struggles.

technology. Practical knowledge of the industrial arts; the application of better processes and new inventions.

Tennis Court Oath, 1789. The resolve of the Third Estate declaring itself to be the true National Assembly of France; was the beginning of the defiance of royal authority and, therefore, the beginning of the Revolution.

theocracy. Rule by a religious minority in a union of church and state.

Thermidorean Reaction, July, 1794. The turning point of the French Revolution when the moderates gained control of the National Convention and brought an end to the Reign of Terror.

Third Reich. Name adopted by Hitler for the National Socialist government in Germany. The two preceding Reich's or empires were the Holy Roman Empire and the German Empire established by Bismarck in 1871.

Third Republic. The French republic established after the downfall of Napoleon III and which lasted until the fall of France in 1940.

totalitarianism. State control of every aspect of the life of a nation in order to carry out the ideology of a single political party; is the opposite of individualism. Fascist and Communist governments are likely to be totalitarian. Very roughly comparable to the eighteenth century absolute monarchies.

Triple Entente, 1907. The alliance between France, Great Britain, and Russia preceding World War I.

Truman Doctrine, 1947. Policy begun by President Truman of giving military and economic aid to countries threatened by Communist subversion; first put in effect by appropriations to aid Greece and Turkey.

trusteeship. See *mandates.*

"Twenty-One Demands," 1915. Extensive demands made by Japan against China which would have subordinated China to Japan. The United States vigorously protested the ultimatum to China as a violation of the Open Door policy. The Washington Naval Conference in 1921-1922 finally settled the uneasiness that Japanese demands had caused.

ultramontanism. In various countries of Europe Catholics looked for guidance beyond the Alps to the Roman papacy.

utilitarianism. The philosophy developed by Jeremy Bentham and John Stuart Mill that judged institutions by their usefulness in providing for the happiness of man; their ideas were liberal and humanitarian.

United Nations Relief and Rehabilitation Administration (UNRRA). The agency created in 1945 to aid liberated countries.

Vichy Regime. The French government with its capital set up at Vichy after the downfall of France in 1940; was dominated by the Nazis.

Washington Naval Conference, 1921-1922. A conference of the leading naval powers resulting in the Four-Power Treaty, the Five-Power Treaty, and the Nine-Power Pact.

Weimar Republic. The German government established after the downfall of the regime of Kaiser William II in 1918; its constitution was written at the old liberal, cultural city of Weimar.

Westernizers. See *Slavophils.*

Westminster, Statute of, 1931. Act of the British Parliament by which the dominions were formally recognized as equal in status with Britain.

workmen's compensation laws. Also called employers' liability laws. State and federal laws that make employers liable for injuries on the job sustained by workers. Employers protect themselves by insurance against accidents.

World Court. Popular name for the Permanent Court of International Justice; drawn up as a part of the League of Nations. The United States did not become a member but four prominent American jurists served it as judges.

Yalta Conference, 1945. Most publicized wartime conference of the Allied leaders. They met at Yalta in Russia where many important decisions were made relating to ending the war against Japan and the disposition of territories won from the defeated powers.

Young Italy. The organization of Mazzini's to work for Italian unity and freedom.

Young Plan, 1929. A revision of the Dawes Plan by a committee under the American banker Owen D. Young; reduced Germany's reparations payments.

Young Turks. A nationalist movement to reform and modernize the Turkish empire. The movement aroused subject people to resist Turkish rule.

Zionism. Movement to establish a national homeland for the Jews.

Zollverein. The customs union established by Prussia which helped bring about the unification of Germany; German word for any customs union.

Rulers and Governments of Leading European States Since 1500

Austria (beginning with the Holy Roman Empire)

Maximilian I, *1493-1519*
Charles V, *1519-1556*
Ferdinand I, *1556-1564*
Maximilian II, *1564-1576*
Rudolf II, *1576-1612*
Matthias I, *1612-1619*
Ferdinand II, *1619-1637*
Ferdinand III, *1637-1657*
Leopold I, *1658-1705*
Joseph I, *1705-1711*
Charles VI, *1711-1740*
Maria Theresa, *1740-1780*. Married Francis, Duke of Lorraine, who ruled as Holy Roman Emperor, *1745-1765*
Joseph II, *1765-1790*, Emperor; ruled Hapsburg domains *1780-1790*
Leopold II, *1790-1792*
Francis II, *1792-1806*. The Holy Roman Empire ended in *1806*. Francis II in *1804* assumed the title of Emperor of Austria as Francis I, *1804-1835*
Ferdinand I, *1835-1848*
Francis Joseph I, *1848-1916*
Charles I, *1916-1918*. In 1918 the territories of the Hapsburg Monarchy were taken over by Austria, Czechoslovakia, Hungary, Poland, Italy, Rumania, and Yugoslavia.

Belgium

Under the rule of Spanish kings, *1516-1713*
Under the rule of Austrian monarchs, *1713-1797*
Under the rule of Revolutionary and Napoleonic France, *1797-1815*
Part of Netherlands, *1815-1830*
Leopold I, *1831-1865*

Leopold II, *1865-1909*
Albert, *1909-1934*
Leopold III, *1934-1951*
Baudouin I, *1951-*

England, Great Britain

Henry VII, *1485-1509*
Henry VIII, *1509-1547*
Edward VI, *1547-1553*
Mary I, *1553-1558*
Elizabeth I, *1558-1603*
James I, *1603-1625*
Charles I, *1625-1649*
Commonwealth and Protectorate under Cromwell, *1649-1660*
Charles II, *1660-1685*
James II, *1685-1688*
William III and Mary II, *1689-1694*
William III, *1694-1702*
Anne, *1702-1714*
George I, *1714-1727*
George II, *1727-1760*
George III, *1760-1820*
George IV, *1820-1830*
William IV, *1830-1837*
Victoria, *1837-1901*
Edward VII, *1901-1910*
George V, *1910-1936*
Edward VIII, *1936*
George VI, *1936-1952*
Elizabeth II, *1952-*

France

Louis XI, *1461-1483*
Charles VIII, *1483-1498*
Louis XII, *1498-1515*
Francis I, *1515-1547*

Henry II, *1547-1559*
Francis II, *1559-1560*
Charles IX, *1560-1574*
Henry III, *1574-1589*
Henry IV, *1589-1610*
Louis XIII, *1610-1643*
Louis XIV, *1643-1715*
Louis XV, *1715-1774*
Louis XVI, *1774-1792*
First Republic, *1792-1799*
Consulate, *1799-1804*
First Empire, Napoleon I, *1804-1814*
Louis XVIII, *1814-1824*
Charles X, *1824-1830*
Louis Philippe, *1830-1848*
Second Republic, *1848-1852*
Second Empire, Napoleon III, *1852-1870*
Third Republic, *1870-1940*
Vichy Regime, *1940-1944*
Provisional Government, *1945-1946*
Fourth Republic, *1946-1958*
Fifth Republic, *1958-*

Germany (beginning with Prussia)

Frederick William, the "Great Elector" of Brandenburg and Duke of Prussia, *1640-1688*

Frederick III, *1688-1713*, Elector of Brandenburg and Duke of Prussia. In 1701 Frederick III became King of Prussia as Frederick I, *1701-1713*

Frederick William I, *1713-1740*

Frederick II, *1740-1786*

Frederick William II, *1786-1797*

Frederick William III, *1797-1840*

Frederick William IV, *1840-1861*

William I, *1861-1888;* Emperor of Germany, *1871-1888*

Frederick III, *1888*

William II, *1888-1918*

Weimar Republic, *1918-1933*
Third Reich, Hitler dictatorship, *1933-1945*
Military government of victorious powers, *1945-1949*
Federal Republic of Germany (West Germany), *1949-*
German Democratic Republic (East Germany), *1949-*

Italy (beginning with Sardinia)

Victor Amadeus II, *1720-1730*. Victor Amadeus II, Duke of Savoy, acquired the island of Sardinia and in 1720 assumed the title of King of Sardinia
Charles Emmanuel III, *1730-1773*
Victor Amadeus III, *1773-1796*
Charles Emmanuel IV, *1796-1802*
Victor Emmanuel I, *1802-1821*
Charles Felix, *1821-1831*
Charles Albert, *1831-1849*
Victor Emmanuel II, *1849-1878*. In 1861 Victor Emmanuel II assumed the title of King of Italy, *1861-1878*
Humbert I, *1878-1900*
Victor Emmanuel III, *1900-1946*
Humbert II, *1946*
Republic of Italy, *1946-*

Netherlands (Holland)

Under rule of Spanish kings, *1516-1581*
William the Silent, stadholder, *1581-1584*
Maurice, *1584-1625*
Frederick Henry, *1625-1647*
William II, *1647-1650*
John De Witt, grand pensionary, *1650-1672*
William III, stadholder, *1672-1702*. (also King of England from 1689)
William IV, stadholder, *1711-1751*
William V, *1751-1795*
Republic under French control, *1795-1806*
Louis Bonaparte, *1806-1810*

Part of France, *1810-1813*
William I, king, *1813-1840*
William II, *1840-1849*
William III, *1849-1890*
Wilhelmina, *1890-1948*
Juliana, *1948-*

Papacy (Popes with brief pontificates omitted)

Alexander VI, *1492-1503*
Julius II, *1503-1513*
Leo X, *1513-1521*
Clement VII, *1523-1534*
Paul III, *1534-1549*
Pius IV, *1559-1565*
Pius V, *1566-1572*
Gregory XIII, *1572-1585*
Sixtus V, *1585-1590*
Clement VIII, *1592-1605*
Paul V, *1605-1621*
Urban VIII, *1623-1644*
Innocent X, *1644-1655*
Alexander VII, *1655-1667*
Clement X, *1670-1676*
Innocent XI, *1676-1689*
Innocent XII, *1691-1700*
Clement XI, *1700-1721*
Benedict XIII, *1724-1730*
Clement XII, *1730-1740*
Benedict XIV, *1740-1758*
Clement XIII, *1758-1769*
Pius VI, *1775-1799*
Pius VII, *1800-1823*
Leo XII, *1823-1829*
Gregory XVI, *1831-1846*
Pius IX, *1846-1878*
Leo XIII, *1878-1903*

Pius X, *1903-1914*
Benedict XV, *1914-1922*
Pius XI, *1922-1939*
Pius XII, *1939-1958*
John XXIII, *1958-1963*
Paul VI, *1963-*

Russia

Ivan III, *1462-1505*
Basil III, *1505-1533*
Ivan IV, *1533-1584*
Theodore I, *1584-1598*
Boris Godunov, *1598-1603*
Time of Troubles, *1604-1613*
Michael (Romanov), *1613-1645*
Alexis I, *1645-1676*
Theodore III, *1676-1682*
Ivan V and Peter I, *1682-1689*
Peter I (the Great), *1682-1725*
Catherine I, *1725-1727*
Peter II, *1727-1730*
Anna, *1730-1740*
Ivan VI, *1740-1741*
Elizabeth, *1741-1762*
Peter III, *1762*
Catherine II, *1762-1796*
Paul, *1796-1801*
Alexander I, *1801-1825*
Nicholas I, *1825-1855*
Alexander II, *1855-1881*
Alexander III, *1881-1894*
Nicholas II, *1894-1917*
Revolution, Civil War, *1917-1920*
Union of Soviet Socialist Republics, *1922-*
  Soviet Communist Dictators:
    Lenin, *1917-1924*

Stalin, *1924-1953*
Malenkov, *1953-1955*
Bulganin, *1955-1958*
Khrushchev, *1958-1964*
Brezhnev, Secretary of the party; Kosygin, Premier, *1964-*

Spain

Ferdinand and Isabella, *1479-1504*
Ferdinand, *1504-1516*
Charles I, *1516-1556* (Holy Roman Emperor Charles V, *1519-1556*)
Philip II, *1556-1598*
Philip III, *1598-1621*
Philip IV, *1621-1665*
Charles II, *1665-1700*
Philip V, *1700-1746*
Ferdinand VI, *1746-1759*
Charles III, *1759-1788*
Charles IV, *1788-1808*
Joseph Bonaparte, *1808-1813*
Ferdinand VII, *1813-1833*
Isabella II, *1833-1868*
Amadeo, *1871-1873*
Republic, *1873-1874*
Alphonso XII, *1875-1885*
Regency of Maria Cristina, *1885-1902*
Alphonso XIII, *1902-1931*
Republic, *1931-1936*
Civil War, *1936-1939*
Francisco Franco, dictator, *1939-*

Selected Documents

The Monroe Doctrine, 1823

At the proposal of the Russian Imperial Government, made through the minister of the Emperor, residing here, a full power and instructions have been transmitted to the minister of the United States at St. Petersburg to arrange by amicable negotiation the respective rights and interests of the two nations on the northwest coast of this continent. A similar proposal has been made by His Imperial Majesty, to the Government of Great Britain, which has likewise been acceded to. The Government of the United States has been desirous by this friendly proceeding of manifesting the great value which they have invariably attached to the friendship of the Emperor and their solicitude to cultivate the best understanding with his Government. In the discussions to which this interest has given rise and in the arrangements by which they may terminate the occasion has been judged proper for asserting as a principle in which the rights and interests of the United States are involved, that the American continents, by the free and independent condition which they have assumed and maintain, are henceforth not to be considered as subjects for future colonization by any European powers. . . .

It was stated at the commencement of the last session that a great effort was then making in Spain and Portugal to improve the condition of the people of those countries, and that it appeared to be conducted with extraordinary moderation. It need scarcely be remarked that the result has been so far very different from what was then anticipated. Of events in that quarter of the globe, with which we have so much intercourse, and from which we derive our origin, we have always been anxious and interested spectators. The citizens of the United States cherish sentiments the most friendly in favor of the liberty and happiness of their fellowmen on that side of the Atlantic. In the wars of the European powers in matters relating to themselves we have never taken any part, nor does it comport with our policy so to do. It is only when our rights are invaded or seriously menaced that we resent injuries or make preparation for our defense. With the movements in this hemisphere we are of necessity more immediately connected, and by causes which must be obvious to all enlightened and impartial observers. The political system of the allied powers is essentially different in this respect from that of America. This difference proceeds from that which exists in their respective Governments, and to the defence of our own, which has been achieved by the loss of so much blood and treasure, and matured by the wisdom of their most enlightened citizens, and under which we have enjoyed unexampled felicity, this whole nation is devoted. We owe it, therefore, to candor and to the amicable relations existing between the United States and those powers to declare that we should consider any attempt on their part to extend their system to any portions of this hemisphere as dangerous to our peace and safety. With the existing colonies or dependencies of any European power we have not interfered and shall not interfere. But with the Governments who have declared their independence and maintained it, and whose independence we have, on great consideration and on just principles, acknowledged, we could not view any interposition for the purpose of oppressing them, or controlling in any other manner their destiny, by any European power in any other light than as the manifestation of an unfriendly disposition towards the United States. In the war between those new Governments and Spain we declared our neutrality at the time of their recognition, and to this we have adhered, and shall continue to adhere, provided no change shall occur which, in the judgment of the competent authorities of this Government, shall make a corresponding change on the part of the United States indispensable to their security.

The late events in Spain and Portugal shew that Europe is still unsettled. Of this important fact, no stronger proof can be adduced, than that the allied powers should have thought it proper, on any principle satisfactory to themselves, to have interposed by force in the internal concerns of Spain. To what extent such interposition may be carried, on the same principle, is a question, in which all independent powers whose governments differ from theirs are interested, even those most remote, and surely none more so than the United States. Our policy in regard to Europe, which was adopted at an early stage of the wars which have so long agitated that quarter of the globe, nevertheless remains the same, which is, not to interfere in the internal concerns of any of its powers; to consider the Government *de facto* as the legitimate government for us; to cultivate friendly relations with it, and to preserve those relations by a frank, firm, and manly policy, meeting in all instances the just claims of every power, submitting to injuries from none. But in regard to those continents circumstances are eminently and conspicuously different. It is impossible that the allied powers should extend their political systems to any portion of either continent without endangering our peace and happiness; nor can anyone believe, that our southern brethren, if left to themselves, would adopt it of their own accord. It is equally impossible, therefore, that we should behold such interposition in any form with indifference. If we look to the comparative strength and resources of Spain and those new governments, and their distance from each other, it must be obvious that she can never subdue them. It is still the true policy of the United States to leave the parties to themselves, in the hope that other powers will pursue the same course.

From *A Compilation of the Messages and Papers of the Presidents,* 1789-1897, ed. by James D. Richardson, 10 vols., II (1896) 207ff.

Carlsbad Decrees, 1819

Supervision of the Universities

The sovereign shall make choice for each university of an extraordinary commissioner furnished with suitable powers.

The duty of this commissioner shall be to watch over the most rigorous observation of the laws and disciplinary regulations; to observe carefully the spirit with which the professors and tutors are guided in their public and private lectures; to endeavour, without interfering directly in the scientific courses, or in the method of instruction, to give the instruction a salutary direction, suited to the future destiny of the students and to devote a constant attention to the maintenance of good order among the youths.

2. The governments of the states reciprocally engage to remove from their universities and other establishments of instruction, the professors and other public teachers against whom it may be proved, that in departing from their duty, in overstepping the bounds of their duty, in abusing their legitimate influence over the minds of youth, by the propagation of pernicious dogmas, hostile to order and public tranquillity, or in sapping the foundation of existing establishments, they have shown themselves incapable of executing the important functions entrusted to them.

3. The laws long since made against secret or unauthorized associations at the universities shall be maintained in all their force and vigour, and shall be particularly extended with so much the more severity against the well-known society formed some years ago under the name of the General Burschenschaft, as it has correspondence between the different universities.

Press Censorship

1. As long as the present decree shall be in force, no writing appearing in the form of a daily paper or periodical pamphlet, which does not contain more than 20 printed leaves, shall be issued from the press without the previous consent of the public authority. . . .

4. Each government of the confederation is accountable for the writings published under its jurisdiction. . . .

6. The Diet will proceed also, of its own authority, against every publication comprised in Article I in whatever state of Germany it may be published, if . . . it may have compromised the dignity of the Germanic body, or the internal peace of Germany. . . .

Committee of Investigation

1. In 15 days . . . an extraordinary commission of inquiry, . . . shall assemble in the city of Mayence. . . .

2. The object of this commission is to make careful and detailed inquiries respecting the facts, the origin, and the multiplied ramifications of the secret revolutionary and demagogic associa-

tions directed against the political constitution and internal repose, as well of the Confederation in general as of the individual members thereof.

From "Appendix to the Chronicle,"
The Annual Register . . . for the Year 1819 (1820), 159-162.

The Communist Manifesto, 1848

A specter is haunting Europe—the specter of Communism. All the powers of Old Europe have entered into a holy alliance to exorcise this specter; Pope and Czar, Metternich and Guizot, French Radicals and German police-spies.

Where is the party in opposition that has not been decried as communistic by its opponents in power? Where the opposition that has not hurled back the branding reproach of Communism, against the more advanced opposition parties, as well as against its reactionary adversaries?

Two things result from this fact.

I. Communism is already acknowledged by all European powers to be in itself a power.

II. It is high time that Communists should openly, in the face of the whole world, publish their views, their aims, their tendencies, and meet this nursery tale of the specter of Communism with a Manifesto of the party itself.

To this end Communists of various nationalities have assembled in London, and sketched the following Manifesto to be published in the English, French, German, Italian, Flemish and Danish languages.

Bourgeois and Proletarians

The history of all hitherto existing society is the history of class struggles.

Freeman and slave, patrician and plebeian, lord and serf, guildmaster and journeyman, in a word, oppressor and oppressed, stood in constant opposition to one another, carried on an uninterrupted, now hidden, now open fight, that each time ended, either in a revolutionary reconstitution of society at large, or in the common ruin of the contending classes.

In the earlier epochs of history we find almost everywhere a complicated arrangement of society into various orders, a manifold gradation of social rank. In ancient Rome we have patricians, knights, plebeians, slaves; in the middle ages, feudal lords, vassals, guild-masters, journeymen, apprentices, serfs; in almost all of these classes, again, subordinate gradations.

The modern bourgeois society that has sprouted from the ruins of feudal society, has not done away with class antagonisms. It has but established new classes, new conditions of oppression, new forms of struggle in place of the old ones.

Our epoch, the epoch of the bourgeoisie, possesses, however, this distinctive feature; it has simplified the class antagonisms. Society as a whole is more and more splitting up into two great hostile camps, into two great classes directly facing each other: Bourgeoisie and Proletariat.

From the serfs of the middle ages sprang the chartered burghers of the earliest towns. From these burgesses the first elements of the bourgeoisie were developed.

The discovery of America, the rounding of the Cape, opened up fresh ground for the rising bourgeoisie. The East-Indian and Chinese markets, the colonization of America, trade with the colonies, the increase in the means of exchange and in commodities generally, gave to commerce, to navigation, to industry, an impulse never before known, and thereby, to the revolutionary element in the tottering feudal society, a rapid development.

The feudal system of industry, under which industrial production was monopolized by closed guilds, now no longer sufficed for the growing wants of the new market. The manufacturing system took its place. The guild-masters were pushed on one side by the manufacturing middle class; division of labor between the different corporate guilds vanished in the face of division of labor in each single workshop.

Meantime the markets kept ever growing, the demand ever rising. Even manufacture no longer sufficed. Thereupon steam and machinery revolutionized industrial production. The place of manufacture was taken by the giant, Modern Industry, the place of the industrial middle class, by industrial millionaires, the leaders of whole industrial armies, the modern bourgeois.

Modern Industry has established the world's market, for which the discovery of America paved the way. This market has given an immense development to commerce, to navigation, to communication by land. This development has, in its turn, reacted on the extension of industry; and in proportion as industry, commerce, navigation, railways extended, in the same proportion, the bourgeoisie developed, increased its capital, and pushed into the background every class handed down from the Middle Ages.

We see, therefore, how the modern bourgeoisie is itself the product of a long course of development, of a series of revolutions in the modes of production and of exchange.

Each step in the development of the bourgeoisie was accompanied by a corresponding political advance of that class. An oppressed class under the sway of the feudal nobility, an armed and self-governing association in the mediaeval commune, here independent urban republic (as in Italy and Germany), there taxable "third estate" of the monarchy (as in France), afterwards, in the period of manufacture proper, serving either the semi-feudal or the absolute monarchy as a counterpoise against the nobility, and, in fact, corner-stone of the great monarchies in general, the bourgeoisie has at last, since the establishment of Modern Industry and of the world's market, conquered for itself, in the modern representative State, exclusive political sway. The executive of the modern State is but a committee for managing the common affairs of the whole bourgeoisie.

The bourgeoisie, historically, has played a most revolutionary part.

The bourgeoisie, wherever it has got the upper hand, has put an end to all feudal, patriarchal, idyllic relations. It has pitilessly torn asunder the motley feudal ties that bound man to his "natural superiors," and has left remaining no other nexus between man and man than naked self-interest, than callous "cash payment." It has drowned the most heavenly ecstasies of religious fervor, of chivalrous enthusiasm, of Philistine sentimentalism, in the icy water of egotistical calculation. It has resolved personal worth into exchange value, and in place of the numberless indefeasible chartered freedoms, has set up that single, unconscionable freedom—Free Trade. In one word, for exploitation, veiled by religious and political illusions, it has substituted naked, shameless, direct, brutal exploitation.

The bourgeoisie has stripped of its halo every occupation hitherto honored and looked up to with reverent awe. It has converted the physician, the lawyer, the priest, the poet, the man of science, into its paid wage-laborers.

The bourgeoisie has torn away from the family its sentimental veil, and has reduced the family relation to a mere money relation.

The bourgeoisie has disclosed how it came to pass that the brutal display of vigor in the Middle Ages, which reactionists so much admire, found its fitting complement in the most slothful indolence. It has been the first to show what man's activity can bring about. It has accomplished wonders far surpassing Egyptian pyramids, Roman aqueducts, and Gothic cathedrals; it has conducted expeditions that put in the shade all former Exoduses of nations and crusades.

The bourgeoisie cannot exist without constantly revolutionizing the instruments of production, and thereby the relations of production, and with them the whole relations of society. Conservation of the old modes of production in unaltered form, was, on the contrary, the first condition of existence for all earlier industrial classes. Constant revolutionizing of production, uninterrupted disturbance of all social conditions, everlasting uncertainty and agitation, distinguish the bourgeois epoch from all earlier ones. All fixed, fast-frozen relations, with their train of ancient and venerable prejudices and opinions, are swept away; all new-formed ones become antiquated before they can ossify. All that is solid melts into air, all that is holy is profaned, and man is at last compelled to face with sober senses his real conditions of life, and his relations with his kind.

The need of a constantly expanding market for its products chases the bourgeoisie over the whole surface of the globe. It must nestle everywhere, settle everywhere, establish connections everywhere.

The bourgeoisie has through its exploitation of the world's market given a cosmopolitan character to production and consumption in every country. To the great chagrin of reactionists, it has drawn from under the feet of industry the national ground on which it stood. All old established national industries have been destroyed or are daily being destroyed. They are dislodged by new industries, whose introduction becomes a life and death question for all civilized nations, by industries that no longer work up indigenous raw material, but raw material drawn from the remotest zones, industries whose products are consumed, not only at home, but in every quarter of the globe. In place of the old wants, satisfied by the productions of the country, we find new wants, requiring for their satisfaction the products of distant lands and climes. In place of the old local and national seclusion and self-sufficiency we have had intercourse in every direction, universal interdependence of nations. And as in material, so also in intellectual production. The intellectual creations of individual nations become common property. National onesidedness and narrowmindedness become more and more impossible, and from the numerous national and local literatures, there arises a world-literature.

The bourgeoisie, by the rapid improvement of all instruments of production, by the immensely facilitated means of communication, draws all, even the most barbarian, nations into civilization. The cheap prices of its commodities are the heavy artillery with which it batters down all Chinese walls, with which it forces the barbarians' intensely obstinate hatred of foreigners to capitulate. It compels all nations, on pain of extinction, to adopt the bourgeois mode of production; it compels them to introduce what it calls civilization into their midst, *i.e.,* to become bourgeois themselves. In one word, it creates a world after its own image.

The bourgeoisie has subjected the country to the rule of the towns. It has created enormous cities, has greatly increased the urban population as compared with the rural, and has thus rescued a considerable part of the population from the idiocy of rural life. Just as it has made the country dependent on the towns, so it has made barbarian and semi-barbarian countries dependent on the civilized ones, nations of peasants on nations of bourgeois, the East on the West.

The bourgeoisie keeps more and more doing away with the scattered state of the population, of the means of production, and of property. It has agglomerated population, centralized means of production, and has concentrated property in a few hands. The necessary consequence of this was political centralization. Independent, or but loosely connected provinces, with separate interests, laws, governments, and systems of taxation, became lumped together into one nation, with one government, one code of laws, one national class interest, one frontier, and one customs tariff.

The bourgeoisie, during its rule of scarce one hundred years, has created more massive and more colossal productive forces than have all preceding generations together. Subjection of Nature's forces to man, machinery, application of chemistry to industry and agriculture, steam-navigation, railways, electric telegraphs, clearing of whole continents for cultivation, canalization of rivers . . . what earlier century had even a presentiment that such productive forces slumbered in the lap of social labor?

We see then: the means of production and of exchange on whose foundation the bourgeoisie built itself up, were generated in feudal society. At a certain stage in the development of these means of production and of exchange, the conditions under which feudal society produced and exchanged, the feudal organization of agriculture and manufacturing industry, in one word, the feudal relations of property, became no longer compatible with the already developed productive forces; they became so many fetters. They had to burst asunder; they were burst asunder.

Into their places stepped free competition, accompanied by a social and political constitution adapted to it, and by the economical and political sway of the bourgeois class.

A similar movement is going on before our own eyes. Modern bourgeois society with its relations of production, of exchange, and of property, a society that has conjured up such gigantic means of production and of exchange, is like the sorcerer, who is no longer able to control the powers of the nether world whom he has called up by his spells. For many a decade past the history of industry and commerce is but the history of the revolt of modern productive forces against modern conditions of production, against the property relations that are the conditions for the existence of the bourgeoisie and of its rule. It is enough to mention the commercial crises that by their periodical return put on its trial, each time more threateningly, the existence of the bourgeois society. In these crises a great part not only of the existing products, but also of the previously created productive forces, is periodically destroyed. In these crises there breaks out an epidemic that, in all earlier epochs, would have seemed an absurdity—the epidemic of overproduction. Society sudenly finds itself put back into a state of momentary barbarism; it appears as if a famine, a universal war of devastation, had cut off the supply of every means of subsistence; industry and commerce seem to be destroyed; and why? because there is too much civilization, too much means of subsistence, too much industry, too much commerce. The productive forces at the disposal of society no longer tend to further the development of the conditions of bourgeois property; on the contrary, they have become too powerful for these conditions, by which they are fettered, and as soon as they overcome these fetters, they bring disorder into the whole of bourgeois society, endanger the existence of bourgeois property. The conditions of bourgeois society are too narrow to comprise the wealth created by them. And how does the bourgeoisie get over these crises? On the one hand by enforced destruction of a mass of productive forces; on the other, by the conquest of new markets, and by the more thorough exploitation of the old ones. That is to say, by paving the way for more extensive and more destructive crises, and by diminishing the means whereby crises are prevented.

The weapons with which the bourgeoisie felled feudalism to the ground are now turned against the bourgeoisie itself.

But not only has the bourgeoisie forged the weapons that bring death to itself; it has also called into existence the men who are to wield those weapons—the modern working class—the proletarians.

In proportion as the bourgeoisie, *i.e.*, capital, is developed, in the same proportion is the proletariat, the modern working class, developed; a class of laborers, who live only so long as they find work, and who find work only so long as their labor increases capital. These laborers, who must sell themselves piecemeal, are a commodity, like every other article of commerce, and are consequently exposed to all the vicissitudes of competition, to all the fluctuations of the market.

Owing to the extensive use of machinery and to division of labor, the work of the proletarians has lost all individual character, and, consequently all charm for the workman. He becomes an appendage of the machine, and it is only the most simple, most monotonous, and most easily acquired knack, that is required of him. Hence, the cost of production of a workman is restricted almost entirely to the means of subsistence that he requires for his maintenance, and for the propagation of his race. But the price of a commodity, and therefore also of labor, is equal to its cost of production. In proportion, therefore, as the repulsiveness of the work increases, the wage decreases. Nay, more, in proportion as the use of machinery and division of labor increases, in the same proportion the burden of toil also increases, whether by prolongation of the working hours, by increase of the work enacted in a given time, or by increased speed of the machinery, etc.

Modern industry has converted the little workshop of the patriarchal master into the great factory of the industrial capitalist. Masses of laborers, crowded into factories, are organized like soldiers. As privates of the industrial army they are placed under the command of a perfect hierarchy of officers and sergeants. Not only are they the slaves of the bourgeois class, and of the bourgeois State, they are daily and hourly enslaved by the machine . . . and, above all, by the individual bourgeois manufacturer himself. The more openly this despotism proclaims gain to be its end and aim, the more petty, the more hateful and the more embittering it is.

The less skill and exertion of strength implied in manual labor, in other words, the more modern industry becomes developed, the more is the labor of men superseded by that of women. Differences of age and sex have no longer any distinctive social validity for the working class. All are instruments of labor, more or less expensive to use, according to age and sex.

No sooner is the exploitation of the laborer by the manufacturer, so far at an end, that he receives his wages in cash, than he is set upon by the other portions of the bourgeoisie, the landlord, the shopkeeper, the pawnbroker, etc.

The lower strata of the Middle class—the small tradespeople, shopkeepers, and retired tradesmen generally, the handicraftsmen and peasant—all these sink gradually into the proletariat, partly because their diminutive capital does not suffice for the scale on which modern industry is carried on, and is swamped in the competition with the large capitalists, partly because their specialized skill is rendered worthless by new methods of production. Thus the proletariat is recruited from all classes of the population.

The proletariat goes through various stages of development. With its birth begins its struggle with the bourgeoisie. At first the contest is carried on by individual laborers, then by the workpeople of a factory, then by the operatives of one trade, in one locality, against the individual bourgeois who directly exploits them. They direct their attacks not against the bourgeois conditions of production, but against the instruments of production themselves; they destroy imported wares that compete with their labor, they smash to pieces machinery, they set factories ablaze, they seek to restore by force the vanished status of the workman of the Middle Ages.

At this stage the laborers still form an incoherent mass scattered over the whole country, and broken up by their mutual competition. If anywhere they unite to form more compact bodies, this is not yet the consequence of their own active union, but of the union of the bourgeoisie, which class, in order to attain its own political ends, is compelled to set the whole proletariat in motion, and is moreover yet, for a time, able to do so. At this stage, therefore, the proletarians do not fight their enemies, but the enemies of their enemies, the remnants of absolute monarchy, the landowners, the non-industrial bourgeois, the petty bourgeoisie. Thus the whole historical movement is concentrated in the hands of the bourgeoisie; every victory so obtained is a victory for the bourgeoisie.

But with the development of industry the proletariat not only increases in number; it becomes concentrated in greater masses, its strength grows and it feels that strength more. The various interests and conditions of life within the ranks of the proletariat are more and more equalized, in proportion as machinery obliterates all distinctions of labor, and nearly everywhere reduces wages to the same low level. The growing competition among the bourgeois, and the resulting commercial crises, make the wages of the workers even more fluctuating. The unceasing improvement of machinery, ever more rapidly developing, makes their livelihood more and more precarious; the collisions between individual workmen and individual bourgeois take more and more the character of collisions between two classes. Thereupon the workers begin to form combinations (Trades' Unions) against the bourgeois; they club together in order to keep up the rate of wages; they found permanent associations in order to make provision beforehand for these occasional revolts. Here and there the contest breaks out into riots.

Now and then the workers are victorious, but only for a time. The real fruit of their battles lies not in the immediate result but in the ever-improved means of communication that are created by modern industry, and that place the workers of different localities in contact with one another. It was just this contact that was needed to centralize the numerous local struggles, all of the same character, into one national struggle between classes. But every class struggle is a political struggle. And that union, to attain which the burghers of the Middle Ages, with their miserable highways, required centuries, the modern proletarians, thanks to railways, achieve in a few years.

This organization of the proletarians into a class, and consequently into a political party, is continually being upset again by the competition between the workers themselves. But it ever rises up again; stronger, firmer, mightier. It compels legislative recognition of particular interests of the workers, by taking advantage of the divisions among the bourgeoisie itself. Thus the ten-hours' bill in England was carried.

Altogether collisions between the classes of the old society further, in many ways, the course of development of the proletariat. The bourgeoisie finds itself involved in a constant battle. At first with the aristocracy; later on, with those portions of the bourgeoisie itself, whose interests have become antagonistic to the progress of industry; at all times with the bourgeoisie of foreign countries. In all these countries it sees itself compelled to appeal to the proletariat, to ask for its help, and thus to drag it into the political arena. The bourgeoisie itself, therefore, supplies the proletariat with weapons for fighting the bourgeoisie.

Further, as we have already seen, entire sections of the ruling classes are, by the advance of industry, precipitated into the proletariat, or are at least threatened in their conditions of existence. These also supply the proletariat with fresh elements of enlightenment and progress.

Finally, in times when the class struggle nears the decisive hour, the process of dissolution going on within the ruling class, in fact, within the whole range of an old society, assumes such a violent, glaring character, that a small section of the ruling class cuts itself adrift, and joins the revolutionary class, the class that holds the future in its hands. Just as, therefore, at an earlier period, a section of the nobility went over to the bourgeoisie, so now a portion of the bourgeoisie goes over to the proletariat, and in particular, a portion of the bourgeoisie ideologists, who have raised themselves to the level of comprehending theoretically the historical movement as a whole.

Of all the classes that stand face to face with the bourgeoisie today the proletariat alone is a really revolutionary class. The other classes decay and finally disappear in the face of modern industry; the proletariat is its special and essential product.

The lower middle class, the small manufacturer, the shopkeeper, the artisan, the peasant, all these fight against the bourgeoisie to save from extinction their existence as fractions of the middle class. They are therefore not revolutionary, but conservative. Nay, more, they are reactionary, for they try to roll back the wheel of history. If by chance they are revolutionary, they are so only in view of their impending transfer into the proletariat; they thus defend not their present, but their future interests, they desert their own standpoint to place themselves at that of the proletariat.

The "dangerous class," the social scum, that passively rotting class thrown off by the lowest layers of old society, may, here and there, be swept into the movement by a proletarian revolution; its conditions of life, however, prepare it far more for the part of a bribed tool of reactionary intrigue.

In the conditions of the proletariat, those of the old society at large are already virtually swamped. The proletarian is without property; his relation to his wife and children has no longer anything in common with the bourgeois family relations; modern industrial labor, modern subjection to capital, the same in England as in France, in America as in Germany, has stripped him of every trace of national character. Law, morality, religion, are to him so many bourgeois prejudices, behind which lurk in ambush just as many bourgeois interests.

All the preceding classes that got the upper hand sought to fortify their already acquired status by subjecting society at large to their conditions of appropriation. The proletarians cannot become masters of the productive forces of society, except by abolishing their own previous mode of appropriation, and thereby also every other previous mode of appropriation. They have nothing of their own to secure and to fortify; their mission is to destroy all previous securities for, and insurances of, individual property.

All previous historical movements were movements of minorities, or in the interest of minorities. The proletarian movement is the self-conscious, independent movement of the immense majority, in the immense majority. The proletariat, the lowest stratum of our present society, cannot stir, cannot raise itself up, without the whole super-incumbent strata of official society being sprung into the air.

Though not in substance, yet in form, the struggle of the proletariat with the bourgeoisie is at first a national struggle. The proletariat of each country must, of course, first of all settle matters with its own bourgeoisie.

In depicting the most general phases of the development of the proletariat, we traced the more or less veiled civil war, raging within existing society, up to the point where that war breaks out into open revolution, and where the violent overthrow of the bourgeoisie lays the foundation for the sway of the proletariat.

Hitherto every form of society has been based, as we have already seen, on the antagonism of oppressing and oppressed classes. But in order to oppress a class certain conditions must be assured to it under which it can, at least, continue its slavish existence. The serf, in the period of serfdom, raised himself to membership in the commune, just as the petty bourgeois, under the yoke of feudal absolutism, managed to develop into a bourgeois. The modern laborer, on the contrary, instead of rising with the progress of industry, sinks deeper and deeper below the conditions of existence of his own class. He becomes a pauper, and pauperism develops more rapidly than population and wealth. And here it becomes evident that the bourgeoisie is unfit any longer to be the ruling class in society and to impose its conditions of existence upon society as an over-riding law. It is unfit to rule because it is incompetent to assure an existence to its slave within his slavery, because it cannot help letting him sink into such a state that it has to feed him instead of being fed by him. Society can no longer live under this bourgeoisie, in other words its existence is no longer compatible with society.

The essential condition for the existence, and for the sway of the bourgeois class, is the formation and augmentation of capital; the condition for capital is wage-labor. Wage-labor rests exclusively on competition between the laborers. The advance of industry, whose involuntary promoter is the bourgeoisie, replaces the isolation of the laborers, due to competition, by their revolutionary combination, due to association. The development of modern industry, therefore, cuts from under its feet the very foundation on which the bourgeoisie produces and appropriates products. What the bourgeoisie therefore produces, above all, are its own gravediggers. Its fall and the victory of the proletariat are equally inevitable. . . .

Position of the Communists in Relation to the Various Existing Opposition Parties

. . . The Communists fight for the attainment of the immediate aims, for the enforcement of the momentary interests of the working class; but in the movement of the present they also represent and take care of the future of that movement. In France the Communists ally themselves with the Social-Democrats, against the conservative and radical bourgeoisie, reserving, however, the right to take up a critical position in regard to phrases and illusions traditionally handed down from the great Revolution.

In Switzerland they support the Radicals, without losing sight of the fact that this party consists of antagonistic elements, partly of Democratic Socialists, in the French sense, partly of radical bourgeois.

In Poland they support the party that insists on an agrarian revolution, as the prime condition for national emancipation, that party which fomented the insurrection of Cracow in 1846.

In Germany they fight with the bourgeoisie whenever it acts in a revolutionary way against the absolute monarchy, the feudal squirearchy, and the petty bourgeoisie.

But they never cease, for a single instant, to instill into the working class the clearest possible recognition of the hostile antagonism between bourgeoisie and proletariat, in order that the German workers may straightway use, as so many weapons against the bourgeoisie the social and political conditions that the bourgeoisie must necessarily introduce along with its supremacy, and in order that, after the fall of the reactionary classes in Germany, the fight against the bourgeoisie itself may immediately begin.

The Communists turn their attention chiefly to Germany, because that country is on the eve of a bourgeois revolution that is bound to be carried out under more advanced conditions of European civilization, and with a much more developed proletariat, than that of England was in the seventeenth, and of France in the eighteenth century, and because the bourgeois revolution in Germany will be but the prelude to an immediately following proletarian revolution.

In short, the Communists everywhere support every revolutionary movement against the existing social and political order of things.

In all these movements they bring to the front, as the leading question in each, the property question, no matter what its degree of development at the time.

Finally, they labor everywhere for the union and agreement of the democratic parties of all countries.

The Communists disdain to conceal their views and aims. They openly declare that their ends can be attained only by the forcible overthrow of all existing social conditions. Let the ruling classes tremble at a Communistic revolution. The proletarians have nothing to lose but their chains. They have a world to win.

Working men of all countries, unite!

Karl Marx and Friedrich Engels, *Manifesto of the Communist Party*, Authorized English Translation, ed. Friedrich Engels (1888), 7-15.

The Ems Telegram, 1870

Under this conviction I made use of the royal authorisation communicated to me through Abeken, to publish the contents of the telegram; and in the presence of my two guests I reduced the telegram by striking out words, but without adding or altering, to the following form:

"After the news of the renunciation of the hereditary Prince of Hohenzollern had been officially communicated to the imperial government of France by the royal government of Spain, the French ambassador at Ems further demanded of his Majesty the King that he would authorise him to telegraph to Paris that his Majesty the King bound himself for all future time never again to give his consent if the Hohenzollerns should renew their candidature. His Majesty the King thereupon decided not to receive the French ambassador again, and sent to tell him through the aide-de-camp on duty that his Majesty had nothing further to communicate to the ambassador."

The difference in the effect of the abbreviated text of the Ems telegram as compared with that produced by the original was not the result of stronger words but of the form, which made this announcement appear decisive, while Abeken's version would only have been regarded as a fragment of a negotiation still pending, and to be continued at Berlin.

After I had read out the concentrated edition to my two guests, Moltke remarked: "Now it has a different ring; it sounded before like a parley; now it is like a flourish in answer to a challenge." I went on to explain: "If in execution of his Majesty's order I at once communicate this text, which contains no alteration in or addition to the telegram not only to the newspapers, but also by telegraph to all our embassies, it will be known in Paris before midnight, and not only on account of its contents, but also on account of the manner of its distribution, will have the effect of a red rag upon the Gallic bull. Fight we must if we do not want to act the part of the vanquished without a battle. Success, however, essentially depends upon the impression which the origination of the war makes upon us and others; it is important that we should be the party attacked, and this Gallic overweening and touchiness will make us if we announce in the face of Europe, so far as we can without the speaking-tube of the Reichstag, that we fearlessly meet the public threats of France."

Bismarck The Man and the Statesman,
trans. by A. J. Butler, Vol. II (1898), 278-280.

Alexander II's Ukase Emancipating The Serfs, 1861

By grace of God, we, Alexander II, Emperor and Autocrat of all the Russias, King of Poland, Grand Duke of Finland, etc., to all our faithful subjects make known:

In considering the various classes and conditions of which the State is composed we came to the conviction that the legislation of the empire having wisely provided for the organization of the upper and middle classes and having defined with precision their obligations, their rights, and their privileges, has not attained the same degree of efficiency as regards the peasants attached to the soil, thus designated because either from ancient laws or from custom they have been hereditarily subjected to the authority of the proprietors, on whom it was incumbent at the same time to provide for their welfare. In the most favourable cases this state of things has established patriarchal relations founded upon a solicitude sincerely equitable and benevolent on the part of the proprietors, and on an affectionate submission on the part of the peasants; but in proportion as the simplicity of morals diminished, as the diversity of the mutual relations became complicated, as the paternal character of the relations between the proprietors and the peasants became weakened, and moreover, as the seigneurial authority fell sometimes into hands exclusively occupied with their personal interests, those bonds of mutual good-will slackened, and a wide opening was made for an arbitrary sway, which weighed upon

the peasants, was unfavourable to their welfare and made them indifferent to all progress under the conditions of their existence.

These facts had already attracted the notice of our predeces-
sors of glorious memory, and they had taken measures for improving the conditions of the peasants; but among those measures some
were not stringent enough, insomuch that they remained subordinate to the spontaneous initiative of such proprietors who showed
themselves animated with liberal intentions; and others, called forth
by peculiar circumstances, have been restricted to certain localities
or simply adopted as an experiment. . . .

We thus came to the conviction that the work of a serious
improvement of the condition of the peasants was a sacred inheri-
tance bequeathed to us by our ancestors, a mission which, in the
course of events, Divine Providence called upon us to fulfil.

Having invoked the Divine assistance, we have resolved to
carry this work into execution.

In virtue of the new dispositions the peasants attached to the
soil will be invested within a term fixed by the law with all the
rights of free cultivators.

The proprietors retaining their rights of property on all the
land belonging to them, grant to the peasants for a fixed regulated
rental the full enjoyment of their close. In this state, which must be
a transitory one, the peasants shall be designated as "temporarily
bound."

At the same time, they are granted the right of purchasing
their close, and, with the consent of the proprietors, they may
acquire in full property the arable lands and other appurtenances
which are allotted to them as a permanent holding. By the acquisition in full property of the quantity of land fixed, the peasants are
free from their obligations towards the proprietors for land thus
purchased, and they enter definitively into the condition of free
peasants—landholders.

Although these dispositions, general as well as local, and the
special supplementary rules for some particular localities, for the
lands of small proprietors, and for the peasants who work in the
manufactories and establishments of the proprietors, have been, as
far as was possible, adapted to economical necessities and local
customs, nevertheless, to preserve the existing state where it presents

reciprocal advantages, we leave it to the proprietors to come to amicable terms with the peasants, and to conclude transactions relative to the extent of the territorial allotment and to the amount of rental . . . observing, rules to guarantee the inviolability of such agreements.

Aware of all the difficulties of the reform we have undertaken, we place above all things our confidence in the goodness of Divine Providence, who watches over the destinies of Russia.

We also count upon the generous devotion of our faithful nobility, and we are happy to testify to that body the gratitude it has deserved from us, as well as from the country, for the disinterested support it has given to the accomplishment of our designs. Russia will not forget that the nobility, acting solely upon its respect for the dignity of man and its love for its neighbour, has spontaneously renounced rights given to it by serfdom actually abolished, and laid the foundation of a new future, which is thrown open to the peasants. We also entertain the firm hope that it will also nobly exert its ulterior efforts to carry out the new regulation by maintaining good order, in a spirit of peace and benevolence, and that each proprietor will complete, within the limits of his property, the great civic act accomplished by the whole body, by organizing the existence of the peasants domiciliated on his estates, and of his domestics, under mutual advantageous conditions, thereby giving to the country population the example of a faithful and conscientious execution of the regulations of the State.

When the first news of this great reform meditated by the Government became diffused among the rural populations, who were scarcely prepared for it, it gave rise, in some instances, to misunderstandings among individuals more intent upon liberty than mindful of the duties which it imposes. But, generally, the good sense of the country has not been wanting. It has not misunderstood either the inspirations of natural reason, which says that every man who accepts freely the benefits of society owes it in return the fulfilment of certain positive obligations; nor the teachings of the Christian law, which enjoins that "every one be subject unto the higher powers" (St. Paul to the Romans, xiii. 1); and to "render to all their dues," and above all, to whomsoever it belongs, tribute, custom, respect and honour (*Ibid.*, xiii. 7). It has understood that the proprietors would not be deprived of rights legally acquired, except for a fit and sufficient indemnity, or by a voluntary concession on their part; that it would be contrary to all equity to accept this enjoyment of the lands conceded by the proprietors without accepting also towards them equivalent charges.

And now we hope with confidence that the freed serfs, in the presence of the new future which is opened before them, will appreciate and recognize the considerable sacrifices which the nobility have made on their behalf. They will understand that the blessing of an existence supported upon the base of guaranteed property, as well as a greater liberty in the administration of their goods, entails upon them, with new duties towards society and themselves, the obligation of justifying the protecting designs of the law by a loyal and judicious use of the rights which are now accorded to them. For if men do not labour themselves to insure their own well-being under the shield of the laws, the best of those laws cannot guarantee it to them. . . .

And now, pious and faithful people, make upon thy forehead the sacred sign of the cross, and join thy prayers to ours to call down the blessing of the Most High upon thy first free labours, the sure pledge of thy personal well-being and of the public prosperity.

ALEXANDER.

The Annual Register, 1861 (1862), 207-211.

De Rerum Novarum, 1891
(Encyclical Letter of Pope Leo XIII "On the Condition of Labor")

That the spirit of revolutionary change, which has long been disturbing the nations of the world, should have passed beyond the sphere of politics and made its influence felt in the cognate sphere of practical economics is not surprising. The elements of the conflict now raging are unmistakable in the vast expansion of industrial pursuits and the marvellous discoveries of science; in the changed relations between masters and workmen; in the enormous fortunes of some few individuals, and the utter poverty of the masses; in the increased self-reliance and closer mutual combination of the working classes; as also, finally, in the prevailing moral degeneracy. The momentous gravity of the state of things now obtaining fills every mind with painful apprehension; wise men are discussing it; practical men are proposing schemes; popular meetings, legislatures, and rulers of nations are all busied with it. . . .

The great mistake made in regard to the matter now under consideration is to take up with the notion that class is naturally hostile to class, and that the wealthy and the workingmen are intended by nature to live in mutual conflict. So irrational and so false is this view, that the direct contrary is the truth. Just as the symmetry of the human frame is the resultant of the disposition of the bodily members, so in a State is it ordained by nature that these two classes should dwell in harmony and agreement, and should, as it were, groove into one another, so as to maintain the balance of the body politic. Each needs the other: Capital cannot do without Labor, nor Labor without Capital. Mutual agreement results in pleasantness of life and the beauty of good order; while perpetual conflict necessarily produces confusion and savage barbarity. Now, in preventing such strife as this, and in uprooting it, the efficacy of Christian institutions is marvellous and manifold. First of all, there is no intermediary more powerful than Religion (whereof the Church is the interpreter and guardian) in drawing the rich, and the poor bread-winners, together, by reminding each class of its duties to the other, and especially of the obligations of justice. Thus Religion teaches the laboring man and the artisan to carry out honestly and fairly all equitable agreements freely entered into; never to injure the property, nor to outrage the person, of an employer; never to resort to violence in defending their own cause, nor to engage in riot or disorder; and to have nothing to do with men of evil principles, who work upon the people with artful promises, and excite foolish hopes which usually end in useless regrets, followed by insolvency. Religion teaches the wealthy owner and the employer that their work-people are not to be accounted their bondsmen; that in every man they must respect his dignity and worth as a man and as a Christian; that labor is not a thing to be ashamed of, if we lend ear to right reason and to Christian philosophy, but is an honorable calling, enabling a man to sustain his life in a way upright and creditable; and that it is shameful and inhuman to treat men like chattels to make money by, or to look upon them merely as so much muscle or physical power. Again, therefore, the Church teaches that, as Religion and things spiritual and mental are among the workingman's main concerns, the employer is bound to see that the worker has time for his religious duties; that he be not exposed to corrupting influences and dangerous occasions, and that he be not led away to neglect his home and family, or to squander his earnings. Furthermore, the employer must never tax his work-people beyond their strength, or employ them in work unsuited to their sex or age. His great and principal duty is to give every one a fair wage. Doubtless, before deciding whether wages are adequate, many things have to be considered; but wealthy owners and all masters of labor should be mindful of this—that to exercise pressure upon the indigent and the destitute for the sake of gain, and to gather one's profit out of the need of another, is condemned by all laws, human and divine. To defraud any one of wages that are his due is a crime which cries to the avenging anger of Heaven. *Behold, the hire of the laborers . . . which by fraud hath been kept back by you, crieth aloud; and the cry of them hath entered into the ears of the Lord of Sabaoth.* Lastly, the rich must religiously refrain from cutting down the workmen's earnings, whether by force, by fraud, or by usurious dealing, and with all the greater reason because the laboring man is, as a rule, weak and unprotected, and because his slender means should in proportion to their scantiness be accounted sacred.

Whenever the general interest or any particular class suffers, or is threatened with mischief which can in no other way be met or prevented, the public authority must step in to deal with it. Now, it interests the public, as well as the individual, that peace and good order should be maintained: that family life should be carried on in accordance with God's laws and those of nature; that religion should be reverenced and obeyed; that a high standard of morality should prevail, both in public and private life, that the sanctity of justice should be respected, and that no one should injure another with impunity; that the members of the commonwealth should grow up to man's estate strong and robust, and capable, if need be, of guarding and defending their country. If by a strike, or other combination of workmen, there should be imminent danger of disturbance to the public peace, or if circumstances were such as that among the laboring population the ties of family life were relaxed; if religion were found to suffer through the operatives not having time and opportunity afforded them to practise its duties; if in workshops and factories there were danger to morals through the mixing of the sexes or from other harmful occasions of evil; or if employers laid burdens upon their workmen which were unjust, or degraded them with conditions repugnant to their dignity as human beings, finally, if health were endangered by excessive labor, or by work unsuited to sex or age—in such cases, there can be no question but that, within certain limits, it would be right to invoke the aid and authority of the law. The limits must be determined by the nature of the occasion which calls for the law's interference—the principle being that the law must not undertake more, nor proceed further, than is required for the remedy of the evil or the removal of the mischief.

Rights must be religiously respected wherever they exist, and it is the duty of the public authority to prevent and to punish injury, and to protect every one in the possession of his own. Still, when there is a question of defending the rights of individuals, the poor and helpless have a claim to especial consideration. The richer class have many ways of shielding themselves, and stand less in need of help from the State; whereas those who are badly off have no resources of their own to fall back upon, and must chiefly depend upon the assistance of the State. And it is for this reason that wage-earners, who are undoubtedly among the weak and necessitous, should be specially cared for and protected by the Government.

Here, however, it is expedient to bring under special notice certain matters of moment. It should ever be borne in mind that the chief thing to be realized is the safeguarding of private property by legal enactment and public policy. Most of all it is essential, amid such a fever of excitement, to keep the multitude within the line of duty; for if all may justly strive to better their condition, neither justice nor the common good allows any individual to seize upon that which belongs to another, or, under the futile and shallow

pretext of equality, to lay violent hands on other people's possessions. Most true it is that by far the larger part of the workers
prefer to better themselves by honest labor rather than by doing
any wrong to others. But there are not a few who are imbued with
evil principles and eager for evolutionary change, whose main purpose is to stir up tumult and bring about measures of violence. The
authority of the State should intervene to put restraint upon such
firebrands, to save the working classes from their seditious arts, and
protect lawful owners from spoliation.

When working men have recourse to a strike, it is frequently
because the hours of labor are too long, or the work too hard, or
because they consider their wages insufficient. The grave incon-
venience of this not uncommon occurrence should be obviated by
public remedial measures; for such paralyzing of labor not only
affects the masters and their work-people alike, but is extremely
injurious to trade and to the general interests of the public; moreover, on such occasions, violence and disorder are generally not
far distant, and thus it frequently happens that the public peace
is imperilled. The laws should forestall and prevent such troubles
from arising; they should lend their influence and authority to the
removal in good time of the causes which lead to conflicts between
employers and employed. . . .

If we turn now to things external and corporeal, the first concern of all is to save the poor workers from the cruelty of greedy
speculators, who use human beings as mere instruments of money-
making. It is neither just nor human so to grind men down with
excessive labor as to stupefy their minds and wear out their bodies.
Man's powers, like his general nature, are limited, and beyond these
limits he cannot go. His strength is developed and increased by
use and exercise, but only on condition of due intermission and
proper rest. Daily labor, therefore, should be so regulated as not to
be protracted over longer hours than strength admits. How many
and how long the intervals of rest should be must depend on the
nature of the work, on circumstances of time and place, and on
the health and strength of the workmen. Those who work in mines
and quarries, and extract coal, stone, and metals from the bowels
of the earth, should have shorter hours in proportion as their labor

is more severe and trying to health. Then, again, the season of the year should be taken into account; for not infrequently a kind of labor is easy at one time which at another is intolerable or exceedingly difficult. Finally, work which is quite suitable for a strong man cannot reasonably be required from a woman or a child. And, in regard to children, great care should be taken not to place them in workshops and factories until their bodies and minds are sufficiently developed. For just as very rough weather destroys the buds of spring, so does too early an experience of life's hard toil blight the young promise of a child's faculties and render any true education impossible. Women, again, are not suited for certain occupations; a woman is by nature fitted for home work, and it is that which is best adapted at once to preserve her modesty and to promote the good bringing up of children and the well-being of the family. As a general principle it may be laid down that a workman ought to have leisure and rest proportionate to the wear and tear of his strength; for waste of strength must be repaired by cessation from hard work. . . .

In the last place—employers and workmen may of themselves effect much in the matter we are treating, by means of such associations and organizations as afford opportune aid to those who are in distress, and which draw the two classes more closely together. Among these may be enumerated societies for mutual help; various benevolent foundations established by private persons to provide for the workman, and for his widow or his orphans, in case of sudden calamity, in sickness, and in the event of death; and what are called "patronages," or institutions for the care of boys and girls, for young people, as well as homes for the aged.

The most important of all are workingmen's unions; for these virtually include all the rest. History attests what excellent results were brought about by the artificers' guilds of olden times. They were the means of affording not only many advantages to the workmen, but in no small degree of promoting the advancement of art. . . . Such unions should be suited to the requirements of this our age—an age of wider education, of different habits, and of far more numerous requirements in daily life. It is gratifying to know that there are actually in existence not a few associations of this nature, consisting either of workmen alone, or of workmen and employers together; but it were greatly to be desired that they should become more numerous and more efficient. . . .

Excerpts from "De Rerum Novarum" in Leo XIII, *The Great Encyclical Letters of Pope Leo XIII* (1903), 208-239.

Platform of the Populist Party, 1892

We declare, therefore—

First.—That the union of the labor forces of the United States this day consummated shall be permanent and perpetual; may its spirit enter into all hearts for the salvation of the Republic and the uplifting of mankind.

Second.—Wealth belongs to him who creates it, and every dollar taken from industry without an equivalent is robbery. "If any will not work, neither shall he eat." The interests of rural and civil labor are the same; their enemies are identical.

Third.—We believe that the time has come when the railroad corporations will either own the people or the people must own the railroads; and should the government enter upon the work of owning and managing all railroads, we should favor an amendment to the constitution by which all persons engaged in the government service shall be placed under a civil-service regulation of the most rigid character, so as to prevent the increase of the power of the national administration by the use of such additional government employes.

FINANCE.—We demand a national currency, safe, sound, and flexible issued by the general government only, a full legal tender for all debts, public and private, and that without the use of banking corporations; a just, equitable, and efficient means of distribution direct to the people, at a tax not to exceed 2 per cent, per annum, to be provided as set forth in the sub-treasury plan of the Farmers' Alliance, or a better system; also by payments in discharge of its obligations for public improvements.

1. We demand free and unlimited coinage of silver and gold at the present legal ratio of 16 to 1.
2. We demand that the amount of circulating medium be speedily increased to not less than $50 per capita.
3. We demand a graduated income tax.
4. We believe that the money of the country should be kept as much as possible in the hands of the people, and hence we demand that all State and national revenues shall be limited to the necessary expenses of the government, economically and honestly administered.
5. We demand that postal savings banks be established by the government for the safe deposit of the earnings of the people and to facilitate exchange.

TRANSPORTATION.—Transportation being a means of exchange and a public necessity, the government should own and operate the railroads in the interest of the people. The telegraph and telephone, like the postoffice system, being a necessity for the transmission of news, should be owned and operated by the government in the interest of the people.

LAND.—The land, including all the natural sources of wealth, is the heritage of the people, and should not be monopolized for speculative purposes, and alien ownership of land should be prohibited. All land now held by railroads and other corporations in excess of their actual needs, and all lands now owned by aliens should be reclaimed by the government and held for actual settlers only.

From Edward McPherson, *A Handbook of Politics for 1892*, p. 269ff.

President Fillmore's Letter to The Emperor of Japan, 1853

Millard Fillmore, President of the United States of America,
to his Imperial Majesty, the Emperor of Japan.

Great and good Friend: I send you this public letter by Commodore Matthew C. Perry, an officer of the highest rank in the navy of the United States, and commander of the squadron now visiting your imperial majesty's dominions.

I have directed Commodore Perry to assure your imperial majesty that I entertain the kindest feelings toward your majesty's person and government, and that I have no other object in sending him to Japan but to propose to your imperial majesty that the United States and Japan should live in friendship and have commercial intercourse with each other.

The Constitution and laws of the United States forbid all interference with the religious or political concerns of other nations. I have particularly charged Commodore Perry to abstain from every act which could possibly disturb the tranquility of your imperial majesty's dominions.

The United States of America reach from ocean to ocean, and our Territory of Oregon and State of California lie directly opposite to the dominions of your imperial majesty. Our steamships can go from California to Japan in eighteen days.

Our great State of California produces about sixty millions of dollars in gold every year, besides silver, quicksilver, precious stones, and many other valuable articles. Japan is also a rich and fertile country, and produces many very valuable articles. Your imperial majesty's subjects are skilled in many of the arts. I am desirous that our two countries should trade with each other, for the benefit both of Japan and the United States.

We know that the ancient laws of your imperial majesty's government do not allow of foreign trade, except with the Chinese and the Dutch; but as the state of the world changes and new governments are formed, it seems to be wise, from time to time, to make new laws. There was a time when the ancient laws of your imperial majesty's government were first made.

About the same time America, which is sometimes called the New World, was first discovered and settled by the Europeans. For a long time there were but a few people, and they were poor. They have now become quite numerous; their commerce is very extensive; and they think that if your imperial majesty were so far to change the ancient laws as to allow a free trade between the two countries it would be extremely beneficial to both.

If your imperial majesty is not satisfied that it would be safe altogether to abrogate the ancient laws which forbid foreign trade, they might be suspended for five or ten years, so as to try the experiment. If it does not prove as beneficial as was hoped, the ancient laws can be restored. The United States often limit their treaties with foreign States to a few years, and then renew them or not, as they please.

I have directed Commodore Perry to mention another thing to your imperial majesty. Many of our ships pass every year from California to China; and great numbers of our people pursue the whale fishery near the shores of Japan. It sometimes happens, in stormy weather, that one of our ships is wrecked on your imperial majesty's shores. In all such cases we ask, and expect, that our unfortunate people should be treated with kindness, and that their property should be protected, till we can send a vessel and bring them away. We are very much in earnest in this.

Commodore Perry is also directed by me to represent to your imperial majesty that we understand there is a great abundance of coal and provisions in the Empire of Japan. Our steamships, in crossing the great ocean, burn a great deal of coal, and it is not convenient to bring it all the way from America. We wish that our steamships and other vessels should be allowed to stop in Japan and supply themselves with coal, provisions, and water. They will pay for them in money, or anything else your imperial majesty's subjects may prefer; and we request your imperial majesty to appoint a convenient port, in the southern part of the Empire, where our vessels may stop.

These are the only objects for which I have sent Commodore

Perry, with a powerful squadron, to pay a visit to your imperial majesty's renowned city of Yedo: friendship, commerce, a supply of coal and provisions, and protection for our shipwrecked people.

We have directed Commodore Perry to beg your imperial majesty's acceptance of a few presents. They are of no great value in themselves; but some of them may serve as specimens of the articles manufactured in the United States, and they are intended as tokens of our sincere and respectful friendship.

May the Almighty have your imperial majesty in His great and holy keeping!

In witness whereof, I have caused the great seal of the United States to be hereunto affixed, and have subscribed the same with my name, at the city of Washington, in America, the seat of my government, on the thirteenth day of the month of November, in the year one thousand eight hundred and fifty-two.

Your good friend,
Millard Fillmore.
Edward Everett,
SECRETARY OF STATE.

From Francis L. Hawks (ed.), *Narrative of the Expedition of an American Squadron to the China Seas and Japan, Performed in the Years 1852, 1853, and 1854, under the Command of Commodore M. C. Perry, United States Navy* (1856), 256-257.

Bethmann-Hollweg Note on The Eve of World War I, 1914

EXHIBIT 2

The Chancellor to the Governments of Germany. Confidential. Berlin, July 28, 1914.

You will make the following report to the Government to which you are accredited:

In view of the facts which the Austrian Government has published in its note to the Servian Government, the last doubt must disappear that the outrage to which the Austro-Hungarian successor to the throne has fallen a victim, was prepared in Servia, to say the least with the connivance of members of the Servian government and army. It is a product of the pan-Serb intrigues which for a series of years have become a source of permanent disturbance for the Austro-Hungarian Monarchy and for the whole of Europe.

The pan-Serb chauvinism appeared especially marked during the Bosnian crisis. Only to the far-reaching self-restraint and moderation of the Austro-Hungarian government and the energetic intercession of the powers is it to be ascribed that the provocations to which Austria-Hungary was exposed at that time, did not lead to a conflict. The assurance of future well-behaviour, which the Servian government gave at that time, it has not kept. Under the very eyes, at least with the tacit sufferance of official Servia, the pan-Serb propaganda has meanwhile continued to increase in scope and intensity. It would be compatible neither with its dignity nor with its right to self-preservation if the Austro-Hungarian government persisted to view idly any longer the intrigues beyond the frontier, through which the safety and the integrity of the monarchy are permanently threatened. With this state of affairs, the action as well as the demands of the Austro-Hungarian Government can be viewed only as justifiable.

The reply of the Servian government to the demands which the Austro-Hungarian government put on the 23rd inst. through its representative in Belgrade, shows that the dominating factors in Servia are not inclined to cease their former policies and agitation. There will remain nothing else for the Austro-Hungarian government than to press its demands, if need be through military action, unless it renounces for good its position as a great power.

Some Russian personalities deem it their right as a matter of course and a task of Russia's to actively become a party to Servia in the conflict between Austria-Hungary and Servia. For the European conflagration which would result from a similar step by Russia, the *Nowoje Wremja* believes itself justified in making Germany responsible in so far as it does not induce Austria-Hungary to yield.

The Russian press thus turns conditions upside down. It is not Austria-Hungary which has called forth the conflict with Servia, but it is Servia which, through unscrupulous favor toward pan-Serb aspirations, even in parts of the Austro-Hungarian monarchy, threatens the same in her existence and creates conditions, which eventually found expression in the wanton outrage at Sarajevo. If Russia believes that it must champion the cause of Servia in this matter, it certainly has the right to do so. However, it must realize that it makes the Serb activities its own, to undermine the conditions of existence of the Austro-Hungarian monarchy, and that thus it bears the sole responsibility if out of the Austro-Servian affair, which all other great powers desire to localize, there arises a European war. This responsibility of Russia's is evident and it weighs the more heavily as Count Berchtold [Hungary's Foreign Minister] has officially declared to Russia that Austria-Hungary has no intention to acquire Servian territory or to touch the existence of the Servian Kingdom, but only desires peace against the Servian intrigues. . . .

The attitude of the Imperial government in this question is clearly indicated. The agitation conducted by the pan-Slavs in Austria-Hungary has for its goal, with the destruction of the Austro-Hungarian monarchy, the scattering or weakening of the triple alliance with a complete isolation of the German Empire in consequence. Our own interest therefore calls us to the side of Austria-Hungary. The duty, if at all possible, to guard Europe against a universal war, points to the support by ourselves of those endeavors which aim at the localization of the conflict, faithful to the course of those policies which we have carried out successfully for forty-four years in the interest of the preservation of the peace of Europe.

Should, however, against our hope, through the interference of Russia the fire be spread, we should have to support, faithful to our duty as allies, the neighbor-monarchy with all the power at our command. We shall take the sword only if forced to it, but then in the clear consciousness that we are not guilty of the calamity which war will bring upon the peoples of Europe.

From *The German White-Book* (Only authorized translation, 1914), 34-37.

Count Bernstorff's Message to The United States on The Resumption of Unrestricted Submarine Warfare, Jan. 31, 1917

Washington, *January 31, 1917.*

Mr. Secretary of State: Your excellency was good enough to transmit to the Imperial Government a copy of the message which the President of the United States of America addressed to the Senate on the 22 instant. The Imperial Government has given it the earnest consideration which the President's statements deserve, inspired as they are by a deep sentiment of responsibility. It is highly gratifying to the Imperial Government to ascertain that the main tendencies of this important statement correspond largely to the desires and principles professed by Germany. These principles especially include self-government and equality of rights for all nations. Germany would be sincerely glad if in recognition of this principle countries like Ireland and India, which do not enjoy the benefits of political independence, should now obtain their freedom. The German people also repudiate all alliances which serve to force the countries into a competition for might and to involve them in a net of selfish intrigues. On the other hand, Germany will gladly cooperate in all efforts to prevent future wars. The freedom of the seas, being a preliminary condition of the free existence of nations and the peaceful intercourse between them, as well as the open door for the commerce of all nations, has always formed part of the leading principles of Germany's political program. All the more the Imperial Government regrets that the attitude of her enemies who are so entirely opposed to peace makes it impossible for the world at present to bring about the realization of these lofty ideals. Germany and her allies were ready to enter now into a discussion of peace and had set down as basis the guaranty of existence, honor, and free development of their peoples. Their aims, as has been expressly stated in the note of December 12, 1916, were not directed towards the destruction or annihilation of their enemies and were according to their conviction perfectly compatible with the rights of the other nations. As to Belgium for which such warm and cordial sympathy is felt in the United States, the Chancellor had declared only a few weeks previously that its annexation had never formed part of Germany's intentions. The peace to be signed with Belgium was to provide for such conditions in that country, with which Germany desires to maintain friendly neighborly relations, that Belgium should not be used again by Germany's enemies for the purpose of instigating continuous hostile intrigues. Such precautionary measures are all the more necessary, as Germany's enemies have repeatedly stated not only in speeches delivered by their leading men, but also in the statutes of the economical conference in Paris, that it is their intention not to treat Germany as an equal, even after peace has been restored, but to continue their hostile attitude and especially to wage a systematical economical war against her.

The attempt of the four allied powers to bring about peace has failed owing to the lust of conquest of their enemies, who desired to dictate the conditions of peace. Under the pretense of following the principle of nationality our enemies have disclosed their real aims in this war, viz. to dismember and dishonor Germany, Austria-Hungary, Turkey, and Bulgaria. To the wish of reconciliation they oppose the will of destruction. They desire a fight to the bitter end.

A new situation has thus been created which forces Germany to new decisions. Since two years and a half England is using her naval power for a criminal attempt to force Germany into submission by starvation. In brutal contempt of international law the group of powers led by England does not only curtail the legitimate trade of their opponents but they also by ruthless pressure compel neutral countries either to altogether forego every trade not agreeable to the Entente powers or to limit it according to their arbitrary decrees. The American Government knows the steps which have been taken to cause England and her allies to return to the rules of international law and to respect the freedom of the seas. The English Government, however, insists upon continuing its war of starvation, which does not at all affect the military power of its opponents, but compels women and children, the sick and the aged to suffer, for their country, pains and privations which endanger the vitality of the nation. Thus British tyranny mercilessly increases the sufferings of the world indifferent to the laws of humanity, indifferent to the protests of the neutrals whom they severely harm, indifferent even to the silent longing for peace among England's own allies. Each day of the terrible struggle causes new destruction, new sufferings. Each day shortening the war will, on both sides, preserve the life of thousands of brave soldiers and be a benefit to mankind.

The Imperial Government could not justify before its own conscience, before the German people, and before history the neglect of any means destined to bring about the end of the war. Like the President of the United States the Imperial Government had hoped to reach this goal by negotiations. After the attempts to come to an understanding with the Entente powers have been answered by the latter with the announcement of an intensified continuation of the war, the Imperial Government—in order to serve the welfare of mankind in a higher sense and not to wrong its own people—is now compelled to continue the fight for existence, again forced upon it, with the full employment of all the weapons which are at its disposal.

Sincerely trusting that the people and Government of the United States will understand the motives for this decision and its necessity, the Imperial Government hopes that the United States may view the new situation from the lofty heights of impartiality and assist, on their part, to prevent further misery and avoidable sacrifice of human life.

Enclosing two memoranda regarding the details of the contemplated military measures at sea, I remain

J. Bernstorff

U. S. Department of State,
Papers Relating to the Foreign Relations of the United States,
1917, Supplement I, the World War (1931), 97-101.

Wilson's Fourteen Points, 1918

We entered this war because violations of right had occurred which touched us to the quick and made the life of our own people impossible unless they were corrected and the world secure once for all against their recurrence. What we demand in this war, therefore, is nothing peculiar to ourselves. It is that the world be made fit and safe to live in; and particularly that it be made safe for every peace-loving nation which, like our own, wishes to live its own life, determine its own institutions, be assured of justice and fair dealing by the other peoples of the world as against force and selfish aggression. All the peoples of the world are in effect partners in this interest, and for our own part we see very clearly that unless justice be done to others it will not be done to us. The programme of the world's peace, therefore, is our programme: and as we see it, is this:

I. Open covenants of peace, openly arrived at, after which there shall be no private international understandings of any kind, but diplomacy shall proceed always frankly and in the public view

II. Absolute freedom of navigation upon the seas, outside territorial waters, alike in peace and in war, except as the seas may be closed in whole or in part by international action for the enforcement of international covenants.

III. The removal, so far as possible, of all economic barriers and the establishment of an equality of trade conditions among all the nations consenting to the peace and associating themselves for its maintenance.

IV. Adequate guarantees given and taken that national armaments will be reduced to the lowest point consistent with domestic safety.

V. A free, open-minded, and absolutely impartial adjustment of all colonial claims, based upon a strict observance of the principle that in determining all such questions of sovereignty the interests of the populations concerned must have equal weight with the equitable claims of the government whose title is to be determined.

VI. The evacuation of all Russian territory and such a settlement of all questions affecting Russia as will secure the best and freest cooperation of the other nations of the world in obtaining for her an unhampered and unembarrassed opportunity for the independent determination of her own political development and national policy, and assure her of a sincere welcome into the society of free nations under institutions of her own choosing; and, more than a welcome, assistance also of every kind that she may need and may herself desire. The treatment accorded Russia by her sister nations in the months to come will be the acid test of their good will, of their comprehension of her needs as distinguished from their own interests, and of their intelligent and unselfish sympathy.

VII. Belgium, the whole world will agree, must be evacuated and restored, without any attempt to limit the sovereignty which she enjoys in common with all other free nations. No other single act will serve to restore confidence among the nations in the laws which they have themselves set and determined for the government of their relations with one another. Without this healing act, the whole structure and validity of international law is forever impaired.

VIII. All French territory should be freed and the invaded portions restored, and the wrong done to France by Prussia in 1871 in the matter of Alsace-Lorraine, which has unsettled the peace of the world for nearly fifty years, should be righted, in order that peace may once more be made secure in the interest of all.

IX. A readjustment of the frontiers of Italy should be effected along clearly recognizable lines of nationality.

X. The peoples of Austria-Hungary, whose place among the nations we wish to see safeguarded and assured, should be accorded the freest opportunity of autonomous development.

XI. Rumania, Serbia, and Montenegro should be evacuated; occupied territories restored; Serbia accorded free access to the sea; and the relations of the several Balkan states to one another determined by friendly counsel along historically established lines of allegiance and nationality; and international guarantees of the political and economic independence and territorial integrity of the several Balkan states should be entered into.

XII. The Turkish portions of the present Ottoman Empire should be assured a secure sovereignty, but the other nationalities which are now under Turkish rule should be assured an undoubted security of life and an absolutely unmolested opportunity of autonomous development, and the Dardanelles should be permanently opened as a free passage to the ships and commerce of all nations under international guarantees.

XIII. An independent Polish state should be erected which

should include the territories inhabited by indisputably Polish populations, which should be assured a free and secure access to the sea, and whose political and economic independence and territorial integrity should be guaranteed by international covenant.

XIV. A general association of nations must be formed under specific covenants for the purpose of affording mutual guarantees of political independence and territorial integrity to great and small states alike.

We have spoken now, surely, in terms too concrete to admit of any further doubt or question. An evident principle runs through the whole programme I have outlined. It is the principle of justice to all peoples and nationalities, and their right to live on equal terms of liberty and safety with one another, whether they be strong or weak.

Foreign Relations of the United States, 1918, Sup. I, Vol. I, 13-17.

The Pact of Paris, 1928

THE BRIAND-KELLOGG MULTILATERAL TREATY
FOR THE RENUNCIATION OF WAR

THE PRESIDENT OF THE GERMAN REICH, THE PRESIDENT OF THE UNITED STATES OF AMERICA, HIS MAJESTY THE KING OF THE BELGIANS, THE PRESIDENT OF THE FRENCH REPUBLIC, HIS MAJESTY THE KING OF GREAT BRITAIN, IRELAND AND THE BRITISH DOMINIONS BEYOND THE SEAS, EMPEROR OF INDIA, HIS MAJESTY THE KING OF ITALY, HIS MAJESTY THE EMPEROR OF JAPAN, THE PRESIDENT OF THE REPUBLIC OF POLAND, THE PRESIDENT OF THE CZECHO-SLOVAK REPUBLIC,

Deeply sensible of their solemn duty to promote the welfare of mankind;

Persuaded that the time has come when a frank renunciation of war as an instrument of national policy should be made to the end that the peaceful and friendly relations now existing between their peoples may be perpetuated;

Convinced that all changes in their relations with one another should be sought only by pacific means and be the result of a peaceful and orderly process, and that any signatory Power which shall hereafter seek to promote its national interests by resort to war should be denied the benefits furnished by this treaty;

Hopeful that, encouraged by their example, all the other nations of the world will join in this humane endeavor and by adhering to the present Treaty as soon as it comes into force bring their peoples within the scope of its beneficent provisions, thus uniting the civilized nations of the world in a common renunciation of war as an instrument of their national policy.

Have decided to conclude a Treaty . . . and have agreed upon the following articles:

ARTICLE I

The High Contracting Parties solemnly declare in the names of their respective peoples that they condemn recourse to war for the solution of international controversies, and renounce it as an instrument of national policy in their relations with one another.

ARTICLE II

The High Contracting Parties agree that the settlement or solution of all disputes or conflicts of whatever nature or of whatever origin they may be, which may arise among them, shall never be sought except by pacific means.

ARTICLE III

The present Treaty shall be ratified by the High Contracting Parties named in the Preamble in accordance with their respective constitutional requirements, and shall take effect as between them as soon as all their several instruments of ratification shall have been deposited at Washington.

This Treaty shall, when it has come into effect as prescribed in the preceding paragraph, remain open as long as may be necessary for adherence by all the other Powers of the world. Every instrument evidencing the adherence of a Power shall be deposited at Washington and the Treaty shall immediately upon such deposit become effective as between the Power thus adhering and the other Powers parties hereto.

It shall be the duty of the Government of the United States to furnish each Government named in the Preamble and every Government subsequently adhering to this Treaty with a certified copy of the Treaty and of every instrument of ratification or adherence. It shall also be the duty of the Government of the United States telegraphically to notify such Governments immediately upon the deposit with it of each instrument of ratification or adherence.

From United States Department of State, *The General Pact for the Renunciation of War, Text of the Pact, Signed, Notes and Other Papers* (1928), pp. 1-3.

Mussolini's Statement of Fascist Doctrine, 1923

Anti-individualistic, the Fascist conception of life stresses the importance of the State and accepts the individual only in so far as his interests coincide with those of the State, which stands for the conscience and the universal will of man as a historic entity. It is opposed to classical liberalism which arose as a reaction to absolutism and exhausted its historical function when the State became the expression of the conscience and will of the people. Liberalism denied the State in the name of the individual; Fascism reasserts the rights of the State as expressing the real essence of the individual. And if liberty is to be the attribute of living men and not of abstract dummies invented by individualistic liberalism, then Fascism stands for liberty, and for the only liberty worth having, the liberty of the State and of the individual within the State. The Fascist conception of the State is all-embracing; outside of it no human or spiritual values can exist, much less have value. Thus understood, Fascism is totalitarian, and the Fascist State—a synthesis and a unit inclusive of all values—interprets, develops, and potentiates the whole life of a people.

No individuals or groups (political parties, cultural associations, economic unions, social classes) [exist] outside the State. Fascism is therefore opposed to Socialism to which unity within the State (which amalgamates classes into a single economic and ethical reality) is unknown, and which sees in history nothing but the class struggle. Fascism is likewise opposed to trade-unionism as a class weapon. But when brought within the orbit of the State, Fascism recognises the real needs which gave rise to socialism and trade-unionism, giving them due weight in the guild or corporative system in which divergent interests are coordinated and harmonised in the unity of the State.

Grouped according to their several interests, individuals form classes; they form trade-unions when organised according to their several economic activities; but first and foremost they form the State, which is no mere matter of numbers, the sum of the individuals forming the majority. Fascism is therefore opposed to that form of democracy which equates a nation to the majority, lowering it to the level of the largest number; but it is the purest form of democracy if the nation be considered—as it should be—from the point of view of quality rather than quantity, as an idea, the mightiest because the most ethical, the most coherent, the truest, expressing itself in a people as the conscience and will of the few, if not, indeed, of one, and tending to express itself in the conscience and the will of the mass, of the whole group ethnically moulded by natural and historical conditions into a nation, advancing, as one conscience and one will, along the self-same line of development and spiritual formation. Not a race, nor a geographically defined region, but a people, historically perpetuating itself; a multitude unified by an idea and imbued with the will to live, the will to power, self-consciousness, personality.

In so far as it is embodied in a State, this higher personality becomes a nation. It is not the nation which generates the State; that is an antiquated naturalistic concept which afforded a basis for XIXth century publicity in favor of national governments. Rather is it the State which creates the nation, conferring volition and therefore real life on a people made aware of their moral unity.

Fascism is now clearly defined not only as a régime but as a doctrine. This means that Fascism, exercising its critical faculties on itself and on others, has studied from its own special standpoint and judged by its own standards all the problems affecting the material and intellectual interests now causing such grave anxiety to the nations of the world, and is ready to deal with them by its own policies.

First of all, as regards the future development of mankind,— and quite apart from all present political considerations—Fascism does not, generally speaking, believe in the possibility or utility of perpetual peace. It therefore discards pacifism as a cloak for cowardly supine renunciation in contra-distinction to self-sacrifice. War alone keys up all human energies to their maximum tension and sets the seal of nobility on those peoples who have the courage to face it. All other tests are substitutes which never place a man face to face with himself before the alternative of life or death. Therefore all doctrines which postulate peace at all costs are in- compatible with Fascism. Equally foreign to the spirit of Fascism, even if accepted as useful in meeting special political situations— are all internationalistic or League superstructures which, as history shows, crumble to the ground whenever the heart of nations is deeply stirred by sentimental, idealistic or practical considerations. Fascism carries this anti-pacifistic attitude into the life of the in- dividual. "I don't care a damn" (*me ne frego*)—the proud motto of the fighting squads scrawled by a wounded man on his band- ages, is not only an act of philosophic stoicism, it sums up a doc- trine which is not merely political: it is evidence of a fighting spirit which accepts all risks. It signifies a new style of Italian life. The Fascist accepts and loves life; he rejects and despises suicide as cowardly. Life as he understands it means duty, elevation, con- quest; life must be lofty and full, it must be lived for oneself but above all for others, both near by and far off, present and future.

The population policy of the régime is the consequence of these premises. The Fascist loves his neighbor, but the word "neighbor" does not stand for some vague and unseizable concep- tion. Love of one's neighbor does not exclude necessary educa- tional severity; still less does it exclude differentiation and rank. Fascism will have nothing to do with universal embraces; as a member of the community of nations it looks other peoples straight in the eyes; it is vigilant and on its guard; it follows others in all their manifestations and notes any changes in their interests; and it does not allow itself to be deceived by mutable and fallacious appearances.

Such a conception of life makes Fascism the resolute negation of the doctrine underlying so-called scientific and Marxian socialism, the doctrine of historic materialism which would explain the history of mankind in terms of the class-struggle and by changes in the processes and instruments of production, to the exclusion of all else.

That the vicissitudes of economic life—discoveries of raw materials, new technical processes, scientific inventions—have their importance, no one denies; but that they suffice to explain human history to the exclusion of other factors is absurd. Fascism believes now and always in sanctity and heroism, that is to say in acts in which no economic motive—remote or immediate—is at work. Having denied historic materialism, which sees in men mere puppets on the surface of history, appearing and disappearing on the crest of the waves while in the depths the real directing forces move and work, Fascism also denies the immutable and irreparable character of the class struggle which is the natural outcome of this economic conception of history; above all it denies that the class struggle is the preponderating agent in social transformations. Having thus struck a blow at socialism in the two main points of its doctrine, all that remains of it is the sentimental aspiration—old as humanity itself—toward social relations in which the sufferings and sorrows of the humbler folk will be alleviated. But here again Fascism rejects the economic interpretation of felicity as something to be secured socialistically, almost automatically, at a given stage of economic evolution when all will be assured a maximum of material comfort. Fascism denies the materialistic conception of happiness as a possibility, and abandons it to the economists of the mid-eighteenth century. This means that Fascism denies the equation: well-being = happiness, which sees in men mere animals, content when they can feed and fatten, thus reducing them to a vegetative existence pure and simple.

After socialism, Fascism trains its guns on the whole block of democratic ideologies, and rejects both their premises and their practical applications and implements. Fascism denies that numbers, as such, can be the determining factor in human society; it denies the right of numbers to govern by means of periodical consultations; it asserts the irremediable and fertile and beneficent inequality of men who cannot be levelled by any such mechanical and extrinsic device as universal suffrage. Democratic régimes may be described as those under which the people are, from time to time, deluded into the belief that they exercise sovereignty, while all the time real sovereignty resides in and is exercised by other and sometimes irresponsible and secret forces. Democracy is a kingless régime infested by many kings who are sometimes more exclusive, tyrannical, and destructive than one, even if he be a tyrant.

The Fascist negation of socialism, democracy, liberalism, should not, however, be interpreted as implying a desire to drive the world backwards to positions occupied prior to 1789, a year commonly referred to as that which opened the demo-liberal century. History does not travel backwards. The Fascist doctrine has not taken De Maistre as its prophet. Monarchical absolutism is of the past, and so is ecclesiolatry. Dead and done for are feudal privileges and the division of society into closed, uncommunicating casts. Neither has the Fascist conception of authority anything in common with that of a police-ridden State.

The Fascist State expresses the will to exercise power and to command. Here the Roman tradition is embodied in a conception of strength. Imperial power, as understood by the Fascist doctrine, is not only territorial, or military, or commercial; it is also spiritual and ethical. An imperial nation, that is to say a nation which directly or indirectly is a leader of others, can exist without the need of conquering a single square mile of territory. Fascism sees in the imperialistic spirit—i. e. in the tendency of nations to expand—a manifestation of their vitality. In the opposite tendency, which would limit their interests to the home country, it sees a symptom of decadence. Peoples who rise or rearise are imperialistic; renunciation is characteristic of dying peoples. The Fascist doctrine is that best suited to the tendencies and feelings of a people which, like the Italian, after lying fallow during centuries of foreign servitude, is now reasserting itself in the world.

But imperialism implies discipline, the coordination of efforts, a deep sense of duty and a spirit of self-sacrifice. This explains many aspects of the practical activity of the régime, and the direction taken by many of the forces of the State, as also the severity which has to be exercised towards those who would oppose this spontaneous and inevitable movement of XXth century Italy by agitating outgrown ideologies of the XIXth century, ideologies rejected wherever great experiments in political and social transformations are being dared.

Never before have the peoples thirsted for authority, direction, order, as they do now. If each age has its doctrine, then innumerable symptoms indicate that the doctrine of our age is the Fascist. That it is vital is shown by the fact that it has aroused a faith; that this faith has conquered souls is shown by the fact that Fascism can point to its fallen heroes and its martyrs.

Benito Mussolini,
Fascism: Doctrine and Institutions (1935), 10-22, 30-31.

Atlantic Charter, 1941

Over a week ago I held several important conferences at sea with the British Prime Minister. Because of the factor of safety to British, Canadian, and American ships, and their personnel, no prior announcement of these meetings could properly be made.

At the close, a public statement by the Prime Minister and the President was made. I quote it for the information of the Congress and for the record:

"The President of the United States and the Prime Minister, Mr. Churchill, representing His Majesty's Government in the United Kingdom, have met at sea.

"They have been accompanied by officials of their two Governments, including high-ranking officers of their military, naval, and air services.

"The whole problem of the supply of munitions of war, as provided by the Lease-Lend Act, for the armed forces of the United States, and for those countries actively engaged in resisting aggression, has been further examined.

"Lord Beaverbrook, the Minister of Supply of the British Government, has joined in these conferences. He is going to proceed to Washington to discuss further details with appropriate officials of the United States Government. These conferences will also cover the supply problems of the Soviet Union.

"The President and the Prime Minister have had several conferences. They have considered the dangers to world civilization arising from the policies of military domination by conquest upon which the Hitlerite government of Germany and other governments associated therewith have embarked, and have made clear the steps which their countries are respectively taking for their safety in the face of these dangers.

"They have agreed upon the following joint declaration:

"*Joint declaration of the President of the United States of America and the Prime Minister, Mr. Churchill, representing His Majesty's Government in the United Kingdom, being met together, deem it right to make known certain common principles in the national policies of their respective countries on which they base their hopes for a better future for the world.*

"*First, their countries seek no aggrandizement, territorial or other;*

"*Second, they desire to see no territorial changes that do not accord with the freely expressed wishes of the peoples concerned;*

"*Third, they respect the right of all peoples to choose the form of government under which they will live; and they wish to see sovereign rights and self-government restored to those who have been forcibly deprived of them;*

"*Fourth, they will endeavor, with due respect for their existing obligations, to further the enjoyment by all states, great or small, victor or vanquished, of access, on equal terms, to the trade and to the raw materials of the world which are needed for their economic prosperity;*

"*Fifth, they desire to bring about the fullest collaboration between all nations in the economic field with the object of securing, for all, improved labor standards, economic advancement, and social security;*

"*Sixth, after the final destruction of the Nazi tyranny, they hope to see established a peace which will afford to all nations the means of dwelling in safety within their own boundaries, and which will afford assurance that all the men in all the lands may live out their lives in freedom from fear and want;*

"Seventh, such a peace should enable all men to traverse the high seas and oceans without hindrance;

"Eighth, they believe that all of the nations of the world, for realistic as well as spiritual reasons, must come to the abandonment of the use of force. Since no future peace can be maintained if land, sea, or air armaments continue to be employed by nations which threaten, or may threaten, aggression outside of their frontiers, they believe, pending the establishment of a wider and permanent system of general security, that the disarmament of such naions is essential. They will likewise aid and encourage all other practicable measures which will lighten for peace-loving peoples the crushing burden of armaments.

FRANKLIN D. ROOSEVELT
WINSTON S. CHURCHILL"

U. S. Department of State, *Peace and War: United States Foreign Policy, 1931-1941,* Department of State Publication 1933 (1943), 717-720.

Churchill's "Iron Curtain" Speech, 1946

A shadow has fallen upon the scenes so lately lighted by the Allied victory. Nobody knows what Soviet Russia and its Communist international organisation intends to do in the immediate future, or what are the limits, if any, to their expansive and proselytising tendencies. I have a strong admiration and regard for the valiant Russian people and for my wartime comrade, Marshal Stalin. There is deep sympathy and goodwill in Britain—and I doubt not here also—towards the peoples of all the Russias and a resolve to persevere through many differences and rebuffs in establishing lasting friendships. We understand the Russian need to be secure on her western frontiers by the removal of all possibility of German aggression. We welcome Russia to her rightful place among the leading nations of the world. We welcome her flag upon the seas. Above all, we welcome constant, frequent and growing contacts between the Russian people and our own people on both sides of the Atlantic. It is my duty however, for I am sure you would wish me to state the facts as I see them to you, to place before you certain facts about the present position in Europe.

From Stettin in the Baltic to Trieste in the Adriatic, an iron curtain has descended across the Continent. Behind that line lie all the capitals of the ancient states of Central and Eastern Europe. Warsaw, Berlin, Prague, Vienna, Budapest, Belgrade, Bucharest and Sofia, all these famous cities and the populations around them lie in what I must call the Soviet sphere, and all are subject in one form or another, not only to Soviet influence but to a very high and, in many cases, increasing measure of control from Moscow. Athens alone—Greece with its immortal glories—is free to decide its future at an election under British, American and French observation. The Russian-dominated Polish Government has been encouraged to make enormous and wrongful inroads upon Germany, and mass expulsions of millions of Germans on a scale grievous and undreamed-of are now taking place. The Communist parties, which were very small in all these Eastern States of Europe, have been raised to pre-eminence and power far beyond their numbers and are seeking everywhere to obtain totalitarian control. Police governments are prevailing in nearly every case, and so far, except in Czechoslovakia, there is no true democracy.

Turkey and Persia are both profoundly alarmed and disturbed at the claims which are being made upon them and at the pressure being exerted by the Moscow Government. An attempt is being made by the Russians in Berlin to build up a quasi-Communist party in their zone of Occupied Germany by showing special favours to groups of left-wing German leaders. At the end of the fighting last June, the American and British Armies withdrew westwards, in accordance with an earlier agreement, to a depth at some points of 150 miles upon a front of nearly four hundred miles, in order to allow our Russian allies to occupy this vast expanse of territory which the Western Democracies had conquered.

If now the Soviet Government tries, by separate action, to

build up a pro-Communist Germany in their areas, this will cause new serious difficulties in the British and American zones, and will give the defeated Germans the power of putting themselves up to auction between the Soviets and the Western Democracies. Whatever conclusions may be drawn from these facts—and facts they are —this is certainly not the Liberated Europe we fought to build up. Nor is it one which contains the essentials of permanent peace.

The safety of the world requires a new unity in Europe, from which no nation should be permanently outcast. It is from the quarrels of the strong parent races in Europe that the world wars we have witnessed, or which occurred in former times, have sprung. Twice in our own lifetime we have seen the United States, against their wishes and their traditions, against arguments, the force of which it is impossible not to comprehend, drawn by irresistible forces, into these wars in time to secure the victory of the good cause, but only after frightful slaughter and devastation had occurred. Twice the United States has had to send several millions of its young men across the Atlantic to find the war; but now war can find any nation, wherever it may dwell between dusk and dawn. Surely we should work with conscious purpose for a grand pacification of Europe, within the structure of the United Nations and in accordance with its Charter. That I feel is an open cause of policy of very great importance.

In front of the iron curtain which lies across Europe are other causes for anxiety. In Italy the Communist Party is seriously hampered by having to support the Communist-trained Marshal Tito's claims to former Italian territory at the head of the Adriatic. Nevertheless the future of Italy hangs in the balance. Again one cannot imagine a regenerated Europe without a strong France. All my public life I have worked for a strong France and I never lost faith in her destiny, even in the darkest hours. I will not lose faith now. However, in a great number of countries, far from the Russian frontiers and throughout the world, Communist fifth columns are established and work in complete unity and absolute obedience to the directions they receive from the Communist centre. Except in the British Commonwealth and in the United States where Communism is in its infancy, the Communist parties or fifth columns constitute a growing challenge and peril to Christian civilisation. These are sombre facts for anyone to have to recite on the morrow of a victory gained by so much splendid comradeship in arms and in the cause of freedom and democracy.

On the other hand I repulse the idea that a new war is inevitable; still more that it is imminent. It is because I am sure that our fortunes are still in our own hands and that we hold the power to save the future, that I feel the duty to speak out now that I have the occasion and the opportunity to do so. I do not believe that Soviet Russia desires war. What they desire is the fruits of war and the indefinite expansion of their power and doctrines. But what we have to consider here to-day while time remains, is the permanent prevention of war and the establishment of conditions of freedom and democracy as rapidly as possible in all countries. Our difficulties and dangers will not be removed by closing our eyes to them. They will not be removed by mere waiting to see what happens; nor will they be removed by a policy of appeasement. What is needed is a settlement, and the longer this is delayed, the more difficult it will be and the greater our dangers will become.

From what I have seen of our Russian friends and Allies during the war, I am convinced that there is nothing they admire so much as strength, and there is nothing for which they have less respect than for weakness, especially military weakness. For that reason the old doctrine of a balance of power is unsound. We cannot afford, if we can help it, to work on narrow margins, offering temptations to a trial of strength. If the Western Democracies stand together in strict adherence to the principles of the United Nations Charter, their influence for furthering those principles will be immense and no one is likely to molest them. If however they become divided or falter in their duty and if these all-important years are allowed to slip away then indeed catastrophe may overwhelm us all.

Last time I saw it all coming and cried aloud to my own fellow-countrymen and to the world, but no one paid any attention. Up till the year 1933 or even 1935, Germany might have been saved from the awful fate which has overtaken her and we might all have been spared the miseries Hitler let loose upon mankind.

There never was a war in all history easier to prevent by timely action than the one which has just desolated such great areas of the globe. It could have been prevented in my belief without the firing of a single shot, and Germany might be powerful, prosperous and honoured to-day; but no one would listen and one by one we were all sucked into the awful whirlpool. We surely must not let that happen again. This can only be achieved by reaching now, in 1946, a good understanding on all points with Russia under the general authority of the United Nations Organisation and by the maintenance of that good understanding through many peaceful years, by the world instrument, supported by the whole strength of the English-speaking world and all its connections. . . .

Let no man underrate the abiding power of the British Empire and Commonwealth. Because you see the 46 millions in our island harassed about their food supply, of which they only grow one half, even in war-time, or because we have difficulty in restarting our industries and export trade after six years of passionate war effort, do not suppose that we shall not come through these dark years of privation as we have come through the glorious years of agony, or that half a century from now, you will not see 70 or 80 millions of Britons spread about the world and united in defence of our traditions, our way of life, and of the world causes which you and we espouse. If the population of the English-speaking Commonwealths be added to that of the United States with all that such co-operation implies in the air, on the sea, all over the globe and in science and in industry, and in moral force, there will be no quivering, precarious balance of power to offer its temptation to ambition or adventure. On the contrary, there will be an overwhelming assurance of security. If we adhere faithfully to the Charter of the United Nations and walk forward in sedate and sober strength seeking no one's land or treasure, seeking to lay no arbitrary control upon the thoughts of men; if all British moral and material forces and convictions are joined with your own in fraternal association, the highroads of the future will be clear, not only for us but for all, not only for our time, but for a century to come.

From Winston S. Churchill,
The Sinews of Peace: Postwar Speeches, ed. Randolph S. Churchill
(1949), 100-105. Published by Houghton Mifflin Company, owners
of the copyright.

Reproduced with permission.

The Truman Doctrine, 1947

The gravity of the situation which confronts the world today
necessitates my appearance before a joint session of the Congress.

The foreign policy and the national security of this country
are involved.

One aspect of the present situation, which I wish to present
to you at this time for your consideration and decision, concerns
Greece and Turkey.

The very existence of the Greek state is today threatened by
the terrorist activities of several thousand armed men, led by Communists, who defy the government's authority at a number of points,
particularly along the northern boundaries. A commission appointed
by the United Nations Security Council is at present investigating
disturbed conditions in northern Greece and alleged border violations along the frontier between Greece on the one hand and
Albania, Bulgaria, and Yugoslavia on the other.

Meanwhile, the Greek Government is unable to cope with the
situation. The Greek Army is small and poorly equipped. It needs
supplies and equipment if it is to restore the authority of the
Government throughout Greek territory.

Greece must have assistance if it is to become a self-supporting and self-respecting democracy.

The United States must supply this assistance. We have already extended to Greece certain types of relief and economic aid
but these are inadequate.

There is no other country to which democratic Greece can
turn.

No other nation is willing and able to provide the necessary
support for a democratic Greek Government.

The British Government, which has been helping Greece, can give no further financial or economic aid after March 31. Great Britain finds itself under the necessity of reducing or liquidating its commitments in several parts of the world, including Greece.

We have considered how the United Nations might assist in this crisis. But the situation is an urgent one requiring immediate action, and the United Nations and its related organizations are not in a position to extend help of the kind that is required.

It is important to note that the Greek Government has asked for our aid in utilizing effectively the financial and other assistance we may give to Greece, and in improving its public administration. It is of the utmost importance that we supervise the use of any funds made available to Greece, in such a manner that each dollar spent will count toward making Greece self-supporting, and will help to build an economy in which a healthy democracy can flourish.

No government is perfect. One of the chief virtues of a democracy, however, is that its defects are always visible and under democratic processes can be pointed out and corrected. The Government of Greece is not perfect. Nevertheless it represents 85 percent of the members of the Greek Parliament who were chosen in an election last year. Foreign observers, including 692 Americans, considered this election to be a fair expression of the views of the Greek people.

The Greek Government has been operating in an atmosphere of chaos and extremism. It has made mistakes. The extension of aid by this country does not mean that the United States condones everything that the Greek Government has done or will do. We have condemned in the past, and we condemn now, extremist measures of the right or the left. We have in the past advised tolerance, and we advise tolerance now.

Greece's neighbor, Turkey, also deserves our attention.

The future of Turkey as an independent and economically sound state is clearly no less important to the freedom-loving peoples of the world than the future of Greece. The circumstances in which Turkey finds itself today are considerably different from those of Greece. Turkey has been spared the disasters that have beset Greece. And during the war, the United States and Great Britain furnished Turkey with material aid.

Nevertheless, Turkey now needs our support.

Since the war, Turkey has sought financial assistance from Great Britain and the United States for the purpose of effecting that modernization necessary for the maintenance of its national integrity.

That integrity is essential to the preservation of order in the Middle East.

The British Government has informed us that, owing to its own difficulties, it can no longer extend financial or economic aid to Turkey.

As in the case of Greece, if Turkey is to have the assistance it needs, the United States must supply it. We are the only country able to provide that help.

I am fully aware of the broad implications involved if the United States extends assistance to Greece and Turkey, and I shall discuss these implications with you at this time.

One of the primary objectives of the foreign policy of the United States is the creation of conditions in which we and other nations will be able to work out a way of life free from coercion. This was a fundamental issue in the war with Germany and Japan. Our victory was won over countries which sought to impose their will, and their way of life, upon other nations.

To insure the peaceful development of nations, free from coercion, the United States has taken a leading part in establishing the United Nations. The United Nations is designed to make possible lasting freedom and independence for all its members. We shall not realize our objectives, however, unless we are willing to help free peoples to maintain their free institutions and their national integrity against aggressive movements that seek to impose upon them totalitarian regimes. This is no more than a frank recognition that totalitarian regimes imposed on free peoples, by direct or indirect aggression, undermine the foundations of international peace and hence the security of the United States.

The peoples of a number of countries of the world have recently had totalitarian regimes forced upon them against their will.

The Government of the United States has made frequent protests against coercion and intimidation, in violation of the Yalta agreement, in Poland, Rumania, and Bulgaria. I must also state that in a number of other countries there have been similar developments.

At the present moment in world history nearly every nation must choose between alternative ways of life. The choice is too often not a free one.

One way of life is based upon the will of the majority, and is distinguished by free institutions, representative government, free elections, guaranties of individual liberty, freedom of speech and religion, and freedom from political oppression.

The second way of life is based upon the will of a minority forcibly imposed upon the majority. It relies upon terror and oppression, a controlled press and radio, fixed electrons, and the suppression of personal freedoms.

I believe that it must be the policy of the United States to support free peoples who are resisting attempted subjugation by armed minorities or by outside pressures.

I believe that we must assist free peoples to work out their own destinies in their own way.

I believe that our help should be primarily through economic and financial aid, which is essential to economic stability and orderly political processes.

The world is not static and the status quo is not sacred. But we cannot allow changes in the status quo in violation of the Charter of the United Nations by such methods as coercion, or by such subterfuges as political infiltration. In helping free and independent nations to maintain their freedom, the United States will be giving effect to the principles of the Charter of the United Nations.

It is necessary only to glance at a map to realize that the survival and integrity of the Greek nation are of grave importance in a much wider situation. If Greece should fall under the control of an armed minority, the effect upon its neighbor, Turkey, would be immediate and serious. Confusion and disorder might well spread throughout the entire Middle East.

Moreover, the disappearance of Greece as an independent state would have a profound effect upon those countries in Europe whose peoples are struggling against great difficulties to maintain their freedoms and their independence. . . .

It would be an unspeakable tragedy if these countries, which have struggled so long against overwhelming odds, should lose that victory for which they sacrificed so much. Collapse of free institutions and loss of independence would be disastrous not only for them but for the world. Discouragement and possibly failure would quickly be the lot of neighboring peoples striving to maintain their freedom and independence.

Should we fail to aid Greece and Turkey in this fateful hour, the effect will be far reaching to the West as well as to the East.

We must take immediate and resolute action.

I therefore ask the Congress to provide authority for assistance to Greece and Turkey in the amount of $400,000,000 for the period ending June 30, 1948. In requesting these funds, I have taken into consideration the maximum amount of relief assistance which would be furnished to Greece out of the $350,000,000 which I recently requested that the Congress authorize for the prevention of starvation and suffering in countries devastated by the war.

In addition to funds, I ask the Congress to authorize the detail of American civilian and military personnel to Greece and Turkey, at the request of those countries, to assist in the tasks of reconstruction, and for the purpose of supervising the use of such financial and material assistance as may be furnished. I recommend that authority also be provided for the instruction and training of selected Greek and Turkish personnel.

Finally, I ask that the Congress provide authority which will permit the speediest and most effective use, in terms of needed commodities, supplies, and equipment, of such funds as may be authorized.

If further funds, or further authority, should be needed for purposes indicated in this message, I shall not hesitate to bring the situation before the Congress. On this subject the executive and legislative branches of the Government must work together.

This is a serious course upon which we embark.

I would not recommend it except that the alternative is much more serious.

The United States contributed $341,000,000,000 toward

winning World War II. This is an investment in world freedom and world peace.

The assistance that I am recommending for Greece and Turkey amounts to little more than one-tenth of 1 percent of this investment. It is only common sense that we should safeguard this investment and make sure that it was not in vain.

The seeds of totalitarian regimes are nurtured by misery and want. They spread and grow in the evil soil of poverty and strife. They reach their full growth when the hope of a people [dies].

We must keep that hope alive.

The free peoples of the world look to us for support in maintaining their freedoms.

If we falter in our leadership, we may endanger the peace of the world—and we shall surely endanger the welfare of our own Nation.

Great responsibilities have been placed upon us by the swift movement of events.

I am confident that the Congress will face these responsibilities squarely.

From U. S. Congress, *Congressional Record*, 80th Congress, 1st Session, XCIII, 1980-1981.

"Point Four" Program, 1949

We must embark on a bold new program for making the benefit of our scientific advances and industrial progress available for the improvement and growth of underdeveloped areas. More than half the people of the world are living in conditions approaching misery. For the first time in history, humanity possesses the knowledge and the skill to relieve the suffering of these people.

The United States is preeminent among nations in the development of industrial and scientific techniques. The material resources which we can afford to use for the assistance of other peoples are limited. But our imponderable resources in technical knowledge are constantly growing and are inexhaustible.

I believe that we should make available to peace-loving peoples the benefits of our store of technical knowledge in order to help them realize their aspirations for a better life. And, in cooperation with other nations, we should foster capital development in areas needing development.

Our aim should be to help the free peoples of the world, through their own efforts, to produce more food, more clothing, more materials for housing, and more mechanical power to lighten their burdens.

Only by helping the least fortunate of its members to help themselves can the human family achieve the decent, satisfying life that is the right of all people.

Democracy alone can supply the vitalizing force to stir the peoples of the world into triumphant action, not only against their human oppressors, but also against their ancient enemies—hunger, misery, and despair.

From Inaugural Address of President Harry S. Truman (January 20, 1949) in Senate Document 4, 81st Congress, 1st Session (1949), 3-4.

North Atlantic Treaty, 1949

PREAMBLE. The Parties to this Treaty reaffirm their faith in the purposes and principles of the Charter of the United Nations and their desire to live in peace with all peoples and all governments.

They are determined to safeguard the freedom, common heritage and civilization of their peoples, founded on the principles of democracy, individual liberty and the rule of law.

They seek to promote stability and well-being in the North Atlantic area.

They are resolved to unite their efforts for collective defense and for the preservation of peace and security.

They therefore agree to this North Atlantic Treaty:

Article 1. The Parties undertake, as set forth in the Charter of the

United Nations, to settle any international disputes in which they may be involved by peaceful means in such a manner that international peace and security, and justice, are not endangered, and to refrain in their international relations from the threat or use of force in any manner inconsistent with the purposes of the United Nations. . . .

Article 3. In order more effectively to achieve the objectives of this Treaty, the Parties, separately and jointly, by means of continuous and effective self-help and mutual aid, will maintain and develop their individual and collective capacity to resist armed attack. . . .

Article 5. The Parties agree that an armed attack against one or more of them in Europe or North America shall be considered an attack against them all; and consequently they agree that, if such an armed attack occurs, each of them, in exercise of the right of individual or collective self-defense recognized by Article 51 of the Charter of the United Nations, will assist the Party or Parties so attacked by taking forthwith, individually and in concert with the other Parties, such action as it deems necessary, including the use of armed force, to restore and maintain the security of the North Atlantic area.

Any such armed attack and all measures taken as a result thereof shall immediately be reported to the Security Council. Such measures shall be terminated when the Security Council has taken the measures necessary to restore and maintain international peace and security.

Article 6. For the purpose of Article 5 an armed attack on one or more of the Parties is deemed to include an armed attack on the territory of any of the Parties in Europe or North America, on the Algerian departments of France, on the occupation forces of any Party in Europe, on the islands under the jurisdiction of any Party in the North Atlantic area north of the Tropic of Cancer or on the vessels or aircraft in this area of any of the Parties. . . .

Article 9. The Parties hereby established a council, on which each of them shall be represented, to consider matters concerning the implementation of this Treaty. The council shall be so organized as to be able to meet promptly at any time. The council shall set up such subsidiary bodies as may be necessary; in particular it shall establish immediately a defense committee which shall recommend measures for the implementation of Articles 3 and 5.

Article 10. The Parties may, by unanimous agreement, invite any other European state in a position to further the principles of this Treaty and to contribute to the security of the North Atlantic area to accede to this Treaty. . . .

Article 11. This Treaty shall be ratified and its provisions carried out by the Parties in accordance with their respective constitutional processes. The instruments of ratification shall be deposited as soon as possible with the Government of the United States of America, which will notify all the other signatories of each deposit. The Treaty shall enter into force between the states which have ratified it as soon as the ratifications of the majority of the signatories, including the ratifications of Belgium, Canada, France, Luxembourg, the Netherlands, the United Kingdom and the United States, have been deposited and shall come into effect with respect to other states on the date of the deposit of their ratifications.

Article 12. After the Treaty has been in force for ten years, or at any time thereafter, the Parties shall, if any of them so requests, consult together for the purpose of reviewing the Treaty, having regard for the factors then affecting peace and security in the North Atlantic area, including the development of universal as well as regional arrangements under the Charter of the United Nations for the maintenance of international peace and security.

Article 13. After the Treaty has been in force for twenty years, any Party may cease to be a party one year after its notice of denunciation has been given to the Government of the United States of America, which will inform the Governments of the other Parties of the deposit of each notice of denunciation.

Article 14. This Treaty, of which the English and French texts are equally authentic, shall be deposited in the archives of the Government of the United States of America. Duly certified copies thereof will be transmitted by that Government to the Governments of the other signatories.

Done at Washington, the fourth day of April, 1949.

"A Decade of American Foreign Policy: 1941-1949," *Senate Document* 123, 81st Congress, 1st Session (1940), 1328-1330.

The Marshall Plan, 1947

I need not tell you gentlemen that the world situation is very serious. That must be apparent to all intelligent people. I think one difficulty is that the problem is one of such enormous complexity that the very mass of facts presented to the public by press and radio make it exceedingly difficult for the man in the street to reach a clear appraisement of the situation. Furthermore, the people of this country are distant from the troubled areas of the earth and it is hard for them to comprehend the plight and consequent reactions of the long-suffering peoples, and the effect of those reactions on their governments in connection with our efforts to promote peace in the world.

In considering the requirements for the rehabilitation of Europe, the physical loss of life, the visible destruction of cities, factories, mines, and railroads was correctly estimated, but it has become obvious during recent months that this visible destruction was probably less serious than the dislocation of the entire fabric of European economy. For the past 10 years conditions have been highly abnormal. The feverish preparation for war and the more feverish maintenance of the war effort engulfed all aspects of national economies. . . . Under the arbitrary and destructive Nazi rule, virtually every possible enterprise was geared into the German war machine. Long-standing commercial ties, private institutions, banks, insurance companies, and shipping companies disappeared, through loss of capital, absorption through nationalization, or by simple destruction. In many countries, confidence in the local currency has been severely shaken. The breakdown of the business structure of Europe during the war was complete. Recovery has been seriously retarded by the fact that two years after the close of hostilities a peace settlement with Germany and Austria has not been agreed upon. But even given a more prompt solution of these difficult problems, the rehabilitation of the economic structure of Europe quite evidently will require a much longer time and greater effort than had been foreseen.

There is a phase of this matter which is both interesting and serious. The farmer has always produced the foodstuffs to exchange with the city dweller for the other necessities of life. This division of labor is the basis of modern civilization. At the present time it is threatened with breakdown. The town and city industries are not producing adequate goods to exchange with the food-producing farmer. Raw materials and fuel are in short supply. Machinery is lacking or worn out. The farmer or the peasant cannot find the goods for sale which he desires to purchase. So the sale of his farm produce for money which he cannot use seems to him an unprofitable transaction. He, therefore, has withdrawn many fields from crop cultivation and is using them for grazing. He feeds more grain to stock and finds for himself and his family an ample supply of food, however short he may be on clothing and the other ordinary gadgets of civilization. Meanwhile people in the cities are short of food and fuel. So the governments are forced to use their foreign money and credits to procure these necessities abroad. This process exhausts funds which are urgently needed for reconstruction. Thus a very serious situation is rapidly developing which bodes no good for the world. The modern system of division of labor upon which the exchange of products is based is in danger of breaking down.

The truth of the matter is that Europe's requirements for the next three or four years of foreign food and other essential products —principally from America—are so much greater than her present ability to pay that she must have substantial additional help or face economic, social, and political deterioration of a very grave character.

The remedy lies in breaking the vicious circle and restoring the confidence of the European people in the economic future of their own countries and of Europe as a whole. The manufacturer and the farmer throughout wide areas must be able and willing to exchange their products for currencies, the continuing value of which is not open to question.

Aside from the demoralizing effect on the world at large and the possibilities of disturbances arising as a result of the desperation of the people concerned, the consequences to the economy of the United States should be apparent to all. It is logical that the

United States should do whatever it is able to do to assist in the return of normal economic health in the world, without which there can be no political stability and no assured peace. Our policy is directed not against any country or doctrine but against hunger, poverty, desperation, and chaos. Its purpose should be the revival of a working economy in the world so as to permit the emergence of political and social conditions in which free institutions can exist. Such assistance, I am convinced, must not be on a piecemeal basis as various crises develop. Any assistance that this Government may render in the future should provide a cure rather than a mere palliative. Any government that is willing to assist in the task of recovery will find full cooperation, I am sure, on the part of the United States Government. Any government which maneuvers to block the recovery of other countries cannot expect help from us. Furthermore, governments, political parties, or groups which seek to perpetuate human misery in order to profit therefrom politically or otherwise will encounter the opposition of the United States.

It is already evident that, before the United States Government can proceed much further in its efforts to alleviate the situation and help start the European world on its way to recovery, there must be some agreement among the countries of Europe as to the requirements of the situation and the part those countries themselves will take in order to give proper effect to whatever action might be undertaken by this Government. It would be neither fitting nor efficacious for this Government to undertake to draw up unilaterally a program designed to place Europe on its feet economically. This is the business of the Europeans. The initiative, I think, must come from Europe. The role of this country should consist of friendly aid in the drafting of a European program and of later support of such a program so far as it may be practical for us to do so. The program should be a joint one, areed to by a number [of], if not all, European nations.

From *A Decade of American Foreign Policy: Basic Documents,* 1941-49, Senate Document 123, 81st Congress, 1st Session (1950), 1268-1270.

Index